# Child Growth and Development 13/14
*Twentieth Edition*

## EDITORS

**Ellen N. Junn**
*San Jose State University*

Ellen Junn is the provost and vice president for academic affairs and professor of psychology at San Jose State University. She received her BS with distinction in psychology and with high honors from the University of Michigan and her MA and PhD in cognitive and developmental psychology from Princeton University. Dr. Junn's areas of research include college teaching effectiveness, educational equity, faculty development, and public policy as it affects children and families. She served as a Past President for the California Association for the Education of Young Children and as a Governing Board member of the National Association for the Education of Young Children.

**Chris J. Boyatzis**
*Bucknell University*

Chris Boyatzis is professor of psychology at Bucknell University and Director of the Bucknell in Denmark program. He received a BA with distinction in psychology from Boston University and his MA and PhD in developmental psychology from Brandeis University. His primary interests are religious and spiritual development and cultural influences on child development. He is president of Div. 36, Psychology of Religion, of the American Psychological Association, and is Associate Editor of the APA journal, *Psychology of Religion and Spirituality* as well as serving on the editorial board of four other journals.

**ANNUAL EDITIONS: CHILD GROWTH AND DEVELOPMENT, TWENTIETH EDITION**

Published by McGraw-Hill, a business unit of The McGraw-Hill Companies, Inc., 1221 Avenue of the Americas, New York, NY 10020. Copyright © 2014 by The McGraw-Hill Companies, Inc. All rights reserved. Previous editions © 2013, 2012, and 2011. Printed in the United States of America. No part of this publication may be reproduced or distributed in any form or by any means, or stored in a database or retrieval system, without the prior written consent of The McGraw-Hill Companies, Inc., including, but not limited to, in any network or other electronic storage or transmission, or broadcast for distance learning.

Some ancillaries, including electronic and print components, may not be available to customers outside the United States.

This book is printed on acid-free paper.

Annual Editions® is a registered trademark of The McGraw-Hill Companies, Inc.
Annual Editions is published by the **Contemporary Learning Series** group within the McGraw-Hill Higher Education division.

1 2 3 4 5 6 7 8 9 0 QDB/QDB 1 0 9 8 7 6 5 4 3

ISBN: 978-0-07-813594-1
MHID: 0-07-813594-X
ISSN: 1075-5217 (print)
ISSN: 2162-1780 (online)

Developmental Editor: *Jade Benedict*
Content Licensing Specialist: *Rita Hingtgen*
Marketing Director: *Adam Kloza*
Marketing Manager: *Nathan Edwards*
Project Manager: *Melissa M. Leick*
Cover Designer: *Studio Montage, St. Louis, MO*
Buyer: *Nichole Birkenholz*
Media Project Manager: *Sridevi Palani*

Compositor: Laserwords Private Limited
Cover Image Credits: © Rolf Bruderer/Getty Images (inset);
© Image Source/Getty Images (background)

www.mhhe.com

# Editors/Academic Advisory Board

Members of the Academic Advisory Board are instrumental in the final selection of articles for each edition of ANNUAL EDITIONS. Their review of articles for content, level, and appropriateness provides critical direction to the editors and staff. We think that you will find their careful consideration well reflected in this volume.

## ANNUAL EDITIONS: Child Growth and Development 13/14
20th Edition

## EDITORS

**Ellen N. Junn**
*California State University, Fresno*

**Chris J. Boyatzis**
*Bucknell University*

## ACADEMIC ADVISORY BOARD MEMBERS

# Editors/Academic Advisory Board continued

# Preface

In publishing ANNUAL EDITIONS we recognize the enormous role played by the magazines, newspapers, and journals of the public press in providing current, first-rate educational information in a broad spectrum of interest areas. Many of these articles are appropriate for students, researchers, and professionals seeking accurate, current material to help bridge the gap between principles and theories and the real world. These articles, however, become more useful for study when those of lasting value are carefully collected, organized, indexed, and reproduced in a low-cost format, which provides easy and permanent access when the material is needed. That is the role played by ANNUAL EDITIONS.

We are delighted to welcome you to this twentieth edition of *Annual Editions: Child Growth and Development 13/14*. The amazing sequence of events of prenatal development that lead to the birth of a baby is an awe-inspiring process. Perhaps more intriguing is the question of what the future may hold for this newly arrived baby. For instance, will this child become a doctor, a lawyer, an artist, a beggar, or a thief? Although philosophers and prominent thinkers such as Charles Darwin and Sigmund Freud have long speculated about the importance of infancy on subsequent development, not until the 1960s did the scientific study of infants and young children flourish.

Since then, research and theory in infancy and childhood have exploded, resulting in a wealth of new knowledge about child development. Past accounts of infants and young children as passive, homogeneous organisms have been replaced with investigations aimed at studying infants and young children at a "microlevel"—as active individuals with many inborn competencies who are capable of shaping their own environment—as well as at a "macrolevel"—by considering the larger context surrounding the child. In short, children are not "blank slates," and development does not take place in a vacuum; children arrive with many skills and grow up in a complex web of social, historical, political, economic, and cultural spheres.

As was the case for previous editions, we hope to achieve at least four major goals with this volume. First, we hope to present you with the latest research and thinking to help you better appreciate the complex interactions that characterize human development in infancy and childhood. Second, in light of the feedback we received on previous editions, we have placed greater emphasis on important contemporary issues and challenges, exploring topics such as understanding development in the context of current societal and cultural influences. Third, attention is given to articles that also discuss effective, practical applications. Finally, we hope that this anthology will serve as a catalyst to help students become more effective future professionals and parents.

To achieve these objectives, we carefully selected articles from a variety of sources, including scholarly research journals and texts as well as semiprofessional journals and popular publications. Every selection was scrutinized for readability, interest level, relevance, and currency. In addition, we listened to the valuable input and advice from members of our board, consisting of faculty from a range of institutions of higher education, including community and liberal arts colleges as well as research and teaching universities. We are most grateful to the advisory board as well as to the excellent editorial staff of McGraw-Hill/Contemporary Learning Series.

*Annual Editions: Child Growth and Development* is organized into five major units. Unit 1 includes articles regarding some advances in trying to prevent and help premature babies, as well as how genetic and prenatal stress can affect development. Unit 2 presents information regarding brain development, perception, memory, and language in infants and young children, as well as information on schooling. Unit 3 focuses on social and emotional development, including peers, gender socialization and play, bullying and antisocial behavior, as well as issues of institutional deprivation, antisocial behavior, and resiliency. Unit 4 is devoted to parenting and family issues such as infant attachment, discipline, effects of divorce, sibling interactions, cultural differences in parental control and gay and lesbian parents. Finally, Unit 5 focuses on larger cultural and societal influences such as media and marketing, and on special challenges (e.g., obesity, autism, and traumatic situations such as coping with terrorism, war or natural disasters).

Instructors for large lecture courses may wish to adopt this anthology as a supplement to a basic text, whereas instructors for smaller sections might also find the readings effective for promoting student presentations or for stimulating discussions and applications. Whatever format is utilized, it is our hope that the instructor and the students will find the readings interesting, illuminating, and provocative.

As the title indicates, *Annual Editions: Child Growth and Development* is by definition a volume that undergoes continual review and revision. Thus, we welcome and encourage your comments and suggestions for future editions of this volume. Simply fill out and return the article rating form found at the end of this book. Best wishes, and we look forward to hearing from you!

Ellen N. Junn
*Editor*

Chris J. Boyatzis
Editor

# The Annual Editions Series

## VOLUMES AVAILABLE

Adolescent Psychology

Aging

American Foreign Policy

American Government

Anthropology

Archaeology

Assessment and Evaluation

Business Ethics

Child Growth and Development

Comparative Politics

Criminal Justice

Developing World

Drugs, Society, and Behavior

Dying, Death, and Bereavement

Early Childhood Education

Economics

Educating Children with Exceptionalities

Education

Educational Psychology

Entrepreneurship

Environment

The Family

Gender

Geography

Global Issues

Health

Homeland Security

Human Development

Human Resources

Human Sexualities

International Business

Management

Marketing

Mass Media

Microbiology

Multicultural Education

Nursing

Nutrition

Physical Anthropology

Psychology

Race and Ethnic Relations

Social Problems

Sociology

State and Local Government

Sustainability

Technologies, Social Media, and Society

United States History, Volume 1

United States History, Volume 2

Urban Society

Violence and Terrorism

Western Civilization, Volume 1

Western Civilization, Volume 2

World History, Volume 1

World History, Volume 2

World Politics

# Contents

# UNIT 1
## Conception to Birth

# UNIT 2
## Cognition, Language, and Learning

The concepts in bold italics are developed in the article. For further expansion, please refer to the Topic Guide.

The concepts in bold italics are developed in the article. For further expansion, please refer to the Topic Guide.

# UNIT 3
## Social and Emotional Development

The concepts in bold italics are developed in the article. For further expansion, please refer to the Topic Guide.

# UNIT 4
## Parenting and Family Issues

The concepts in bold italics are developed in the article. For further expansion, please refer to the Topic Guide.

# UNIT 5
# Cultural and Societal Influences

The concepts in bold italics are developed in the article. For further expansion, please refer to the Topic Guide.

The concepts in bold italics are developed in the article. For further expansion, please refer to the Topic Guide.

# Correlation Guide

The *Annual Editions* series provides students with convenient, inexpensive access to current, carefully selected articles from the public press. **Annual Editions: Child Growth and Development 13/14** an easy-to-use reader that presents articles on important topics such as *fertility technology, prenatal development, brain development,* and many more. For more information on *Annual Editions* and other *McGraw-Hill Contemporary Learning Series* titles, visit www.mhhe.com/cls.

This convenient guide matches the units in **Annual Editions: Child Growth and Development 13/14** with the corresponding chapters in one of our best-selling McGraw-Hill Child Development textbooks by Papalia.

| **Annual Editions: Child Growth and Development 13/14** | **A Child's World: Infancy Through Adolescence, 12/e by Papalia** |
|---|---|
| **Unit 1:** Conception to Birth | **Chapter 3:** Forming a New Life: Conception, Heredity, and Environment <br> **Chapter 4:** Pregnancy and Prenatal Development |
| **Unit 2:** Cognition, Language, and Learning | **Chapter 7:** Cognitive Development during the First Three Years <br> **Chapter 10:** Cognitive Development in Early Childhood <br> **Chapter 13:** Cognitive Development in Middle Childhood |
| **Unit 3:** Social and Emotional Development | **Chapter 8:** Psychosocial Development during the First Three Years <br> **Chapter 11:** Psychosocial Development in Early Childhood |
| **Unit 4:** Parenting and Family Issues | **Chapter 4:** Pregnancy and Prenatal Development |
| **Unit 5:** Cultural and Societal Influences | **Chapter 1:** Studying a Child's World <br> **Chapter 2:** A Child's World: How We Discover It |

# Topic Guide 13/14

This topic guide suggests how the selections in this book relate to the subjects covered in your course. You may want to use the topics listed on these pages to search the Web more easily.

On the following pages a number of websites have been gathered specifically for this book. They are arranged to reflect the units of this Annual Editions reader. You can link to these sites by going to www.mhhe.com/cls.

**All the articles that relate to each topic are listed below the bold-faced term.**

## Aggression
20. The Role of Neurobiological Deficits in Childhood Antisocial Behavior

## Antisocial behavior
27. Parental Divorce and Children's Adjustment

## Attachment
6. New Advances in Understanding Sensitive Periods in Brain Development
25. Children of Lesbian and Gay Parents
26. Evidence of Infants' Internal Working Models of Attachment
34. More Support Needed for Trauma Interventions

## Autism
36. The Positives of Caregiving: Mothers' Experiences Caregiving for a Child with Autism

## Birth and birth defects
1. Prenatal Origins of Neurological Development: A Critical Period for Fetus *and* Mother
2. Genes in Context: Gene–Environment Interplay and the Origins of Individual Differences in Behavior
3. Effects of Prenatal Social Stress on Offspring Development: Pathology or Adaptation?

## Brain development
1. Prenatal Origins of Neurological Development: A Critical Period for Fetus *and* Mother
3. Effects of Prenatal Social Stress on Offspring Development: Pathology or Adaptation?
6. New Advances in Understanding Sensitive Periods in Brain Development
20. The Role of Neurobiological Deficits in Childhood Antisocial Behavior

## Child abuse
34. More Support Needed for Trauma Interventions

## Cognitive development
5. The Other-Race Effect Develops during Infancy: Evidence of Perceptual Narrowing
6. New Advances in Understanding Sensitive Periods in Brain Development
7. Contributions of Neuroscience to Our Understanding of Cognitive Development
8. Infant Feeding and Cognition: Integrating a Developmental Perspective
9. Do Babies Learn from Baby Media?
10. Social Cognitive Development: A New Look
11. Running on Empty? How Folk Science Gets by With Less
26. Evidence of Infants' Internal Working Models of Attachment

## Cross-cultural issues
5. The Other-Race Effect Develops during Infancy: Evidence of Perceptual Narrowing
28. The Role of Parental Control in Children's Development in Western and East Asian Countries
30. Sibling Experiences in Diverse Family Contexts

## Culture
23. Culture, Peer Interaction, and Socioemotional Development
25. Children of Lesbian and Gay Parents
33. Independence and Interdependence in Children's Developmental Experiences
34. More Support Needed for Trauma Interventions
38. The Human Child's Nature Orientation

## Development
1. Prenatal Origins of Neurological Development: A Critical Period for Fetus *and* Mother
6. New Advances in Understanding Sensitive Periods in Brain Development
23. Culture, Peer Interaction, and Socioemotional Development
25. Children of Lesbian and Gay Parents
26. Evidence of Infants' Internal Working Models of Attachment
32. Siblings Play Formative, Influential Role as 'Agents of Socialization'
34. More Support Needed for Trauma Interventions

## Developmental disabilities
12. Children's Reading Comprehension Difficulties: Nature, Causes, and Treatments
35. ADHD among Preschoolers

## Discipline
28. The Role of Parental Control in Children's Development in Western and East Asian Countries
29. The Case Against Spanking: Physical Discipline is Slowly Declining as Some Studies Reveal Lasting Harms for Children

## Eating/Feeding
8. Infant Feeding and Cognition: Integrating a Developmental Perspective

## Economic issues
31. The Effects of Parental Undocumented Status on the Developmental Contexts of Young Children in Immigrant Families

## Education/School
9. Do Babies Learn from Baby Media?
12. Children's Reading Comprehension Difficulties: Nature, Causes, and Treatments
20. The Role of Neurobiological Deficits in Childhood Antisocial Behavior
35. ADHD among Preschoolers

## Emotional development
7. Contributions of Neuroscience to Our Understanding of Cognitive Development
17. Don't!: The Secret of Self-Control
23. Culture, Peer Interaction, and Socioemotional Development
25. Children of Lesbian and Gay Parents
26. Evidence of Infants' Internal Working Models of Attachment
34. More Support Needed for Trauma Interventions

## Evolution
38. The Human Child's Nature Orientation

# Internet References

The following Internet sites have been selected to support the articles found in this reader. These sites were available at the time of publication. However, because websites often change their structure and content, the information listed may no longer be available. We invite you to visit www.mhhe.com/cls for easy access to these sites.

## Annual Editions: Child Growth and Development 13/14

### General Sources

**American Academy of Pediatrics**
www.aap.org

This organization provides data for optimal physical, mental, and social health for all children.

**CYFERNet**
www.cyfernet.org

The Children, Youth, and Families Education Research Network is sponsored by the Cooperative Extension Service and USDA's Cooperative State Research Education and Extension Service. This site provides practical research-based information in areas including health, childcare, family strengths, science, and technology.

**KidsHealth**
http://kidshealth.org

This site was developed to help parents find reliable children's health information. Enter the Parents site to find such topics as General Health, Nutrition and Fitness, First Aid and Safety, Growth and Development, Positive Parenting, and more.

**National Institute of Child Health and Human Development**
www.nichd.nih.gov

The NICHD conducts and supports research on the reproductive, neurobiological, developmental, and behavioral processes that determine and maintain the health of children, adults, families, and populations.

### UNIT 1: Conception to Birth

**World Baby Report**
worldbabyreport.com

Extensive information on caring for infants can be found at this site. There are also links to numerous other related sites.

**Children's Nutrition Research Center (CNRC)**
www.bcm.tmc.edu/cnrc

CNRC, one of six USDA/ARS (Agricultural Research Service) facilities, is dedicated to defining the nutrient needs of healthy children, from conception through adolescence, and pregnant and nursing mothers. The *Nutrition and Your Child* newsletter is of general interest and can be accessed from this site.

**Zero to Three: National Center for Infants, Toddlers, and Families**
www.zerotothree.org

This national organization is dedicated solely to infants, toddlers, and their families. It is headed by recognized experts in the field and provides technical assistance to communities, states, and the federal government. The site provides information that the organization gathers and disseminates through its publications.

### UNIT 2: Cognition, Language, and Learning

**Educational Resources Information Center (ERIC)**
www.ed.gov/about/pubs/intro/pubdb.html

This website is sponsored by the U.S. Department of Education and will lead to numerous documents related to elementary and early childhood education, as well as other curriculum topics and issues.

**National Association for the Education of Young Children (NAEYC)**
www.naeyc.org

The National Association for the Education of Young Children provides a useful link from its home page to a site that provides resources for "Parents."

**Project Zero**
http://pzweb.harvard.edu

Harvard Project Zero, a research group at the Harvard Graduate School of Education, has investigated the development of learning processes in children and adults for 30 years. Today, Project Zero is building on this research to help create communities of reflective, independent learners, to enhance deep understanding within disciplines, and to promote critical and creative thinking. Project Zero's mission is to understand and enhance learning, thinking, and creativity in the arts and other disciplines for individuals and institutions.

**Vandergrift's Children's Literature Page**
www.scils.rutgers.edu/special/kay/sharelit.html

This site provides information about children's literature and links to a variety of resources related to literacy for children.

### UNIT 3: Social and Emotional Development

**Max Planck Institute for Psychological Research**
www.mpg.de/english/institutesProjectsFacilities/instituteChoice/psychologische_forschung

Results from several behavioral and cognitive development research projects are available on this site.

**National Child Care Information Center (NCCIC)**
www.occ-archive.org

Information about a variety of topics related to childcare and development is available on this site. Links to the *Child Care Bulletin,* which can be read online, and to the ERIC database of online and library-based resources are available.

**Serendip**
http://serendip.brynmawr.edu/serendip

Organized into five subject areas (brain and behavior, complex systems, genes and behavior, science and culture, and science education), Serendip contains interactive exhibits, articles, links to other resources, and a forum area for comments and discussion.

# Internet References

## UNIT 4: Parenting and Family Issues

### The National Association for Child Development (NACD)
www.nacd.org

This international organization is dedicated to helping children and adults reach their full potential. Its home page presents links to various programs, research, and resources in topics related to the family and society.

### National Council on Family Relations
www.ncfr.com

This NCFR home page will lead you to articles, research, and a lot of other resources on important issues in family relations, such as stepfamilies, couples, and divorce.

### Parenting and Families
www.cyfc.umn.edu

The University of Minnesota's Children, Youth, and Family Consortium site will lead you to many organizations and other resources related to divorce, single parenting, and stepfamilies, as well as information about other topics of interest in the study of children's development and the family.

### Parentsplace.com: Single Parenting
www.parentsplaceonline.org/resource-library/single-parenting

This resource focuses on issues concerning single parents and their children. Although the articles range from parenting children from infancy through adolescence, most of the articles deal with middle childhood.

### National Stepfamily Resource Center
www.stepfam.org

This website is dedicated to educating and supporting stepfamilies and to creating a positive family image.

## UNIT 5: Cultural and Societal Influences

### Association to Benefit Children (ABC)
www.a-b-c.org

ABC presents a network of programs that includes child advocacy, education for disabled children, care for HIV-positive children, employment, housing, foster care, and daycare.

### Children's Defense Fund
www.childrensdefense.org

CDF is a national proponent and advocate of policies and programs that safeguard children's needs in the areas of amelioration of poverty, protection from abuse and neglect, and increased access to healthcare and quality education.

### Children Now
www.childrennow.org

Children Now uses research and mass communications to make the well-being of children a top priority across the nation. Current articles include information on the influence of media on children, working families, and health.

### Council for Exceptional Children
www.cec.sped.org

This is the home page for the Council for Exceptional Children, a large professional organization that is dedicated to improving education for children with exceptionalities, students with disabilities, and/or the gifted child. It leads to the ERIC Clearinghouse on disabilities and gifted education and the National Clearinghouse for Professions in Special Education.

### Prevent Child Abuse America
www.preventchildabuse.org

Dedicated to their child abuse prevention efforts, PCAA's site provides fact sheets and reports that include statistics, a public opinion poll, a 50-state survey, and other resource materials.

# UNIT 1

# Conception to Birth

## Unit Selections

1. **Prenatal Origins of Neurological Development: A Critical Period for Fetus and Mother,** Laura M. Glynn and Curt A. Sandman
2. **Genes in Context: Gene–Environment Interplay and the Origins of Individual Differences in Behavior,** Frances A. Champagne and Rahia Mashoodh
3. **Effects of Prenatal Social Stress on Offspring Development: Pathology or Adaptation?,** Sylvia Kaiser and Norbert Sachser

## Learning Outcomes

- Explain how the fetus is active in its own brain development and shapes its mother's brain development as well.

- Evaluate the evidence this unit: Does it support genetic determinism, the notion that genes will dictate development? If not, what view does the evidence support about nature and nurture, and about the child's role in its own growth?

- Describe the "books in a library" metaphor to fellow students who have not read this article to help them understand epigenetics.

- Compare and contrast the effects of prenatal social stress on offspring development for animals and humans. Discuss the ethical complications of conducting human studies on this topic.

- Explain the theoretical basis for why prenatal social stress on developing offspring might yield positive, ameliorative benefits for those offspring rather than only negative pathologies.

- Evaluate the differential effects of prenatal social stress on developing offspring as a function of the sex of the offspring. Provide a rationale that might explain these differential effects for male versus female offspring.

## Student Website

www.mhhe.com/cls

## Internet References

**World Baby Report**
worldbabyreport.com
**Children's Nutrition Research Center (CNRC)**
www.bcm.tmc.edu/cnrc
**Zero to Three: National Center for Infants, Toddlers, and Families**
www.zerotothree.org

Carefree ideas of starting a family as exemplified by the nursery rhyme, *"First comes love. Then comes marriage. Then comes baby in a baby carriage,"* do not always hold true in light of the latest scientific findings regarding prenatal development. In the past, most attention has focused on the vital role that the mother must play in safeguarding her unborn fetus' health during pregnancy. However, the authors of "Prenatal Origins of Neurological Development: A Critical Period for Fetus *and* Mother" provide evidence that the prenatal environment and the mother's hormones can interact to reciprocally alter both the fetus' and the mother's brain structures and functions that may have long term adaptive effects.

Parents often wonder how their children can be so remarkably different from one another even as infants. How influential are genes over environment or visa versa? This question of nature versus nurture is addressed by the authors of "Genes in Context: Gene-Environment Interplay and the Origins of Individual Differences in Behavior" who explain how the environment can determine which genes become activated or remain silent early in development, leading to individual differences. Similarly, in, "Effects of Prenatal Social Stress on Offspring Development: Pathology or Adaptation?" the authors cite new research showing that prolonged prenatal stress can result in hormonal changes that may affect the masculinization of the baby.

All of these articles highlight the powerful and enduring effects of the prenatal environment in shaping and supporting the genetic foundations of a given infant, and underscore the critical importance of optimal prenatal development.

©JGI/Jamie Grill/Blend Images LLC
Pregnant Asian woman caressing stomach

# Prenatal Origins of Neurological Development: A Critical Period for Fetus *and* Mother

LAURA M. GLYNN AND CURT A. SANDMAN

In Britain, at the turn of the last century, there was a noticeable decline in population. Birth rates were low and infant mortality was high. Moreover, two thirds of the young men who volunteered to fight in the South African war were rejected because of physical frailties. In an enlightened response, one county enlisted an "army" of midwives to interview and assist all women during and after pregnancy. This intervention was intended to improve the health of mothers and their children, but a secondary consequence was meticulous record keeping of pregnancy histories and birth outcomes (Barker, 1998). These early-life-history records, combined with national health records from later in life, formed the basis of the developmental origins of disease model, or the Barker hypothesis, which asserts that prenatal exposures to adversity have implications for poor physical health across the life span. There now is substantial evidence that adverse intrauterine exposures increase subsequent risk for a range of outcomes including hypertension, heart disease, diabetes, obesity, and polycystic ovary disease, as well as psychiatric illnesses such as schizophrenia, mood disorders, and suicide. We and others are taking a prospective, interdisciplinary approach to examine the consequences of intrauterine experience on fetal central nervous system (CNS) development. A parallel focus of our research program is the role of the prenatal period in CNS development of the mother. Accumulating evidence indicates that pregnancy remodels the architecture of the maternal brain, an effect that persists across the life span and is conserved across species.

## Fetal Programming of CNS Development

Each developing organism plays an active role in its own construction (Denver, 1997). The human fetus has evolved mechanisms to acquire information about the environment and guide its development. The human placenta is both a sensory and effector organ that incorporates and transduces information from its maternal environment into the fetal-developmental program. The fetal–placental unit's detection of stress signals from the maternal environment (e.g., cortisol) "informs" the fetus that there may be a threat to survival. This information primes or advances the placental clock, resulting in earlier delivery (McLean et al., 1995) and escape from the hostile environment. Concurrently, the fetus adjusts its developmental trajectory, modifying its nervous system to ensure survival.

Most existing human studies of prenatal influences on development rely on retrospective designs in which birth phenotype (i.e., being born early or small) is determined archivally and is used to predict adult health (the logic is that these birth phenotypes reflect adverse intrauterine experience). The obvious limitations with this approach are that the prenatal environment cannot be characterized accurately and that it cannot be separated from the deleterious effects of being born early or small. A critical next step that is currently being undertaken is the prospective study of variations in the prenatal environment and how these influence postnatal development. Among these prospective studies, the majority have consistently reported that adversity in utero predicts behavioral and emotional disturbances. In particular, elevated prenatal psychological and biological stress signals repeatedly have been linked to hypothalamic-pituitary-adrenal (HPA) axis function and fearful temperament and also to internalizing and externalizing behavioral problems in childhood and adolescence (Davis, Glynn, Waffarn, & Sandman, 2011; O'Connor et al., 2005; Talge, Neal, Glover, & Health, 2007; Van den Bergh & Marcoen, 2004).

Fewer studies have examined the effects of prenatal stress on human cognitive development. However, there is evidence that maternal cortisol and psychological distress during the prenatal period are associated with delayed cognitive development, at least through adolescence (Talge et al., 2007). The first study showing that a mother's elevated pregnancy-specific anxiety (i.e., anxiety about her pregnancy and the health of her fetus) early in her pregnancy was associated with reduced gray matter volumes in her 6- to 9-year-old children was recently published (Buss, Davis, Muftuler, Head, & Sandman, 2010). The affected regions were those associated with higher cognitive functions including reasoning, planning, attention, working and recall memory, language, and social and emotional processing.

# If Interested in the Role of Prenatal Experience, Study the Fetus

Even more current work has begun to study the development of the fetus, because this approach allows the direct examination of intrauterine environment on the developing human, independent from birth phenotype and the effects of the postnatal environment. Fetal activity has been linked to maternal anxiety, depression, anger, and pregnancy-specific stress and also to maternal cortisol. However, assessment of the fetal response (usually heart rate or movement) to extrauterine stimuli (e.g., tones or vibroacoustic stimuli) across gestation provides a more sensitive assessment of the developing CNS. Elevations in placental corticotropin-releasing hormone (pCRH) are associated with diminished ability of the fetus to detect and respond to stimulation, and overexposure to maternal endogenous opiates with delayed ability to habituate to a repeated stimulus (Sandman, Davis, Buss, & Glynn, in press). The direct study of programming effects on the fetus represents an important approach for understanding prenatal influences, independent from postnatal influences.

# Beyond Fetal Programming: The Predictive Adaptive Response

Recently, an alternative conceptual framework to the Barker Hypothesis has emerged. Instead of assuming that pathology is the only outcome of fetal exposure to adversity, the predictive adaptive response (PAR) model proposes that the developing organism makes adjustments based on the predicted postnatal environment. When the PAR does not match the environment (i.e., the prediction is inaccurate), the mismatch results in disease states. For example, the fetus exposed to an impoverished intrauterine environment will prepare for, and perhaps thrive in, a postnatal environment of nutritional scarcity. However, if that same fetus is instead born into an environment of nutritional abundance, its developmental adjustments may result in an increased risk for obesity, diabetes, and cardiovascular disease. There is persuasive support for the PAR model from studies examining a mismatch between prenatal and postnatal nutrient environments. More recently, an examination of consistency of another indicator of early life adversity, maternal depression, provides further support for the PAR model by demonstrating that congruous prenatal and postnatal environments confer an adaptive advantage in motor and mental development during an infant's first year of life, even when the environments are unfavorable (Sandman, Davis & Glynn, in press).

# Maternal Programming

In the life span of the human female, no other naturally occurring hormone exposures are more extreme than those experienced during the perinatal period. A substantial amount of literature indicates that other, less extreme endocrine events, such as puberty and menopause, are associated with changes in human brain structure and function. In contrast, almost nothing is known about how the hormone exposures linked to reproductive experience influence the brain and behavior of human mothers. Rodent models have confirmed that reproduction produces neurological changes that persist throughout the life span and that these changes are not confined to those areas of the brain directly involved in maternal behaviors. For example, alterations have been observed also in brain regions associated with emotion (amygdala) and memory (hippocampus). Our studies have examined the influence of reproductive experience on the structure and function of women's brains—a process we term "maternal programming."

The existence of hormonal control of onset and maintenance of maternal behavior in nonhuman species (largely rodents) is well established. What little is known about humans is largely consistent with this literature, suggesting that in humans, too, the hormone exposures of pregnancy prime the maternal brain for the challenges of motherhood. Specifically, there are a small number of studies demonstrating that prenatal estrogen, cortisol, and oxytocin exposures influence the quality of early postpartum maternal care and the ability to respond to infant signals. Furthermore, new findings indicate that the early postpartum period is one in which gray matter volumes increase in brain regions implicated in maternal motivation and behavior and that mothers who have the most positive feelings toward their infants show the largest increases (Kim et al., 2010).

Species from rats to humans show a decline in physiological and behavioral responses to stress during pregnancy. Late in gestation, women exhibit a dampened cortisol response to HPA challenge and show decreased blood pressure, heart rate, and catecholamine responses to psychological and physical challenges (de Weerth & Buitelaar, 2005). In parallel to these physiological changes, pregnant women also experience diminished psychological responses to stress (Glynn, Wadhwa, Dunkel Schetter, Chicz-DeMet, & Sandman, 2001). There is reason to believe that the down-regulation of stress responding during pregnancy serves an adaptive purpose, providing some protection for mother and fetus from the adverse effects of stress. It has been shown that early exposures to stress are more likely to result in preterm birth than are later exposures (Glynn et al., 2001), and women who do not show the normative, protective decrease in stress responding during pregnancy are at increased risk for preterm delivery (Glynn, Dunkel Schetter, Hobel, & Sandman, 2008).

Up to 80% of women report impaired cognitive function during pregnancy. This observation is supported by empirical investigations of memory function during pregnancy. A meta-analysis of the 17 studies published over the last decade indicated deficits in two components of memory during pregnancy that persist into the postpartum period: recall memory and the executive component of working memory (Henry & Rendell, 2007).

The largest prospective study of human memory function during pregnancy was recently published, and for the first time, potential endocrine mechanisms (estradiol and cortisol) associated with impaired prenatal and postpartum memory function were identified (Glynn, 2010).

At present, essentially nothing is known about how reproduction alters the brain structure of women. However, it is extremely likely that the dramatic hormone exposures of pregnancy do result in permanent changes for several reasons. First, the massive fluctuations in estrogens dwarf those seen at any other time in development, and it is known that these hormones have effects on human brain structure and function. Second, adult neurogenesis is modulated by reproduction—for example, in rats, pregnancy enhances production of neuronal progenitors in the forebrain subventricular zone, stimulating the formation of new olfactory neurons (Shingo et al., 2003). Third, animal models demonstrate that changes in CNS structure associated with reproduction endure across the life span. Fourth, findings from animal models also indicate that the effects of pregnancy and parturition may be additive—with each successive litter, the effects of pregnancy on cognition and stress responding are amplified.

# How Might the Fetus Program the Mother?

It is becoming increasingly recognized that maternal signals shape the development of the fetus. However, it is not as widely acknowledged that this is only one side of a bidirectional relationship; specifically, fetal or placental signals may also shape the development of the maternal brain and behavior. It is possible that the fetus exerts these influences through endocrine, cellular, and behavioral routes. Corticotropin-releasing hormone (CRH) is a 41-amino-acid neuropeptide that is synthesized primarily in the paraventricular nucleus of the hypothalamus and has a major role in regulating pituitary-adrenal function and the physiological response to stress. During pregnancy the placenta also expresses the genes for CRH, and placental CRH (pCRH) increases across gestation, reaching levels in the maternal circulation observed only in the hypothalamic portal system (i.e., the blood vessels that carry regulatory hormones from the hypothalamus to the pituitary) during conditions of physiological stress. Little is known about the possible influences of pCRH on the maternal brain. In the nonpregnant state, CRH is believed to play a role in the etiology of depression. Because of the dramatic increase in pCRH during pregnancy and a demonstrated link between CRH and depression in the nonpregnant state, it is possible that pCRH exposures may present a risk for postpartum depression. To date, one report provides evidence consistent with this possibility (Yim et al., 2009) and more broadly demonstrates that a fetal endocrine signal may affect neurological function in the mother.

Fetal behavior represents a second pathway through which the fetus might shape the mother. DiPietro and colleagues (DiPietro, Irizarry, Costigan, & Gurewitsch, 2004) applied time-series analysis to longitudinal data from mother-fetus pairs and found that, beginning at 20 weeks of gestation until term, fetal movement stimulated rises in maternal heart rate and skin conductance. Currently the pathway through which fetal movements might determine maternal sympathetic arousal is unknown. However, it is unlikely that this occurs through conscious perception of these movements. (At term, women detect as few as 16% of fetal movements.) Given that the influence does not operate through conscious channels, DiPietro et al. propose that the most likely local mechanism is through perturbations of the uterine wall. They further suggest that the sympathetic activation in response to the fetal movement signal may begin to prepare the woman for the new demands of motherhood by redirecting maternal resources away from competing but less relevant environmental demands. This finding raises the additional provocative question of whether the degree of prenatal synchrony between mother and fetus might set the stage for postnatal mother–infant interaction.

A third possible route, the cellular, involves what is called fetal microchimerism: Fetal cells cross the placenta and enter the maternal circulation. In humans, fetal cells have been detected in a range of maternal tissues years after delivery. Relevant to maternal programming are findings demonstrating the presence of fetal cells in the brains of pregnant mice (Tan et al., 2005). These fetal cells are capable of taking on a range of attributes including neuron-, astrocyte- and oligodendrocyte-like types (the latter two are glial cells that provide support and protection for neurons in the brain). Whether these fetal cells have any functional or physiological significance has yet to be demonstrated. However, the fetal cells were preferentially found in the region of the olfactory bulb, an area critical for offspring recognition. It is possible that pregnancy changes the attraction of specific brain areas for fetal cells.

# Emerging Moderating Variables: Fetal Sex and Timing of Exposures
## Fetal sex

The concept that the sex of the fetus is important in understanding neurological development is by no means novel. However, there are some issues that are unique to the prenatal period that deserve consideration. First, fetal sex is an additional factor that has the potential to alter the prenatal endocrine milieu. For example, levels of human chorionic gonadatropin (hCG; a hormone produced by the embryo and later by placental cells) differ depending on fetal sex. Second, there are sex differences in the structure and function of the placenta, including placental cytokine expression, insulin-like growth factor pathways, and glucocorticoid receptor expression and function that may play a central role in fetal development. Furthermore, Clifton (2010) has posited that sex-specific differences in adaptation to adversity exist. Specifically, female fetuses make multiple adaptations in placental gene and protein expression in response to intrauterine adversity to ensure survival in the event of possible additional prenatal adversity.

In contrast, males "take a minimalist approach" when faced with a similar hostile prenatal environment and do not adjust their developmental trajectories—a strategy that places the male fetus at risk if additional adversity is encountered. A third consideration is that fetal sex moderates trajectories of fetal CNS development—there is some evidence that female fetuses exhibit more precocious CNS development (Sandman, Davis, et al., in press).

## The importance of timing

The effects of timing stress exposure during gestation are determined by multiple factors. First, it is established that timing of such exposure will have different effects on the fetus depending on the timetable of development of organ systems. Second, the maternal–fetal endocrine milieu and the regulation of maternal–fetal endocrine exposures are highly dynamic. Third, as we discussed, women become progressively less sensitive to perturbations in their environments, and so, as gestation advances, exposure to adversity stress may be less likely to shape CNS development. Taken together, these timing-dependent vulnerabilities in both mother and fetus are consistent with findings suggesting that the same signal may exert influences at certain gestational periods but not at others. For example, pregnancy-specific anxiety early in gestation, but not later, influences gray matter volumes in children (Buss et al., 2010). Or in the case of the mother, only estrogen levels early in gestation are predictive of the decline in maternal memory function during pregnancy (Glynn, 2010). The timetable of maternal and fetal vulnerabilities also may explain how the same signal can have opposite effects depending upon the timing of exposure. For example, early elevations in maternal cortisol have been linked to lower levels of toddler mental development, whereas late elevations predict enhanced mental development (Davis & Sandman, 2010).

## Conclusions

The fetal programming "movement" has had a significant impact on medicine and basic science. Despite the fact that this area of research is in its embryonic stage, the findings have created a paradigm shift. It now is essential to consider fetal experience in order to fully understand human development. Like early-life brain development, the reconstruction of the maternal brain may similarly represent a critical period for CNS development. The vast majority of women give birth to at least one child. As a result, a significant proportion of the adult population has its neurological abilities and functions distinctly altered by the transient state of pregnancy, and yet the extent, persistence, and consequences of these alterations are largely unknown. Elucidation of the role of the prenatal period in the development of both mother and child cannot be achieved by a single level of analysis, because multiple interrelated pathways (biological, environmental, psychosocial, and genetic) are implicated in these processes. Progress will be greatest with collaborations between basic, social, and epidemiological scientists and with the application of prospective, multilevel, longitudinal approaches.

In addition to increasing understanding of the contribution of the prenatal period to CNS development, investigations of prenatal influences have potential to make intervention possible, improving maternal and child health. For clinical syndromes such as phenylketonuria, Down syndrome, and others, there are standard prenatal tests available to provide information and guide treatment. In the next 5 to 10 years, a more comprehensive understanding of the factors influencing "normal" fetal neurological development will emerge. For example, we may identify factors that impair child outcomes and also those that optimize them. Similarly, it is possible that the early identification of women at risk for postpartum depression or compromised maternal care could be achieved. With comprehensive characterization of maternal and fetal programming, specific and successful interventions could be realized.

## Suggested Readings

Barker, D.J.P. (1998). (See References). A book describing the work that laid the foundation for the developmental origins of disease model, or the Barker Hypothesis.

Clifton, V.L. (2010). (See References). A provocative new review describing the sexual dimorphism of the placenta and its implications.

Diamond, M.C., Johnson, R.E., & Ingram, C. (1971). Brain plasticity induced by environment and pregnancy. *International Journal of Neuroscience, 2,* 171–178. This paper provides some of the earliest evidence that pregnancy is associated with changes in brain structure.

Gluckman, P.D., & Hanson, M.A. (2004). Living with the past: Evolution, development, and patterns of disease. *Science, 305,* 1733–1736. This paper provides a full discussion of the predictive adaptive response.

Kinsley, C.H., & Lambert, K.G. (2006). The maternal brain. *Scientific American, 294,* 72–79. A comprehensive, accessible review of evidence for the neural plasticity associated with pregnancy and reproduction derived from animal models.

## References

Barker, D.J.P. (1998). *Mothers, babies and health in later life.* Edinburgh, UK: Harcourt Brace.

Buss, C., Davis, E.P., Muftuler, L.T., Head, K., & Sandman, C.A. (2010). High pregnancy anxiety during mid-gestation is associated with decreased gray matter density in 6–9-year-old children. *Psychoneuroendocrinology, 35,* 141–153.

Clifton, V.L. (2010). Sex and the human placenta: Mediating differential strategies of fetal growth and survival. *Placenta, 24,* S33–S39.

Davis, E.P., Glynn, L.M., Waffarn, F., & Sandman, C.A. (2011). Prenatal maternal stress programs infant stress regulation. *Journal of Child Psychology and Psychiatry, 52,* 119–129.

Davis, E.P., & Sandman, C.A. (2010). The timing of prenatal exposure to maternal cortisol and psychosocial stress is associated with human infant cognitive development. *Child Development, 81,* 131–138.

Denver, R.J. (1997). Environmental stress as a developmental cue: Corticotropin-releasing hormone is a proximate mediator of adaptive phenotypic plasticity in amphibian metamorphosis. *Hormones and Behavior, 31,* 161–171.

de Weerth, C., & Buitelaar, J.K. (2005). Physiological stress reactivity in human pregnancy—A review. *Neuroscience & Biobehavioral Reviews, 29*, 295–312.

DiPietro, J.A., Irizarry, R.A., Costigan, K.A., & Gurewitsch, E.D. (2004). The psychophysiology of the maternal-fetal relationship. *Psychophysiology, 41*, 510–520.

Glynn, L.M. (2010). Giving birth to a new brain: Hormone exposures of pregnancy influence human memory. *Psychoneuroendocrinology, 35*, 1148–1155.

Glynn, L.M., Dunkel Schetter, C., Hobel, C.J., & Sandman, C.A. (2008). Pattern of perceived stress and anxiety in pregnancy predicts preterm birth. *Health Psychology, 27*, 43–51.

Glynn, L.M., Wadhwa, P.D., Dunkel Schetter, C., Chicz-DeMet, A., & Sandman, C.A. (2001). When stress happens matters: Effect of earthquake timing on stress responsivity in pregnancy. *American Journal of Obstetrics & Gynecology, 184*, 637–642.

Henry, J.D., & Rendell, P.G. (2007). A review of the impact of pregnancy on memory function. *Journal of Clinical and Experimental Neuropsychology, 29*, 793–803.

Kim, P., Leckman, J.F., Mayes, L.C., Feldman, R., Wang, X., & Swain, J.E. (2010). The plasticity of human maternal brain: Longitudinal changes in brain anatomy during the early postpartum period. *Behavioral Neuroscience, 124*, 695–700.

McLean, M., Bisits, A., Davies, J., Woods, R., Lowry, P., & Smith, R. (1995). A placental clock controlling the length of human pregnancy. *Nature Medicine, 1*, 460–463.

O'Connor, T.G., Ben-Shiomo, Y., Heron, J., Golding, J., Adams, D., & Glover, V. (2005). Prenatal anxiety predicts individual differences in cortisol in pre-adolescent children. *Biological Psychiatry, 58*, 211–217.

Sandman, C.A., Davis, E.P., Buss, C., & Glynn, L.M. (in press). Exposure to prenatal psychobiological stress exerts programming influences on the mother and her fetus. *Neuroendocrinology*.

Sandman, C.A., Davis, E.P., & Glynn, L.M. (in press). Prescient human fetuses thrive. *Psychological Science*.

Shingo, T., Gregg, C., Enwere, E., Fujikawa, H., Hassam, R., Geary, C., . . . Weiss, S. (2003). Pregnancy-stimulated neurogenesis in the adult female forebrain mediated by prolactin. *Science, 299*, 117–120.

Talge, N.M., Neal, C., Glover, V., & Early Stress, Translational Research and Prevention Science Network: Fetal and Neonatal Experience on Child and Adolescent Mental Health. (2007). Antenatal maternal stress and long-term effects on child neuro-development: How and why? *Journal of Child Psychology and Psychiatry, 48*, 245–261.

Tan, X.-W., Liao, H., Sun, L., Okabe, M., Xiao, Z.-C., & Dawe, G.S. (2005). Fetal microchimerism in the maternal mouse brain: A novel population of fetal progenitor or stem cells able to cross the blood-brain barrier? *Stem Cells, 23*, 1443–1452.

Van den Bergh, B.R., & Marcoen, A. (2004). High antenatal maternal anxiety is related to ADHD symptoms, externalizing problems, and anxiety in 8- and 9-year-olds. *Child Development, 75*, 1085–1087.

Yim, I.S., Gynn, L.M., Dunkel Schetter, C., Hobel, C.J., Chicz-DeMet, A., & Sandman, C.A. (2009). Elevated corticotropin-releasing hormone in human pregnancy increases the risk of postpartum depressive symptoms. *Archives of General Psychiatry, 66*, 162–169.

# Critical Thinking

1. How does the fetus actively guide its development?

2. Explain the bidirectional relationship between maternal and fetal signals. How do the intrauterine and maternal environments interact?

3. What is maternal programming and how might it be adaptive?

**LAURA GLYNN,** Crean School of Health and Life Sciences, Chapman University, One University Drive, Orange, CA 92866 E-mail: lglynn@chapman.edu. **CURT A. SANDMAN,** Professor Emeritus, Department of Psychiatry and Human Behavior at the University of California, Irvine.

From *Current Directions in Psychological Science,* December 05, 2011, pp. 384–389. Copyright © 2011 by the Association for Psychological Science. Reprinted by permission of Sage Publications via Rightslink.

# Genes in Context

## *Gene–Environment Interplay and the Origins of Individual Differences in Behavior*

Frances A. Champagne and Rahia Mashoodh

Historically, the question of the origins of individual differences in personality, aptitudes, and even physical features has led to debates over nature *versus* nurture. However, it is becoming increasingly clear that creating a division between genes and environment limits our understanding of the complex biological processes through which individual differences are achieved. The reality that the interaction between genes and environment is a critical feature of development is emerging as a central theme in laboratory studies and longitudinal analyses in human populations. However, appreciating the existence of this interaction is simply the first step in broadening our theoretical approach to the study of behavior. To move forward, we must ask "What do genes do?" and "How do genes and environments interact?" Recent studies combining molecular biology with the study of behavior may provide insight into these issues and perhaps even call into question our current understanding of mechanisms involved in the transmission of traits across generations. Here we will highlight these new findings and illustrate the importance of putting genes in context.

## Laboratory and Longitudinal Approaches to Gene–Environment Interactions

Though recent advances in our ability to detect genetic variations have led to rapid progress in the study of gene-by-environment (G × E) effects, clues that G × E was critical in considering the origins of behavior have been available for a long time. In 1958, Cooper and Zubek published a report in which rats selectively bred to be either "maze-dull" or "maze-bright" were reared after weaning in either "enriched" environments containing increased sensory stimuli or "impoverished" environments containing limited sensory stimuli (Cooper & Zubek, 1958). In the rats reared under standard conditions, stable and heritable group differences in cognitive ability were observed in adulthood. However, maze-dull animals reared in an enriched environment showed a significant improvement in learning ability, and mazebright animals reared under impoverished conditions showed a significant decline in performance. This study provides evidence that, even when considering a genetically derived characteristic, our prediction of behavior must incorporate knowledge of the environmental context of development.

A more recent example of G × E comes from the Dunedin longitudinal study (Caspi et al., 2003), which explored the roles of variation in a gene that alters serotonin levels and exposure to stressful life events across a 20-year period in determining risk of depression. Levels of serotonin within neural circuits are altered by the number of serotonin transporter proteins, and in humans there are genetic variations that lead to either high or low levels of the serotonin transporter. The serotonin system has been implicated in variations in mood, and this system is the target of most pharmacological interventions in the treatment of depression. Among individuals within the Dunedin study, risk of depression was predicted by the interaction of serotonin transporter genotype and the number of stressful life events experienced. Thus, no differences in risk of depression emerged as a function of genotype when the number of stressful life events was low. However, when an individual had experienced a high frequency of stressful events, genotype effects were observed, with individuals possessing the low-serotonin-transporter-level gene variant being at greater risk of depression. Though certain genetic variations can lead to risk or resilience to psychological disorder (see Kim-Cohen & Gold, 2009, this issue), this "potential" may not be observed unless variation in the environment is considered.

## Contextual Determinants of Gene Function

Empirical findings from G × E studies raise an important question: "If the effects of genetic variation can vary depending on characteristics of the environment, then what are environments doing to genes to alter their impact?" To address this question, we must first address the following question: "What do genes do?" Historically, *gene* was a term used to describe a unit of heritable material. Since the discovery of DNA, the study of genetics has come to mean the study of DNA, with *gene* defined as a particular sequence of DNA. Due to the complex nature of DNA, it is perhaps easier to employ an analogy that conveys the basic notions of gene function. Think of an individual's

DNA as books in a library that have been ordered and arranged very precisely by a meticulous librarian. These books contain a wealth of knowledge and the potential to inspire whoever should choose to read them. Asking what DNA does is like asking what a book in this library does. Books sit on a shelf waiting to be read. Once read, the information in those books can have limitless consequences. Likewise, DNA sits in our cells and waits to be read by an enzyme called RNA polymerase, leading to the production of messenger RNA (mRNA)—a process referred to as *transcription* (Figure 1a). The mRNA transcript is a copy of the DNA sequence that can further be "translated" into protein. The reading, or *expression,* of DNA can, like the books in our library, have limitless consequences. However, without the active process that triggers such expression, this potential may never be realized. Importantly, it is the environment around the DNA that contains those critical factors that make it possible to read the DNA (Figure 1b; also see Cole, 2009, for extended discussion of the regulation of gene expression).

The control of gene expression is ultimately determined by how accessible the sequence of DNA is to factors within the cell that are involved in transcription. Influences that determine the expression of DNA without altering the sequence of DNA are referred to as epigenetic, meaning "in addition to genetic." One particular epigenetic mechanism that may have consequences for long-term changes in gene activity is DNA methylation (Figure 1c). DNA can become modified through the addition of a methyl chemical group to particular sites within the gene sequence. DNA methylation typically reduces the accessibility of DNA and can lead to "silencing" of the gene (Razin, 1998). In the library analogy, one can think of multiple factors that will influence the likelihood a book will or will not be read. Even books containing very valuable information may sit undisturbed and unread, gradually collecting dust. This may be particularly true if the book is hard to get to. It may be located on a shelf that is particularly difficult to reach or blocked by some piece of furniture. DNA methylation reduces the likelihood of transcription much in the same way that shifting furniture in a library can reduce the likelihood that a book will be read. The gene is there, but sits unread, collecting dust.

# Environmental Influences on Gene Activity

A recent breakthrough in our understanding of gene–environment interplay comes from studies exploring the epigenetic processes that are altered by an individual's experiences during development. Based primarily on studies in rodents, these paradigms address the question raised by G × E research: "What are environments doing to genes to alter their impact?" In rodents, variations in maternal care lead to individual differences in the expression of genes that alter the stress response. Low levels of glucocorticoid receptors (*GR*) within the hippocampus, a brain region critical for learning and memory, result in a prolonged response to stress. Analysis of DNA methylation within the regulatory region of the *GR* gene indicates that low levels of maternal care are associated with elevated levels of DNA methylation, which epigenetically silence this gene (Weaver et al., 2004). Moreover, the epigenetic status of the *GR* gene can be targeted pharmacologically in adulthood. Treatment with a drug that promotes increases in accessibility of DNA results

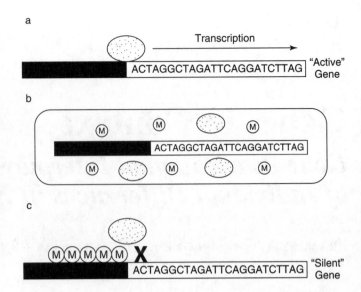

**Figure 1** Illustration of the epigenetic control of gene expression and the environmental context of DNA. As shown in the top panel (a), genes consist of a sequence of DNA consisting of "C," "T," "A," and "G" nucleotides preceded by a promotor region of DNA (the black bar). The promoter region responds to factors that control the likelihood of transcription (reading of the DNA). In order for transcription to occur, enzymes that "read" the DNA (the gray oval) must bind to the promotor region of the gene. When this occurs, the gene is "active" and can alter the function of the cell. The environmental context of the gene, shown in the middle panel (b), includes factors that increase gene activity (i.e., enzymes that read the DNA, shown as gray ovals) and factors that decrease gene activity (i.e., methyl groups, illustrated as circles labeled "M"); these factors will determine the likelihood that a gene will be expressed. When a methyl chemical group attaches to the promotor region, as shown in the bottom panel (c), the enzymes that transcribe DNA are blocked and the gene becomes "silent"; this is referred to as DNA methylation.

in decreased *GR* methylation and a dramatic shift in the phenotype of adult offspring who received low levels of maternal care (Weaver et al., 2004). Conversely, when adult offspring who experienced high levels of care are treated with a drug that increases the availability of methyl groups within the brain, they become indistinguishable from offspring who received low levels of maternal care (Weaver et al., 2005). These dynamic alterations in DNA methylation in adulthood have also been observed in studies of learning and memory (Miller & Sweatt, 2007). The experience of learning is associated with rapid changes in methylation of genes within the hippocampus, and if DNA methylation is inhibited there will be impairment in memory for the experience. These studies illustrate the role of epigenetic mechanisms in shaping the activity of the genome in response to environmental cues and demonstrate the plasticity that is possible through shifts in DNA methylation.

The prenatal period is characterized by rapid changes in brain development and is thus a sensitive time during which the quality of the environment can exert sustained effects on functioning. In rodents, exposure to chronic variable stress during the first trimester is associated with increased methylation of the regulatory region of the *GR* gene (Mueller & Bale, 2008). This effect could potentially be mediated by (a) stress-induced decreases in postnatal maternal behavior (Champagne & Meaney, 2006), (b) alterations to gene expression in the placenta (Mueller & Bale, 2008) that may restrict access of the fetus to maternal resources, or (c) a direct influence of maternal stress hormone on fetal gene expression. Modification to the fetal "epigenome" can also be achieved through variations in maternal diet during pregnancy. A striking example of this phenomenon comes from work with a mouse model in which a mutation of the *Agouti* gene leads to alterations in coat color and metabolism. The severity of the effects of this mutation depends on the level of DNA methylation of the *Agouti* gene; high levels of DNA methylation will epigenetically silence this mutation and induce a "pseudoagouti" mouse that is comparable in phenotype to a mouse without the mutation. When pregnant female mice with the *Agouti* mutation are placed on a diet that is rich in methyl groups, the methylation status of this gene is altered such that offspring develop a pseudo-agouti phenotype (Dolinoy, 2008). Thus, experience-dependent change in the epigenetic status of genes is not limited to the postnatal period.

# Implications of Gene–Environment Interplay for Psychological Functioning

The molecular processes described in laboratory studies may also be critical in understanding the origins of individual differences in humans. Analyses of DNA methylation in cells extracted from fetal cord blood suggest that antenatal maternal depression and anxiety during the third trimester can lead to increased levels of DNA methylation of the GR gene promotor region, having consequences for the stress response of infants at 3 years of age (Oberlander et al., 2008). These effects emerge even in the absence of depression-induced decreases in postnatal mother–infant interactions. The stability of DNA methylation also permits analysis of the epigenetic status of genes in postmortem brain tissue, which can be correlated to life experiences and psychological functioning. In a recent study, DNA methylation of ribosomal genes in hippocampal tissue of suicide victims with a history of abuse and neglect was compared to that of controls. Elevated levels of methylation were detected in ribosomal RNA genes among suicide victims (McGowan et al., 2008), and this effect was found to be specific to the hippocampus. Ribosomes are critical for the production of proteins and thus serve as a critical link between the expression of genes and the level of protein created.

Studies of monozygotic (MZ) twins also provide important insights into epigenetic effects in humans. Comparison of the gene expression of 3-year-old and 50-year-old MZ twins indicates a higher level of discordance in patterns of gene expression among older twins that is associated with increasing differences in DNA methylation in older compared to younger twins (Fraga et al., 2005). Though it is unknown whether concordance in young twins is due to germ-line (the cells that transmit genetic material across generations) or prenatal factors and whether the emerging discordance is random or driven by specific environmental events,

there is evidence that epigenetic variation in MZ twins may account for differential risk of mental illness. Analysis of methylation patterns within the catechol-O-methyltransferase *(COMT)* gene in tissue samples from 5-year-old MZ twins indicates varying degrees of discordance, with some MZ twin pairs showing a high degree of discordance and others being very similar in epigenetic status (Mill et al., 2006). *COMT* is an enzyme involved in the inactivation of neurotransmitters such as dopamine and norepinephrine, and disruptions in these neurotransmitter systems have been implicated in many forms of psychopathology. The divergence in methylation of the *COMT* gene within these twin pairs may predict differential risk of neurodevelopmental disorder in later life. Incorporating epigenetic analysis into twin studies represents a novel approach to the study of the origins of individual differences.

# Transmission of Traits across Generations: Rethinking Inheritance

In addition to shaping developmental trajectories within an individual's life span, DNA methylation may also have implications for the transmission of traits from one generation to the next. There are two distinct pathways through which this transmission can occur: (a) the behavioral transmission of traits through experience-dependent changes in the methylation of genes, and (b) environmental effects that change DNA methylation in germ cells and are thus transmitted through the germ line of subsequent generations. An example of the first pathway comes from studies of the transmission of maternal care across generations. Variations in maternal care in rodents have been demonstrated to alter the epigenetic status of hypothalamic estrogen receptors of female offspring (Champagne et al., 2006). These receptors are critical in regulating maternal behavior and coordinate the sensitivity of females to hormonal cues. Experience of low levels of maternal care in infancy is associated with increased estrogen receptor promotor methylation, decreased receptor expression, and subsequent decreases in the adult maternal behavior of these offspring. Thus, there is a behavioral transmission of individual differences in maternal care across generations. Interestingly, the quality of environmental conditions experienced by these females at later periods in development can alter this transgenerational inheritance. Prolonged social isolation from peers and prenatal stress can lead to reductions in maternal care that are passed on to subsequent generations (Champagne & Meaney, 2006, 2007). These studies, which are conducted in rodents that have limited genetic variability, suggest that similarities in traits between parental and offspring generations involve far more than the inheritance of genes.

Though epigenetic characteristics of DNA are dynamic in response to environmental cues, these modifications are also stable and heritable. Thus, both genetic and epigenetic factors are transmitted down cell lineages with consequences for the activity of genes within these lineages. However, when considering the question of inheritance at the level of an individual, we must know whether epigenetic patterns within the germ line are correlated to those patterns found within the developing organism. In rodents, prenatal exposure to endocrine disruptors leads to abnormal methylation patterns in sperm cells that are observed several generations beyond the point of initial exposure (Anway, Cupp, Uzumcu, & Skinner, 2005). This germ-line epigenetic inheritance of environmentally induced effects provides further support for the notion that the transmission of traits across generations is not limited in scope to the inheritance of DNA.

# Conclusion

Just as a library is more than a collection of books, the genome is more than just DNA. The challenge for the field of epigenetics is to determine the origins of the "uniqueness" of each individual's library by exploring the relationship between genetic and epigenetic variation. Though there are many basic questions to be addressed regarding the pathways whereby specific experiences target particular genes, this field of research certainly has promise in uncovering the nature of experience-dependent changes in development both within and across generations. Advances in tools available to study these effects in humans will be critically important in further exploring the role of epigenetics within the broad field of psychological science.

# Recommended Readings

Champagne, F.A. (2008). Epigenetic mechanisms and the transgenerational effects of maternal care. *Frontiers of Neuroendocrinology, 29,* 386–397. Provides a thorough review of the potential role of epigenetic factors in mediating the effects of maternal care within and across generations.

Jirtle, R.L., & Skinner, M.K. (2007). Environmental epigenomics and disease susceptibility. *Nature Reviews Genetics, 8,* 253–262. A review of our current understanding of environmentally induced epigenetic changes and the influence of these processes on individual risk of disease.

Maher, B. (2008). Personal genomes: The case of the missing heritability. *Nature, 456,* 18–21. An interesting commentary on the relationship between heritability estimates and the biological processes that determine the relationship between genes and behavior.

Meaney, M.J. (2001). Maternal care, gene expression, and the transmission of individual differences in stress reactivity across generations. *Annual Review of Neuroscience, 24,* 1161–1192. A review of the profound influence of maternal care on gene expression and behavior of offspring.

# References

Anway, M.D., Cupp, A.S., Uzumcu, M., & Skinner, M.K. (2005). Epigenetic transgenerational actions of endocrine disruptors and male fertility. *Science, 308,* 1466–1469.

Caspi, A., Sugden, K., Moffitt, T.E., Taylor, A., Craig, I.W., Harrington, H., et al. (2003). Influence of life stress on depression: Moderation by a polymorphism in the 5-HTT gene. *Science, 301,* 386–389.

Champagne, F.A., & Meaney, M.J. (2006). Stress during gestation alters postpartum maternal care and the development of the offspring in a rodent model. *Biological Psychiatry, 59,* 1227–1235.

Champagne, F.A., & Meaney, M.J. (2007). Transgenerational effects of social environment on variations in maternal care and behavioral response to novelty. *Behavioral Neuroscience, 121,* 1353–1363.

Champagne, F.A., Weaver, I.C., Diorio, J., Dymov, S., Szyf, M., & Meaney, M.J. (2006). Maternal care associated with methylation of the estrogen receptor-alpha1b promoter and estrogen receptor alpha expression in the medial preoptic area of female offspring. *Endocrinology, 147,* 2909–2915.

Cole, S.W. (2009). Social regulation of human gene expression. *Current Directions in Psychological Science, 18,* 132–137.

Cooper, R.M., & Zubek, J.P. (1958). Effects of enriched and restricted early environments on the learning ability of bright and dull rats. *Canadian Journal of Psychology, 12,* 159–164.

Dolinoy, D.C. (2008). The Agouti mouse model: An epigenetic biosensor for nutritional and environmental alterations on the fetal epigenome. *Nutrition Reviews, 66*(Suppl 1), S7–S11.

Fraga, M.F., Ballestar, E., Paz, M.F., Ropero, S., Setien, F., Ballestar, M.L., et al. (2005). Epigenetic differences arise during the lifetime of monozygotic twins. *Proceedings of the National Academy of Sciences, USA, 102,* 10604–10609.

Kim-Cohen, J., & Gold, A.L. (2009). Measured gene–environment interactions and mechanisms promoting resilient development. *Current Directions in Psychological Science, 18,* 138–142.

McGowan, P.O., Sasaki, A., Huang, T.C., Unterberger, A., Suderman, M., Ernst, C., et al. (2008). Promoter-wide hypermethylation of the ribosomal RNA gene promoter in the suicide brain. *PLoS ONE, 3,* e2085.

Mill, J., Dempster, E., Caspi, A., Williams, B., Moffitt, T., & Craig, I. (2006). Evidence for monozygotic twin (MZ) discordance in methylation level at two CpG sites in the promoter region of the catechol-O-methyltransferase (COMT) gene. *American Journal of Medical Genetics B: Neuropsychiatric Genetics, 141,* B421–B425.

Miller, C.A., & Sweatt, J.D. (2007). Covalent modification of DNA regulates memory formation. *Neuron, 53,* 857–869.

Mueller, B.R., & Bale, T.L. (2008). Sex-specific programming of offspring emotionality after stress early in pregnancy. *Journal of Neuroscience, 28,* 9055–9065.

Oberlander, T.F., Weinberg, J., Papsdorf, M., Grunau, R., Misri, S., & Devlin, A.M. (2008). Prenatal exposure to maternal depression, neonatal methylation of human glucocorticoid receptor gene (NR3C1) and infant cortisol stress responses. *Epigenetics, 3,* 97–106.

Razin, A. (1998). CpG methylation, chromatin structure and gene silencing-a three-way connection. *EMBO Journal, 17,* 4905–4908.

Weaver, I.C., Cervoni, N., Champagne, F.A., D'Alessio, A.C., Sharma, S., Seckl, J.R., et al. (2004). Epigenetic programming by maternal behavior. *Nature Neuroscience, 7,* 847–854.

Weaver, I.C., Champagne, F.A., Brown, S.E., Dymov, S., Sharma, S., Meaney, M.J., et al. (2005). Reversal of maternal programming of stress responses in adult offspring through methyl supplementation: Altering epigenetic marking later in life. *Journal of Neuroscience, 25,* 11045–11054.

# Critical Thinking

1. What are some environmental factors, from maternal diet, stress, or exposure to toxins, that can influence genetic processes in the fetus?

2. What is DNA methylation, and how does it illustrate the interplay of genes and environment?

3. How is the field of epigenetics a new way of thinking beyond the simple nature vs. nurture debate?

Address correspondence to **FRANCES A. CHAMPAGNE**, Columbia University, Department of Psychology, 406 Schermerhorn Hall, 1190 Amsterdam Avenue, New York, NY 10027; e-mail: fac2105@columbia.edu.

From *Current Directions in Psychological Science,* June, 2009, pp. 127–131. Copyright © 2009 by the Association for Psychological Science. Reprinted by permission of Sage Publications via Rightslink.

# Effects of Prenatal Social Stress on Offspring Development
## *Pathology or Adaptation?*

Sylvia Kaiser and Norbert Sachser

Ontogeny is the development of an individual from the moment the egg is fertilized until death. Most research on *behavioral* ontogeny has focused on the early postnatal phase, probably because socialization and learning processes are thought to play their most important role during this time. However, there is growing evidence that environmental influences before birth also have impact on the individual's development later in life (de Weerth, Buitelaar, & Mulder, 2005). In particular, stressors acting on the mother during pregnancy can have distinct and long-term effects on behavior, reproductive functions, and the immune, neuroendocrine and autonomic systems of her offspring (de Kloet, Sibug, Helmerhorst, & Schmidt, 2005).

In most experimental studies on the effects of prenatal stress, pregnant female animals have been subjected to nonsocial stressors (e.g., bright light, restraint). Interpretation of these studies is difficult, because such artificial stressors typically do not occur in those animals' natural environments (Kaiser & Sachser, 2005). In their natural habitats, animals have to cope with a variety of stressors that depend on their ecological niche. They have to adjust to the physical environment (e.g., weather) and to the biotic world that surrounds them (e.g., predators, food shortage). A major part of an individual's biotic environment consists of other members of the same species, which can be defined as that individual's "social world." In fact, a majority of human and animal daily expectations, motivations, and behaviors are directed toward encounters with conspecifics. On the one hand, this social world can support welfare and health (e.g., through the effects of social support). On the other hand, it can result in severe stress, eventually leading to disease and even death (e.g., in the case of social defeat, social instability, or crowding; von Holst, 1998). Thus, the social environment represents a very influential stressor, which, during pregnancy, can be crucial for the development of the offspring (Kaiser & Sachser, 2005).

## Effects of the Prenatal Social Environment on Offspring Development and Behavior
### *Animal Studies*

The most comprehensive insights from studies of nonhuman animals regarding prenatal social influences on offspring development have been derived from studies in guinea pigs (Kaiser & Sachser, 2005). For example, when compared to daughters whose mothers had lived in a stable social environment during pregnancy (that is, group composition was kept constant, with one male and five females), female guinea pigs whose mothers had lived in an unstable social environment (every third day, two females from different groups were exchanged) showed conspicuous behavioral masculinization (e.g., displaying high levels of male-typical courtship behavior) later in life, increased testosterone concentrations, and a male-typical distribution pattern of androgen receptors in parts of the limbic system (Kaiser, Kruijver, Swaab, & Sachser, 2003). Compared to male guinea pigs whose mothers had lived in a stable social environment, those whose mothers had lived in an unstable social environment during pregnancy showed behavioral infantilization (e.g., displaying behavioral patterns usually shown only by very young male guinea pigs, such as sitting in close bodily contact), delayed development of the adrenocortical system, and down-regulation of androgen receptor expression in the limbic system (Kaiser, Kruijver, Straub, Sachser, & Swaab, 2003).

Studies of prenatal social influences on offspring development have been conducted only in a few other species (e.g., mice, rats, squirrel monkeys). Although a variety of different social stressors have been applied in these experiments (e.g., crowding, social confrontation, changing group membership), a common characteristic of all approaches is the induction of social instability. In general, under such conditions, the number of interactions with conspecifics increases and the predictability and controllability of social encounters dramatically decline. Interestingly, modern stress research shows that, in animals as well as in humans, situations of uncertainty or unpredictability are a major source of stress responses (von Holst, 1998).

When all experimental studies on prenatal social stress are compared, some general conclusions can be drawn: Female offspring show a masculinization of behavior, endocrine state, and brain development. Male offspring show a less pronounced expression of male-typical traits (e.g., demasculinization, feminization) and/or a delay in development. In addition, there are some indications that both sexes might have a more or less severe impairment of reproductive functions (cf., Kaiser & Sachser, 2005).

## Human Studies

The long-lasting effects of prenatal stress on offspring are also well known in humans: Children of mothers who were stressed during pregnancy develop higher risk of different diseases (including cardiovascular illness and diabetes) and may experience physical and cognitive developmental delays (e.g., Huizink, Mulder, & Buitelaar, 2004; Wadhwa, 2005). However, only limited data concerning the effects of *social* stressors during pregnancy on human offspring later in life are available. Those few studies, however, point to distinct effects on behavioral and physiological development. For instance, family discord during pregnancy leads to behavioral disturbances in children, and such children are more likely to develop psychopathological disorders such as autism (Ward, 1990; unfortunately, it is not mentioned whether this finding is controlled for postnatal effects). Similarly, moderate to severe stressors combined with low levels of social support during pregnancy reduce children's head circumference at birth, pointing to the effects of prenatal stress on brain development (Glynn & Sandman, 2006). Children whose mothers experienced high levels of daily hassles and pregnancy-specific anxiety show lower mental and motor developmental scores at 8 months of age after correcting for postnatal stress (Buitelaar, Huizink, Mulder, Robles de Medina, & Visser, 2003).

# Effects of Prenatal Social Stress: Pathology or Adaptation?

Researchers typically interpret the characteristic traits of individuals who were exposed to adverse environmental stimuli (stressors) during pregnancy as deviations from some standard considered optimal, and phenotypic differences in offspring are frequently called pathological. Alternatively, and in accordance with current evolutionary theory, these traits might also represent adaptive maternal effects; that is, the offspring's fitness is enhanced by maternal adjustments to the current environmental conditions.

Adaptation through maternal effects—that is, control and/or modulation of the offspring's phenotype—has become a key concept in modern evolutionary biology (see, e.g., Groothuis,

Müller, von Engelhardt, Carere, & Eising, 2005; Mousseau & Fox, 1998) and numerous studies to reveal the mechanism underlying these phenomena are currently underway. Particular maternal hormonal responses to environmental stimuli represent a potential tool by which development of offspring can be influenced. Indeed, in different bird species, mothers' deposition of androgens into the yolk of their eggs varies with environmental factors or social conditions, and experimental studies have shown effects of enhanced androgen levels on offspring traits such as competitiveness or growth (Groothuis, Müller, von Engelhardt, Carere, & Eising, 2005). Results of two recent studies in wild spotted hyenas and guinea pigs suggest that prenatal androgen exposure can adaptively influence offspring phenotype (in terms of aggression, sexual behavior, and testosterone responsiveness to social challenge) regularly in mammals as well (Dloniak, French, & Holekamp, 2006; Kemme, Kaiser, & Sachser, 2007). If such traits result in enhancement of fitness parameters such as social dominance or reproductive benefits, we can speak of an adaptive phenotype.

## Possible Benefits of Altered Phenotypes

The questions arise: What is the benefit of being a masculinized daughter? And what is the benefit for sons who show less pronounced expression of male-typical traits and/or a delay in development?

Consider the case of fluctuations in the density of natural populations of mammals. Under high-density conditions, social instability is a common trait, whereas low population densities are characterized by stable social situations (von Holst, 1998). Hence, different pregnant females may experience very different degrees of social stability in their natural habitats. If a pregnant female living in a high-density population has the possibility of preprogramming her daughters in such a way that they will gain maximum reproductive success in that high-density situation, it would seem reasonable for her to masculinize them in order to make them more robust and/or more competitive. These and other masculine traits facilitate the attainment of dominant social positions, which in turn help to defend important resources such as food and shelter (which are scarce in high-density situations) more efficiently. However, frequently a characteristic feature of masculinized females is impairment of reproductive function later in life (Kaiser & Sachser, 2005). Thus, under high-density conditions, there is likely to be a trade-off between the benefits of a behaviorally and endocrinologically masculinized phenotype and the costs of decreased reproductive success. Although decreased reproductive success might seem inconsistent with the idea of enhanced fitness, under such conditions, masculinized females might fare better than nonmasculinized females; the latter may often fail to reproduce at all because of lower social status that prevents access to resources necessary for reproduction. Under low-density conditions, however, sufficient resources are available and competitive abilities are less important. Under such conditions, it would seem more beneficial to invest time and energy in reproductive effort rather than to build and maintain a male-typical phenotype for defending resources. Thus, under low-density conditions, reproductive success would be higher in nonmasculinized females than in masculinized ones (Kaiser & Sachser, 2005).

The argument is similar for sons. Around the time of sexual maturity, they can find themselves in different situations. Consider a low-density condition with only a few males of the same age and some females present. In such a situation, the best strategy to maximize reproductive success would be to fight for the access to a copulation partner, because usually the winners will mate. Under such conditions, mothers will maximize their own fitness if they program their sons prenatally in a way that maximizes the timely expression of male-typical traits. In contrast, when animals live at high densities in large, age-graded populations, a different situation exists: Under such conditions, in many species, high-ranking (alpha) males almost exclusively sire all the offspring. Remarkably, males usually do not attain an alpha position until well beyond the age of sexual maturity (e.g., mandrills; Setchell, Charpentier, & Wickings, 2005). A male born in a high-density population should avoid agonistic encounters at too early an age, because this will not result in reproductive success. By neither signaling sexual interest in females nor displaying other signs of sexual maturity, a pubescent male is less likely to be attacked by the alpha males. This strategy should change, however, around the time of social maturity in order to attain the alpha position that is required for reproductive success. Thus, under conditions of high density, mothers may provide their sons with a more adaptive reproductive strategy by programming them prenatally in a way that delays development and/or diminishes expression of male-typical traits until social maturity is attained (Kaiser & Sachser, 2005).

Currently, much experimental animal research is being conducted to test such hypotheses on the adaptive value of prenatal maternal programming (Dloniak, French, & Holekamp, 2006; Kemme, Kaiser, & Sachser, 2007).

## Human Studies

Similar arguments for the adaptive value of the response to prenatal-stress effects in humans have been put forward. For example, Bateson et al. (2004) hypothesize that a period of starvation during pregnancy tells the developing fetus that food is probably going to be scarce in the future. Babies of such mothers often show small body weight and correspondingly modified metabolism. These traits are not necessarily pathological, inasmuch as they help the baby to cope with environments of low food availability. The proposed mechanism for these persistent effects into adulthood involves alteration in set points for various aspects of basic metabolism (e.g., glucoregulation, adiposity, and blood pressure; Roseboom, de Rooij, & Painter, 2006).

For ethical reasons, in humans it is not feasible to experimentally manipulate hormonal levels during early development or exposure to stress in pregnant mothers. Nevertheless,

good evidence that the behavioral phenotype of daughters can be shaped by prenatal androgens does exist. For example, girls with congenital adrenal hyperplasia (an autosomal recessive disorder that causes elevated adrenal androgens) are exposed to elevated androgen concentrations during fetal development, and this results in a masculinized phenotype—revealed, for example, by increased rough-and-tumble play (Hines, 2006). Other evidence shows that androgen levels in women can be affected by environmental situations: Testosterone concentrations increase, for example, in periods of high-intensity exercise (Bergeron et al., 1991). We therefore propose that androgen concentrations in pregnant women may change as a result of environmental factors and that these changed androgen concentrations may influence fetal central-nervous-system differentiation during early development, thereby shaping the behavioral phenotype of the offspring later in life. Whether or not this specific phenotype represents an adaptive adjustment to the environmental conditions under which the mother has lived during pregnancy remains to be determined.

## Conclusion

Studies of animals and humans clearly show that severe stressors acting upon a pregnant female can have profoundly negative effects on the later development and health of her offspring. In such cases, prenatal stress results in pathology and no discussion about adaptive function seems appropriate. Recent experimental animal studies of prenatal stress, when considered from an evolutionary perspective, draw attention to an additional hypothesis: that variation in behavioral phenotype brought about by prenatal stressors may represent an adaptation to the prevailing environmental situation. From this point of view, deviations from the behavioral and physiological standard, such as masculinized daughters and infantilized sons, should not be regarded as pathological but may rather be seen as representing adaptations to the offspring's likely environment. It is timely and exciting to test whether some of the individual variation among members of our species might not reflect the action of similar, and perhaps now vestigial, processes. Accordingly the central hypothesis is this: We share the same mechanisms with nonhuman mammals that allow infants to be preadapted to the world their mothers live in during pregnancy. In particular, we assume that the environment in which a pregnant woman lives affects her endocrine state, which in turn influences fetal brain development, thereby adapting the infant's behavior and physiology to cope successfully with the challenges of the environmental niche of the mother. If so, children of mothers who have lived in a stable social situation during pregnancy will cope better with conditions of social stability later in life than will children whose mothers have lived under unstable social conditions. However, children whose mothers have lived under unstable social conditions during pregnancy might cope better with conditions of social instability later in life than might children of mothers who have lived in stable social situations. Future studies are required to test these hypotheses.

# Recommended Reading

Bateson, P., Barker, D., Clutton-Brock, T., Deb, D., D'Udine, B., Foley, R.A., et al. (2004). Developmental plasticity and human health. *Nature, 430,* 419–421. Discusses developmental plasticity and human health in more details than the current article.

Champagne, F.A., & Curley, J.P. (2005). How social experiences influence the brain. *Current Opinion in Neurobiology, 15,* 704–709. A clearly written, user-friendly, and relatively comprehensive review for readers who wish to expand their knowledge on influences of social experiences on brain development.

de Kloet, E.R., Sibug, R.M., Helmerhorst, F.M., & Schmidt, M. (2005). (See References). A clearly written, user-friendly, and relatively comprehensive review for readers who wish to expand their knowledge on long-lasting effects of early stress on brain programming.

Dufty, A.M., Jr., Clobert, J., & Møller, A.P. (2002). Hormones, developmental plasticity and adaptation. *Trends in Ecology & Evolution, 17,* 190–196. A clearly written, user-friendly, and relatively comprehensive review for readers who wish to expand their knowledge on developmental plasticity and adaptation.

Kaiser, S., & Sachser, N. (2005). (See References). A comprehensive, highly accessible overview of what is known about mechanisms and function of the effects of prenatal social stress.

# References

Bateson, P., Barker, D., Clutton-Brock, T., Deb, D., D'Udine, B., Foley, R.A., et al. (2004). Developmental plasticity and human health. *Nature, 430, 419–421.*

Bergeron, M.E., Maresh, C.M., Kraemer, W.J., Abraham, A., Conroy, B., & Gabaree, C. (1991). Tennis: A physiological profile during match play. *International Journal of Sports Medicine, 12,* 474–479.

Buitelaar, J.K., Huizink, A.C., Mulder, E.J., Robles de Medina, P.G., & Visser, G.H.A. (2003). Prenatal stress and cognitive development and temperament in infants. *Neurobiology of Aging, 24,* S53–S60.

de Kloet, E.R., Sibug, R.M., Helmerhorst, F.M., & Schmidt, M. (2005). Stress, genes and the mechanism of programming the brain for later life. *Neuroscience and Biobehavioral Reviews, 29,* 271–281.

de Weerth, C., Buitelaar, J.K., & Mulder, E.J.H. (Eds.). (2005). Prenatal programming of behaviour, physiology and cognition. *Neuroscience and Biobehavioral Reviews, 29,* 207–384.

Dloniak, S.M., French, J.A., & Holekamp, K.E. (2006). Rank-related maternal effects of androgens on behaviour in wild spotted hyaenas. *Nature, 449,* 1190–1193.

Glynn, L.M., & Sandman, C.A. (2006). The influence of prenatal stress and adverse birth outcome on human cognitive and neurological development. *International Review of Research in Mental Retardation, 32,* 109–129.

Groothuis, T.G.G., Müller, W., von Engelhardt, N., Carere, C., & Eising, C. (2005). Maternal hormones as a tool to adjust offspring phenotype in avian species. *Neuroscience and Biobehavioral Reviews, 29,* 329–352.

Hines, M. (2006). Prenatal testosterone and gender-related behaviour. *European Journal of Endocrinology, 155,* S115–S121.

Huizink, A.C., Mulder, E.J.H., & Buitelaar, J.K. (2004). Prenatal stress and risk for psychopathology: Specific effects or induction of general susceptibility? *Psychological Bulletin, 130,* 115–142.

Kaiser, S., Kruijver, F.P.M., Straub, R.H., Sachser, N., & Swaab, D.F. (2003). Early social stress in male guinea pigs changes social behaviour, and autonomic and neuroendocrine functions. *Journal of Neuroendocrinology, 15,* 761–769.

Kaiser, S., Kruijver, F.P.M., Swaab, D.F., & Sachser, N. (2003). Early social stress in female guinea pigs induces a masculinization of adult behavior and corresponding changes in brain and neuroendocrine function. *Behavioral Brain Research, 144,* 199–210.

Kaiser, S., & Sachser, N. (2005). The effects of prenatal social stress on behaviour: Mechanisms and function. *Neuroscience and Biobehavioral Reviews, 29,* 283–294.

Kemme, K., Kaiser, S., & Sachser, N. (2007). Prenatal maternal programming determines testosterone response during social challenge. *Hormones and Behavior, 51,* 387–394.

Mousseau, T.A., & Fox, C.W. (1998). The adaptive significance of maternal effects. *Trends in Ecology and Evolution, 13,* 403–407.

Roseboom, T., de Rooij, S., & Painter, R. (2006). The Dutch famine and its long-term consequences for adult health. *Early Human Development, 82,* 485–491.

Setchell, J.M., Charpentier, M., & Wickings, E.J. (2005). Sexual selection and reproductive careers in mandrills (*Mandrillus sphinx*). *Behavioral Ecology and Sociobiology, 58,* 474–485.

von Holst, D. (1998). The concept of stress and its relevance for animal behavior. *Advances of the Study of Behavior, 27,* 1–131.

Wadhwa, P.D. (2005). Psychoneuroendocrine processes in human pregnancy influence fetal development and health. *Psychoneuroendocrinology, 30,* 724–743.

Ward, A.J. (1990). A comparison and analysis of the presence of family problems during pregnancy of mothers of "autistic" children and mothers of normal children. *Child Psychiatry and Human Development, 20,* 279–288.

# Critical Thinking

1. Appraise and summarize the research findings regarding human prenatal social stress on babies. Identify and prioritize particular social stressors that appear to have the most negative outcomes on babies.

2. Given the research discussed in this article, what specific steps would you recommend to couples who are seeking to have a baby during times of stress and turbulence?

3. Compare and contrast the negative and positive effects of human prenatal social stress on girls versus boys. Provide a rationale for these differences.

4. Discuss and justify implications of these negative effects on possible interventions and/or policies for pregnant women.

Address correspondence to **SYLVIA KAISER**, Department of Behavioral Biology, University of Muenster, Badestrasse 13, D-48149 Muenster, Germany; e-mail: kaisesy@uni-muenster.de.

# UNIT 2

# Cognition, Language, and Learning

## Unit Selections

## Learning Outcomes

- Describe to a classmate the procedures used to study infant perception of native speech. What were some strengths of the procedure? Are there any shortcomings you know of?

- Explain what distributional learning is in early language development.

- Describe how the experimental procedures in Article 6 are similar to and different from the experimental procedures used in the research in Article 4.

- Critique the concept of "interactive specialization" of the postnatal human brain in terms of the nature-versus-nurture debate by marshaling specific research data from the article to support this theoretical concept.

- Synthesize the merits of the three proposed mechanisms underlying changes in the plasticity of sensitive periods.

- Formulate and argue for policy and practice implications in the area of K–12 policies regarding enhancing second language learning as well as interventions to improve vision for children born with significant visual deficits.

- Evaluate and speculate as to why sensitive periods and plasticity vary both across modalities (e.g., vision vs. language acquisition) and even within modalities (phonology vs. morphosyntax). Hypothesize as to why these variations might exist.

- Explain to a biology major who holds the view "biology is destiny" that genetic and neuroscience research shows that biology is not destiny and that environmental experience is crucial for influencing biology.

- Synthesize the evidence on the different topics in Article 7 (e.g., mirror neurons and imitation) to describe how nature and nurture interact to shape early development.

- Evaluate the information in the article and identify specific research questions that remain to be answered on the link between breast feeding and infant cognition.

- Explain to a new mother or pediatrician why it is dangerous to assume that early infant cognitive ability clearly predicts intelligence later in childhood.

- Explain the research design used to determine whether baby videos affect development.

- Advise new parents on whether baby videos are worth the money and hope invested in them.

- Explain how consciousness is different for an infant, preschooler, and older child.

- Synthesize the six different conditions of a narrative approach to explain how child development entails influences of evolution, biology, proximal social experience, and culture.

- Differentiate between social cognitive understanding in children in terms of judgments of goodness and badness, evaluation of similar and dissimilar others, and mental representations of social relationships. Describe how social cognitive understanding in these areas develops from infancy through childhood.

- Explain differences between adults and children in their level of social cognitive understanding and include reference to comparative data involving other primates.

- Predict young children's potential social understandings of other people based on their past experiences with parents, caregivers, and others in their social network.

- Propose how early experiences with those close to them in infancy and early childhood may influence children's subsequent attitudes and prejudices of others.

- Describe the benefits of "adaptive immaturity" as it pertains to children's positivity bias.

- Explain to a teacher with a multicultural classroom how growing up in different cultures may influence how much children use a positivity bias in judging themselves or others.

- Design a brochure or role-play exercise for parents of young children to help the parents communicate with their children in ways that would increase the children's understanding of science exhibits.

- Describe several different causes for reading comprehension difficulties in children.

- Critique several school-based interventions that may be used to treat reading comprehension problems.

- Convince a school principal that recess is important to children's development and why it should not be sacrificed for more instructional time.

- Prepare a presentation for parents who worry that their children are "falling behind" academically and therefore should spend less time at recess.

- Describe and compare success rates of the various SEL, or Social and Emotional Learning, programs across the country designed to improve student outcomes (e.g., decreases in drug and alcohol use, incidence of depression, violence, PTSD, social anxiety and phobias).

- Justify larger-scale, government-funded efforts to increase SEL training programs for students across the nation. Provide data and rationale to support your case.

- Compare, contrast, and recommend who should be responsible for SEL training—teachers, parents, or others?

- Defend the expansion of SEL training to special groups such as military families and special-education populations.

- When do children first understand other people's feelings and mental states or how to evaluate other people's abilities? Do you think parents and teachers helped teach children to promote this awareness and assessment of others? Do you view yourself as having a high emotional IQ? Explain why or why not. Did you have parents or siblings who talked to you about feelings and people and helped you understand others and learn how to behave in productive ways? If not, did you have friends, teachers, or other adults who helped you develop and build your social skills? Do you think you can improve your social skills as an adult or not? Explain your answer and give examples.

- Organize a debate with pro and con positions on whether spirituality should be discussed in schools during instructional time.

- Identify aspects of young children's social and emotional development that may be enriched if spiritual and philosophical issues are discussed in school.

- Prepare a response to teachers or parents who feel that there is no place in schools for discussions of spirituality. Does allowing children to discuss a topic mean that the school endorses or promotes certain religious beliefs?

**W**e have come a long way from the days when the characterization of cognition of infants and young children included phrases like "tabula rasa" and "booming, buzzing confusion." Infants and young children are no longer viewed by researchers as blank slates, passively waiting to be filled up with knowledge. Today, experts in child development are calling for a reformulation of assumptions about children's cognitive abilities, as well as calling for reforms in the ways we teach children in our schools. Hence, the articles in the first subsection highlight some of the new knowledge of the cognitive abilities of infants and young children, while the second subsection focuses on schooling and learning.

Researchers today continue to discover that babies are developing an impressive array of early perceptual, social, emotional, and cognitive skills during infancy. In "How Do Infants Become Experts at Native-Speech Perception?" the authors describe research that helps explain how infants may process phonetic sounds using category learning to help them become speech-perception experts in their native language. From this perspective, babies are not as passive as once thought, and parents and teachers can provide environments that nurture and support their babies' developing abilities. Another area receiving more interest is the research on whether breast-feeding enhances a baby's cognitive abilities. The author of "Infant Feeding and Cognition" summarizes the research on this topic.

Researchers describe the complex interplay between brain maturational development and external experience in determining the emergence of abilities such as language acquisition, neonate imitation, and factors related to stress reactivity in "New Advances in Understanding Sensitive Periods in Brain Development" and "Contributions of Neuroscience to Our Understanding of Cognitive Development." For example, nurturing touch during infancy has been shown to be a very important factor in promoting growth, reducing stress and reducing depression and other cognitive deficits later in life.

We learn from research in "Do Babies Learn from Baby Media?" that the recent glut of baby-focused videos may not necessarily result in the lofty cognitive advances many of these products promise. On the other hand, social interactions play a key role in helping children develop a theory of mind or the ability to understand other people's points of view and emotional states. Children advance in their understanding of mental states—a critical ingredient for building appropriate social skills and understanding people's good and bad actions—when their parents and teachers engage in rich conversations with them about others who have varying points of view and different emotions as discussed in "Social Cognitive Development: A New Look." Mounting research shows that children need to develop social and emotional intelligence to succeed.

Succeeding in school is an important milestone for children, and reading is a critical component of school success.

©JGI/Jamie Grill/Blend Images LLC
Mixed race baby girl playing with alphabet blocks

The authors of "Children's Reading Comprehension Difficulties: Nature, Causes, and Treatments" describe new school-based interventions that help improve children's comprehension abilities even though they may have mastered basic reading skills.

The adage, "all work and no play" is an important caveat to keep in balance for children coping with the demands of schooling. In "Recess—It's Indispensable!" the author discusses the importance of play for children's healthy development and skill building in spite of increasing trends for parents and schools to reduce or de-emphasize free play as a necessary part of young children's developmental environment.

When and how do children learn about and develop concepts about spirituality? In "Kindergartners Explore Spirituality", the authors describe a creative program with kindergartners that utilizes art, dramatic play, and exploratory writing to help children to experiment with ideas about spirituality, growth, and moral issues.

# Student Website

www.mhhe.com/cls

# Internet References

**Educational Resources Information Center (ERIC)**
www.ed.gov/about/pubs/intro/pubdb.html

**National Association for the Education of Young Children (NAEYC)**
www.naeyc.org

**Project Zero**
http://pzweb.harvard.edu

**Vandergrift's Children's Literature Page**
www.scils.rutgers.edu/special/kay/sharelit.html

# How Do Infants Become Experts at Native-Speech Perception?

JANET F. WERKER, H. HENNY YEUNG, AND KATHERINE A. YOSHIDA

## Phonetic Perception and Its Development

A parent points at a toy and says, "Look at this doll! That's your doll!" Learning words in this scenario requires many perceptual, pragmatic, and referential strategies on the part of an infant, but a first step is recognizing which sound properties distinguish word forms in his or her native language(s). This is not a simple task, given that phonetic input to infants is inherently variable. Consider the spoken tokens of "doll." To a Hindi speaker, the difference between the "d" sounds in "this doll" versus "your doll"— a phonetic contrast between a dental [d̪al] versus a retroflex [ɖal], respectively—would signal two possible word forms (either *lentils* or *branch*). In English, both of those "d" sounds signal just one possible word form— phonetically labeled as an alveolar [dal]. In this article, we ask what developmental processes allow infants to learn native-language phonetic categories like these from the input they receive.

Early work suggested that infants begin life sensitive to all phonetic contrasts and that listening experience functions to maintain perceptual sensitivity only for native phonetic contrasts. For example, young English-learning infants easily discriminate the two Hindi "d" sounds mentioned above, whereas English-speaking adults find this much harder. By 10 months of age, English learners begin perceiving speech in accord with their native language, no longer discriminating these two "d" sounds, whereas Hindi-learning infants perceptually maintain this distinction (Werker & Tees, 1984).[1] Dozens of studies have reported this kind of perceptual attunement in consonant, vowel, and even tone perception within the first year of life (for reviews, see Curtin & Werker, 2007; Gervain & Mehler, 2010), even for bilingual infants, who maintain phonetic contrasts used in both of their native languages (Albareda-Castellot, Pons, & Sebastián-Gallés, 2010; Burns, Yoshida, Hill, & Werker, 2007).

Subsequent work has shown that phonetic development is actually much more complex than this single pattern of maintenance and decline (Best, 1995). Language experience also enhances the discrimination of some native phonetic contrasts (Kuhl et al., 2006) and can realign existing phonetic-category boundaries (Burns et al., 2007). Infants discriminate other contrasts only after early exposure to a language with these distinctions, a fact that suggests that listening experience may induce certain categories (Narayan, Werker, & Beddor, 2010; Sato, Kato, & Mazuka, 2012). Moreover, phonetic perception is not as categorical as was once imagined: Young infants also discriminate some within-category variation (McMurray & Aslin, 2005). Finally, perceptual change continues well beyond the first year of life into later stages of development (Minagawa-Kawai, Mori, Naoi, & Kojima, 2007; Mugitani et al., 2009; Sundara, Polka, & Genesee, 2006).

What processes guide infants' phonetic learning? The input frequency of phonetic tokens is crucial. For example, Anderson, Morgan, and White (2003) showed that phonetic contrasts straddling frequently heard categories become language-specific earlier in development than those straddling less-frequently heard ones. Earlier theoretical models had suggested that token frequency "warps" acoustic-phonetic space, altering perceived similarity in that space (Jusczyk, 1993), or that frequently heard tokens attract acoustically similar ones, forming a "perceptual magnet" (Kuhl et al., 2008). In the following section, we review the literature on distributional learning (DL), which shares the token-counting approach of these previous models but also provides a mechanistic explanation of phonetic learning.

## Distributional Learning (DL) From the Statistical Structure of Language Input

The term "statistical learning" refers to the notion that infants learn some language patterns from the statistical properties of language input, a fact that was first demonstrated by seminal work showing that infants can segment possible "words" in a language by tracking transitional probabilities between syllables (Saffran, Aslin, & Newport, 1996). Proponents of DL similarly suggest that native phonetic categories are identified at least in part by statistical information, but it is the relative frequencies of phonetic tokens in subregions of acoustic-phonetic space, not transitional probabilities, that are tracked. Consider, for example, an English-learning infant who hears the word "doll." Along one phonetic dimension, the infant will hear variation around a central tendency, creating a unimodal distribution. For a Hindi learner, this variation is distributed around two means, one for the dental "d" in [d̪al] and one for the retroflex "d" in [ɖal]. Identifying these distributions could be used to infer the underlying phonetic structure of the native language(s).

Maye and Gerken (2000) demonstrated that adults are able to track phonetic distributions and use them to learn new perceptual categories (see Hayes-Harb, 2007, for a replication). To test DL in infants, Maye, Werker, and Gerken (2002) synthesized an 8-step continuum of "da" sounds[2] whose endpoints were within the same English category (likely still discriminable by these infants; see Pegg & Werker, 1997) but were in two possible categories from a different language. Two distributional environments were created from the continuum tokens. In the "bimodal" condition, the input contained more exemplars of steps 2 and 7, mimicking the variability infants might hear if they were raised in a language with two categories along that continuum. In the "unimodal" condition, the input contained more exemplars of steps 4 and 5, mimicking a language like English, which has only a single "da" category. The 6- to 8-month-olds in the study were presented with these tokens in a semirandom order for just over 2 minutes and tested on their ability to discriminate the endpoints of the continuum (steps 1 and 8) immediately afterward. Infants in the bimodal condition discriminated the endpoints, but infants in the unimodal condition did not.

This work illustrated a mechanism for how perceptual sensitivity to pre-existing phonetic categories is maintained while sensitivity to nonnative categories declines. More recently, Maye, Weiss, and Aslin (2008) showed that DL from bimodal distributions can also enhance phonetic sensitivity to difficult phonetic contrasts. The researchers also showed that DL of a an acoustic/phonetic feature in one context (differences between [da] and [ta] in voice-onset time) also generalized to a new contrast in another context ([ka] and [ga]), suggesting that DL may occur at a more abstract, phonetic-feature level. This implies that the identification of two phonetic categories can also facilitate the learning of related contrasts, even if those latter distinctions are not as clearly demarcated by statistical distributions.

DL seems to be a basic mechanism of perceptual change in the phonetic domain. Like other statistical mechanisms, it is available not only to humans but also to other species (Pons, 2006). Moreover, it functions broadly across domains: For example, visual categories can be inferred from distributional information by both children (Duffy, Huttenlocher, & Crawford, 2006) and adults (Rosenthal, Fusi, & Hochstein, 2001). Recently, Cristià and her colleagues have further shown that DL is evident from at least 4-6 months of age and that it is robust to variability along two features simultaneously—an important demonstration, given that multiple redundant acoustic features cue most speech contrasts (Cristià, McGuire, Seidl, & Francis, 2011).

# Limitations and Challenges to DL

Recent evidence suggests two important limitations to DL. First, the effectiveness of DL as a learning strategy has already begun to decline by 10 months of age, when most native phonetic categories have already emerged. For example, Maye et al. (2002, 2008) found that for 6- to 8-month old infants, 2.3 minutes of exposure to a bimodal or unimodal distribution was required to collapse phonetic categories, but by 10 months of age, infants required more than 4 minutes of exposure—still a small amount, but almost twice as much as before—to reestablish phonetic discrimination of a nonnative contrast in the process of decline (Yoshida, Pons, Maye, & Werker, 2010). In adults, even 20 minutes of exposure brings about smaller perceptual changes than those seen in infants (Hayes-Harb, 2007; Maye & Gerken, 2000). These findings mirror broader age-related changes in phonetic sensitivity, and they raise the possibility that DL may operate most effectively during a sensitive period in early development. This could be because phonetic systems are most open to input in infancy for maturational reasons (Werker & Tees, 2005), because other learning mechanisms become more important as infants develop (see the next section for more details), or because inferred distributions become more resilient to change as more speech input is accumulated.

Second, DL appears to interact with acoustic-phonetic salience. Although infants can use DL to learn many kinds of phonetic distinctions, infants show no evidence of learning certain particularly difficult categories (e.g., a Polish alveolar-palatal fricative; see Cristià et al., 2011). Future work will need to investigate whether DL is sufficient to induce phonetic categories that are not discriminable by infants without previous language experience (e.g., Narayan et al., 2010; Sato et al., 2010). Such studies must ask whether the difficulty in learning particular contrasts from DL training in the laboratory correlates with the relative timing of perceptual change for these same contrasts in natural languages.

An important challenge is to show that there are cues in speech input that would support DL in more naturalistic situations. Several analyses of parental speech input to infants have confirmed that, although imperfect, distributional cues are present that can signal both the number of native-language categories and possible phonetic distinctions in that language (Gauthier, Shi, & Xu, 2007; Vallabha, McClelland, Pons, Werker, & Amano, 2007; Werker et al., 2007). These analyses are supported by results from a compelling correlation study showing that distributional regularity in a mother's speech is predictive of the phonetic-category structure her infant learns (Cristià, 2011).

At the same time, other work has provided convincing empirical challenges to the notion that DL alone can explain phonetic-category learning. For example, some researchers have argued that computational modeling of DL is not viable in examinations of samples of natural conversational speech (Swingley, 2009) or without additional constraints (i.e., the ability of highly predictive distributional hypotheses to inhibit other hypothetical distributions; McMurray, Aslin, & Toscano, 2009). Collectively, these studies have suggested that DL must be supplemented by other learning strategies on the part of the infant.

# Current Directions on Mechanisms of Phonetic Learning

Infants may supplement DL by relying on the fact that individual speech sounds frequently occur in unique perceptual contexts. As originally suggested by Lawrence (1949), who labeled this basic, domain-general learning mechanism *acquired distinctiveness* (AD), such contexts reprioritize the salience of perceptible cues in discrimination tasks. According to an AD-based explanation, the occurrence of value A in context X and value B in context Y is thought to highlight cues that distinguish value A from value B and hence facilitate discrimination (see Hayes-Harb, 2007; Kluender, Lotto, Holt, & Bloedel, 1998 for examples in the phonetic domain). Thus, in cases where distributional information might be muddled, hearing one vowel in context X (i.e., /i/ in 'see') contrasted with a similar vowel in context Y (i.e., /I/ in 'this') could enhance the perceptual distance between those vowels (i.e., /i/ versus /I/; see Swingley, 2009). Such auditory AD contexts have already been shown to highlight phonetic contrasts in 14-month-olds' word-form representations (Thiessen, 2011) and to improve the effectiveness of DL in adults (Feldman, Myers, White, Griffiths, & Morgan, 2011); moreover, they have been hypothesized to do the same for phonetic perception as infants learn native phonetic categories (Feldman et al., 2011; Swingley, 2009).

Of course, infants pay attention to much more than just the auditory stream. For example, redundant information in seen and heard speech can influence DL in infants (Teinonen, Aslin, Alku, & Csibra, 2008). Consider a clearer case of cross-modal AD, in which audio-visual co-occurrences are arbitrary. As young infants begin attending to word referents, the simple co-occurrence of distinct words and objects may further highlight the salience of the relevant phonetic cues. In the scenario described in the introduction of this article, a Hindi-learning infant might hear variability around a dental [d̪al] when his mother is talking about cooking lentils and variability around a retroflex [ɖal] when she points to a branch. An English-learning infant would hear that variability only around an alveolar [dal] when his or her mother talks about a doll.

Yeung and Werker (2009) investigated this exact AD scenario. English-learning 9-month-olds were presented with consistent pairings of a syllable beginning with a dental [d̪a] and a picture of one object as well as a syllable beginning with a retroflex [ɖa] and a picture of another object. Results showed that these infants were able to discriminate this nonnative contrast after seeing such contrastive object-speech pairings; however, infants who had received no training (a control group) or had seen inconsistent pairings between syllables and objects (i.e., [d̪a] presented with Object 1 on some familiarization trials and with Object 2 on others) could not.

This work all suggests that co-occurring contextual cues can facilitate the acquisition of native-language phonetic categories

through learning from AD. However, it is important to note that the very same contexts in which infants learn from AD are also those that can be lexically informative. Such learning situations may allow infants to embed phonetic categorization in the broader context of language acquisition (i.e., word-learning) from very early in life. Specifically, it may be the case that as language-specific categories begin to solidify, and as infants come to treat speech as a means of communication, phonetic learning relies less on basic domain-general strategies and more on linguistically motivated ones. For example, there is some evidence that infants learn phonetic patterns better in face-to-face, contingent live interactions, in which the statistical characteristics of (audiovisual) speech input are presumably constant (Kuhl, Tsao, & Liu, 2003). Future work in infant phonetic learning must further investigate what specific learning mechanisms may supplement DL in such scenarios.

Several important issues must be explored by future work in this field. First, learning mechanisms supplementing DL, such as AD, must be further delineated. What are their characteristics? When do they become active in development, and how do different learning mechanisms interact in cases of conflict? Relatedly, are there clear distinctions between domain-general statistical mechanisms—such as DL or basic learning from co-occurring contexts—and more "sophisticated," lexically related mechanisms? And finally, are there sensitive periods in development during which different learning mechanisms are most effective? Answers to these questions will help provide a more complete picture of just how infants learn native-language speech patterns so early in development.

# Recommended Reading

Cristià, A. (2011). (See References). A study showing that the distributional characteristics in maternal speech guide infant phonetic-category learning.

Gervain, J. & Mehler, J. (2010). (See References). A comprehensive, highly accessible overview of the many ways infant speech perception changes in the first year of life.

Swingley, D. (2009). (See References). A paper that provides a full discussion of challenges to distributional learning for readers who wish to learn more about computational approaches to the issue.

Yeung, H. H., & Werker, J. F. (2009). (See References). The original study identifying acquired distinctiveness as a possible phonetic-category-learning mechanism in infancy.

Yoshida, K. A., Pons, F., Maye, J., & Werker, J. F. (2010). (See References). A recent study that illustrates original research on distributional learning and how it becomes more difficult by 10 months of age.

# Declaration of Conflicting Interests

The author declared no conflict of interest with respect to the authorship or the publication of this article.

# Funding

Preparation of this article was supported in part by NSERC Grant 81103 and the Canada Research Chair Foundation.

# Notes

1. Werker and Tees (1984) originally tested "t" sounds rather than "d" sounds, although subsequent work has tested "d" sounds as well.

2. The original work was done with a voicing continuum, not the Hindi retroflex-dental distinction, but subsequent work has tested that distinction as well.

# References

Albareda-Castellot, B., Pons, F., & Sebastián-Gallés, N. (2010). The acquisition of phonetic categories in bilingual infants: New data from an anticipatory eye movement paradigm. *Developmental Science, 14*, 395–401. doi:10.1111/j.1467-7687.2010.00989.x

Anderson, J. L., Morgan, J. L., & White, K. S. (2003). A statistical basis for speech sound discrimination. *Language and Speech, 46*, 155–182.

Best, C. T. (1995). A direct realist view of cross-language speech perception. In W. Strange (Ed.), *Speech perception and linguistic experience: Issues in cross-language speech research* (pp. 171–204). Timonium, MD: York Press.

Burns, T. C., Yoshida, K. A., Hill, K., & Werker, J. F. (2007). The development of phonetic representation in bilingual and monolingual infants. *Applied Psycholinguistics, 28*, 455–474.

Cristià, A. (2011). Fine-grained variation in caregivers' predicts their infants' category. *Journal of the Acoustical Society of America, 129*, 3271–3280. doi:10.1121/1.3562562

Cristià, A., McGuire, G. L., Seidl, A., & Francis, A. L. (2011). Effects of the distribution of acoustic cues on infants' perception of sibilants. *Journal of Phonetics, 39*, 388–402. doi:10.1016/j.wocn.2011.02.004

Curtin, S., & Werker, J. F. (2007). The perceptual foundations of phonological development. In G. Gaskell (Ed.), *The Oxford handbook of psycholinguistics* (pp. 579–599). Oxford, England: Oxford University Press.

Duffy, S., Huttenlocher, J., & Crawford, L. E. (2006). Children use categories to maximize accuracy in estimation. *Developmental Science, 9*, 597–603. doi:10.1111/j.1467-7687.2006.00538.x

Feldman, N., Myers, E., White, K., Griffiths, T., & Morgan, J. L. (2011). Learners use word-level statistics in phonetic category acquisition. In N. Danis, K. Mesh, & H. Sung (Eds.), *Proceedings of the 35th Annual Boston University Conference on Language Development* (pp. 197–209). Boston, MA: Cascadilla Press.

Gauthier, B., Shi, R., & Xu, Y. (2007). Simulating the acquisition of lexical tones from continuous dynamic input. *Journal of the Acoustical Society of America, 121*, EL190–EL195. doi:10.1121/1.2716160

Gervain, J., & Mehler, J. (2010). Speech perception and language acquisition in the first year of life. *Annual Review of Psychology, 61*, 191–218. doi:10.1146/annurev.psych.093008.100408

Hayes-Harb, R. (2007). Lexical and statistical evidence in the acquisition of second language phonemes. *Second Language Research, 23*, 1–31.

Jusczyk, P. W. (1993). From general to language-specific capacities: The WRAPSA model of how speech perception develops. *Journal of Phonetics, 21*, 3–28.

Kluender, K. R., Lotto, A. J., Holt, L. L., & Bloedel, S. L. (1998). Role of experience for language-specific functional mappings of vowel sounds. *Journal of the Acoustical Society of America, 104*, 3568–3582.

Kuhl, P. K., Conboy, B. T., Coffey-Corina, S., Padden, D., Rivera-Gaxiola, M., & Nelson, T. (2008). Phonetic learning as a pathway to language: New data and native language magnet theory expanded (NLM-e). *Philosophical Transactions of the Royal Society of London B: Biological Sciences, 363*, 979–1000. doi:10.1098/rstb.2007.2154

Kuhl, P. K., Stevens, E., Hayashi, A., Deguchi, T., Kiritani, S., & Iverson, P. (2006). Infants show a facilitation effect for native language phonetic perception between 6 and 12 months. *Developmental Science, 9*, F13–F21.

Kuhl, P. K., Tsao, F. M., & Liu, H. M. (2003). Foreign-language experience in infancy: Effects of short-term exposure and social interaction on phonetic learning. *Proceedings of the National Academy of Sciences, USA, 100*, 9096–9101.

Lawrence, D. H. (1949). Acquired distinctiveness of cues: I. Transfer between discriminations on the basis of familiarity with the stimulus. *Journal of Experimental Psychology, 39*, 770–784.

Maye, J., & Gerken, L. (2000). Learning phonemes without minimal pairs. In S. C. Howell, S. A. Fish, & T. Keith-Lucas (Eds.), *Proceedings of the 24th Annual Boston University Conference on Language Development* (pp. 522–533). Somerville, MA: Cascadilla Press.

Maye, J., Weiss, D. J., & Aslin, R. N. (2008). Statistical phonetic learning in infants: Facilitation and feature generalization. *Developmental Science, 11*, 122–134.

Maye, J., Werker, J. F., & Gerken, L. (2002). Infant sensitivity to distributional information can affect phonetic discrimination. *Cognition, 82*, B101–B111.

McMurray, B., & Aslin, R. N. (2005). Infants are sensitive to within-category variation in speech perception. *Cognition, 95*, B15–B26. doi:10.1016/j.cognition.2004.07.005

McMurray, B., Aslin, R. N., & Toscano, J. C. (2009). Statistical learning of phonetic categories: Insights from a computational approach. *Developmental Science, 12*, 369–378. doi:10.1111/j.1467-7687.2009.00822.x

Minagawa-Kawai, Y., Mori, K., Naoi, N., & Kojima, S. (2007). Neural attunement processes in infants during the acquisition of a language-specific phonemic contrast. *Journal of Neuroscience, 27*, 315–321. doi: 10.1523/jneurosci.1984-06.2007

Mugitani, R., Pons, F., Fais, L., Dietrich, C., Werker, J. F., & Amano, S. (2009). Perception of vowel length by Japanese- and English-learning infants. *Developmental Psychology, 45*, 236–247. doi:10.1037/a0014043

Narayan, C. R., Werker, J. F., & Beddor, P. S. (2010). The interaction between acoustic salience and language experience in developmental speech perception: Evidence from nasal place discrimination. *Developmental Science, 13*, 407–420. doi:10.1111/j.1467-7687.2009.00898.x

Pegg, J. E., & Werker, J. F. (1997). Adult and infant perception of two English phones. *The Journal of the Acoustical Society of America, 102*, 3742–3753. Retrieved from www.ncbi.nlm.nih.gov/pubmed/9407666

Pons, F. (2006). The effects of distributional learning on rats' sensitivity to phonetic information. *Journal of Experimental Psychology: Animal Behavior Processes, 32*, 97–101. doi:10.1037/0097-7403.32.1.97

Rosenthal, O., Fusi, S., & Hochstein, S. (2001). Forming classes by stimulus frequency: Behavior and theory. *Proceedings of the National Academy of Sciences, USA, 98*, 4265–4270. doi:10.1073/pnas.071525998

Saffran, J. R., Aslin, R. N., & Newport, E. L. (1996). Statistical learning by 8-month-old infants. *Science, 274,* 1926–1928.

Sato, Y., Kato, M., & Mazuka, R. (2012). Development of single/geminate obstruent discrimination by Japanese infants: Early integration of durational and nondurational cues. *Developmental Psychology, 48,* 18–34. doi:10.1037/a0025528

Sato, Y., Sogabe, Y., and Mazuka, R. (2010). Discrimination of phonemic vowel length by Japanese infants. *Developmental Psychology, 46,* 106–119.

Sundara, M., Polka, L., & Genesee, F. (2006). Language-experience facilitates discrimination of /d-th/ in monolingual and bilingual acquisition of English. *Cognition, 100,* 369–388. doi:10.1016/j.cognition.2005.04.007

Swingley, D. (2009). Contributions of infant word learning to language development. *Philosophical Transactions of the Royal Society B: Biological Sciences, 364,* 3617–3632. doi:10.1098/rstb.2009.0107

Teinonen, T., Aslin, R. N., Alku, P., & Csibra, G. (2008). Visual speech contributes to phonetic learning in 6-month-old infants. *Cognition, 108,* 850–855. doi:10.1016/j.cognition.2008.05.009

Thiessen, E. D. (2011). When variability matters more than meaning: The effect of lexical forms on use of phonemic contrasts. *Developmental Psychology, 47,* 1448–1458. doi:10.1037/a0024439

Vallabha, G. K., McClelland, J. L., Pons, F., Werker, J. F., & Amano, S. (2007). Unsupervised learning of vowel categories from infant-directed speech. *Proceedings of the National Academy of Sciences, USA, 104,* 13273–13278.

Werker, J. F., Pons, F., Dietrich, C., Kajikawa, S., Fais, L., & Amano, S. (2007). Infant-directed speech supports phonetic category learning in English and Japanese. *Cognition, 103,* 147–162.

Werker, J. F., & Tees, R. C. (1984). Cross-language speech perception: Evidence for perceptual reorganization during the first year of life. *Infant Behavior & Development, 7,* 49–63.

Werker, J. F., & Tees, R. C. (2005). Speech perception as a window for understanding plasticity and commitment in language systems of the brain. *Developmental Psychobiology, 46,* 233–251. doi:10.1002/dev.20060

Yeung, H. H., & Werker, J. F. (2009). Learning words' sounds before learning how words sound: 9-month-olds use distinct objects as cues to categorize speech information. *Cognition, 113,* 234–243. doi:10.1016/j.cognition.2009.08.010

Yoshida, K. A., Pons, F., Maye, J., & Werker, J. F. (2010). Distributional phonetic learning at 10 months of age. *Infancy, 15,* 420–433. doi:10.1111/j.1532-7078.2009.00024.x

## Critical Thinking

1. What exactly is distributional learning (DL) and how does it work? Provide an example of the DL mechanism.

2. Of the phonetic-learning mechanisms listed, which do you think provides the strongest evidence that leads to native-language listening expertise?

3. Make sense of the 8-step continuum Maye and Gerken used to test DL in infants. How reliable is this testing on 6- and 8-month-old infants?

**JANET F. WERKER,** Department of Psychology, University of British Columbia, 2136 West Mall, Vancouver, BC V6T IZ4, Canada E-mail: jwerker@psych.ubc.ca

# The Other-Race Effect Develops during Infancy
## *Evidence of Perceptual Narrowing*

Experience plays a crucial role in the development of face processing. In the study reported here, we investigated how faces observed within the visual environment affect the development of the face-processing system during the 1st year of life. We assessed 3-, 6-, and 9-month-old Caucasian infants' ability to discriminate faces within their own racial group and within three other-race groups (African, Middle Eastern, and Chinese). The 3-month-old infants demonstrated recognition in all conditions, the 6-month-old infants were able to recognize Caucasian and Chinese faces only, and the 9-month-old infants' recognition was restricted to own-race faces. The pattern of preferences indicates that the other-race effect is emerging by 6 months of age and is present at 9 months of age. The findings suggest that facial input from the infant's visual environment is crucial for shaping the face-processing system early in infancy, resulting in differential recognition accuracy for faces of different races in adulthood.

DAVID J. KELLY ET AL.

Human adults are experts at recognizing faces of conspecifics and appear to perform this task effortlessly. Despite this impressive ability, however, adults are more susceptible to recognition errors when a target face is from an unfamiliar racial group, rather than their own racial group. This phenomenon is known as the *other-race effect* (ORE; see Meissner & Brigham, 2001, for a review). Although the ORE has been widely reported, the exact mechanisms that underlie reduced recognition accuracy for other-race faces, and precisely when this effect emerges during development, remain unclear.

The ORE can be explained in terms of a modifiable face representation. The concept of a multidimensional *face-space* architecture, first proposed by Valentine (1991), has received much empirical support. According to the norm-based coding model, individual face exemplars are represented as vectors within face-space according to their deviation from a prototypical average. The prototype held by each person represents the average of all faces that person has ever encoded and is therefore unique. Although it is unclear which dimensions are most salient and used for recognition, it is likely that dimensions vary between individuals and possibly within each person over time. The prototype (and therefore the entire face-space) continually adapts and is updated as more faces are observed within the environment. Consequently, individuating face-space dimensions of a person living in China are expected to be optimal for recognition of other Chinese persons, but not, for example, for recognition of African individuals.

Other authors have hypothesized that the dimensions of the face prototype present at birth are broad and develop according to the type of facial input received (Nelson, 2001). According to this account, predominant exposure to faces from a single racial category tunes face-space dimensions toward that category. Such tuning might be manifested at a behavioral level in differential responding to own- versus other-race faces, for example, in spontaneous visual preference and a recognition advantage for own-race faces.

Recent findings regarding spontaneous preference have confirmed the impact of differential face input on the tuning of the face prototype during early infancy. It has been demonstrated that selectivity based on ethnic facial differences emerges very early in life, with 3-month-old infants preferring to look at faces from their own group, as opposed to faces from other ethnic groups (Bar-Haim, Ziv, Lamy, & Hodes, 2006; Kelly et al., 2005, 2007). We (Kelly et al., 2005) have shown that this preference is not present at birth, which strongly suggests that own-group preferences result from differential exposure to faces from one's particular ethnic group. In addition, Bar-Haim et al. (2006) tested a population of Ethiopian infants who had been raised in an absorption center while their families awaited housing in Israel. These infants were frequently exposed to both Ethiopian and Israeli adults and subsequently demonstrated no preference for either African or Caucasian faces when presented simultaneously.

Collectively, these results provide strong evidence that faces observed in the visual environment have a highly influential role in eliciting face preferences during infancy. Additional evidence supporting this conclusion comes from a study concerning gender preference (Quinn, Yahr, Kuhn, Slater, & Pascalis, 2002), which showed that 3- to 4-month-old infants raised primarily by a female caregiver demonstrate a visual preference for female over male faces, whereas infants raised primarily by a male caregiver prefer to look at male rather than female faces.

Although the literature on differential face recognition contains discrepancies regarding the onset of the ORE, evidence points toward an early inception. Some of the initial investigations reported onset at 8 (Feinman & Entwhistle, 1976) and 6 (Chance, Turner, & Goldstein, 1982) years of age. More recent studies have found the ORE to be present in 5-year-olds (Pezdek, Blandon-Gitlin, & Moore, 2003) and 3-year-olds (Sangrigoli & de Schonen, 2004a). In addition, Sangrigoli and de Schonen (2004b) showed that 3-month-old Caucasian infants were able to recognize an own-race face, but not an Asian face, as measured by the visual paired-comparison (VPC) task. However, the effect disappeared if infants were habituated to three, as opposed to one, other-race face exemplars. Thus, although the ORE may be present at 3 months of age, it is weak enough to be eliminated after only a few instances of exposure within an experimental session.

Additional lines of evidence indicate that the face representation undergoes change throughout development. At 6 months of age, infants are able to individuate human and monkey faces, and although the ability to individuate human faces is maintained in later development, the ability to individuate monkey faces is absent in 9-month-old infants and in adults (Pascalis, de Haan, & Nelson, 2002). Although the face-processing system appears to adapt toward own-species faces, it still retains flexibility for within-species categories of faces (i.e., other-race faces). Korean adults adopted by French families during childhood (ages 3–9 years) demonstrated a recognition deficit for Korean faces relative to their ability to recognize European faces (Sangrigoli, Pallier, Argenti, Ventureyra, & de Schonen, 2005). Their pattern of performance was comparable to that of the native French people who were tested in the same study.

The purpose of the study reported here was to clarify the developmental origins of the ORE during the first months of life. Using the VPC task, we assessed the ability of 3-, 6-, and 9-month-old Caucasian infants to discriminate within own-race (Caucasian) faces and within three categories of other-race faces (African, Middle Eastern, and Chinese). This task measures relative interest in the members of pairs of stimuli, each consisting of a novel stimulus and a familiar stimulus observed during a prior habituation period. Recognition of the familiar stimulus is inferred from the participant's tendency to fixate on the novel stimulus. Previous studies have found that 3-month-old infants can perform this task even when they are exposed to different views of faces (e.g., full view vs. 3/4 profile) during the habituation period and the recognition test (Pascalis, de Haan, Nelson, & de Schonen, 1998). We also varied face views between familiarization and testing, a procedure that is preferable to using identical pictures in the habituation and testing phases because it ensures that face recognition—as opposed to picture recognition (i.e., image matching)—is tested. Our selection of

which age groups to test was based on previous research demonstrating that the ORE is found in infancy (3-month-olds; Sangrigoli & de Schonen, 2004b) and that the face-processing system appears to undergo a period of tuning between 6 and 9 months of age (Pascalis et al., 2002).

# Method
## Participants

In total, 192 Caucasian infants were included in the final analysis. There were 64 subjects in each of three age groups: 3-month-olds (age range = 86–102 days; 33 females, 31 males), 6-month-olds (age range = 178–196 days; 31 females, 33 males), and 9-month-olds (age range = 268–289 days; 30 females, 34 males). All participants were healthy, full-term infants. Within each age group, the infants were assigned in equal numbers ($n = 16$) to the four testing conditions (Caucasian, African, Middle Eastern, and Chinese). The infants were recruited from the maternity wing of the Royal Hallamshire Hospital, Sheffield, United Kingdom. In each age group, we tested additional infants who were excluded from the final analysis. Twenty-two 3-month-old infants were excluded because of failure to habituate ($n = 4$), side bias during testing (> 95% looking time to one side; $n = 15$), or fussiness ($n = 3$); sixteen 6-month-old infants were excluded because of failure to habituate ($n = 7$), side bias during testing ($n = 3$), parental interference ($n = 2$), or fussiness ($n = 4$); and eleven 9-month-old infants were excluded because of a failure to habituate ($n = 3$) or fussiness ($n = 8$).

## Stimuli

The stimuli were 24 color images of male and female adult faces (age range = 23–27 years) from four different ethnic groups (African, Asian, Middle Eastern, and Caucasian). All faces had dark hair and dark eyes so that the infants would be unable to demonstrate recognition on the basis of these features. The images were photos of students. The Africans were members of the African and Caribbean Society at the University of Sheffield; the Asians were Han Chinese students from Zhejiang Sci-Tech University, Hangzhou, China; the Middle Easterners were members of the Pakistan Society at the University of Sheffield; and the Caucasians were psychology students at the University of Sheffield.

For each ethnic group, we tested male and female faces in separate conditions. The images for each combination of ethnic group and gender consisted of a habituation face and two test faces, a novel face and the familiar face in a new orientation. The two faces in the test phase were always in the same orientation, and this orientation differed from the orientation of the face seen during habituation. In one orientation condition, infants were habituated to full-view faces and saw test faces in 3/4-profile views; in the other orientation condition, the views were reversed. Equal numbers of infants were assigned to the two orientation conditions.

All photos were taken with a Canon S50 digital camera and subsequently cropped using Adobe Photoshop to remove the neck and background details. All individual pictures were then mounted on a uniform dark-gray background, and the stimuli were resized to the same dimensions to ensure uniformity. Sixteen independent observers rated a pool of 32 faces for attractiveness and distinctiveness, using a scale from 1 to 10, and the final set of 24 faces was selected so as to match gender, attractiveness, and distinctiveness within each face pair.

## Procedure

All infants were tested in a quiet room at the department of psychology at the University of Sheffield. They were seated on their mother's lap, approximately 60 cm from a screen onto which the images were projected. Each infant was randomly assigned to one of the four ethnic-group conditions (African, Asian, Middle Eastern, or Caucasian). Within each of these four conditions, infants were tested with either male or female faces; testing was counterbalanced appropriately, with half the infants assigned to the male-faces condition and half the infants assigned to the female-faces condition. Equal numbers of infants were tested in the male and female conditions. Before the session started, all mothers were instructed to fixate centrally above the screen and to remain as quiet as possible during testing.

### Habituation Phase

Each infant was first presented with a single face projected onto a screen measuring 45 cm × 30 cm. The face measured 18 cm × 18 cm (14° visual angle). The experimenter observed the infant's eye movements on a control monitor from a black-and-white closed-circuit television camera (specialized for low-light conditions) that was positioned above the screen. Time was recorded and displayed on the control monitor using a Horita (Mission Viejo, CA) II TG-50 time coder; video was recorded at 25 frames per second.

The experimenter recorded the infant's attention to the face by holding down the "z" key on a keyboard whenever the infant fixated on the image. When the infant looked away from the image, the experimenter released the key. If the infant's attention was averted for more than 2 s, the image disappeared from the screen. The experimenter then presented the image again and repeated the procedure. The habituation phase ended when the infant's looking time on a presentation was equal to or less than 50% of the average looking time from the infant's first two presentations. Thus, our measure of looking time was the sum of looking time across all presentations until the habituation criterion was reached.

### Test Phase

The test phase consisted of two trials. First, two face images (novel and familiar), each measuring 18 cm × 18 cm (14° visual angle), were presented on the screen. The images were separated by a 9-cm gap and appeared in the bottom left and bottom right corners of the screen. When the infant first looked at the images, the experimenter pressed a key to begin a 5-s countdown. At the end of the 5 s, the images disappeared from the screen. The faces then appeared with their left/right position on the screen reversed. As soon as the infant looked at the images, another 5-s countdown was initiated. Eye movements were recorded throughout, and the film was digitized for frame-by-frame analysis by two independent observers who used specialized computer software to code looking time to each of the two faces. The observers were blind to both gender and ethnic-group condition and to the screen positions of the faces being viewed by the infants. The average level of interobserver agreement was high (Pearson $r = .93$). Recognition was inferred from a preference for the novel face stimulus across the two 5-s test trials.

## Results
### Habituation Trials

A preliminary analysis revealed no significant gender differences for stimuli or participants, so data were collapsed across stimulus gender and participant's gender in subsequent analyses. Habituation time (total looking time across trials) was analyzed in a 3 (age: 3, 6, or 9 months) × 4 (face ethnicity: African, Middle Eastern, Chinese, or Caucasian) × 2 (face orientation: full face or 3/4 profile) between-subjects analysis of variance (ANOVA). The ANOVA yielded only a significant effect of age, $F(2, 189) = 73.193$, $p < .0001$, $\eta^2 = .535$. Post hoc Tukey's honestly significant difference (HSD) tests revealed that the habituation times of 6- and 9-month-old infants did not differ significantly, but both 6-month-old ($M = 42.67$ s) and 9-month-old ($M = 38.88$ s) infants habituated significantly more quickly ($p < .0001$) than 3-month-old infants ($M = 70.74$ s). There were no main effects of face ethnicity or face orientation, nor were there any interactions.

### Test Trials

Again, a preliminary analysis yielded no significant gender differences for stimuli or participants, so data were collapsed across stimulus gender and participant's gender in subsequent analyses. Percentage of time spent looking at the novel stimulus, combined from both trials of the test phase, was analyzed in a 3 (age: 3, 6, or 9 months) × 4 (face ethnicity: African, Middle Eastern, Chinese, or Caucasian) × 2 (face orientation: full face or 3/4 view) between-subjects ANOVA. The ANOVA yielded a significant effect of age, $F(2, 189) = 5.133$, $p < .007$, $\eta^2 = .058$. Post hoc Tukey's HSD tests revealed that 3-month-olds ($M = 60.15\%$) showed significantly greater preference for the novel face ($p < .003$) than did 9-month-olds ($M = 53.19\%$). There were no main effects of face ethnicity or face orientation.

To investigate novelty preferences within each age group, we conducted one-way between-groups ANOVAs on the percentage of time spent looking at the novel stimuli in the four face-ethnicity conditions. A significant effect of face ethnicity was found for 9-month-old infants, $F(3, 60) = 3.105$, $p < .033$, $\eta^2 = .134$, but not for 3- or 6-month-old infants. These results suggest that novelty preferences differed between face-ethnicity conditions only within the group of 9-month-old infants.

To further investigate novelty preferences within each age group, we conducted a series of two-tailed $t$ tests to determine whether the time spent looking at novel stimuli differed from the chance level of 50% (see Table 1). The results showed that 3-month-old infants demonstrated significant novelty preferences in all four face-ethnicity conditions, 6-month-old infants

**TABLE 1**   Results of the Novelty-Preference Test, by Age Group and Face Ethnicity

| Age and Face Ethnicity | Mean Time Looking at the Novel Face (%) | t(15) | p | p_rep |
|---|---|---|---|---|
| 3 months | | | | |
| African | 60.88 (16.52) | 2.635 | .019* | .942 |
| Middle Eastern | 57.31 (11.37) | 2.572 | .021* | .937 |
| Chinese | 58.72 (14.07) | 2.479 | .026* | .929 |
| Caucasian | 63.71 (13.47) | 4.072 | .001* | .988 |
| 6 months | | | | |
| African | 55.35 (11.40) | 1.880 | > .05 | .840 |
| Middle Eastern | 56.70 (12.89) | 2.079 | > .05 | .871 |
| Chinese | 56.42 (7.79) | 3.295 | .005* | .965 |
| Caucasian | 58.27 (8.88) | 3.725 | .002* | .979 |
| 9 months | | | | |
| African | 51.33 (10.53) | 0.505 | > .05 | .414 |
| Middle Eastern | 53.51 (8.47) | 1.658 | > .05 | .799 |
| Chinese | 48.23 (13.31) | 0.530 | > .05 | .642 |
| Caucasian | 59.70 (11.16) | 3.476 | .003* | .971 |

Note. Standard deviations are given in parentheses. Asterisks highlight conditions in which the infants viewed novel faces significantly more often than predicted by chance.

demonstrated significant novelty preferences in two of the four conditions (Chinese and Caucasian), and 9-month-old infants demonstrated a novelty preference for Caucasian faces only.

## Discussion

The aim of the current study was to investigate the onset of the ORE during the first months of life, following up on previous findings that 3-month-olds already show a preference for own-race faces (Bar-Haim et al., 2006; Kelly et al., 2005, 2007). The results reported here do not provide evidence for the ORE (as measured by differential recognition capabilities for own- and other-race faces) in 3-month-old infants, but they do indicate that the ORE emerges at age 6 months and is fully present at age 9 months.

Our results are consistent with the notion of general perceptual narrowing during infancy (e.g., Nelson, 2001). Our findings are also consistent with those of Pascalis et al. (2002), further demonstrating that the face-processing system undergoes a period of refinement within the 1st year of life. Collectively, these findings lend weight to the concept of a tuning period between 6 and 9 months of age. However, differences between the present study and the work by Pascalis et al. should be noted. For example, there is the obvious difference that Pascalis et al. found between-species effects, and our study focused on within-species effects. It should not be assumed that identical mechanisms necessarily underlie the reductions in recognition accuracy observed in the two cases. In addition, once the ability to discriminate between nonhuman primate faces has diminished, it apparently cannot be recovered easily (Dufour, Coleman, Campbell, Petit, & Pascalis, 2004; Pascalis et al., 2002), whereas the ORE is evidently modifiable through

exposure to other-race populations (Sangrigoli et al., 2005) or simple training with other-race faces (Elliott, Wills, & Goldstein, 1973; Goldstein & Chance, 1985; Lavrakas, Buri, & Mayzner, 1976). Furthermore, event-related potential (ERP) studies have shown that in 6-month-olds, the putative infant N170 (a face-selective ERP component elicited in occipital regions) is sensitive to inversion for both human and monkey faces, whereas the N170 recorded in adults is sensitive to inversion only for human faces (de Haan, Pascalis, & Johnson, 2002). An adult-like N170 response is not observed in subjects until they are 12 months of age (Halit, de Haan, & Johnson, 2003). The ERP response for other-race faces has not yet been investigated during infancy, but studies with adults have revealed no differences in the N170 response to own- and other-race faces (Caldara et al., 2003; Caldara, Rossion, Bovet, & Hauert, 2004).

Our findings differ from those reported by Sangrigoli and de Schonen (2004b) in the only other study to have investigated the emergence of the ORE during infancy. In their initial experiment, Sangrigoli and de Schonen found that 3-month-old infants discriminated own-race faces, but not other-race faces, as measured by the VPC task. However, numerous methodological differences between our study and theirs (e.g., color stimuli in our study vs. gray-scale stimuli in theirs) could have contributed to these contrasting results. Furthermore, Sangrigoli and de Schonen were able to eliminate the ORE with only a few trials of exposure to multiple exemplars, which suggests that even if the ORE is already present in 3-month-olds, it is weak and reversible. Between Sangrigoli and de Schonen's work and our own, there are now three VPC experiments (one here, two in Sangrigoli & de Schonen)[1] that have been conducted with 3-month-old infants, yet only one has yielded evidence for the ORE. The weight of the evidence thus suggests that a strong and sustainable ORE may not be present at 3 months of age, but rather develops later.

One might ask whether the ORE arises from differences in the variability of faces from different ethnic groups. However, the available evidence indicates that no category of faces has greater homogeneity than any other (Goldstein, 1979a, 1979b). Moreover, the data suggest that the ORE does not exclusively reflect a deficit for non-Caucasian faces: Individuals from many ethnic groups demonstrate poorer recognition of other-race than own-race faces (Meissner & Brigham, 2001). Evidently, a full account of the ORE will involve factors other than heterogeneity.

We have argued elsewhere (Kelly et al., 2007) that the ORE may develop through the following processes: First, predominant exposure to faces from one's own racial group induces familiarity with and a visual preference for such faces. Second, a preference for faces within one's racial group produces greater visual attention to such faces, even when faces from other racial groups are present in the visual environment. Third, superior recognition abilities develop for faces within one's racial group, but not for faces from groups that are infrequently encountered. Although supporting evidence for the first two processes has been obtained previously (Bar-Haim et al., 2006; Kelly et al., 2005, 2007), the data reported here provide the first direct evidence for the third. According to our account, the ORE can be explained by a modifiable face prototype (Valentine, 1991). If each person's face prototype is an average of all faces that person has encoded during his or her lifetime, then one may assume that it will resemble the race of the faces most commonly encountered. Furthermore, one would expect that individuating dimensions will be optimized for recognition of own-race faces, but not other-race faces.

An alternative to the single-prototype account is that people may possess multiple face-spaces that represent different face categories (e.g., gender, race) separately within a global space. In this contrasting scheme, rather than individuating dimensions being unsuitable for recognition of other-race faces, a face-space for other-race faces (e.g., Chinese faces) either does not exist or is insufficiently formed because of a general lack of exposure to those face categories. In both accounts, recognition capabilities improve through exposure to other-race faces. In the case of the single-prototype account, individuating dimensions acquire properties of newly encountered other-race faces that facilitate recognition. Alternatively, in the multiple-face-spaces account, a relevant space for other-race faces develops through similar exposure.

In summary, this is the first study to investigate the emergence of the ORE during infancy by comparing three different age groups' ability to recognize faces from their own race and a range of other races. The data reported here support the idea that very young infants have a broad face-processing system that is capable of processing faces from different ethnic groups. Between 3 and 9 months of age, this system gradually becomes more sensitive to faces from an infant's own ethnic group as a consequence of greater exposure to such faces than to faces from other racial groups. This shift in sensitivity is reflected in the emergence of a deficit in recognition accuracy for faces from unfamiliar groups. Future research should address whether the pattern of results we obtained with Caucasian infants is universal, or whether the ORE emerges at different ages in other populations.

# Note

1. But note that in a recent study using morphed stimuli, Hayden, Bhatt, Joseph, and Tanaka (2007) demonstrated that 3.5-month-old infants showed greater sensitivity to structural changes in own-race faces than in other-race faces.

# References

Bar-Haim, Y., Ziv, T., Lamy, D., & Hodes, R.M. (2006). Nature and nurture in own-race face processing. *Psychological Science, 17,* 159–163.

Caldara, R., Rossion, B., Bovet, P., & Hauert, C.A. (2004). Event-related potentials and time course of the 'other-race' face classification advantage. *Cognitive Neuroscience and Neuropsychology, 15,* 905–910.

Caldara, R., Thut, G., Servoir, P., Michel, C.M., Bovet, P., & Renault, B. (2003). Faces versus non-face object perception and the 'other-race' effect: A spatio-temporal event-related potential study. *Clinical Neurophysiology, 114,* 515–528.

Chance, J.E., Turner, A.L., & Goldstein, A.G. (1982). Development of differential recognition for own- and other-race faces. *Journal of Psychology, 112,* 29–37.

de Haan, M., Pascalis, O., & Johnson, M.H. (2002). Specialization of neural mechanisms underlying face recognition in human infants. *Journal of Cognitive Neuroscience, 14,* 199–209.

Dufour, V., Coleman, M., Campbell, R., Petit, O., & Pascalis, O. (2004). On the species-specificity of face recognition in human adults. *Current Psychology of Cognition, 22,* 315–333.

Elliott, E.S., Wills, E.J., & Goldstein, A.G. (1973). The effects of discrimination training on the recognition of White and Oriental faces. *Bulletin of the Psychonomic Society, 2,* 71–73.

Feinman, S., & Entwhistle, D.R. (1976). Children's ability to recognize other children's faces. *Child Development, 47,* 506–510.

Goldstein, A.G. (1979a). Race-related variation of facial features: Anthropometric data I. *Bulletin of the Psychonomic Society, 13,* 187–190.

Goldstein, A.G. (1979b). Facial feature variation: Anthropometric data II. *Bulletin of the Psychonomic Society, 13,* 191–193.

Goldstein, A.G., & Chance, J.E. (1985). Effects of training on Japanese face recognition: Reduction of the other-race effect. *Bulletin of the Psychonomic Society, 23,* 211–214.

Halit, H., de Haan, M., & Johnson, M.H. (2003). Cortical specialisation for face processing: Face-sensitive event-related potential components in 3- and 12-month-old infants. *NeuroImage, 19,* 1180–1193.

Hayden, A., Bhatt, R.S., Joseph, J.E., & Tanaka, J.W. (2007). The other-race effect in infancy: Evidence using a morphing technique. *Infancy, 12,* 95–104.

Kelly, D.J., Ge, L., Liu, S., Quinn, P.C., Slater, A.M., Lee, K., et al. (2007). Cross-race preferences for same-race faces extend beyond the African versus Caucasian contrast in 3-month-old infants. *Infancy, 11,* 87–95.

Kelly, D.J., Quinn, P.C., Slater, A.M., Lee, K., Gibson, A., Smith, M., et al. (2005). Three-month-olds, but not newborns, prefer own-race faces. *Developmental Science, 8,* F31–F36.

Lavrakas, P.J., Buri, J.R., & Mayzner, M.S. (1976). A perspective on the recognition of other-race faces. *Perception & Psychophysics, 20,* 475–481.

Meissner, C.A., & Brigham, J.C. (2001). Thirty years of investigating the own-race bias in memory for faces: A meta-analytic review. *Psychology, Public Policy, and Law, 7,* 3–35.

Nelson, C.A. (2001). The development and neural bases of face recognition. *Infant and Child Development, 10,* 3–18.

Pascalis, O., de Haan, M., & Nelson, C.A. (2002). Is face processing species-specific during the first year of life? *Science, 296,* 1321–1323.

Pascalis, O., de Haan, M., Nelson, C.A., & de Schonen, S. (1998). Long-term recognition assessed by visual paired comparison in 3- and 6-month-old infants. *Journal of Experimental Psychology: Learning, Memory, and Cognition, 24,* 249–260.

Pezdek, K., Blandon-Gitlin, I., & Moore, C. (2003). Children's face recognition memory: More evidence for the cross-race effect. *Journal of Applied Psychology, 88,* 760–763.

Quinn, P.C., Yahr, J., Kuhn, A., Slater, A.M., & Pascalis, O. (2002). Representation of the gender of human faces by infants: A preference for female. *Perception, 31,* 1109–1121.

Sangrigoli, S., & de Schonen, S. (2004a). Effect of visual experience on face processing: A developmental study of inversion and non-native effects. *Developmental Science, 7,* 74–87.

Sangrigoli, S., & de Schonen, S. (2004b). Recognition of own-race and other-race faces by three-month-old infants. *Journal of Child Psychology and Psychiatry and Allied Disciplines, 45,* 1219–1227.

Sangrigoli, S., Pallier, C., Argenti, A.M., Ventureyra, V.A.G., & de Schonen, S. (2005). Reversibility of the other-race effect in face recognition during childhood. *Psychological Science, 16,* 440–444.

Valentine, T. (1991). A unified account of the effects of distinctiveness, inversion, and race in face recognition. *The Quarterly Journal of Experimental Psychology, 43A,* 161–204.

## Critical Thinking

1. In face recognition and preferences for faces of different races, what role does biological or natural factors play and what role does experience and nurture play?

2. In infants' ability to perceive faces of different races, what is perceptual narrowing and when does it occur?

**DAVID J. KELLY:** University of Sheffield, Sheffield, United Kingdom; **PAUL C. QUINN:** University of Delaware; **ALAN M. SLATER:** University of Exeter, Exeter, United Kingdom; **KANG LEE:** University of Toronto, Toronto, Ontario, Canada; **LIEZHONG GE:** Zeijiang Sci-Tech University, Hangzhou, People's Republic of China; and **OLIVER PASCALIS:** University of Sheffield, Sheffield, United Kingdom

Address correspondence to David J. Kelly, University of Sheffield, Psychology Department, Western Bank, Sheffield, South Yorkshire S10 2TP, United Kingdom, e-mail: david.kelly@sheffield.ac.uk.

**Acknowledgments**—This work was supported by National Institutes of Health Grants HD 46526 and HD 42451 and by an Economic and Social Research Council studentship awarded to David J. Kelly.

# New Advances in Understanding Sensitive Periods in Brain Development

MICHAEL S. C. THOMAS AND MARK H. JOHNSON

The idea that there are "critical" or sensitive periods in neural, cognitive, and behavioral development has a long history. It first became widely known with the phenomenon of *filial imprinting* as famously described by Konrad Lorenz: After a relatively brief exposure to a particular stimulus early in life, many birds and mammals form a strong and exclusive attachment to that stimulus. According to Lorenz, a critical period in development has several features, including the following: Learning or plasticity is confined to a short and sharply defined period of the life cycle, and this learning is subsequently irreversible in the face of later experience. Following the paradigmatic example of filial imprinting in birds, more recent studies on cats, dogs, and monkeys, as well as investigations of bird song and human language development, have confirmed that critical periods are major phenomena in brain and behavioral development (see Michel & Tyler, 2005, for review). However, it rapidly became evident that, even in the prototypical case of imprinting, critical periods were not as sharply timed and irreversible as first thought. For example, the critical period for imprinting in domestic chicks was shown to be extendable in time in the absence of appropriate stimulation, and the learning is reversible under certain circumstances (for review, see Bolhuis, 1991). These and other modifications of Lorenz's original views have led most current researchers to adopt the alternative term *sensitive periods* to describe these widespread developmental phenomena.

A fundamental debate that continues to the present is whether specific mechanisms underlie sensitive periods or whether such periods are a natural consequence of functional brain development. Support for the latter view has come from a recent perspective on developing brain functions. Relating evidence on the neuroanatomical development of the brain to the remarkable changes in motor, perceptual, and cognitive abilities during the first decade or so of a human life presents a formidable challenge. A recent theory, termed *interactive specialization*, holds that postnatal functional brain development, at least within the cerebral cortex, involves a process of increasing specialization, or fine-tuning, of response properties (Johnson, 2001, 2005). According to this view, during postnatal development, the response properties of cortical regions change as they interact and compete with each other to acquire their roles in new computational abilities. That is, some cortical regions begin with poorly defined functions and consequently are partially activated in a wide range of different contexts and tasks. During development, activity-dependent interactions between regions sharpen up their functions, such that a region's activity becomes restricted to a narrower set of stimuli or task demands. For example, a region originally activated by a wide variety of visual objects may come to confine its response to upright human faces. The termination of sensitive periods is then a natural consequence of the mechanisms by which cortical regions become increasingly specialized and finely tuned. Once regions have become specialized for their adult functions, these commitments are difficult to reverse. If this view is correct, sensitive periods in human cognitive development are intrinsic to the process that produces the functional structure of the adult brain.

In order to better understand how sensitive periods relate to the broader picture of vertebrate functional brain development, researchers have addressed a number of specific questions. In any given species are there multiple sensitive periods or just a few (e.g., one per sensory modality)? If there are multiple sensitive periods, do they share common underlying mechanisms? What are the processes that underlie the end of sensitive periods and the corresponding reduction in plasticity?

## Varieties of Sensitive Period

Recent work indicates that there are multiple sensitive periods in the sensory systems that have been studied. For example, within the auditory domain in humans, there are different sensitive periods for different facets of speech processing and other sensitive periods, having different timing, related to basic aspects of music perception. Similarly, in nonhuman-primate visual systems there are, at a minimum, different sensitive periods related to amblyopia (a condition found in early childhood in which one eye develops good vision but the other does not), visual acuity, motion perception, and face processing (see Johnson, 2005, for review).

How these different and varied sensitive periods relate to each other is still poorly understood. But high-level skills like human language involve the integration of many lower-level systems, and plasticity in language acquisition is therefore likely to be the combinatorial result of the relative plasticity of underlying auditory, phonological, semantic, syntactic, and motor systems, along with the developmental interactions among these components. The literature currently available suggests that plasticity tends to reduce in low-level sensory systems before it reduces in high-level cognitive systems (Huttenlocher, 2002).

While it is now agreed that there are multiple sensitive periods even within one sensory modality in a given species, there is still considerable debate as to whether these different sensitive periods reflect common underlying mechanisms or whether different mechanisms and principles operate in each case.

# Mechanisms Underlying Sensitive Periods

A major feature of sensitive periods is that plasticity appears to be markedly reduced at the end of the period. There are three general classes of explanation for this: (a) termination of plasticity due to maturation, (b) self-termination of learning, and (c) stabilization of constraints on plasticity (without a reduction in the underlying level of plasticity).

According to the first view, endogenous changes in the neurochemistry of the brain region in question could increase the rate of pruning of synapses, resulting in the "fossilization" of existing patterns of functional connectivity. Thus, the termination of sensitive periods would be due to endogenous factors, would have a fixed time course, and could be specific to individual regions of the cortex. Empirical evidence on neurochemical changes associated with plasticity (such as expression of glutamatergic and GABA receptors in the human visual cortex) indicate that the periods of neurochemical change can occur around the age of functional sensitive periods. However, this does not rule out the possibility that these neurochemical changes are a consequence of the differences in functional activity due to termination of plasticity for some other reason, rather than its primary cause (Murphy, Betson, Boley, & Jones, 2005).

The second class of mechanism implies that sensitive periods involve self-terminating learning processes. By this, we mean that the process of learning itself could produce changes that reduce the system's plasticity. These types of mechanisms are most consistent with the view of sensitive periods as a natural consequence of typical functional brain development. An important way to describe and understand self-terminating learning comes from the use of computer-simulated neural networks (Thomas & Johnson, 2006). These models demonstrate mechanistically how processes of learning can lead to neurobiological changes that reduce plasticity, rather than plasticity changing according to a purely maturational timetable. Such computer models have revealed that, even where a reduction in plasticity emerges with increasing experience, a range of different specific mechanisms may be responsible for this reduction (see Thomas & Johnson, 2006). For example, it may be that the neural system's computational resources, which are critical for future learning, have been claimed or used up by existing learning, so that any new learning must compete to capture these resources. Unless earlier-learned abilities are neglected or lost, new learning may always be limited by this competition. Another mechanism discovered through modeling is called entrenchment. In this case, prior experience places the system into a state that is nonoptimal

for learning the new skill. It takes time to reconfigure the system for the new task and learning correspondingly takes longer than it would have done had the system been in an uncommitted state. A third mechanism is assimilation, whereby initial learning reduces the system's ability to detect changes in the environment that might trigger further learning.

Evidence from humans relevant to self-terminating sensitive periods is reported by Lewis and Maurer (2005), who have studied the outcome of cases of human infants born with dense bilateral cataracts in both eyes. Such dense bilateral cataracts restrict these infants to near blindness, but fortunately the condition can be rectified with surgery. Despite variation in the age of treatment from 1 to 9 months, infants were found to have the visual acuity of a newborn immediately following surgery to remove the cataracts. However, after only 1 hour of patterned vision, acuity had improved to the level of a typical 6-week-old; and after a further month of visual experience, the gap to age-matched controls was very considerably reduced. These findings correspond well with experiments showing that rearing animals in the dark appears to delay the end of the normal sensitive period. Thus, in at least some cases, plasticity seems to wait for the appropriate type of sensory stimulation. This is consistent with the idea that changes in plasticity can be driven by the learning processes associated with typical development.

Returning to the paradigmatic example of filial imprinting in birds, O'Reilly and Johnson (1994) constructed a computer model of the neural network known to support imprinting in the relevant region of the chick brain. This computer model successfully simulated a range of phenomena associated with imprinting behavior in the chick. Importantly, in both the model and the chick, the extent to which an imprinted preference for one object can be "reversed" by exposure to a second object depends on a combination of the length of exposure to the first object and the length of exposure to the second object (for review, see Bolhuis, 1991). In other words, in the model, the sensitive period was dependent on the respective levels of learning and was self-terminating. Additionally, like the chick, the network generalised from a training object to one that shared some of its features such as color or shape. By gradually changing the features of the object to which the chick was exposed, the chick's preference could be shifted even after the "sensitive period" had supposedly closed. The simulation work demonstrated the sufficiency of simple learning mechanisms to explain the observed behavioral data (McClelland, 2005).

The third class of explanation for the end of sensitive periods is that it represents the onset of stability in constraining factors rather than a reduction in the underlying plasticity. For example, while an infant is growing, the distance between her eyes increases, thereby creating instability in the information to visual cortical areas. However, once the inter-eye distance is fixed in development, the visual input becomes stable. Thus, brain plasticity may be "hidden" until it is revealed by some perturbation to another constraining factor that disrupts vision.

This mechanism offers an attractive explanation of the surprising degree of plasticity sometimes observed in adults, for instance after even brief visual deprivation. Sathian (2005) reported activity in the visual cortex during tactile perception in sighted human adults after brief visual deprivation—activity similar to that observed in those who have suffered long-term visual deprivation. While this line of research initially appears consistent with life-long plasticity, it is important to note that this tactile-induced visual-cortex activity is much greater if vision is lost early in life or was never present. Thus, although there appears to be residual connectivity between sensory systems that can be uncovered by blocking vision in sighted people, there is also a sensitive period during which these connections can be more drastically altered.

# Sensitive Periods in Second Language Acquisition

Given the variety of mechanisms that may underlie sensitive periods, it would be interesting to know how such periods affect the acquisition of higher cognitive abilities in humans. Recent research on learning a second language illustrates one attempt to answer this question. If you want to master a second language, how important is the age at which you start to learn it? If you start to learn a second language as an adult, does your brain process it in a different way from how it processes your first language?

It is often claimed that unless individuals acquire a second language (L2) before mid-childhood (or perhaps before puberty), then they will never reach native-like levels of proficiency in the second language in pronunciation or grammatical knowledge. This claim is supported by deprivation studies showing that the acquisition of a first language (L1) is itself less successful when begun after a certain age. Further, functional brain-imaging studies initially indicated that in L2 acquisition, different areas of the cortex were activated by the L2 than by the L1; only in individuals who had acquired two languages simultaneously were common areas activated (e.g., Kim, Relkin, Lee, & Hirsch, 1997).

However, subsequent research has painted a more complex picture. First, claims for sensitive periods have tended to rely on assessing final level of attainment rather than speed of learning. This is because there is evidence that adults can learn a second language more quickly than children can, even if their final level of attainment is not as high. Indeed adults and children appear to learn a new language in different ways. Children are relatively insensitive to feedback and extract regularities from exposure to large amounts of input, whereas adults adopt explicit strategies and remain responsive to feedback (see, e.g., Hudson Kam & Newport, 2005).

Second, even when the final level of L2 attainment is considered, it has proved hard to find an age after which prospective attainment levels off. That is, there is no strong evidence for a point at which a sensitive period completely closes (see, e.g., Birdsong, 2006). Instead, L2 attainment shows a linear decline with age: The later you start, the lower your final level is likely to be (Birdsong, 2006).

Third, recent functional imaging research has indicated that at least three factors are important in determining the relative brain-activation patterns produced by L1 and L2 during comprehension and production. These are the age of acquisition, the level of usage/exposure to each language, and the level of proficiency attained in L2. Overall, three broad themes have

emerged (Abutalebi, Cappa, & Perani, 2005; Stowe & Sabourin, 2005): (a) The same network of left-hemisphere brain regions is involved in processing both languages; (b) a weak L2 is associated with more widespread neural activity compared to L1 in production (perhaps because the L2 is more effortful to produce) but less activation in comprehension (perhaps because the L2 is less well understood); and (c) the level of proficiency in L2 is more important than age of acquisition in determining whether L1 and L2 activate common or separate areas. In brief, the better you are at your L2, the more similar the activated regions become to those activated by your L1. This finding fits with the idea that certain brain areas have become optimized for processing language (perhaps during the acquisition of L1) and that, in order to become very good at L2, you have to engage these brain areas. The idea that later plasticity is tempered by the processing structures created by earlier learning fits with the interactive-specialization explanation for the closing of sensitive periods.

Finally, in line with the idea that language requires integration across multiple subskills, increasing evidence indicates that sensitive periods differ across the components of language (Neville, 2006; Wartenburger et al., 2003; Werker & Tees, 2005). Plasticity may show greater or earlier reductions for phonology and morphosyntax than it does for lexical-semantics, in which there may indeed be no age-related change at all. In other words, for the late language learner, new vocabulary is easier to acquire than new sounds or new grammar.

# Conclusion

It is important to understand the mechanisms underlying sensitive periods for practical reasons. Age-of-acquisition effects may shape educational policy and the time at which children are exposed to different skills. The reversibility of effects of deprivation on development has important implications for interventions for children with congenital sensory impairments or children exposed to impoverished physical and social environments. And there are clinical implications for understanding the mechanisms that drive recovery from brain damage at different ages.

Exciting vistas for the future include the possibility of using genetic and brain-imaging data to identify the best developmental times for training new skills in individual children, and the possibility that a deeper understanding of the neurocomputational principles that underlie self-terminating plasticity will allow the design of more efficient training procedures (McClelland 2005).

# Recommended Readings

Birdsong, D. (2006). (See References). Discusses recent research on sensitive periods and second-language acquisition.

Huttenlocher, P.R. (2002). (See References). An overview of neural plasticity.

Johnson, M.H. (2005). *Developmental cognitive neuroscience* (2nd ed.). Oxford, UK: Blackwell. An introduction to the relationship between brain development and cognitive development.

Knusden, E.I. (2004). Sensitive periods in the development of brain and behavior. *Journal of Cognitive Neuroscience, 16,* 1412–1425. A discussion of mechanisms of plasticity and sensitive periods at the level of neural circuits.

# References

Abutalebi, J., Cappa, S.F., & Perani, D. (2005). What can functional neuroimaging tell us about the bilingual brain? In J.F. Kroll & A.M.B. de Groot (Eds.), *Handbook of bilingualism* (pp. 497–515). Oxford, UK: Oxford University Press.

Birdsong, D. (2006). Age and second language acquisition and processing: A selective overview. *Language Learning, 56,* 9–49.

Bolhuis, J.J. (1991). Mechanisms of avian imprinting: A review. *Biological Reviews, 66,* 303–345.

Hudson Kam, C.L., & Newport, E.L. (2005). Regularizing unpredictable variation: The roles of adult and child learners in language formation and change. *Language Learning and Development, 1,* 151–195.

Huttenlocher, P.R. (2002). *Neural plasticity: The effects of the environment on the development of the cerebral cortex.* Cambridge, MA: Harvard University Press.

Huttenlocher, P.R., & Dabholkar, A.S. (1997). Regional differences in synaptogenesis in human cerebral cortex. *Journal of Comparative Neurology, 387,* 167–187.

Johnson, M.H. (2001). Functional brain development in humans. *Nature Reviews Neuroscience, 2,* 475–483.

Johnson, M.H. (2005). Sensitive periods in functional brain development: Problems and prospects. *Developmental Psychobiology, 46,* 287–292.

Kim, K.H.S., Relkin, N.R., Lee, K.M., & Hirsch, J. (1997). Distinct cortical areas associated with native and second languages. *Nature, 388,* 171–174.

Lewis, T.L., & Maurer, D. (2005). Multiple sensitive periods in human visual development: Evidence from visually deprived children. *Developmental Psychobiology, 46,* 163–183.

McClelland, J.L. (2005). How far can you go with Hebbian learning and when does it lead you astray? In Y. Munakata & M.H. Johnson (Eds.), *Attention and Performance XXI: Processes of change in brain and cognitive development* (pp. 33–59). Oxford, UK: Oxford University Press.

Michel, G.F., & Tyler, A.N. (2005). Critical period: A history of the transition from questions of when, to what, to how. *Developmental Psychobiology, 46,* 156–162.

Murphy, K.M., Betson, B.R., Boley, P.M., & Jones, D.G. (2005). Balance between excitatory and inhibitory plasticity mechanisms. *Developmental Psychobiology, 46,* 209–221.

Neville, H.J. (2006). Different profiles of plasticity within human cognition. In Y. Munakata & M.H. Johnson (Eds.), *Attention and Performance XXI: Processes of change in brain and cognitive development* (pp. 287–314). Oxford, UK: Oxford University Press.

O'Reilly, R., & Johnson, M.H. (1994). Object recognition and sensitive periods: A computational analysis of visual imprinting. *Neural Computation, 6,* 357–390.

Sathian, K. (2005). Visual cortical activity during tactile perception in the sighted and the visually deprived. *Developmental Psychobiology, 46,* 279–286.

Stowe, L.A., & Sabourin, L. (2005). Imaging the processing of a second language: Effects of maturation and proficiency on the neural processes involved. *International Review of Applied Linguistics in Language Teaching, 43,* 329–353.

Thomas, M.S.C., & Johnson, M.H. (2006). The computational modelling of sensitive periods. *Developmental Psychobiology, 48,* 337–344.

Wartenburger, I., Heekeren, H.R., Abutalebi, J., Cappa, S.F., Villringer, A., & Perani, D. (2003). Early setting of grammatical processing in the bilingual brain. *Neuron, 37,* 159–170.

Werker, J.F., & Tees, R.C. (2005). Speech perception as a window for understanding plasticity and commitment in language systems of the brain. *Developmental Psychobiology, 46,* 233–251.

# Critical Thinking

1. Compare and contrast the concepts of imprinting, sensitive periods, and plasticity. Discuss and make reference to past and current research that supports, refutes, or expands our scientific understanding of these concepts.

2. The article describes three mechanisms (maturation, self-termination of learning, and stabilization of constraints on plasticity) underlying sensitive periods. Elucidate and explain these three possible mechanisms and provide examples for each type.

3. Suppose you are a person who acquires multiple languages with high fluency as an adult. However, your close friend does not share this skill. Based on this article, how would you explain this differential ability to your friend? Are there interventions you could recommend that might improve your friend's second language acquisition skill? Why or why not?

4. Recently, researchers have shown the importance of supporting early interactions and experiences during infancy and preschool to support brain development. Explain how this information has or has not changed your perceptions and interactions with babies as a result. If you were a parent of an infant or toddler, explain in more detail what you would do to optimize their early development?

5. Based on this article, what implications does this research have for policy recommendations concerning interventions with children born with visual impairments? Are similar policy recommendations needed for second language learning in the public schools?

Address correspondence to **MICHAEL S.C. THOMAS**, Developmental Neurocognition Laboratory, School of Psychology, Birkbeck College, University of London, Malet Street, Bloomsbury, London WC1E 7HX, United Kingdom; e-mail: m.thomas@bbk.ac.uk.

**Acknowledgments**—This research was supported by Medical Research Council (MRC) Career Establishment Grant G0300188 to Michael S.C. Thomas, and MRC Grant G9715587 to Mark H. Johnson.

# Contributions of Neuroscience to Our Understanding of Cognitive Development

Adele Diamond and Dima Amso

Neuroscience research has made its greatest contributions to the study of cognitive development by illuminating mechanisms (providing a "how") that underlie behavioral observations made earlier by psychologists. It has also made important contributions to our understanding of cognitive development by demonstrating that the brain is far more plastic at all ages than previously thought—and thus that the speed and extent by which experience and behavior can shape the brain is greater than almost anyone imagined. In other words, rather than showing that biology is destiny, neuroscience research has been at the forefront of demonstrating the powerful role of experience throughout life. Besides the surprising evidence of the remarkable extent of experience-induced plasticity, rarely has neuroscience given us previously unknown insights into cognitive development, but neuroscience does offer promise of being able to detect some problems before they are behaviorally observable.

## Providing Mechanisms That Can Account for Behavioral Results Reported by Psychologists

Here we describe two examples of behavioral findings by psychologists that were largely ignored or extremely controversial until underlying biological mechanisms capable of accounting for them were provided by neuroscience research. One such example concerns cognitive deficits documented in children treated early and continuously for phenylketonuria (PKU). The second example involves neonatal imitation observed by psychologists and mirror neurons discovered by neuroscientists.

## Prefrontal Dopamine System and PKU Cognitive Deficits

Since at least the mid-1980s, psychologists were reporting cognitive deficits in children with PKU that resembled those associated with frontal cortex dysfunction (e.g., Pennington, VanDoornick, McCabe, & McCabe, 1985). Those reports did not impact medical care, however. Doctors were skeptical. No one could imagine a mechanism capable of producing what psychologists claimed to be observing.

PKU is a disorder in the gene that codes for phenylalanine hydroxylase, an enzyme essential for the conversion of phenylalanine (Phe) to tyrosine (Tyr). In those with PKU, that enzyme is absent or inactive. Without treatment, Phe levels skyrocket, resulting in gross brain damage and mental retardation. Phe is an amino acid and a component of all dietary protein. PKU treatment consists primarily of reducing dietary intake of protein to keep Phe levels down, but that has to be balanced against the need for protein. For years, children with PKU were considered adequately treated if their blood Phe levels were below 600 micromoles per liter (µmol/L; normal levels in the general public being 60–120 µmol/L). Such children did not have mental retardation and showed no gross brain damage, although no one disputed that their blood Phe levels were somewhat elevated and their blood Tyr levels were somewhat reduced (Tyr levels were not grossly reduced because even though the hydroxylation of Phe into Tyr was largely inoperative, Tyr is also available in protein). Since Phe and Tyr compete to cross into the brain, a modest increase in the ratio of Phe to Tyr in the bloodstream results in a modest decrease in how much Tyr can reach the brain. Note that this is a global effect—the entire brain receives somewhat too little Tyr. How was it possible to make sense of psychologists' claims that the resulting cognitive deficits were not global but limited to the cognitive functions dependent on prefrontal cortex?

Neuroscience provided a mechanism by which psychologists' findings made sense. Research in neuropharmacology had shown that the dopamine system in prefrontal cortex has unusual properties not shared by the dopamine systems in other brain regions such as the striatum. The dopamine neurons that project to prefrontal cortex have higher rates of firing and dopamine turnover. This makes prefrontal cortex sensitive to modest reductions in Tyr (the precursor of dopamine) that are too small to affect the rest of the brain (Tam, Elsworth, Bradberry, & Roth, 1990). Those unusual properties of the prefrontal dopamine system provide a mechanism by which children treated for PKU could show selective deficits limited to prefrontal cortex. The moderate imbalance in the bloodstream between Phe and Tyr causes a reduction in the amount of Tyr reaching the brain that is large enough to impair the functioning of the prefrontal dopamine system but not large enough to affect the rest of the brain. Diamond and colleagues provided evidence for this mechanism in animal models of PKU and longitudinal study of children (Diamond, 2001). That work, presenting a mechanistic explanation and providing convincing evidence to support it, resulted in a change in the medical guidelines for the treatment of PKU (blood Phe levels should be kept between 120 and 360 μmol/L) that has improved children's lives (e.g., Stemerdink et al., 2000). Also, by shedding light on the role of dopamine in the prefrontal cortex early in development, such work offers insights on the development of cognitive control (executive function) abilities that are relevant to all children.

## Mirror Neurons and Neonate Imitation

In 1977, Meltzoff and Moore created a sensation by reporting that human infants just 12 to 21 days old imitated facial expressions they observed adults making. That was followed by a second demonstration of such imitation in infants as young as 42 minutes (Meltzoff & Moore, 1983). For years, those reports met strong resistance. Such imitation was thought to be far too sophisticated an accomplishment for a neonate. After all, infants can feel but not see their own mouth and tongue movements, and they can see but not feel the mouth and tongue movements of others. To equate their own motor movements with the perception of those same movements by others would seem to involve high-level cross-modal matching.

The discovery of mirror neurons by Rizzolatti and his colleagues, Fadiga, Fogassi, and Gallese (for review, see Rizzolatti & Craighero, 2004) provided a mechanism that could conceivably underlie newborns' ability to show such imitation rather automatically. Mirror neurons fire when an individual executes an action or when an individual observes someone else executing that action. The cross-modal association occurs at the neuronal, single-cell level. It has since been demonstrated that 3-day-old rhesus monkeys also imitate the facial movements of adult humans (Ferrari et al., 2006) and that the close link between perception and action is not limited to vision; hearing a sound associated with an action activates mirror neurons associated with that action just as does the sight of that action (Kohler et al., 2002).

Whereas the preceding examples are of neuroscience elucidating possible neurobiological bases for observed psychological phenomena, we move on to describe phenomena—concerning plasticity and environmental influences—that neuroscientists have brought to the attention of developmentalists.

# Powerful Effects of Early Experience on Brain, Body, Mind, Behavior, and Gene Expression

Ironically, one of the most important findings to emerge from neurobiology is that biology is not destiny. Neuroscience research has shown that experience plays a far larger role in shaping the mind, brain, and even gene expression than was ever imagined. This insight is particularly important in advancing theory in cognitive development, where debates have raged about the importance of nature versus nurture.

Examples of striking experience-induced plasticity abound—for example, the groundbreaking work of Greenough, Merzenich, Maurer, Neville, Pascual-Leone, Taub, Sur, and Kral. Here we highlight work by Schanberg and Meaney, in part because that work emphasizes a sensory system that has received far less attention by psychologists than have vision and audition: the sense of touch.

## Nurturing Touch and Its Importance for Growth

Two independent, elegant lines of work have demonstrated the powerful effects of touch. Schanberg and colleagues have shown that the licking behavior of rat mothers is essential for the growth of rat pups. If rat pups are deprived of this touch for even just 1 hour, DNA synthesis is reduced, growth-hormone secretion is inhibited, and bodily organs lose their capacity to respond to exogenously administered growth hormone (Butler, Suskind, & Schanberg, 1978; Kuhn, Butler, & Schanberg, 1978). Schanberg and colleagues have identified molecular mechanisms through which deprivation of the very specific kind of touch rat mothers administer to their pups produces these effects (e.g., Schanberg, Ingledue, Lee, Hannun, & Bartolome, 2003).

## Nurturing Touch and Its Importance for Reducing Stress Reactivity and for Cognitive Development

Meaney and colleagues have demonstrated that rat moms who more frequently lick and groom their pups produce offspring who, throughout their lives, explore more, are less fearful, show milder reactions to stress, perform better cognitively as adults, and preserve their cognitive skills better into old age (Liu, Diorio, Day, Francis, & Meaney, 2000). It is the mother's behavior that produces these effects rather than a particular genetic profile that produces both a particular mothering style and particular offspring characteristics. Pups of high-licking-and-grooming moms raised by low-licking-and-grooming moms do not show these characteristics, and pups of low-touch moms raised by high-touch moms do show this constellation of attributes (Francis, Diorio, Liu, & Meaney, 1999).

Furthermore, rats tend to raise their offspring the way they themselves were raised, so these effects are transmitted intergenerationally, not through the genome but through behavior. Biological offspring of low-touch moms who are cross-fostered to high-touch moms lick and groom their offspring a lot; in this way the diminished stress response and cognitive enhancement is passed down through the generations (Francis et al., 1999).

Meaney and colleagues have elegantly demonstrated that maternal behavior produces these behavioral consequences through several mechanisms that alter gene expression. Not all genes in an individual are expressed—many are never expressed. Experience can affect which genes are turned on and off, in which cells, and when. For example, methylation (attaching a methyl group to a gene's promoter) stably silences a gene; demethylation reverses that process, typically leading to the gene being expressed. High licking by rat mothers causes demethylation (i.e., activation) of the glucocorticoid receptor gene, hence lowering circulating glucocorticoid (stress hormone) levels as receptors for the stress hormone remove it from circulation.

## Nurturing Touch and Human Cognitive and Emotional Development

Unlike newborn rats, human newborns can see, hear, and smell, as well as feel touch. Yet despite the additional sensory information available to them, touch is still crucial. Human infants who receive little touching grow more slowly, release less growth hormone, and are less responsive to growth hormone that is exogenously administered (Frasier & Rallison, 1972). Throughout life, they show larger reactions to stress, are more prone to depression, and are vulnerable to deficits in cognitive functions commonly seen in depression or during stress (Lupien, King, Meaney, McEwen, 2000).

Touch plays a powerful role for human infants in promoting optimal development and in counteracting stressors. Massaging babies lowers their cortisol levels and helps them gain weight (Field et al., 2004). The improved weight gain from neonatal massage has been replicated cross-culturally, and cognitive benefits are evident even a year later. It is not that infants sleep or eat more; rather, stimulating their body through massage increases vagal (parasympathetic nervous system) activity, which prompts release of food-absorption hormones. Such improved vagal tone also indicates better ability to modulate arousal and to attend to subtle environmental cues important for cognitive development. Passive bodily contact also has substantial stress-reducing, calming, and analgesic effects for infants and adults (e.g., Gray, Watt, & Blass, 2000). Thus, besides "simple touch" being able to calm our jitters and lift our spirits, the right kind of touch regularly enough early in life can improve cognitive development, brain development, bodily health throughout life, and gene expression.

# Future Directions

Neuroscience may be able to make extremely important contributions to child development by building on repeated demonstrations that differences in neural activity patterns precede and predict differences in cognitive performance. Often, when the brain is not functioning properly, people can compensate so their performance does not suffer until the neural system becomes too dysfunctional or until performance demands become too great. Thus, an underlying problem may exist but not show up behaviorally until, for example, the academic demands of more advanced schooling exceed a child's ability to compensate.

So far, differences in neural activity patterns have been demonstrated to precede and predict differences in cognitive performance only in adults. For example, Bookheimer and colleagues tested older adults (ranging in age from 47 to 82 years) with a genetic predisposition for Alzheimer's disease, selected because they performed fully comparably to controls across diverse cognitive tasks. Nevertheless, functional neuroimaging revealed that the brains of several of the genetically predisposed individuals already showed predicted differences. Two years later, those individuals showed the cognitive impairments predicted by their earlier neural activity patterns (Bookheimer et al., 2000). Similarly, adults in the early stages of other disorders may show no behavioral evidence of a cognitive deficit while neuroimaging shows their brains are compensating or working harder to achieve that behavioral equivalence. As the disease progresses, the compensation is no longer sufficient and the cognitive deficit becomes evident (e.g., Audoin et al., 2006).

What this suggests is that functional neuroimaging in developing children may perhaps be able to detect evidence of learning disorders—such as attentional, sensory-processing, language, or math deficits—before there is behavioral evidence of a problem. Already, research is being undertaken to see if infants' neural responses to auditory stimuli might be predictive of later linguistic problems (e.g., Benasich et al., 2006). The earlier a problem can be detected, the better the hope of correcting it or of putting environmental compensations in place.

## Recommended Readings

Diamond, A. (2001). (See References). Summarizes studies with young children and animals showing the role of maturation of prefrontal cortex in the early emergence of executive function abilities and the importance of dopamine for this.

Grossman, A.W., Churchill, J.D., Bates, K.E., Kleim, J.A., & Greenough, W.T. (2002). A brain adaptation view of plasticity: Is synaptic plasticity an overly limited concept? *Progress in Brain Research, 138,* 91–108. Argues that synaptic, even neuronal, plasticity is but a small fraction of the range of brain changes that occur in response to experience, and that there are multiple forms of brain plasticity governed by mechanisms that are at least partially independent, including non-neuronal changes.

Meaney, M.J. (2001). Maternal care, gene expression, and the transmission of individual differences in stress reactivity across generations. *Annual Review of Neuroscience, 24,* 1161–1192. Provides an overview of research demonstrating that naturally occurring variations in maternal care modify the expression of genes affecting offspring's cognitive development as well as their ability to cope with stress throughout life, and that these changes are passed down intergenerationally (epigenetic inheritance).

Meltzoff, A.N., & Decety, J. (2003). What imitation tells us about social cognition: A rapprochement between developmental psychology and cognitive neuroscience. *Philosophical Transactions of the Royal Society of London – B: Biological Sciences, 358,* 491–500. Reviews the psychological evidence concerning imitation in human neonates and the neurophysiological evidence of a common coding at the single cell level (in mirror neurons) between perceived and generated actions.

Neville, H.J., & Bavelier, D. (2002). Human brain plasticity: Evidence from sensory deprivation and altered language experience. *Progress in Brain Research, 138,* 177–188. Summarizes research, using behavioral measures and neuroimaging, on individuals with altered visual, auditory, and/or language experience, showing ways in which brain development can, and cannot, be modified by environmental input, and how that varies by the timing of the altered input and by specific subfunctions within language or vision.

## References

Audoin, B., Au Duong, M.V., Malikova, I., Confort-Gouny, S., Ibarrola, D., Cozzone, P.J., et al. (2006). Functional magnetic resonance imaging and cognition at the very early stage of MS. *Journal of the Neurological Sciences, 245,* 87–91.

Benasich, A.A., Choudhury, N., Friedman, J.T., Realpe Bonilla, T., Chojnowska, C., & Gou, Z. (2006). Infants as a prelinguistic model for language learning impairments: Predicting from event-related potentials to behavior. *Neuropsychologia, 44,* 396–441.

Bookheimer, S.Y., Strojwas, M.H., Cohen, M.S., Saunders, A.M., Pericak-Vance, M.A., Mazziota, J.C., et al. (2000). Patterns of brain activation in people at risk for Alzheimer's disease. *New England Journal of Medicine, 343,* 450–456.

Butler, S.R., Suskind, M.R., & Schanberg, S.M. (1978). Maternal behavior as a regulator of polyamine biosynthesis in brain and heart of the developing rat pup. *Science, 199,* 445–447.

Diamond, A. (2001). A model system for studying the role of dopamine in prefrontal cortex during early development in humans. In C. Nelson & M. Luciana (eds.), *Handbook of developmental cognitive neuroscience* (pp. 433–472). Cambridge, MA: MIT Press.

Field, T., Hernandez-Reif, M., Diego, M., Feijo, L., Vera, Y., & Gil, K. (2004). Massage therapy by parents improves early growth and development. *Infant Behavior & Development, 27,* 435–442.

Ferrari, P.F., Visalberghi, E., Paukner, A., Fogassi, L., Ruggiero, A., & Suomi, S. (2006). Neonatal imitation in rhesus macaques. *PLoS Biology, 4,* 1501–1508.

Francis, D., Diorio, J., Liu, D., & Meaney, M.J. (1999). Nongenomic transmission across generations of maternal behavior and stress responses in the rat. *Science, 286,* 1155–1158.

Frasier, S.D., & Rallison, M.L. (1972). Growth retardation and emotional deprivation: Relative resistance to treatment with human growth hormone. *Journal of Pediatrics, 80,* 603–609.

Gray, L., Watt, L., & Blass, E.M. (2000). Skin-to-skin contact is analgesic in healthy newborns. *Pediatrics, 105,* 1–6.

Kohler, E., Keysers, C., Umiltà, M.A., Fogassi, L., Gallese, V., & Rizzolatti, G. (2002). Hearing sounds, understanding actions: Action representation in mirror neurons. *Science, 297,* 846–848.

Kuhn, C.M., Butler, S.R., & Schanberg, S.M. (1978). Selective depression of serum growth hormone during maternal deprivation in rat pups. *Science, 201,* 1034–1036.

Liu, D., Diorio, J., Day, J.C., Francis, D.D., & Meaney, M.J. (2000). Maternal care, hippocampal synaptogenesis and cognitive development in rats. *Nature Neuroscience, 3,* 799–806.

Lupien, S.J., King, S., Meaney, M.J., & McEwen, B.S. (2000). Child's stress hormone levels correlate with mother's socioeconomic status and depressive state. *Biological Psychiatry, 48,* 976–980.

Meltzoff, A.N., & Moore, M.K. (1977). Imitation of facial and manual gestures by human neonates. *Science, 198,* 75–78.

Meltzoff, A.N., & Moore, M.K. (1983). Newborn infants imitate adult facial gestures. *Child Development, 54,* 702–709.

Pennington, B.F., VanDoornick, W.J., McCabe, L.L., & McCabe, E.R.B. (1985). Neuropsychological deficits in early treated phenylketonuric children. *American Journal of Mental Deficiency, 89,* 467–474.

Rizzolatti, G., & Craighero, L. (2004). The mirror-neuron system. *Annual Review of Neuroscience, 27,* 169–192.

Schanberg, S.M., Ingledue, V.F., Lee, J.Y., Hannun, Y.A., & Bartolome, J.V. (2003). PKC mediates maternal touch regulation of growth-related gene expression in infant rats. *Neuropsychopharmacology, 28,* 1026–1030.

Stemerdink, B.A., Kalverboer, A.F., van der Meere, J.J., van der Molen, M.W., Huisman, J., de Jong, L.W., et al. (2000). Behaviour and school achievement in patients with early and continuously treated phenylketonuria. *Journal of Inherited Metabolic Disorders, 23,* 548–562.

Tam, S.Y., Elsworth, J.D., Bradberry, C.W., & Roth, R.H. (1990). Mesocortical dopamine neurons: High basal firing frequency predicts tyrosine dependence of dopamine synthesis. *Journal of Neural Transmission, 81,* 97–110.

# Critical Thinking

1. How does neuroscience help us understand mechanism or "the how" of cognitive development?

2. What evidence is there that nurturing touch affects babies in positive ways, and what are some biological processes that are triggered by such nurturing touch?

3. How do mirror neurons help explain how very young infants are able to imitate facial expressions?

Address correspondence to **ADELE DIAMOND,** Canada Research Chair Professor of Developmental Cognitive Neuroscience, Department of Psychiatry, University of British Columbia, 2255 Wesbrook Mall, Vancouver, British Columbia, V6T 2A1, Canada; e-mail: adele.diamond @ubc.ca.

**Acknowledgments**—AD gratefully acknowledges grant support from the National Institute on Drug Abuse (R01 #DA19685) during the writing of this paper.

# Infant Feeding and Cognition: Integrating a Developmental Perspective

Elizabeth Soliday

I n recent years, a number of major medical organizations, including the American Academy of Pediatrics (AAP, 2005), the American College of Obstetricians and Gynecologists (2002), and the U.S. Department of Health and Human Services, Office on Women's Health (U.S. DHHS, 2000), have recommended exclusive breastfeeding for infants during the first 6–12 months of life. These recommendations, which have had tremendous influence on professional practice and hospital maternity care, are based primarily on strong evidence that breastfeeding confers numerous health advantages on children, ranging from pediatric immunological benefits (AAP, 2005) to fewer gastrointestinal disorders (Wang & Wu, 1996) and lower risk of childhood obesity (Arenz, Ruckerl, Koletzko, & von Kries, 2004).

Recently, the AAP, along with other medical organizations, has additionally recommended breastfeeding partly on the basis of evidence that it "has been associated with slightly enhanced performance on tests of cognitive development" (AAP Section on Breastfeeding; AAP, 2005, p. 496). However, cognitive benefits related to breastfeeding are viewed more tentatively by DHHS policymakers, who caution that "observations . . . that . . . cognitive function of these [breastfed] children is greater than in non-breastfed children . . . [have] not been conclusively proven" (U.S. DHHS, 2000, p. 11). The conflicting views of the AAP and the DHHS reflect the current controversy surrounding claims of superior cognitive abilities in breastfed infants.

The controversy actually has a long history. Ever since the first published report of higher IQ scores in children breastfed as infants (Hoefer & Hardy, 1929), researchers have questioned whether such differences in IQ scores might be related to sociodemographic differences between breastfed and formula-fed groups. Specifically, compared with mothers who do not breastfeed, breastfeeding mothers typically are older and have more education, higher family incomes, more stable family circumstances (e.g., Fergusson, Beautrais, & Silva, 1982; Pollock, 1994), and higher IQs (Jacobson, Chiodo, & Jacobson, 1999; Morrow-Tlucak, Haude, & Ernhart, 1988). In addition, extended breastfeeding is associated with higher maternal and paternal education, urban dwelling, and nonsmoking (Pollock;

Taylor & Wadsworth, 1984), as well as having fewer children and fewer psychiatric symptoms (Taylor & Wadsworth). All these factors could be related to higher IQ scores in children. Nevertheless, reviews of effects of feeding practices on children's cognitive abilities generally conclude that even with rigorous statistical control of sociodemographic variables, small score advantages remain in breastfed samples (e.g., Jain, Concato, & Leventhal, 2002; Koo, 2003; Kramer & Kakuma, 2002; Uauy, Hoffman, Mena, Llanos, & Birch, 2003).

Given that studies of infant feeding and cognition have triggered profound changes in professional practice policies, despite the lack of strong evidence for significant cognitive benefits, an integrative perspective on current research is needed. Developmental scientists, whose publications in this area are far outnumbered by those of medical professionals, have a great deal to offer in understanding the influences that infant feeding practices may have on cognitive outcomes. Therefore, the aim of this article was to call attention to primary issues that, though essential, have previously been given only cursory mention in the literature dealing with infant feeding and cognitive outcome. These issues include the following:

- Clearly defining "infant feeding"
- Identifying the mechanism(s) of cognitive effect of various types of infant feeding
- Addressing the stability of cognitive ability scores
- Questioning the clinical significance of the magnitude of score differences typically found
- Providing constructive recommendations for practice and policy.

## Clarifying Definitions of Infant Feeding and Associated Language

Synthesizing studies of the relation between infant feeding and cognitive ability is complicated by differences in how researchers define infant feeding. Across studies, for example, "breastfeeding" includes natural, exclusive breastfeeding, the delivery of breastmilk by one or another artificial means, or the delivery of breastmilk by any means with or without formula supplementation and with or without solid foods. This author recommends defining infant feeding by two dimensions: *feeding method* and *feeding substance*. The first dimension refers to the manner in which food is transmitted to the infant and includes natural breastfeeding and/or artificial (intravenous, parenteral, naso-gastric tube, or bottle) delivery systems. *The second dimension* refers to the substance the infant is fed, which can include human milk, commercially prepared formulas, a mixture of both, other liquids (such as juice), and/or solid foods. In general, *breastfeeding* encompasses both method and substance, whereas *artificial feeding* typically refers to an artificial method and a prepared breastmilk substitute. In addition, across studies, the language used to describe feeding-related differences is inconsistent and does not reflect an attempt to set breastfeeding as the normative standard to which other methods should necessarily be compared. Recognizing this difficulty, rather than discuss "advantages" or "benefits" associated with breastfeeding, this article presumes breastfeeding to be the normative standard. Alternative feeding methods are discussed in terms of their advantages or disadvantages, as the data indicate.

One final issue related to defining feeding *substance* that complicates easy and timely synthesis of this literature is the evolution of infant formula composition. Infant formulas have progressed from raw milk recipes to evaporated milk to current preparations patterned after breastmilk. Formula compositions are continually evolving, and any formula under study typically reflects what was designated as safe and effective at the time.

# Identifying Mechanism of Effect on Cognitive Outcomes

## Long-Chain Polyunsaturated Fatty Acids

The prevailing theory for the poorer cognitive performance of bottle-fed infants is that some artificially prepared formulas lack two long-chain polyunsaturated fatty acids (LC-PUFAs) present in breastmilk: arachadonic acid (ARA) and docosahexanoic acid (DHA). DHA and ARA have been identified as critical nutrients in the development of central nervous system neurons and in cell function. For example, DHA and ARA enhance glucose uptake in neuronal cells, increasing the energy available for functions such as signaling and receiving messages (Innis, 2003; Lapillonne, Clark, & Heird, 2003). Emerging evidence suggests that these LC-PUFAs also affect the expression of genes involved in visual and brain development and function (Innis; Uauy, Mena, & Rojas, 2000). From a functional perspective, these cellular properties may translate into cognitive performance, including general intellectual performance, problem solving, and memory (Das, 2003; Innis & Uauy, 2003).

ARA and DHA can be obtained only through dietary intake, specifically of meat, seafood, and eggs. Humans can also metabolize ARA and DHA from their dietary precursors, linoleic acid (LA) and α-linoleic acid (α-LA), which are found in a wide variety of foods. Until recently, infant formulas manufactured in the United States contained only LA and α-LA. This was primarily due to concerns about the safety (i.e., shelf life) of adding DHA and ARA to infant formulas and to the assumption that full-term infants can metabolize DHA and ADA from precursors. However, researchers have begun to suggest that particularly in the early months, infants are, at best, highly inefficient at metabolizing ARA and DHA from precursors, possibly because of the immaturity of their metabolic system (Das, 2003). Consequently, recent improvements in the production of DHA and ARA, together with accumulating evidence of the benefits of DHA and ARA for visual and cognitive performance, led the U.S. Department of Agriculture in 2002 to issue a statement urging, though not requiring, manufacturers to include DHA and ARA in infant formulas (FDA/CFSAN Office of Nutritional Products, 2002).

Although researchers have proposed that ARA and DHA are responsible for differences in cognitive ability scores between breastfed and artificially fed infants, authors of six individual methodologically sound studies stated that the mechanisms of effect are as yet not well understood (e.g., Gomez-Sanchiz, Canete, Rodero, Baeza, & Avila, 2003; Wigg et al., 1998). To more clearly establish whether LC-PUFAs are the mechanism behind these group differences, researchers have used experimental designs that control potential confounding effects of feeding *method* by randomly assigning infants fed by the same artificial method to different *substances,* that is, formulas varying in nutritional composition including DHA and/or ARA supplements. If the factor driving cognitive score differences between breastfed and bottle-fed groups were LC-PUFAs, then one would expect infants consuming formula supplemented with LC-PUFAs to perform no differently from breastfed infants (i.e., a substance effect) and that formula-supplemented and breastfed groups would have higher scores than infants fed standard formula.

In general, studies involving random assignment to supplemented formulas have yielded equivocal results. Of the six available studies conducted with full-term infants, none was entirely consistent with the hypothesis that formula supplementation with LC-PUFAs negates the disadvantage presumably arising from their absence in standard formula and/or artificial feeding. For example, one study reported higher Bayley scale scores in breastfed groups than in formula-fed groups, including those whose formulas were supplemented with DHA and ARA (Makrides, Neumann, Simmer, Pater, & Gibson, 1995). Across similar studies, researchers found no particular advantage for *any* group, including breastfed infants (e.g., Agostoni et al., 1997; Auestad et al., 2001, 2003; Lucas et al., 1999). One study using specific skill measures (habituation, problem solving) found significant benefits associated with LC-PUFA supplementation only for infants considered small for gestational age and/or who showed growth deceleration (Willatts, Forsyth, DiModugno, Varma, & Colvin, 1998). Further, the results of one study ran *contrary* to theoretical predictions, with infants who were fed formula supplemented with DHA performing significantly *worse* than those who were fed breastmilk or standard formula (Scott et al., 1998).

Although studies focusing solely on LC-PUFAs as the mechanism behind cognitive differences between groups are inconclusive, directing attention to individual differences in LC-PUFA status—which varies among newborns by as much as 100 percent (Agostoni et al., 1997; Foreman-van Drongelen, van Houwelinger, Blanco, & Hornstra, 1995) and continues to vary throughout infancy (Innis & Uauy, 2003; Uauy, Mena, & Peirano, 2001)—may be key in identifying the role of LC-PUFA in infant cognition. Such an approach would require three steps: (a) measuring LC-PUFAs early, to use as a control variable; (b) establishing that LC-PUFA intake translates into physiological differences in the nutrient; and (c) correlating LC-PUFA physiological measures and cognitive test scores.

Relevant to the second of these steps, three studies have found a significant relationship between dietary intake of LC-PUFAs and their physiological availability, as measured by levels of either erythrocytes or red blood cell membrane phospholipids, or both (Auestad et al., 2001; Lapillonne, Brossard, Claris, Reygrobellet, & Salle, 2000). The next step, establishing an association between physiological availability of LC-PUFAs and cognitive test scores, is perhaps the most interesting for developmentalists, and support for such an association is emerging. For example, Agostoni et al. (1997) reported a correlation of .62 between LC-PUFA concentrations and developmental quotient at age 4 months, and Helland et al. (2003) reported a correlation of .23 between infant LC-PUFA and Mental Processing Composite scores on the Kauffman Assessment Battery at age 4 years. Similar findings have been reported for specific skill measures, including language and visual-motor problem-solving scores (Innis, Gilley, & Werker, 2001; Voigt et al., 2002).

Although evidence for a correlation between LC-PUFA concentrations and cognitive ability scores is growing, a limitation of current laboratory measures of LC-PUFAs should be noted. Because direct measurement of LC-PUFA accumulation in brain tissue of live infants is impossible (Clandinin et al., 1980), the measures that are used are typically of circulating LC-PUFAs, which are proximal measures of brain LC-PUFAs. According to Das (2003), the average daily LC-PUFA intake in 750 ml of human milk is 60 mg, of which approximately 5 mg reaches the brain. Thus, a great loss of LC-PUFAs appears to occur in the metabolic process, and proximal measures may not be reliable indicators.

### *Behavioral Mechanisms*

As yet, researchers have not addressed specific caregiver behaviors associated with infant feeding that may account for differences in cognitive ability across feeding methods. Several researchers have examined how home environment quality, which theoretically reflects parenting processes associated with children's cognitive performance (Bradley & Caldwell, 1984), contributes to feeding-related differences in cognitive ability. But perhaps because home environment quality is a distal measure of feeding behavior, findings regarding its influence are equivocal: Two studies found significant effects of home

environment quality beyond feeding effects, including maternal IQ and parenting skills (Jacobson et al., 1999; Wigg et al., 1998), and two did not (Morrow-Tlucak et al., 1988; Paine, Makrides, & Gibson, 1999).

In perhaps the only available study of specific maternal behaviors pertaining to infant feeding and cognitive outcomes, Feldman and Eidelman (2003) examined how mother–infant interaction moderated the relationship between feeding substance and cognitive outcomes. Eighty-six premature infants were divided into three study groups according to the proportion of breastmilk-to-formula they received (primarily by nasogastric tube) prior to hospital discharge: substantial (<75 percent), intermediate (50 percent), and minimal (<25 percent). Videotapes of mother–infant interactions at 37 weeks of gestation revealed that mothers of infants in the substantial group—that is, the mothers who provided the greater amounts of breastmilk—provided significantly greater affectionate touch to their infants. At 6 months of age, infants in the substantial group scored significantly higher on the Bayley Mental Development Index than those in the two lower groups. This relationship was moderated by affectionate touch at 37 weeks, with infants in the substantial group who experienced affectionate touch most frequently scoring highest on the Bayley scales. These results indicate that even when feeding substance has a demonstrated effect on cognitive outcomes, maternal behavior still has an important role. Further studies of specific maternal behaviors during feeding interactions across methods will help clarify relationships among feeding method, behavior, and cognitive abilities.

## Stability of Cognitive Test Scores

The extent to which feeding-related cognitive differences found in infancy persist remains to be established. Although randomized studies do not generally support the idea of LC-PUFA-related differences in early infancy, differences may emerge later. For example, Makrides, Neumann, Simmer, Pater, and Gibson (2000) followed infants randomly assigned to consume standard or LC-PUFA-supplemented formula for 1 year, as well as a group of breastfed infants. No differences on Bayley scales resulted among the groups at age 1 year, but at age 2, breastfed infants scored significantly higher. Auestad et al. (2001) suggested that feeding-related differences may emerge as children experience increasing cognitive and/or social stressors throughout development.

On the other hand, establishing "stability" of global cognitive test scores from early infancy into childhood is in itself problematic. Well-normed, widely used infant developmental assessments such as the Bayley scales are useful for determining whether a child's global functioning is within normal limits *at the time of measurement* (Rose, Feldman, & Jankowski, 2003). But because the brain is only 75 percent developed at birth and continues to grow through age 6 (Hanaoka, Takashima, & Morooka, 1998), early developmental test results reflect children's functioning at considerably less than full capacity. It therefore follows that infant developmental measures have weak predictive ability (Sternberg, Grigorenko, & Bundy, 2001). In addition, owing to infants' limited verbal abilities, tests of infant cognition tend to rely on sensorimotor and perceptual skills, whereas most childhood IQ tests rely on language abilities. It is no surprise, then, that the median correlation between the scores on developmental tests administered in the first 6 months and those on IQ tests administered between ages 2 and 4 years is a modest 0.21 and that the correlation between infant measures and IQ scores between ages 5 and 7 plummets to near 0 (Kopp & McCall, 1982).

# Practical and Clinical Significance of Score Differences by Feeding Method and Substance

In the studies reviewed here, reported global cognitive ability scores were typically in the average range for both breastfed and artificially fed groups, consistent with the majority of research in this area. In studies reporting significant feeding-related differences, breastfed infants generally scored 2 to 3 points higher than their formula-fed counterparts. However, factoring in measurement error, a 2- to 3-point difference between groups would likely be negated by placing scores within 95 percent confidence intervals. At a population level, one might argue that raising IQ 3 points could reduce the number of individuals scoring in the range of mental retardation. However, such an argument assumes that raising IQ from 70 to 73 is as plausible as raising it from 100 to 103, yet individuals with IQs in the range of mental retardation likely differ in qualitative ways from those scoring nearer to average (Strickland, 2000). Certainly, it seems improbable that neurological deficits leading to significant IQ deficits could be ameliorated by boosting a single dietary nutrient (Dobbing, 1981).

Along similar lines, researchers have suggested a potential LC-PUFA threshold effect achieved by dietary intake in well-nourished women (Helland et al., 2001). Though clinical levels for LC-PUFA are yet to be established, current guidelines for LC-PUFA supplementation are based primarily on well-nourished, Caucasian breastfeeding mothers who consume Western diets. Breastmilk samples taken from women in non-Western cultures do not typically meet recommendations currently in place for formula supplementation. In light of cultural variation in breastmilk LC-PUFAs, establishing upper and lower clinical limits for formula supplements and breast-milk becomes even more important. Linking dietary limits to the upper and lower bounds of intellectual, cognitive, and behavioral functioning remains to be done and is especially important on an international scale.

Discussion of global cognitive abilities leads to questions of appropriate assessment of feeding influences. Because the infants assessed in Western studies generally appear to be functioning within normal limits, the likelihood of differences on global scales such as the Bayley is smaller than might be found on specific skill measures. Measures of specific cognitive skills such as visual recognition memory, attention and problem solving, novelty preference, and processing speed may reveal subtle differences. Furthermore, measures of specific cognitive skills

can improve predictive validity for later IQ and language functioning because the constructs are more consistent across development. For example, a meta-analysis indicated that the median predictive correlation between infant visual recognition memory and later cognition was approximately 0.45 (McCall & Carriger, 1993), and in a preterm sample, 6-month-olds' novelty preference scores correlated 0.53–0.66 with 2- to 6-year-olds' Stanford-Binet and Wechsler Preschool and Primary Scale of Intelligence (WPPSI) scores, respectively (Rose & Wallace, 1985).

Other measures that may provide greater sensitivity and predictive validity include neuroimaging and psychophysiological techniques. One of the more promising assessments involves event-related potentials (ERPs), fluctuations in the brain's electrical activity in response to particular stimuli. ERP measures are thought to reflect intermittent synchronization of small groups of cortical neurons, indicating which brain areas are working under specific conditions such as memory tasks or problem solving (Thomas, 2003). Another objective measure is the brainstem auditory evoked response (BAER), a noninvasive measure of brainstem function. BAER tests have detected feeding-related brain differences between breastfed and formula-fed infants, possibly resulting from more rapid axonal growth, synaptic function, and/or myelination in breastfed infants (Amin, Merle, Orlando, Dalzell, & Guillet, 2000); similar tests have also found differences between infants fed a formula supplemented with DHA and those fed the same formula without supplementation (Unay et al., 2004). Other measures of the brain's electrical activity have detected differences in cortical maturity in day-old newborns as a function of prenatal feeding substance (Helland et al., 2001). Though appealing, one should note that the clinical significance of these measures is yet to be established.

# Practice and Policy Recommendations

Substantial evidence points to the physical health benefits of breastfeeding, and on this basis alone, developmentalists have ample reason to join medical professionals in promoting the practice. However, research on the cognitive benefits of breastfeeding is currently characterized by equivocal findings and by emerging data on individual differences in metabolism of essential nutrients in brain development. Consequently, wholesale advocacy of breastfeeding as cognitively advantageous is unwarranted, and until a number of issues are resolved, it seems wisest to adopt the cautious view of DHHS scientists in not promoting any particular feeding method or substance as cognitively beneficial.

Because the question of feeding effects on cognitive outcomes has been used in developing professional practice and hospital policies, these outstanding issues need to be resolved, and developmentalists should advocate for improved research practices in this area. For developmentalists specializing in infant feeding outcomes, using specific cognitive skill measures and laboratory measures of LC-PUFA status, as well as providing context on the clinical utility of findings, may help lead to clearer conclusions and related policies. In addition, direct and indirect effects of feeding method on the development of a broader range of outcomes, including variables such as behavioral inhibition, prosocial behavior, psychopathology, and social competence, are yet to be explored.

Furthermore, the question of infant feeding effects extends beyond research in which infant feeding is the central focus. For example, given the centrality of feeding in early infant care, one would expect it to have some influence on infant behavior, including temperament (e.g., Worobey, 1998). Because infant feeding is theoretically related to neurodevelopment, one might also expect there to be an association between self-regulation and feeding practices. Childhood obesity researchers have only begun exploring how early feeding practices influence later pediatric health, and many questions remain.

On a broader scale, the cultural context in which feeding practices take place should be addressed. Family traditions, public health measures, and social policies associated with infant feeding practices vary greatly across cultures—worth considering in light of the international origins of this research. In addition, infant feeding practices often vary widely within nations; in the United States, for example, approaches to infant feeding vary among ethnic subgroups due to complex interactions among individual, social, cultural, and environmental factors. In the end, historical, systemic, and individual forces always have and will continue to influence infant feeding practices, which must ultimately have some bearing on outcomes at the individual level.

# References

Agostoni, C., Trojan, S., Bellu, R., Riva, E., Bruzzese, M. G., & Giovannini, M. (1997). Developmental quotient at 24 months and fatty acid composition of diet in early infancy: A follow up study. *Archives of Disease in Childhood, 76,* 421–424.

American Academy of Pediatrics. (2005). Policy Statement—Breastfeeding and the use of human milk [section on breastfeeding]. *Pediatrics, 115,* 496–506.

American College of Obstetricians and Gynecologists. (2002). *Breastfeeding: Maternal and infant aspects.* ACOG Educational Bulletin No. 258. Washington, DC: Author.

Amin, S. B., Merle, K. S., Orlando, M. S., Dalzell, L. E., & Guillet, R. (2000). Brainstem maturation in premature infants as a function of enteral feeding type. *Pediatrics, 106,* 318–322.

Arenz, S., Ruckerl, R., Koletzko, B., & von Kries, R. (2004). Breastfeeding and childhood obesity—A systematic review. *International Journal of Obesity & Related Metabolic Disorders, 28,* 1247–1256.

Auestad, N., Halter, R., Hall, R. T., Blatter, M., Bogle, M. L., Burks, W., et al. (2001). Growth and development in term infants fed long-chain polyunsaturated fatty acids: A double-masked, randomized, parallel, prospective, multivariate study. *Pediatrics, 108,* 372–381.

Auestad, N., Scott, D. T., Janowsky, J. S., Jacobsen, C., Carroll, R. E., Montalto, M. B., et al. (2003). Visual, cognitive and language assessment at 39 months: A follow-up study of children fed formulas containing long-chain polyunsaturated fatty acids to 1 year of age. *Pediatrics, 112*(3), e177–e183.

Bradley, R. H., & Caldwell, B. M. (1984). The relation of infants' home environments to achievement test performance in first grade: A follow-up study. *Child Development, 55,* 803–809.

Clandinin, M. T., Chappell, J. E., Leong, S., Heim, T., Swyer, P. R., & Chance, G. W. (1980). Extrauterine fatty acid accretion in infant brain: Implications for fatty acid requirements. *Early Human Development, 4,* 131–138.

Das, U. N. (2003). Long-chain polyunsaturated fatty acids in the growth and development of the brain and memory. *Nutrition, 19,* 62–65.

Dobbing, J. (1981). Nutritional growth restriction and the nervous system. In A. N. Davison, R. H. S. Thompson (Eds.), *The molecular basis of neuropathology* (pp. 221–223). New York: Edward Arnold.

FDA/CFSAN Office of Nutritional Products. (2002, July). *Labeling and dietary supplements.* Retrieved August 7, 2006, from www.cfsan.fda.gov/~dms/qa-inf20.html

Feldman, R., & Eidelman, A. I. (2003). Direct and indirect effects of breast milk on the neurobehavioral and cognitive development of premature infants. *Developmental Psychobiology, 43*(2), 109–119.

Fergusson, D. M., Beautrais, A. L., & Silva, P. A. (1982). Breastfeeding and cognitive development in the first seven years of life. *Social Science & Medicine, 16,* 1705–1708.

Foreman-van Drongelen, M. M., van Houwelinger, A. C., Blanco, C. E., & Hornstra, G. (1995). Comparison between essential fatty acid status of preterm and term infants, measured in umbilical vessel walls. *Early Human Development, 42,* i241–i251.

Gomez-Sanchiz, M., Canete, R., Rodero, I., Baeza, J. E., & Avila, O. (2003). Influence of breast-feeding on mental and psychomotor development. *Clinical Pediatrics, 42*(1), 35–42.

Hanaoka, S., Takashima, S., & Morooka, K. (1998). Study of the maturation of the child's brain using 31P-MRS. *Pediatric Neurology, 18,* 305–310.

Helland, I. B., Saugstad, O. D., Smith, L., Saarem, K., Solvoll, K., Ganes, T., et al. (2001). Similar effects on infants of n-3 and n-6 fatty acids supplementation to pregnant and lactating women. *Pediatrics, 108*(5), 82–91.

Helland, I. B., Smith, L., Saarem, K., Saugstad, O. D., & Drevon, C. A. (2003). Maternal supplementation with very-long-chain n-3 fatty acids during pregnancy and lactation augments children's IQ at 4 years of age. *Pediatrics, 111*(1), e39–e44.

Hoefer, C., & Hardy, M. C. (1929). Later development of breast fed and artificially fed infants. *JAMA, 92,* 615–619.

Innis, S. M. (2003). Perinatal biochemistry and physiology of long-chain polyunsaturated fatty acids. *Journal of Pediatrics, 143*(4 supplement), S1–S8.

Innis, S. M., Gilley, J., & Werker, G. (2001). Are human long-chain polyunsaturated fatty acids related to visual and neural development in breastfed term infants? *Journal of Pediatrics, 139,* 532–538.

Innis, S. M., & Uauy, R. (2003). Mechanisms of action of LCPUFA effects on infant growth and neurodevelopment: Perinatal biochemistry and physiology of LCPUFA discussion. *Journal of Pediatrics, 143*(4 supplement), S96–S109.

Jacobson, S. W., Chiodo, L. M., & Jacobson, J. L. (1999). Breastfeeding effects on intelligence quotient in 4- and 11-year-old children. *Pediatrics, 103*(5), e71.

Jain, A., Concato, J., & Leventhal, J. M. (2002). How good is the evidence linking breastfeeding and intelligence? *Pediatrics, 109,* 1044–1053.

Koo, W. W. K. (2003). Efficacy and safety of docosahexaenoic acid and arachidonic acid addition to infant formulas: Can one buy better vision and intelligence? *Journal of the American College of Nutrition, 22*(2), 101–107.

Kopp, C. B., & McCall, R. B. (1982). Predicting later mental performance for normal, at-risk, and handicapped infants. In P. B. Bates & O. B. Brim (Eds.), *Lifespan development and behavior* (pp. 33–61). New York: Academic Press.

Kramer, M. S., & Kakuma, R. (2002). *The optimal duration of exclusive breastfeeding: A systematic review.* Geneva, Switzerland: World Health Organization.

Lapillonne, A., Brossard, N., Claris, O., Reygrobellet, B., & Salle, B. L. (2000). Erythrocyte fatty acid composition in term infants fed human milk or a formula enriched with a low eicosapentanoic acid fish oil for 4 months. *European Journal of Pediatrics, 159,* 49–53.

Lapillonne, A., Clarke, S. D., & Heird, W. C. (2003). Plausible mechanisms for effects of long-chain polyunsaturated fatty acids on growth. *Journal of Pediatrics, 143*(4 supplement), S9–S16.

Lucas, A., Stafford, M., Morley, R., Abbott, R., Stephenson, T., MacFadyen, U., et al. (1999). Efficacy and safety of long-chain polyunsaturated fatty acid supplementation of infant-formula milk: A randomized trial. *Lancet, 354,* 1948–1954.

Makrides, M., Neumann, M., Simmer, K., Pater, J., & Gibson, R. (1995). Are long-chain polyunsaturated fatty acids essential nutrients in infancy? *Lancet, 345,* 1463–1468.

Makrides, M., Neumann, M., Simmer, K., Pater, J., & Gibson, R. (2000). A critical appraisal of the role of dietary long-chain polyunsaturated fatty acids on neural indices of term infants: A randomized, controlled trial. *Pediatrics, 105*(1), 32–38.

McCall, R. B., & Carriger, M. S. (1993). A meta-analysis of infant habituation and recognition memory performance as predictors of later IQ. *Child Development, 64,* 57–79.

Morrow-Tlucak, M., Haude, R. H., & Ernhart, C. B. (1988). Breastfeeding and cognitive development in the first 2 years of life. *Social Science & Medicine, 26,* 635–639.

Paine, B. J., Makrides, M., & Gibson, R. A. (1999). Duration of breastfeeding and Bayley's Mental Development Index at 1 year of age. *Journal of Paediatrics and Child Health, 35,* 82–85.

Pollock, J. I. (1994). Long-term associations with infant feeding in a clinically advantaged population of babies. *Developmental Medicine and Child Neurology, 36,* 429–440.

Rose, S. A., Feldman, J. F., & Jankowski, J. J. (2003). The building blocks of cognition. *Journal of Pediatrics, 143*(4 supplement), S54–S61.

Rose, S. A., & Wallace, I. F. (1985). Visual recognition memory: A predictor of later cognitive functioning in preterms. *Child Development, 56,* 843–852.

Scott, D. T., Janowsky, J. S., Carroll, R. E., Taylor, J. A., Auestad, N., & Montalto, M. B. (1998). Formula supplementation with long-chain polyunsaturated fatty acids: Are there developmental benefits? *Pediatrics, 102*(5), e59.

Sternberg, R. J., Grigorenko, E. L., & Bundy, D. A. (2001). The predictive value of IQ. *Merrill-Palmer Quarterly, 47*(1), 1–41.

Strickland, B. R. (2000). Misassumptions, misadventures, and the misuse of psychology. *American Psychologist, 55,* 331–338.

Taylor, B., & Wadsworth, J. (1984). Breast feeding and child development at five years. *Developmental Medicine and Child Neurology, 26,* 73–80.

Thomas, K. M. (2003). Assessing brain development using neuro-physiologic and behavioral measures. *Journal of Pediatrics, 143*(4 supplement), S46–S53.

Uauy, R., Hoffman, D. R., Mena, P., Llanos, A., & Birch, E. E. (2003). Term infant studies of DHA and ARA supplementation on neurodevelopment: Results of randomized controlled trials. *Journal of Pediatrics, 143*(4 supplement), S17–S25.

Uauy, R., Mena, P., & Peirano, P. (2001). Mechanisms for nutrient effects on brain development and cognition. *Nutrition and Brain, 5,* 41–72.

Uauy, R., Mena, P., & Rojas, C. (2000). Essential fatty acids in early life: Structural and functional role. *Proceedings of the Nutrition Society, 59,* 3–15.

Unay, B., Sarici, S. U., Ulas, U. H., Akin, R., Alpay, F., & Gokay, E. (2004). Nutritional effects on auditory brainstem evoked potentials in healthy term infants. *Archives of Disease in Childhood. Fetal and Neonatal Edition, 89,* F177–F179.

U.S. Department of Health and Human Services, Office on Women's Health. (2000). *HHS blueprint for action on breastfeeding.* Washington, DC: Author.

Voigt, R. G., Jensen, C. L., Fraley, J. K., Rozelle, J. C., Brown, F. R., III, & Heird, W. C. (2002). Relationship between omega3 long-chain polyunsaturated fatty acid status during early infancy and neurodevelopmental status at 1 year of age. *Journal of Human Nutrition & Dietetics, 15,* 111–120.

Wang, Y. S., & Wu, S. Y. (1996). The effect of exclusive breastfeeding on development and incidence of infection in infants. *Journal of Human Lactation, 12,* 27–30.

Wigg, N. R., Tong, S., McMichael, A. J., Baghurst, P. A., Vimpani, G., & Roberts, R. (1998). Does breast feeding at six months predict cognitive development? *Australian and New Zealand Journal of Public Health, 22,* 232–236.

Willatts, P., Forsyth, J. S., DiModugno, M. K., Varma, S., & Colvin, M. (1998). Effect of long-chain polyunsaturated fatty acids in infant formula on problem solving at 10 months of age. *Lancet, 352,* 688–691.

Worobey, J. (1998). Feeding method and motor activity in 3-month-old human infants. *Perceptual and Motor Skills, 86,* 883–895.

# Critical Thinking

1. What are the biological reasons why breast feeding would promote infant cognitive development?

2. The article raises concerns about the link between breast feeding and infant cognitive growth. Why are the researchers not convinced that we know enough about this link? What is some new information that we must obtain about feeding practices or cognitive growth?

# Do Babies Learn from Baby Media?

Judy S. DeLoache et al.

One of the most remarkable marketing phenomena of recent history was ignited by the 1997 release of the first Baby Einstein video (The Baby Einstein Co., Littleton, CO), which was followed by a host of other videos and DVDs designed and marketed specifically for infants and very young children. American parents alone spend hundreds of millions of dollars yearly on these products, with the Baby Einstein series leading in popularity and sales worldwide.

Most companies that market these DVDs feature quotes from parents touting the virtues of the company's products. In these testimonials on websites and in advertisements, parents frequently mention the remarkable degree of attention that children pay to the DVDs (as well as the fact that their children's absorption in the DVDs enables them to get household chores done and even take the occasional shower). Prominently featured are parent testimonials that their children learn a great deal from watching infant DVDs. Our own experience with parents of young children has led us to suspect that a substantial proportion believe that infants benefit from commercial media products, and recent research indicates that 40 percent of mothers of young children believe that their children learn from television (Rideout, 2007).

But how well do infants actually learn from visual media? Because development typically proceeds at a very rapid pace in the first years of life, parents may misattribute ordinary developmental progress to their children's media exposure. For example, on one commercial website, a parent reported that her 18-month-old child had very few words until she started watching one of the company's videos, at which point her vocabulary "suddenly blossomed." However, a very well-documented phenomenon in early language development is the "word spurt," a rapid increase in the acquisition of new words during the second year of life (e.g., Benedict, 1979; Goldfield & Reznick, 1990). It would be easy for parents to

misattribute their children's sudden linguistic advances to recent video experience.

Although several empirical studies have examined the relation between early television viewing and a variety of outcome measures, most have been large-scale surveys yielding correlational data (e.g., Rideout, Vandewater, & Wartella, 2003; Schmidt, Rich, Rifas-Shiman, Oken, & Taveras, 2009; Zimmerman, Christakis, & Meltzoff, 2007). Only a relatively small number of laboratory studies have examined specific aspects of young children's interaction with visual media (see Anderson & Pemipek, 2005; DeLoache & Chiong, 2009).

Further, only a few of those studies have specifically focused on infants' *learning* from video. In one such study (Kuhl, Tsao, & Liu, 2003), 9-month-olds from English-speaking families watched several presentations, either live or video, of an adult speaking Mandarin. A month later, the researchers tested whether this exposure had prolonged the infants' sensitivity to the Mandarin speech sounds. Only children whose Mandarin exposure had occurred in live interactions showed any impact of that experience.

Laboratory studies of infants' imitation of simple actions presented on video have established that 12- to 30-month-olds are able to reproduce a modest number of observed actions (e.g., Barr & Hayne, 1999; Hayne, Herbert, & Simcock, 2003; McCall, Parke, & Kavanaugh, 1977). Imitation is substantially better, however, when children experience the same demonstrations live.

Young children's word learning from commercial television has also been examined. A large-scale parent survey reported a negative correlation between vocabulary size and television exposure: For every hour of baby media that infants between 8 and 16 months of age watched on their own, they were reported to know 6 to 8 fewer words (Zimmerman et al., 2007). Krcmar, Grela, and Lin (2007) obtained similar results in a laboratory study, in which children under 22 months of age learned few object names presented on a clip from a Tele-tubbies television episode.

In a recent experimental investigation of early learning from video, Robb, Richert, and Wartella (2009) assessed word learning from home viewing of a commercial DVD designed to teach words to young children. According to parent reports, the 12- to 15-month-old participants learned relatively few of the words featured on the DVD: Children who had substantial exposure to it performed no better than did those with none. These results are intriguing, but the fact that the primary data were parent reports is of some concern.

Accordingly, we conducted an experiment using objective testing to directly examine the extent to which infants learn from a very popular commercial infant DVD promoted to foster word learning. Six aspects of the study were designed to ensure a highly valid assessment of the potential for early learning from video: (a) The entire experiment was conducted in the children's own homes. (b) The conditions mimicked everyday situations in which young children view videos. (c) A best-selling video was used. (d) The children received extensive exposure to the video. (e) They were tested for their understanding of the specific words featured on the video. (f) The tester was blind to the condition to which each child had been randomly assigned.

## Method

### Participants

Participants were 72 infants between 12 and 18 months of age ($M = 14.7$ months). They were recruited from a large metropolitan area and a small city. The sample was predominantly White and middle-class. None of the infants had had any exposure to the target DVD. Eighteen children (including approximately equal numbers of girls and boys) were randomly assigned to each of four conditions.

### Materials

A best-selling commercial DVD designed and marketed for infants from "12 months of age and up" was used in the research. The 39-min DVD depicts a variety of scenes of a house and yard. A voice labels common household objects, each of which is named three times, with several minutes intervening between the repetitions of a given label. In addition, during the first and last labeling of a given object, a person is shown producing a manual sign for the object.

### Conditions

In the three experimental conditions, the experimenter made three home visits to each family. During the first visit, the experimenter gave detailed oral and written instructions to the parents. The experimental conditions included two video conditions: video with interaction and video with no interaction. In both of these conditions, parents gave their children substantial experience with the DVD in their own homes over 4 weeks. To ensure that they followed the instructions, we asked them to complete a daily log of their child's experience with the video. Parents in the parent-teaching (non-video) condition estimated how often they had attempted to teach their children the target words. On the second and third home visits in all three of these conditions, the experimenter checked to make sure the parents had been following the protocol.

In the *video-with-interaction condition,* the child and a parent watched the DVD together at least five times a week over a 4-week period, for a total of 10 or more hours of viewing time in 20 or more viewing episodes. (Some advertisements for baby videos recommend that parents watch with their children.) Parents were instructed to interact with their child in whatever way seemed natural to them while viewing the video. This condition mimicked the common everyday experience of young children and parents watching television together.

In the *video-with-no-interaction* condition, the children watched the video alone, but had the same total amount of exposure to it as did the children in the video-with-interaction condition. (The parents were almost always in the room with their infants, but were not watching television with them.) This condition mimicked another common situation, in which young children watch television on their own while their parents are nearby but engaged in other activities.

In the *parent-teaching* condition, the children were not exposed to the video at all. Instead, the parents were given a list of the 25 words featured on the video and were instructed simply to "try to teach your child as many of these words as you can in whatever way seems natural to you."

The fourth condition, in which there was no intervention, was the control condition. It provided a baseline of normal vocabulary growth against which performance in the three intervention groups could be compared.

### Testing

During the initial home visit, each child was tested for knowledge of 13 of the 25 words featured on the video in order to establish an individualized set of target words for that child. (As Table S1 in the Supplemental Material available online shows, children in the target age range perform around or below chance when tested for their knowledge of the majority of these words.) On each of 13 trials, the child was shown a pair of replica objects—a target representing an object featured in the video (e.g., clock, table, tree) and a distractor that did not appear in the video (e.g., fan, plate, fence). The experimenter named the target and asked the child to point to the appropriate object (e.g., "Can you show me the table?"). The names of the objects that a child failed to identify became that child's individualized set of target words. The number of target words ranged from 5 to 12; the mean number (6.4–6.9) did not differ across the four groups.

On the final visit, the child's knowledge of his or her target words was tested to determine how much word learning had taken place over the 4 weeks. The testing was conducted in the same way as in the initial visit, except that two trials were given for each of the child's target words, with the words presented in one order for the first set of trials and in the reverse order for the second. To be credited with knowing a word, the child had to choose the correct object on both trials; this criterion minimized the likelihood that children would be counted as knowing a word after simply guessing correctly. Parents in the video conditions completed a brief questionnaire concerning their and their child's experience with the video.

## Results

Figure 1 shows the percentage of their target words that the children got correct on the posttest. Only the performance of the parent-teaching group was above chance ($p < .05$). The result of primary importance is clear: Children who had extensive exposure to a popular infant video over a full month, either with a parent or alone, did not learn any more new words than did children with no exposure to the video at all.

The absence of learning from experience with the video was not due to lack of attention to it. Representative comments from the logs of parents whose children were in the video groups include the following: "She was practically glued to the screen today"; "She was very quiet today—stared intently at the screen and ignored me when I asked her to talk"; "She loves the blasted thing. It's crack for babies!"

As Figure 1 shows, performance was highest in the parent-teaching group—those children who had no exposure to the video, but whose parents had attempted to teach them new words during everyday interactions. Preliminary examination of the individual scores indicated that the data were not normally distributed, so a median test was performed on the proportion of target words that the children in the four conditions identified on the posttest. There was a significant overall difference among the groups, $\chi^2 (3, N = 72) = 10.03$, $p < .05$. Post hoc tests indicated that the performance of the parent-teaching group was significantly better than that

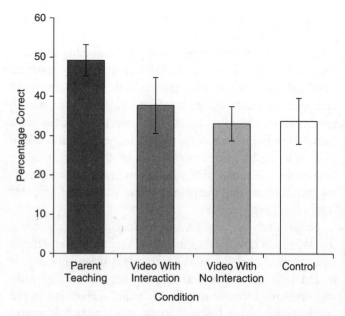

**Figure 1** Children's mean performance on the posttest as a function of group. Each child was tested on an individualized set of target words. Error bars represent standard errors of the mean.

of all three of the other groups—video-with-interaction group: $\chi^2 (1, N = 36) = 4.0$, $p < .05$; video-with-no-interaction group: $\chi^2 (1, N = 36) = 11.11$, $p = .001$; and control group: $\chi^2 (1, N = 36) = 4.0$, $p < .05$. Neither of the video conditions differed from the control condition. Thus, significantly more learning occurred in the context of everyday parent-child interactions than in front of television screens.

Finally, the parents' assessment of how much their children had learned from the DVD was unrelated to the children's performance on the posttest: Children whose parents thought that they had learned a substantial amount from their experience with the DVD performed no better than did children of less sanguine parents. There was, however, a significant correlation ($r = .64$, $p < .01$) between parents' own liking for the DVD and their estimate of how much their children had learned: The more a parent liked the DVD, the more he or she believed the child had learned from it.

## Discussion

The results of this study provide a clear answer to our original question: Infants between 12 and 18 months of age learned very little from a highly popular media product promoted for this age group. Even with the substantial amount of exposure that they had to the video, the infants learned only a few of the words featured on it. Because great care was taken to ensure that the video-viewing conditions were as natural as possible, the results should be generalizable to young children's everyday experience.

These results are consistent with a body of theory and research that has established that very young children often fail to use information communicated to them via symbolic media, including pictures, models, and video (e.g., DeLoache, 2004; Troseth, Pierroutsakos, & DeLoache, 2004). For example, 2-year-olds who watch a live video of an adult hiding a desirable toy in the room next-door fail to find the toy when encouraged to search for it immediately afterward (Troseth, 2003a, 2003b; Troseth & DeLoache, 1998). This and related results indicate that infants and very young children have difficulty understanding the relation between what they see on a screen and the real world.

An additional finding from this experiment is directly relevant to the possibility that parents may misattribute normal developmental progress to their infants' video exposure. Parents who had a favorable attitude toward the DVD thought that their children had learned more from it than did parents who were less positively disposed to the DVD. There was, in fact, no difference in how many words were learned by the children of these two groups of parents. This result suggests that much of the enthusiasm expressed in parent testimonials about baby video products is misplaced.

In summary, the research reported here supports two important conclusions. First, parents whose infants have experience with baby videos tend to misattribute normal developmental change to that experience, thereby overestimating the impact of the videos on their children's development. Second, the degree to which babies actually learn from baby videos is negligible.

# References

Anderson, D.R., & Pempek, T.A. (2005). Television and very young children. *American Behavioral Scientist, 48,* 505–522.

Barr, R., & Hayne, H. (1999). Developmental changes in imitation from television during infancy. *Child Development, 70,* 1067–1081.

Benedict, H. (1979). Early lexical development: Comprehension and production. *Journal of Child Language, 6,* 183–200.

DeLoache, J.S. (2004). Becoming symbol-minded. *Trends in Cognitive Sciences, 8,* 66–70.

DeLoache, J.S., & Chiong, C. (2009). Babies and baby media. *American Behavioral Scientist, 52,* 1115–1135.

Goldfield, B.A., & Reznick, J.S. (1990). Early lexical acquisition: Rate, content, and the vocabulary spurt. *Journal of Child Language, 17,* 171–184.

Hayne, H., Herbert, J., & Simcock, G. (2003). Imitation from television by 24- and 30-month-olds. *Developmental Science, 6,* 254–261.

Krcmar, M., Grela, B., & Lin, K. (2007). Can toddlers learn vocabulary from television? An experimental approach. *Media Psychology, 10,* 41–63.

Kuhl, P.K., Tsao, F.M., & Liu, H.M. (2003). Foreign-language experience in infancy: Effects of short-term exposure and social interaction on phonetic learning. *Proceedings of the National Academy of Sciences, USA, 100,* 9096–9101.

McCall, R.B., Parke, R.D., & Kavanaugh, R.D. (1977). Imitation of live and televised models by children one to three years of age. *Monographs of the Society for Research in Child Development, 42*(5, Serial No. 173).

Rideout, V. (2007). *Parents, children, and media.* Menlo Park, CA: Henry J. Kaiser Family Foundation.

Rideout, V.J., Vandewater, E.A., & Wartella, E.A. (2003). *Zero to six: Electronic media in the lives of infants, toddlers and preschoolers.* Menlo Park, CA: Henry J. Kaiser Family Foundation.

Robb, M., Richert, R., & Wartella, E. (2009). Just a talking book? Word learning from watching baby videos. *British Journal of Developmental Psychology, 27,* 27–45.

Schmidt, M.E., Rich, M., Rifas-Shiman, S.L., Oken, E., & Taveras, E.M. (2009). Television viewing in infancy and child cognition at 3 years of age in a US cohort. *Pediatrics, 123,* 370–375.

Troseth, G.L. (2003a). Getting a clear picture: Young children's understanding of a televised image. *Developmental Science, 6,* 247–253.

Troseth, G.L. (2003b). TV guide: 2-year-olds learn to use video as a source of information. *Developmental Psychology, 39,* 140–150.

Troseth, G.L., & DeLoache, J.S. (1998). The medium can obscure the message: Young children's understanding of video. *Child Development, 69,* 950–965.

Troseth, G.L., Pierroutsakos, S.L., & DeLoache, J.S. (2004). From the innocent to the intelligent eye: The early development of pictorial competence. In R.V. Kail (Ed.), *Advances in child development and behavior,* Volume 32 (pp. 1–35). New York, NY: Academic Press.

Zimmerman, F.J., Christakis, D.A., & Meltzoff, A. (2007). Television and DVD/video viewing in children younger than 2 years. *Archives of Pediatric & Adolescent Medicine, 69,* 473–479.

# Critical Thinking

1. Why might parents be so inclined to buy educational videos for their babies? Are some parents more likely to buy them than others? What findings from the research in the article suggest that parents are likely to believe the videos work, even when they don't?

2. Describe some strengths of the experimental design in this study. How did the researchers determine that children's vocabulary didn't improve due to any type of video? How did the researchers create the "parent teaching" condition?

3. Does this article prove to you that educational baby videos are not beneficial for all aspects of infant development, or just some? What are some other infant outcomes that could be studied to learn if educational videos have an effect on behaviors other than vocabulary?

**Acknowledgments**—We thank Monica Ehrbacher for her very helpful statistical advice.

**Declaration of Conflicting Interests**—The authors declared that they had no conflicts of interest with respect to their authorship or the publication of this article.

**Funding**—This research was supported by National Institutes of Health Grant HD 25271, as well as by National Science Foundation Grant 0819508, both to the first author.

**Supplemental Material**—Additional supporting information may be found at http://pss.sagepub.com/content/by/supplemental-data

# Social Cognitive Development: A New Look

## Kristina R. Olson and Carol S. Dweck

The study of social cognitive development is undergoing a renaissance. A large part of this renaissance stems from research employing methods and theories from the study of cognitive development to ask questions of importance for children's social development. Of course, research on theory of mind (Leslie, 1987; Wellman, 1990; Wimmer & Perner, 1983), imitation (Gergely, Bekkering, & Kiraly, 2002; Meltzoff, 1995; Meltzoff & Borton, 1979), and intentionality and agency (Baldwin, 2000; Gergely, Nadasdy, Csibra, & Biro, 1995; Johnson, Slaughter, & Carey, 1998; Premack & Premack, 1997; Tomasello, Carpenter, Call, Behne, & Moll, 2005; Woodward, 1998) has been thriving for some time, and, in many researchers' minds, social cognitive development is synonymous with these concepts. However, never before have so many researchers in the area of cognitive development brought their tools and perspectives to bear on children's social development. In this article, we focus on emerging work, providing a "thin slice" of research coming from a cognitive development perspective that examines the development of children's social judgments and representations.[1] This work is exciting not only because it brings the ingenious methods of cognitive development to the social domain but also because it illuminates children's social functioning and relationships, topics that cognitive developmentalists have seldom addressed in the past.

As we describe elsewhere (Olson & Dweck, 2008), social cognitive development is the study of socially relevant mental representations and mental processes across development. Key aspects of social cognitive development concern how these representations and processes are shaped by particular antecedents (such as culture or parental practices) and how these representations and processes influence important outcomes for the child (such as children's well-being or relationships). Thus, here, we highlight current work on social judgments and representations because we see it as having important implications for both.

## Judgments of Goodness and Badness

A noteworthy body of work is emerging on infants' and young children's social judgments. At the simplest level, this work is concerned with how children decide who is good or bad or helpful or harmful; it examines when these kinds of social judgments first emerge and what information children use to make them.

In some of the most provocative work on social judgments, Kuhlmeier, Wynn, and Bloom (2003) showed infants episodes in which a "climber" (a geometric, self-propelled figure) was attempting, but failing, to go up a hill. In one episode, a "helper" aided the climber, and in another episode, a "hinderer" pushed the climber back down. Through use of looking-time measures, the researchers found that 12-month-old infants (but not 5-month-old infants) looked longer when the climber approached the helper than when it approached the hinderer, indicating, the authors suggest, that the 12-month-olds found the reunion with the helper to be the more satisfying ending. This work was replicated and extended by Hamlin, Wynn, and Bloom (2007), who found that both 6- and 10-month-olds, when encouraged to choose their preferred object, reached for the helper over the hinderer. These results suggest that infants as young as 6 months attend to the good or bad actions of individuals and that perhaps some of the bases of social and moral judgments emerge quite early.

Do children distinguish between different kinds of "good" actors, for example, those who differ in the degree of their generosity? McCrink, Santos, and Bloom (2006) had children receive rewards from two puppets and then select the puppet that was "nicer." In key trials, the puppets differed in the number of rewards they possessed and the number they gave to the participant. The experimenters varied the absolute number and the proportion of rewards given. They discovered that whereas 4-year-olds preferred a puppet who had given a greater absolute number of rewards, 5-year-olds used a combination of absolute number and proportion and adults relied on proportion only. These results suggest that children's understanding of important moral concepts such as sharing changes across development and, as a result, their social evaluations of sharers do as well.

Do children use only people's *actions* to decide whether those people are good or bad? New research with preschoolers and elementary-aged children has asked whether children might also evaluate people on the basis of things that happen to them, even things that may be out of their control, such as lucky or unlucky events that befall them (Olson, Banaji, Dweck, & Spelke, 2006; Olson, Dunham, Dweck, Spelke, & Banaji, 2008). This work has found that children as young as 3 years judge lucky individuals to be nicer than unlucky individuals and that this preference for the lucky holds regardless of whether the events are trivial (e.g., getting splashed by a passing car) or more extreme (such as having one's house destroyed by a tornado). This phenomenon has also been shown in children in Japan (Olson et al., 2008). Finally, the luck preference appears to spread to new members of groups; children prefer an individual who merely shares group membership with lucky people over an individual who shares group membership with unlucky people, despite the fact that the individuals being evaluated were themselves neither lucky nor unlucky (Olson et al., 2006). Understanding the extent of this generalization and the relationship between luck attitudes and prejudice is a task for future research. For example, it could exacerbate prejudice and discrimination if members of disadvantaged groups experience more unlucky events and receive more negative evaluations as a result.

As the Olson et al. (2006) work suggests, often one learns about a person as part of a community of people. Does it matter for social judgments if that community is portrayed in subtly different ways? Master, Markman, and Dweck (2008) asked how young children represent individuals depending on whether they are presented as members of a continuum or members of a category. In a series of studies, they showed 4-year-olds a set of six schematized faces that ranged from broadly smiling to seriously frowning, with the two middle faces crossing the boundary from smiling to frowning. They then either described the first three, one at a time, as "nice" and the last three as "mean" (category condition) or described them in gradations from "really nice" to "really mean" (continuum condition).

They then assessed social expectations and judgments: Who would share, who would hit, with whom did the participant want to play, how much did the participants like each one, and how would participants distribute presents to them? Those in the category condition made a much sharper differentiation between the middle two faces on all measures than did those in the continuum condition, whereas those in the continuum condition showed more differentiation *within* the categories. Future work can explore how the "continuum" representation, which captures many social stimuli, may lead children both to maintain important distinctions among people that category representations may obscure and to avoid the sharp breaks between groups that the category representation encourages.

# Evaluations of Similar and Dissimilar Others

Social judgments can also be made on the basis of similarity or dissimilarity to the self. Thus, another topic that is receiving considerable attention is the extent to which children prefer similar to dissimilar others. For example, Markson and Fawcett (2007) discovered that 3-year-old children view those with shared toy preferences, food preferences, or hair color as more desirable playmates than those with different preferences. Thus, early on children can make important social judgments on the basis of common interests and perceptual similarity.

Other researchers have been concerned with the extent to which children prefer others who share their group membership. Historically, these studies have focused on racial, ethnic, and gender groups (e.g., Clark & Clark, 1947; Maccoby & Jacklin, 1974;

for reviews, see Aboud, 1988; Ruble, Martin, & Berenbaum, 2006). New work in these areas, coming from a cognitive development perspective, is employing looking-time, reaching, and choice tasks with young children. These studies ask questions about when children notice group differences and when they use these differences to make decisions, such as whom to play with or what toys or activities are desirable (e.g., Bar-Haim, Ziv, Lamy, & Hodes, 2006; Diesendruck & ha Levi, 2006; Kelly et al., 2007; Shutts, Banaji, & Spelke, 2007).

Another direction this work has moved in is to examine social categories other than race and gender. For example, work by Kinzler, Dupoux, and Spelke (2007) has examined native language and native accent as social category markers. Using an array of different methods appropriate to different ages, they have found that 5- to 6-month-olds preferentially attend to the face of someone speaking their language with a native accent over the face of someone speaking a different language or speaking with a foreign accent and that 10-month-old infants will select toys from a native speaker over a foreign-accented speaker of their language. These preferences appear to continue, as 5-year-old children indicate that they would prefer to be friends with speakers of their native language and those with native accents. An important question for future research is how powerful these biases will be in children's actual relationships and what kinds of information can override them.

Several other researchers have been investigating whether young children will even infer liking from an arbitrary similarity. This work builds on past research demonstrating that older children and adolescents will prefer members of their own groups even when those groups have been arbitrarily assigned by the experimenter (Sherif, Harvey, White, Hood, & Sherif, 1961; Turner, Brown, & Tajfel, 1979). Patterson and Bigler (2006) put 3- to 5-year-old children into arbitrary groups by having them wear one of two colors of T-shirts to preschool every day for 3 weeks. At the end of that time, children made more favorable evaluations of peers wearing the same-color T-shirt than of peers wearing the other-color T-shirt, suggesting that even an arbitrary similarity, such as experimentally assigned T-shirt color, can influence even young children's evaluations of others. Dunham (2007) has found similar results with 5-year-olds, but with an even smaller manipulation. He simply asked children to draw a colored coin out of a bag to assign a T-shirt color and then measured children's attitudes and sharing behavior toward members of both groups.

Across these studies, it is clear that early in life, children can and often do make important social judgments, such as whom to approach, whom to play with, and whom they like, on the basis of similarity, be it a common interest or group membership. As we have noted, it will now be important to see how features of children's environment influence these social judgments and how these judgments play out in social interactions.

# Representations of Social Relationships

Exciting new findings are also emerging from the study of infants' and young children's *representations* of people and relationships. Here, too, methods from cognitive development have been used (such as looking-time tasks, resource allocation tasks, and evaluation tasks), and they have illuminated children's expectations of how people will behave and their understanding of the relationships between people.

Attachment theory and research have a long history in social development (e.g., Ainsworth & Bell, 1970; De Wolff & van IJzendoorn, 1997; Main, Kaplan, & Cassidy, 1985; Sroufe, 1985). However, one aspect of Bowlby's (1958) groundbreaking proposal had never been directly investigated in infants: the hypothesis that infants form "internal working models" or mental representations of attachment relationships based on their early experiences with caretakers. These working models are said to consist of children's expectations of how caretakers will behave toward stressed or distressed children (e.g., will they approach them?) and how children under stress will behave toward the caretaker (e.g., will they seek proximity?). Could we detect these internal working models in infants?

Johnson, Dweck, and Chen (2007) employed a looking-time procedure to assess infants' mental representations of attachment relationships. In one study, 14-month-old infants were shown a video interaction between a "child" (represented by a small abstract form) and a "parent" (represented by a larger abstract form). The parent moved away from the child, who was unable to follow, and the child cried repeatedly. Infants watched this episode again and again until they were habituated to (got bored with) the event. Then, on the test trials, the participants either observed the parent return to the distressed child or observed the parent continue to move away from the child. Children previously identified as securely attached to their caregiver looked longer (were more "surprised") when the parent continued moving away from the distressed child than when the parent returned to the child. In contrast, children previously identified as insecurely attached showed little discrimination between the two events. In fact, in follow-up work, they showed the opposite pattern—more surprise when the parent returned (Johnson, 2007)! These results suggest that infants have indeed formed expectations for how caretakers will react to a child in distress.

In a second study, Johnson (2007) showed infants similar videos, except that this time during the habituation trials, the parent returned to a spot near the crying child. During the test trials, as the parent returned, the child either approached or fled from the parent. Consistent with different representations of attachment relationships, securely attached infants expected the distressed child to approach the parent and insecurely attached infants did not. These results importantly demonstrate that infants already have well-formed expectations about human interactions. Although we do not yet know how malleable or how stable these representations are across development, it is reasonable to think that these early representations can have important influences on children's interpersonal interactions. Whereas securely attached infants, when stressed, may be likely to approach others and expect to be helped by them, insecurely attached infants may not recognize or tap into social resources, even when they are available.

Of course, attachment relationships are not the only relationships children understand at an early age. New research by Olson and Spelke (2008) has discovered that children represent reciprocal relationships between unknown individuals. Evolutionary biologists and economists have long argued that it is beneficial to engage in cooperative behaviors including reciprocation (sharing with someone who shared with you) and indirect reciprocation (sharing with someone who shared with someone else). However, in order to engage in these behaviors, individuals must be able to track and represent who has given resources and to whom. As a test of these representations in children, these researchers asked 3.5-year-old children to help a target doll distribute rewards to a series of dolls that had been described as previously sharing with the target, sharing with another doll, or not sharing at all. Although children favored reciprocity over indirect reciprocity, their sharing behavior was consistent with both principles, indicating that they were able to represent these important social relationships. Such behavior suggests that young children have a tendency to reward one another's sharing and that they can track the costs and benefits of sharing with specific individuals.

# Other Sources of New Social Cognitive Developmental Research

In addition to work coming from a cognitive development perspective, the recent surge in research on social cognitive development has been influenced by methods from adult cognitive psychology and from adult social cognition. For example, new research is applying neuroimaging and comparative methods from cognitive psychology to address questions about the underlying mechanisms and phylogenetic origins of social cognitive development. Researchers have recently conducted developmental social cognitive neuroscience studies that examined such topics as differences in how children and adults represent self and social knowledge (Pfeifer, Lieberman, & Dapretto, 2007), differences in children's and adult's understanding of a speaker's intention (Wang, Lee, Sigman, & Dapretto, 2006), and differences in the neural circuitry underlying emotion recognition and display in children with and without autism spectrum disorders (Dapretto et al., 2006; Dawson, Webb, Carver, Panagiotides, & McPartland, 2004). We look forward to what this work can contribute to our understanding of the mechanisms underlying social cognitive development and the light it may shed on similarities and differences between children's and adults' social functioning.

Similarly, by investigating basic social cognitive abilities in other primates, researchers can develop better theories about the causes and uses of such abilities and may even change their theories entirely (e.g., Brosnan & de Waal, 2003; Tomasello, Call, & Hare, 2003; Warneken & Tomasello, 2006). For example, some theories have suggested that cognitive dissonance reduction is the result of complex self-related processes; however, recent evidence of cognitive dissonance reduction in capuchins, who are generally considered to lack a sense of self, suggests either that evaluations of capuchin's sense of self are wrong or that a self-based theory of cognitive dissonance is not likely (Egan, Santos, & Bloom, 2007).

Another source, as we have noted, is the field of adult social cognition. Researchers from this tradition have recently begun to ask about the origins of social cognitive phenomena. For example, a key topic in social cognition research over the past decade has been the measurement of implicit or nonconscious attitudes (e.g., Dovidio, Kawakami, Johnson, Johnson, & Howard, 1997; Fazio & Olson, 2003; Greenwald, McGhee, & Schwartz, 1998). Researchers have now begun to investigate the development of implicit social attitudes (Baron & Banaji, 2006; Rutland, Cameron, Milne, & McGeorge, 2005) in order to understand how attitudes toward specific social groups develop, to understand how explicit and implicit attitudes diverge during development, and to understand the relationship between attitudes and behavior. Such findings may also be of importance for informing future intervention studies that aim to reduce prejudice and stereotyping.

Although modern neuroscience, comparative, and adult social cognitive approaches have not always been concerned with human developmental issues, we see many ways in which they are likely to contribute to the methodological toolbox and theoretical claims of the "new" social cognitive development.

# Conclusions

We believe that the recent surge in work on social cognitive development represents an emerging approach that is unique, that is likely to have staying power, and that builds bridges to other fields including social cognition, comparative psychology, and neuroscience. We are optimistic that the work on social cognitive development will not only continue to identify important socially relevant mental representations and cognitive processes but will also (a) examine the influence of specific antecedents, such as culture or parental practices, on the development of these representations and (b) identify the real-world consequences of these processes, with the goal of promoting greater well-being and more positive social interactions. Our hope is that as the research projects we have described become flourishing research programs—and as others adopt a social cognitive approach—we will have increasingly vigorous methods to address the origins of social outcomes that are meaningful for children.

# Note

1. Much of the work presented here is current work that has been presented at recent conferences, including the 2007 Society for Research in Child Development meeting, the 2007 Cognitive Development Society meeting, the 2007 and 2008 Society for Personality and Social Psychology meetings, and the 2008 International Conference on Infant Studies meeting.

# References

Aboud, F. E. (1988). *Children and prejudice*. New York: Blackwell.

Ainsworth, M. D., & Bell, S. M. (1970). Attachment, exploration, and separation: Illustrated by the behavior of one-year-olds in a strange situation. *Child Development, 41*, 49–67.

Baldwin, D. A. (2000). Interpersonal understanding fuels knowledge acquisition. *Current Directions in Psychological Science, 9*, 40–45.

Bar-Haim, Y., Ziv, T., Lamy, D., & Hodes, R. M. (2006). Nature and nurture in own-race face processing. *Psychological Science, 17*, 159–163.

Baron, A. S., & Banaji, M. R. (2006). The development of implicit attitudes: Evidence of race evaluations from ages 6 and 10 and adulthood. *Psychological Science, 17*, 53–58.

Bowlby, J. (1958). The nature of the child's ties to his mother. *International Journal of Psychoanalysis, 39*, 350–373.

Brosnan, S. F., & de Waal, F. B. (2003). Monkeys reject unequal pay. *Nature, 425*, 297–299.

Clark, K., & Clark, M. (1947). Racial identification and preference in Negro children. In T. M. Newcomb & E. I. Hartley (Eds.), *Readings in social psychology* (pp. 169–178). New York: Holt.

Dapretto, M., Davies, M. S., Pfeifer, J. H., Scott, A. A., Sigman, M., Bookheimer, S. Y., et al. (2006). Understanding emotions in others: Mirror neuron dysfunction in children with autism spectrum disorders. *Nature Neuroscience, 9*, 28–30.

Dawson, G., Webb, S. J., Carver, L., Panagiotides, H., & McPartland, J. (2004). Young children with autism show atypical brain responses to fearful versus neutral facial expressions of emotion. *Developmental Science, 7*, 340–359.

De Wolff, M., & van IJzendoorn, M. H. (1997). Sensitivity and attachment: A meta-analysis on parental antecedents of infant attachment. *Child Development, 68*, 571–591.

Diesendruck, G., & ha Levi, H. (2006). The role of language, appearance, and culture in children's social category-based induction. *Child Development, 77*, 539–553.

Dovidio, J. F., Kawakami, K., Johnson, C., Johnson, B., & Howard, A. (1997). On the nature of prejudice: Automatic and controlled processes. *Journal of Experimental Social Psychology, 33*, 510–540.

Dunham, Y. (2007). *Minimal group biases in childhood*. Talk presented at the meeting of the Cognitive Development Society, Santa Fe, NM.

Egan, L. C., Santos, L. R., & Bloom, P. (2007). The origins of cognitive dissonance: Evidence from children and monkeys. *Psychological Science, 18*, 978–983.

Fazio, R. H., & Olson, M. A. (2003). Implicit measures in social cognition research: Their meaning and uses. *Annual Review of Psychology, 54*, 297–327.

Gergely, G., Bekkering, H., & Kiraly, I. (2002). Rational imitation in preverbal infants. *Nature, 415*, 755.

Gergely, G., Nadasdy, Z., Csibra, G., & Biro, S. (1995). Taking the intentional stance at 12 months of age. *Cognition, 56*, 165–193.

Greenwald, A. G., McGhee, D. E., & Schwartz, J. L. K. (1998). Measuring individual differences in implicit cognition: The implicit association test. *Journal of Personality and Social Psychology, 74*, 1464–1480.

Hamlin, J. K., Wynn, K., & Bloom, P. (2007). Social evaluation in preverbal infants. *Nature, 450*, 557–559.

Johnson, S. C. (2007). *Evidence for infants' working model of attachment*. Presented at the meeting of the Child Development Society, Santa Fe, NM.

Johnson, S. C., Dweck, C. S., & Chen, F. S. (2007). Evidence for infants' internal working models of attachment. *Psychological Science, 18*, 501–502.

Johnson, S. C., Slaughter, V., & Carey, S. (1998). Whose gaze will infants follow? The elicitation of gaze-following in 12-month-olds. *Developmental Science, 1*, 233–238.

Kelly, D. J., Liu, S., Ge, L., Quinn, P. C., Slater, A. M., Lee, K., et al. (2007). Cross-race preferences for same-race faces extend beyond the African versus Caucasian contrast in 3-month-old infants. *Infancy, 11*, 87–95.

Kinzler, K. D., Dupoux, E., & Spelke, E. S. (2007). The native language of social cognition. *Proceedings of the National Academy of Sciences of the United States of America, 104*, 12577–12580.

Kuhlmeier, V., Wynn, K., & Bloom, P. (2003). Attribution of dispositional states by 12-month-olds. *Psychological Science, 14*, 402–408.

Leslie, A. M. (1987). Pretense and representation: The origins of "theory of mind." *Psychological Review, 94,* 412–426.

Maccoby, E. E., & Jacklin, C. N. (1974). *The psychology of sex differences.* Stanford, CA: Stanford University Press.

Main, M., Kaplan, N., & Cassidy, J. (1985). Security in infancy, childhood, and adulthood: A move to the level of representation. *Monographs of the Society for Research in Child Development,* (Serial No. 209), *50,* 66–104.

Markson, L., & Fawcett, C. (2007). *Social influences on children's preferences.* Presented at the meeting of the Cognitive Development Society, Santa Fe, NM.

Master, A., Markman, E. M., & Dweck, C. S. (2008, February). *How thinking in categories or along a continuum affects children's social judgments.* Poster presented at the conference of the Society for Personality and Social Psychology, Albuquerque, NM.

McCrink, K., Santos, L., & Bloom, P. (2006). *Cues to generosity in children and adults.* Presented at the conference of the Society for Research in Child Development, Boston.

Meltzoff, A. (1995). Understanding of the intentions of others: Re-enactment of intended acts by 18-month-old children. *Developmental Psychology, 31,* 838–850.

Meltzoff, A., & Borton, R. W. (1979). Intermodal matching by human neonates. *Nature, 282,* 403–404.

Olson, K. R., Banaji, M. R., Dweck, C. S., & Spelke, E. S. (2006). Children's bias against lucky vs. unlucky people and their social groups. *Psychological Science, 17,* 845–846.

Olson, K. R., Dunham, Y., Dweck, C. S., Spelke, E. S., & Banaji, M. R. (2008). Judgments of the lucky across development and culture. *Journal of Personality and Social Psychology, 94,* 757–776.

Olson, K. R., & Dweck, C. S. (2008). A blueprint for social cognitive development. *Perspectives on Psychological Science, 3,* 193–202.

Olson, K. R., & Spelke, E. S. (2008). Foundations of cooperation in preschool children. *Cognition, 108,* 222–231.

Patterson, M. M., & Bigler, R. S. (2006). Preschool children's attention to environmental messages about groups: Social categorization and the origins of intergroup bias. *Child Development, 77,* 847–860.

Pfeifer, J. H., Lieberman, M. D., & Dapretto, M. (2007). "I know you are but what am I?": Neutral bases of self- and social knowledge retrieval in children and adults. *Journal of Cognitive Neuroscience, 19,* 1323–1337.

Premack, D., & Premack, A. J. (1997). Infants attribute value? To the goal-directed actions of self-propelled objects. *Journal of Cognitive Neuroscience, 9,* 848–856.

Ruble, D. N., Martin, C. L., & Berenbaum, S. A. (2006). Gender development. In N. Eisenberg, W. Damon, & R. M. Lerner (Eds.), *Handbook of child psychology: Vol. 3. Social, emotional, and personality development* (6th ed., pp. 858–932). New York: Wiley.

Rutland, A., Cameron, L., Milne, A., & McGeorge, P. (2005). Social norms and self-presentation: Children's implicit and explicit intergroup attitudes. *Child Development, 76,* 451–466.

Sherif, M., Harvey, O. J., White, B. J., Hood, W. R., & Sherif, C. W. (1961). *Intergroup cooperation and competition: The Robbers Cave experiment.* Norman, OK: University Book Exchange.

Shutts, K., Banaji, M. R., & Spelke, E. S. (2007). *Social categories guide young children's preferences for novel objects.* Presented at the meeting of the Cognitive Development Society, Santa Fe, NM.

Sroufe, L. A. (1985). Attachment classification from the perspective of infant-caregiver relationships and infant temperament. *Child Development, 56,* 1–14.

Tomasello, M., Call, J., & Hare, B. (2003). Chimpanzees understand psychological states—The question is which ones and to what extent. *Trends in Cognitive Sciences, 7,* 153–156.

Tomasello, M., Carpenter, M., Call, J., Behne, T., & Moll, H. (2005). Understanding and sharing intentions: The origins of cultural cognition. *Behavioral and Brain Sciences, 28,* 675–735.

Turner, J. C., Brown, R. J., & Tajfel, H. (1979). Social comparison and group interest in ingroup favouritism. *European Journal of Social Psychology, 9,* 187–204.

Wang, A. T., Lee, S. S., Sigman, M., & Dapretto, M. (2006). Developmental changes in the neural basis of interpreting communicative intent. *Social Cognitive and Affective Neuroscience, 1,* 107–121.

Warneken, F., & Tomasello, M. (2006). Altruistic helping in human infants and young chimpanzees. *Science, 311,* 1301–1303.

Wellman, H. (1990). *The child's theory of mind.* Cambridge, MA: MIT Press.

Wimmer, H., & Perner, J. (1983). Beliefs about beliefs: Representation and constraining function of wrong beliefs in young children's understanding of deception. *Cognition, 13,* 103–128.

Woodward, A. L. (1998). Infants selectively encode the goal object of an actor's reach. *Cognition, 69,* 1–34.

# Critical Thinking

1. Suppose you want to raise your child to perceive others as good, fair, equitable, not prejudiced, and trusting of others. Based on this article, describe what specific steps you might take as a parent during infancy and early childhood.

2. Summarize and evaluate the data on why young children appear to show preference for those who are similar to themselves. What implications does this have for children who are not similar to most others in their age group? How might this preference play a role in discrimination and prejudice and how might one safeguard against a preference for excessive similarity?

3. Assume you are a preschool center director. Based on this research, how might you work with parents and teachers to create an environment that promotes constructive social cognitive understanding for infants and preschoolers in your center.

4. Using data from this article, design a presentation or flier that you could make to give to school boards and other parenting groups about the importance of a child's early social environment to their later fundamental understanding about people and peers.

Correspondence concerning this article should be addressed to **KRISTINA R. OLSON,** Psychology Department, Box 208205, Yale University, New Haven, CT 06520; e-mail: kristina.olson@yale.edu.

From *Child Development Perspectives,* April 2009, pp. 60–65. Copyright © 2009 by the Authors. Published by the Society for Research in Child Development. Reprinted by permission of Wiley-Blackwell.

# Running on Empty? How Folk Science Gets By With Less

FRANK C. KEIL
*Yale University*

Folk science is often thought of as laypeople's mechanistic understandings of the natural and the artifactual worlds. Yet people of all ages have strikingly impoverished mechanistic understandings—often far worse than they assume. At the same time, even very young children have strong interests in mechanistic explanations and persistently seek them out. This fascination with and search for mechanism may support the tracking of causal structures and processes at levels far above that of mechanism. That information, in turn, enables people to bridge their extensive mechanistic gaps by identifying relevant experts. To be able to defer to experts effectively, even without mechanistic understanding, laypeople use a wide array of early-emerging heuristics for inferring causal relations and for evaluating experts and their explanations.

Although people in all cultures appear to have folk-scientific understandings of both nature and constructed devices, those understandings are often largely vacuous when considered at the level of mechanistic knowledge. The depth of this ignorance can be stunning. For example, functionally impossible schematic diagrams of mundane artifacts, such as simple bicycles, are falsely recognized as correct by large proportions of adults, and even by some devoted members of cycling clubs (Lawson, 2006). Thus, a schematic in which a bicycle's chain goes from the rear axle to the front one is endorsed by many adults even though that configuration would make steering impossible.

People's memory for the features of everyday objects, such as pennies, has long been known to be severely flawed. But even at the more abstract level of having a schematic sense of how everyday things work, we have only snatches and fragments—nothing like idealized schematic diagrams—in our heads. The problem is compounded by our sense that we have much more detailed explanatory understandings than we really do (Rozenblit & Keil, 2002), an illusion of explanatory depth that is especially strong in young children (Mills & Keil, 2004).

In short, knowledge of concrete mechanisms eludes not only children but also most adults. We appear to be blissfully gliding along, thinking we understand the world much better than we really do, in effect "running on empty." Yet this ignorance clashes with another well-documented phenomenon: the interest of young children in mechanisms.

Although children may occasionally ask "why" or "how" questions as ways of merely engaging adults, they often expect, and receive, mechanism-rich responses from them. Moreover, if the responses to such questions avoid mention of mechanisms or causal explanations, even preschoolers will persist in asking questions until they get such information (Callanan & Oakes, 1992; Frazier, Gelman, & Wellman, 2009; Mills, Legare, Grant, & Landrum, 2011; Wellman, 2011). They are also clearly able to adjust their course of questioning to pursue their informational needs (Chouinard, 2007), and the ways in which they adjust suggest an interest in and preference for mechanistic information. For example, if a child asks why the sky is blue and is told that all skies are blue, she will be more likely to then ask more "why" questions than she would if she had been given a mechanistic answer about air particles absorbing certain colors of light (such mechanistic answers can also invite further "why" questions, but they do so to a lesser extent).

Children do not always pursue mechanistic information, and important questions remain concerning the contexts and situations that prompt such queries (such as device malfunction; Isaacs, 1930; Legare, 2012), but on many occasions, they do seek out such information and acquire it either through direct experience or through testimony. Why should very young children have such an interest in mechanistic understanding if it seems to evaporate in the minds of all laypeople, leaving behind only the vaguest traces of specific mechanisms and isolated fragments of understanding (diSessa, Gillespie, & Esterly, 2004)?

Answering this question may depend on rethinking folk science as primarily tracking causal patterns at other levels, levels that can powerfully support folk science but cannot yield clockwork senses of how the world works (Keil, 2010). Indeed, there may be distinct advantages to usually having minimalist mechanistic understandings. In addition to sophisticatedly tracking causal patterns that are "above" the level of mechanism, people of all ages use such patterns to infer fertile, or richly articulated, domains of expertise and guide themselves toward knowledge sources, and then use sophisticated strategies to evaluate those sources. In this article, I briefly describe research that has built on these ideas in four ways. Specifically, I consider (a) several different levels at which children, and sometimes even infants, can track causal information in nonmechanistic ways, (b) how children develop the ability to assess which domains are plausible areas of expertise, (c) ways in which young children can have huge mechanistic gaps but manage to infer causal patterns nonetheless, and (d) how children and adults outsource expertise and may actually benefit from illusions of understanding.

# Levels of Tracking of Causal Information

Although mechanistic information may be difficult to remember in detail, attention to mechanism may enable memory for patterns at more abstract, nonmechanistic levels, memories that can be present in human infants and even in some other species. Several such levels are listed in Table 1. For example, at the most abstract level, one can notice *causal relevance* and *causal density*. We notice causal relevance when we track that certain types of properties, such as surface coloration, are typically causally connected to many other properties of most natural categories. In contrast, such causal connections to surface color are typically much less dense for properties of artifact categories (Keil, Smith, Simons, & Levin, 1998; Santos, Sulkowski, Spaepen, & Hauser, 2002). Similarly, one may know that some phenomena are much more causally complex than others even

if the precise nature of that complexity remains unknown (Keil, 2010). At a more specific level, we also track causal powers. For example, preverbal infants believe that only animate intentional agents can create order out of disorder whereas a much wider range of agents can create disorder out of order (Newman, Keil, Kuhlmeier, & Wynn, 2010). They, as well as much older children, may have little sense of the mechanisms that underlie this causal power relation, but they know and use the pattern to interpret their world.

Beyond causal patterns, infants and young children can track broad functional properties of entities and categories. For example, although they are sometimes overly exuberant in ascribing functions to the natural world (Kelemen, 1999), they also know that it is more common to attribute functions to entire artifacts and their component parts than to entire animals (Greif, Kemler-Nelson, Keil, & Gutierrez, 2006). High-level functional inferences are commonplace and often made in the context of observing intentional goal-directed actions by others, an ability present even in infancy (Csibra & Gergely, 2011).

All of these impressive abilities, however, do not translate into having blueprints of how things work, and they are often tacit. Thus, the child who thinks it more appropriate to talk about the functions of entire tools (e.g., what hammers are for) than of entire animals (e.g., what crows are for) may have never explicitly realized that contrast. Moreover, children often can be stunningly misguided about mechanistic details, a pattern that

## Table 1  Ways of Tracking Causal Relations

| Kind of causal pattern | Characteristics | Developmental trajectory | Tacit vs. explicit |
|---|---|---|---|
| Causal relevancy | Tracking what kinds of causal properties are likely to be most explanatorily relevant to a domain | Appears in infancy among humans and some other species; continues to emerge throughout childhood | Tacit |
| Causal density | Tracking causal complexity and interconnectedness of properties for an entity or system | Emerges at least by preschool years; increases in sensitivity in early school years | Initially tacit |
| Causal powers | Knowing that an entity has the power to cause a particular kind of effect | Appears in infancy; expands considerably in preschool years | Both tacit and explicit |
| Functional relations | Knowing that a property or an entity serves a specific function | Appears in late infancy; functional attributions change in scope during preschool and early school years | Mostly explicit for specific functions; the tracking of abstract patterns of functional use (e.g., preference to think of functions of entire artifacts) may be tacit |
| Mechanistic fragments | Knowing the concrete details of isolated components of a system | Knowledge of some small fragments emerges in infancy; knowledge of larger and more numerous fragments develops throughout lifespan | Explicit |
| Full mechanistic details | Having a full mental blueprint of how something works | Develops very rarely and only for restricted domains among a few experts | Explicit |

Note: Although much of the work on folk science has focused on full mechanistic understanding as the endpoint and goal of explanatory knowledge, most tracking of causal patterns occurs instead at levels that do not involve much mechanistic understanding at all. These other levels are intimately involved in identifying appropriate experts for deference and for evaluating the quality of explanations and of experts themselves. More abstract levels of tracking causal patterns may also be more tacit in nature.

has spawned thousands of papers on children's misconceptions. These different levels of analysis (e.g., mechanistic vs. functional) can lead to claims that young children are either sophisticated scientists or hopelessly misguided. Beliefs about essence (Gelman, 2003) provide one example. Even preverbal infants seem to know that animals' insides are more essential to them than their outsides (Newman, Herrmann, Wynn, & Keil, 2008), yet school-age children can show striking errors in understanding how essences are actually physically instantiated in terms of biological components (Newman & Keil, 2008). Children and adults alike can sometimes grasp mechanistic fragments, such as a particular part of a physical or a biological system, but they have difficulty remembering how these fragments all fit together into a coherent system (diSessa et al., 2004).

There also may be a trend whereby, as people move to higher levels of abstraction, their tracking of causal patterns becomes more tacit. This pattern is proposed in the rightmost column in Table 1. It is suggested by cases in which patterns are tracked by preverbal infants and even nonhuman primates. Other suggestive evidence arises when participants express surprise at a pattern in their judgments that is disclosed in experimental debriefings. For example, many participants will report only realizing for the first time in an experiment their strong bias that it makes less sense to talk about the purposes of entire animals than of artifacts (Greif et al., 2006). Similarly, although infants may be strongly biased to prefer intentional agents as the causes of ordering events, even some adults can be startled at the extent to which they try to link intentional agency to departures from randomness (Newman et al., 2010). Future studies are needed to more systematically explore how tacit and explicit awareness of causal patterns vary according to the nature of those patterns and across development.

## Accessing the Fertility of Domains

The tracking of causal patterns above the level of mechanism enables people of all ages to sense when a domain is likely an area of expertise as opposed to common knowledge that one needs no input from others to understand. Although young children show systematic biases in rating psychological phenomena as less complex than biological and physical phenomena (Keil, Lockhart, & Schlegel, 2010), even the youngest children are able to effectively distinguish between domains whose information is self-evident and domains whose understanding is heavily dependent on input from other minds (Keil, 2010). Indeed, there is now an increasing emphasis in the literature on the extent to which concepts are dependent on inputs from other minds (Gelman, 2009; Harris, 2012; Keil, 2010).

One particularly powerful result of children's search for mechanism may be the ways in which inquiry into mechanism instills other forms of knowledge. For example, as children strive to understand mechanisms, the details they learn may fade, but a sense of relative complexity persists; this perception of complexity is remarkably consistent across individuals, especially in the later elementary-school years and beyond (Kominsky, Zamm, & Keil, 2012). More broadly, the quest for mechanism may enable learning about causal relevance and density, powers and function. Thus, investigating mechanisms necessarily entails investigating all the other information as well, much of which may then be abstracted more implicitly and retained more fully than mechanistic information. Moreover, characterizing the degree and specific nature of a domain's complexity may be critical for identifying and evaluating experts.

## Tricks for Tracking Causality

Because mechanistic understanding is weak, we have developed other strategies and heuristics for tracking important causal relations in the world, and we use these methods to discern causal powers and function without having to master mechanism. Consider two such strategies: overimitation and the stability heuristic.

*Overimitation* is the tendency to imitate all actions intentionally performed on a novel device and to automatically encode all those actions as causally central to the operation of the device even if they are mechanistically implausible (Lyons, Damrosch, Lin, Simeone, & Keil, 2011). In one paradigm, preschoolers are shown a "puzzle box" from which they are to retrieve a toy by manipulating knobs, levers, and other parts; however, only some of those parts are causally necessary for the retrieval. If an adult manipulates all the parts to retrieve the toy, observing preschoolers will do so as well, even though the casual connection between manipulating some of those parts and retrieving the toy is implausible. In contrast, chimpanzees drop the implausible steps (Horner & Whiten, 2005). Young humans often assume that others typically act "in good faith" when they operate devices and that all the parts they manipulate on the devices are being manipulated for important causal reasons that are central to the functioning of the device. These assumptions are a powerful, albeit fallible, shortcut toward inferring the causal underpinnings of artifacts. Automatic causal encoding may not always occur, as other social factors can also promote overimitation (Harris, 2012; Over & Carpenter, 2012); important questions about this issue and others remain about the conditions and contexts that promote the learning of causal powers from observations of others' actions.

The *stability heuristic* is used by people to explain changes in causal systems. People tend to assume that most properties of causal systems are fairly stable over time, and when they observe a change, they seek to attribute it to some cause. This heuristic is particularly useful when we don't know which of two parts of a causal system influences the other—when we are trying to identify the direction of the causal relationship. In particular, when considering a causal system with two parts that sometimes change simultaneously and at other times change independently while the corresponding part remains stable, people tend to infer that the more stable part influences the less stable part, but not vice versa (Rottman & Keil, 2012). This heuristic greatly enhances the learning of causal relationships that unfold over time. It is challenging to integrate the learning of such temporal causal patterns into standard models of causal learning that have focused on nontemporal scenarios with independent trials (e.g., Gopnik et al., 2004).

# The Outsourcing of Understanding and the Virtues of Illusions of Knowing

Once an individual has learned that a class of phenomena is sufficiently complex for an understanding of it to warrant the need for outside expertise, the challenge remains of identifying appropriate experts. Three classes of processes converge to make this happen. The first uses abstract causal patterns to match classes of phenomena to appropriate experts. The second uses an array of heuristics to evaluate the likely quality of individual experts. The third examines the internal structure of explanations to assess their quality. Although such skills might seem to emerge late in development and to be hallmarks of sophisticated scientific thought, they start to emerge early and form a foundational framework that guides deference in understanding.

In terms of using causal patterns to seek out appropriate experts, even preschoolers can extrapolate from one thing an expert knows to what else she or he is likely to know, and they do so in ways that go far beyond matching surface similarities. Thus, they will realize that an expert on one problem in biology is more likely to be an expert on another problem in biology than is an expert on a problem in physical mechanics (Lutz & Keil, 2002). Moreover, children use abstract causal schematic patterns to construct such mappings (Keil, Stein, Webb, Billings, & Rozenblit, 2008): When children hear that a person is an expert on a particular phenomenon, they sense some of the core underlying causal patterns associated with that phenomenon and then infer what other phenomena are governed by the same underlying causal patterns. They then assume that the expert is more likely than other people to know about those phenomena as well.

Several heuristics are also used early in life to evaluate experts. For example, young children prefer experts who have made fewer errors in the past and whose opinions agree more often with consensus (Harris & Corriveau, 2011). In addition, by the early school years, children start to be sensitive to conflicts of interest as reasons to doubt experts, assuming that a person's assertions might be suspect if they are strongly aligned with helping achieve a goal (Mills & Keil, 2004).

Finally, expressions of expertise themselves can be evaluated for their internal quality—for instance, in terms of their coherence, simplicity, and informativeness (Frazier et al., 2009; Lombrozo, 2007). More developmental growth seems to be required for this skill, which tends to emerge more dramatically during the elementary-school years, but still well ahead of exposure to formal instruction on the nature of scientific thought. For example, by second grade, children start to understand the vacuous nature of circular arguments and explanations (Baum, Danovitch, & Keil, 2008).

Successful navigation of the division of cognitive labor requires mastery and integration of each of these processes, elements of which all emerge early in life and without explicit instruction. These processes buttress our own partial understandings right from the start. They are not late-acquired nuances of the ways in which we understand the world and form our concepts; they are instead intrinsic to understanding at any age.

## Summary

Even though the youngest child has an intrinsic fascination with mechanism, the most sophisticated adult, outside of narrow areas of expertise, displays yawning gaps in mechanistic knowledge. Yet an interest in mechanism helps even young children build a sense of causal patterns that exist far above the level of mechanisms. That sense, in combination with strategies for identifying and evaluating experts and their explanations, allows us all to ground our incomplete knowledge in more secure footings in other minds. This is hardly a foolproof method, as many cases of public misunderstandings of science reveal, but the early emergence of these strategies suggests that, rather than become overwhelmed with mechanistic details that would swamp any one person's cognitive capacities, even the youngest among us have learned sophisticated ways of relying on the contents of other minds.

## Recommended Reading

Atran, S., & Medin, D. (2008). *The native mind and the cultural construction of nature.* Boston, MA: MIT Press. A detailed exploration of folk biology and how it becomes manifested in specific cultures.

Dunning, D. (2011). The Dunning-Kruger effect: On remaining ignorant of one's own ignorance. *Advances in Experimental Social Psychology, 44,* 247–296. A comprehensive review of different facets of the human bias to overestimate one's knowledge and understanding.

Gelman, S. A., & Legare, C. H. (2011). Concepts and folk theories. *Annual Review of Anthropology, 40,* 379–398. A review of how intuitive theories and their constitutive concepts emerge in development.

Keil, F. C. (2006). Explanation and understanding. *Annual Review of Psychology, 5,* 227–254. A discussion of the literature concerning the cognitive science of explanation.

Strevens, M. (2008). *Depth: An account of scientific explanation.* Cambridge, MA: Harvard University Press. An analysis of the ways in which explanations are constrained by such factors as depth of detail and idealization.

## References

Baum, L. A., Danovitch, J. H., & Keil, F. C. (2008). Children's sensitivity to circular explanations. *Journal of Experimental Child Psychology, 100,* 146–155.

Callanan, M. A., & Oakes, L. M. (1992). Preschoolers' questions and parents' explanations: Causal thinking in everyday activity. *Cognitive Development, 7,* 213–233.

Chouinard, M. M. (2007). Children's questions: A mechanism for cognitive development. *Monographs of the Society for Research in Child Development, 72,* 1–108.

Csibra, G., & Gergely, G. (2011). Natural pedagogy as evolutionary adaptation. *Philosophical Transactions of the Royal Society B, 366,* 1149–1157.

diSessa, A. A., Gillespie, N. M., & Esterly, J. B. (2004). Coherence versus fragmentation in the development of the concept of force. *Cognitive Science, 28,* 843–900.

Frazier, B. N., Gelman, S. A., & Wellman, H. M. (2009). Preschoolers' search for explanatory information within adult-child conversation. *Child Development, 80,* 1592–1611.

Gelman, S. A. (2003). *The essential child.* New York, NY: Oxford University Press.

Gelman, S. A. (2009). Learning from others: Children's construction of concepts. *Annual Review of Psychology, 60,* 115–140.

Gopnik, A., Glymour, C., Sobel, D. M., Schulz, L. E., Kushnir, T., & Danks, D. (2004). A theory of causal learning in children: Causal maps and Bayes nets. *Psychological Review, 111,* 3–32.

Greif, M. L., Kemler-Nelson, D. G., Keil, F. C., & Gutierrez, F. (2006). What do children want to know about animals and artifacts? Domain-specific requests for information. *Psychological Science, 17,* 455–459.

Harris, P. L. (2012). *Trusting what you're told: How children learn from others.* Cambridge, MA: Harvard University Press.

Harris, P. L., & Corriveau, K. H. (2011). Young children's selective trust in informants. *Philosophical Transactions of the Royal Society B, 366,* 1179–1187.

Horner, V., & Whiten, A. (2005). Causal knowledge and imitation/emulation switching in chimpanzees (*Pan troglodytes*) and children (*Homo sapiens*). *Animal Cognition, 8,* 164–181.

Isaacs, N. (1930). Children's "why" questions. In S. Isaacs (Ed.), *Intellectual growth in young children* (pp. 291–349). London, England: George Routledge & Sons.

Keil, F. C. (2010). The feasibility of folk science. *Cognitive Science, 34,* 826–862.

Keil, F. C., Lockhart, K. L., & Schlegel, E. (2010). A bump on a bump? Emerging intuitions concerning the relative difficulty of the sciences. *Journal of Experimental Psychology: General, 139,* 1–15.

Keil, F. C., Smith, W. C., Simons, D. J., & Levin, D. T. (1998). Two dogmas of conceptual empiricism: Implications for hybrid models of the structure of knowledge. *Cognition, 65,* 103–135.

Keil, F. C., Stein, C., Webb, L., Billings, V. D., & Rozenblit, L. (2008). Discerning the division of cognitive labor: An emerging understanding of how knowledge is clustered in other minds. *Cognitive Science, 32,* 259–300.

Kelemen, D. (1999). Functions, goals and intentions: Children's teleological reasoning about objects. *Trends in Cognitive Sciences, 12,* 461–468.

Kominsky, J. F., Zamm, A., & Keil, F. C. (2012). Intuitive complexity in the absence of deep understanding. Manuscript submitted for publication.

Lawson, R. (2006). The science of cycology: Failures to understand how everyday objects work. *Memory & Cognition, 34,* 1667–1675.

Legare, C. H. (2012). Exploring explanation: Explaining inconsistent evidence informs exploratory, hypothesis-testing behavior in young children. *Child Development, 83,* 173–185.

Lombrozo, T. (2007). Simplicity and probability in causal explanation. *Cognitive Psychology, 55,* 232–257.

Lutz, D. R., & Keil, F. C. (2002). Early understanding of the division of cognitive labor. *Child Development, 73,* 1073–1084.

Lyons, D. E., Damrosch, D., Lin, J. K., Simeone, D. M., & Keil, F. C. (2011). Automatic causal encoding and the scope of overimitation. *Proceedings of the Royal Society B: Biological Sciences, 366,* 1158–1167.

Mills, C. M., & Keil, F. C. (2004). Knowing the limits of one's understanding: The development of an awareness of an illusion of explanatory depth. *Journal of Experimental Child Psychology, 87,* 1–32.

Mills, C. M., Legare, C. H., Grant, M. G., & Landrum, A. R. (2011). Determining who to question, what to ask, and how much information to ask for: The development of inquiry in young children. *Journal of Experimental Child Psychology, 110,* 539–560.

Newman, G., Herrmann, P., Wynn, K., & Keil, F. C. (2008). Biases towards internal features in infants' reasoning about objects. *Cognition, 107,* 420–432.

Newman, G., & Keil, F. C. (2008). "Where's the essence?": Developmental shifts in children's beliefs about the nature of essential features. *Child Development, 79,* 1344–1356.

Newman, G. E., Keil, F. C., Kuhlmeier, V. A., & Wynn, K. (2010). Early understandings of the link between agents and order. *Proceedings of the National Academy of Sciences, USA, 107,* 17140–17145.

Over, H., & Carpenter, M. (2012). Putting the social into social learning: Explaining both selectivity and fidelity in children's copying behavior. *Journal of Comparative Psychology, 126,* 182–192.

Rottman, B. M., & Keil, F. C. (2012). Causal structure learning over time: Observations and interventions. *Cognitive Psychology, 64,* 93–125.

Rozenblit, L. R., & Keil, F. C. (2002). The misunderstood limits of folk science: An illusion of explanatory depth. *Cognitive Science, 26,* 521–562.

Santos, L. R., Sulkowski, G. M., Spaepen, G. M., & Hauser, M. D. (2002). Object individuation using property/kind information in rhesus macaques (*Macaca mulatta*). *Cognition, 83,* 241–264.

Wellman, H. M. (2011). Reinvigorating explanations for the study of early cognitive development. *Child Development Perspectives, 5,* 33–38.

## Critical Thinking

1. Why would children be so eager to generate causal explanations for events?

2. What are "mechanistic processes"? In what ways are children and adults similar and different in their understanding of mechanistic processes?

3. How does children's implicit and explicit knowledge affect their folk science?

**FRANK C. KEIL,** Department of Psychology, Yale University, 2 Hillhouse Ave., New Haven, CT 06520 E-mail: frank.keil@yale.edu

From *Current Directions in Psychological Science,* vol. 21, no. 5, 2012, pp. 329–334. Copyright © 2012 by the Association for Psychological Science. Reprinted by permission of Sage Publications via Rightslink.

# Children's Reading Comprehension Difficulties: Nature, Causes, and Treatments

CHARLES HULME AND MARGARET J. SNOWLING

Teaching children to read accurately, fluently, and with adequate comprehension is one of the main goals of early education. Reading is critical because a great deal of formal education depends upon being able to read with understanding. Reading difficulties will inevitably create educational difficulties, which, in turn, are a major source of economic and social disadvantage. But such difficulties may be reduced by suitable early intervention (Heckman, 2006).

Reading comprehension depends on word recognition, and these two skills correlate around 70 in the early grades (see, e.g., Juel, Griffith, & Gough, 1986). However, the less-than-perfect correlation between word recognition and reading comprehension implies that there will be children who have deficits in just one of these skills. It is well established that both these forms of selective reading difficulty are relatively common (see Cain, 2010; Hulme & Snowling, 2009; Stothard & Hulme, 1995; Yuill & Oakhill, 1991). The most widely recognized form of reading disorder is often referred to as dyslexia. Children with dyslexia find learning to recognize printed words inordinately difficult. Dyslexia has been widely studied and is now relatively well understood (Hulme & Snowling, 2009; Vellutino, Fletcher, Snowling, & Scanlon, 2004).

In contrast to dyslexia, children with reading-comprehension impairment (often simply referred to as poor comprehenders) can read aloud accurately and fluently at a level appropriate for their age but fail to understand much of what they read. Although this condition has been studied for many years (e.g., Oakhill, 1984), it still often goes unnoticed in the classroom, because when such children are asked to read a passage aloud they may do so with ease and it is only when they are asked questions about the meaning of what they have read that their problems are revealed. For this reason, reading-comprehension impairment (and the language difficulties that underlie it) may often be a hidden disability. It is likely that many such children and their teachers are unaware that they have a reading problem.

## The Nature and Prevalence of Reading Comprehension Impairment

Reading-comprehension impairment is not identified in the *Diagnostic and Statistical Manual of Mental Disorders, 4th Edition* (DSM-IV; American Psychiatric Association, 1994), and in the current draft of *DSM-5*, children with this profile would be identified as having a form of language impairment. A simple definition of reading-comprehension impairment is that a child must show a deficit in reading comprehension that is markedly discrepant with their reading accuracy. Many widely used tests (e.g., Wechsler Individual Achievment Test, WIAT-II; Wechsler, 2005) contain separate measures of reading accuracy and reading comprehension that have been standardized on the same population, making them ideally suited to identifying these children. It must be emphasized, however, that not all standardized reading-comprehension tests are equivalent and that some tests appear to assess primarily decoding accuracy rather than broader aspects of language comprehension (see Keenan, Betjeman, & Olson, 2008).

In practice the criteria used to identify poor comprehenders have differed widely between studies. Furthermore, given that reading-comprehension skills show a continuous distribution in the population, the cutoff used to define an impairment is to some degree arbitrary (Hulme & Snowling, 2009). Nevertheless, evidence indicates that reading-comprehension impairments are relatively common. Perhaps the best evidence we have comes from the standardization of a new reading test in the United Kingdom (York Assessment for Reading & Comprehension; Snowling et al., 2009) involving a representative sample of 1,324 UK primary-school children. Of the children in this sample, 10.3% showed a greater than 1 standard deviation deficit in reading comprehension compared to reading accuracy. This figure includes some children with average to good reading-comprehension ability but who have exceptionally good decoding skills. To identify children with clinically significant reading-comprehension difficulties, we can select only those children who show this discrepancy and whose reading-comprehension standard scores are equal to or below 90 and whose reading-accuracy scores are 90 or above; 3.3% of the sample met this arguably quite stringent set of criteria for defining a reading-comprehension impairment. Some 28% of these poor comprehenders were children with English as a second language, compared to just 14% of the rest of the sample (see also Lervåg & Aukrust, 2010). In summary, there is little doubt that reading-comprehension impairment is relatively common (and more common in children who are learning to read in a second language).

# The Causes of Reading-Comprehension Impairment

According to the *simple view of reading* (Gough & Tunmer, 1986) reading comprehension (R) is equal to decoding (D) "multiplied by" linguistic comprehension (R = D × C). In this view, adequate reading comprehension depends critically upon the ability both to decode print (translate written language into speech) and to understand spoken language. If either of these components (decoding or linguistic comprehension) is deficient, problems of reading comprehension will ensue. Studies of typically developing children show that variations in reading-comprehension skills are strongly predicted by variations in decoding and listening comprehension, as claimed by the simple view of reading. In addition, behavior-genetic evidence suggests that word recognition and listening comprehension are subject to genetic influence, which together fully account for the genetic influences on reading comprehension (Keenan, Betjeman, Wadsworth, de Fries, & Olson, 2006). Finally, as children get older, the correlation between reading-comprehension and decoding skills tends to decrease somewhat, while the correlation between reading comprehension and listening comprehension increases—suggesting that at older ages, reading comprehension comes to depend relatively more on language-comprehension ability and less on the ability to decode print (Gough, Hoover, & Petersen, 1996).

Given that children with reading-comprehension impairment are defined by having adequate reading accuracy (decoding) coupled with deficient reading comprehension, it follows from the simple view of reading that these children should show deficits on measures of language comprehension. A great deal of evidence bears out this prediction.

Catts, Adlof, and Ellis-Weismer (2006) conducted a large-scale study of eighth graders, many of whom had language impairments. Of the 182 children who took part, 57 had a reading-comprehension impairment (poor comprehension in relation to word-reading ability), 27 had decoding problems (poor word reading in relation to reading-comprehension ability), and 98 were typically developing children of the same age. As expected from the simple view, the children with reading-comprehension impairment showed deficits on a wide range of language measures. We can express the size of the problems shown by the poor comprehenders in terms of effect sizes (Cohen's $d$; the size of the difference between groups in standard deviation units). There were very large effect sizes when comparing the receptive-vocabulary ($d = 1.47$), grammatical-understanding ($d = 1.15$), and listening-comprehension ($d = 1.26$) skills of the poor comprehenders to typically developing children of the same age. In contrast, the poor comprehenders showed essentially normal performance on measures of phonological (speech-sound) skills, whereas children with decoding difficulties showed deficits on these measures but not on measures of vocabulary, grammatical understanding, and listening comprehension. This contrasting profile of language strengths and weaknesses between poor comprehenders and poor decoders shows that these are two different forms of reading problems that arise from different underlying language difficulties.

Another interesting feature of this study was that data were available for the same children when they had been tested earlier in kindergarten and second and fourth grade. A retrospective analysis showed that the poor comprehenders showed poor language scores at all these previous test times. This shows that these children had a stable language deficit and one that might plausibly be a cause of their problems in understanding what they read. Furthermore, approximately 30% of the poor comprehenders met the diagnostic criteria for having a language impairment, compared to approximately 5% of the typical readers.

A similar pattern emerged from an earlier study by Nation, Clarke, Marshall, & Durand (2004), which used a more stringent criterion for identifying children as poor comprehenders. In this study, once again, there were very large effect sizes when comparing the vocabulary ($d = 1.74$) and morphosyntactic ($d = 1.09$) and receptive and expressive language ($d = 1.02$) skills of the poor comprehenders to those of typically developing children of the same age. Some 35% of the poor comprehenders in this study met the criteria for having a language impairment. Finally, in another study by the same group (Nation, Cocksey, Taylor, & Bishop, 2010), a small sample of 8-year-old poor comprehenders showed substantial deficits on measures of vocabulary ($d = .82$), listening comprehension ($d = .88$), and grammatical knowledge ($d = .99 - 1.22$) in comparison to age-matched normal readers, and longitudinal data showed that these deficits were highly stable.

In summary, the evidence reviewed clearly shows that poor comprehenders display broad language difficulties that are present before reading develops and that are therefore likely causes of their later reading-comprehension difficulties. These early-emerging language problems include weak vocabulary knowledge, difficulties in processing grammatical information in spoken language, and poor performance on general measures of language comprehension. For most of these children, their language difficulties are not severe enough for them to be diagnosed as having a language impairment, but a reasonable view would be that most of these children have a subclinical language difficulty, which is manifested clearly in their reading-comprehension problems. We should note that a wide range of other explanations for these children's reading-comprehension difficulties have been considered, including deficits of working memory, problems in making inferences, and problems in monitoring their comprehension of what they are reading (see Cain, 2010; Hulme & Snowling, 2009). In our view, many of these other putative causes may reduce to more basic limitations in oral language comprehension, which are the direct cause of these children's reading comprehension difficulties. If this is the case, interventions to improve oral language comprehension skills should improve these children's reading comprehension.

# Treatments for Reading-Comprehension Impairment

The evidence about how best to treat reading-comprehension impairment is so far limited, but the results from a recent randomized controlled trial paint an optimistic picture (Clarke, Snowling, Truelove, & Hulme, 2010; see also the Reading for Meaning Project, 2010, for more details of the methods and materials used in this study). After initial screening of 1,120 children in 23 school classes, 160 children were identified (8 children in each of 20 classes) as having a relative weakness in reading comprehension compared to reading accuracy.

The children selected were randomly allocated to four groups; three groups received an intervention immediately, while the fourth group waited until the first three groups had completed their intervention. The three interventions were text-comprehension (TC) training, oral-language (OL) training, and a combined (COM) oral-language and text-comprehension training. It is important to note that the OL program involved only oral-language work and no reading or writing. The interventions were delivered in the children's schools by specially trained teaching assistants in three 30-minute sessions each week over 20 weeks. The children's reading and language skills were assessed before the intervention began, immediately after the intervention was completed, and again some 11 months later.

The effects were very clear. Immediately after the intervention was completed, all three intervention groups showed reliable improvements of equivalent size in reading comprehension (as measured by the WIAT-II) in comparison to the control group (increases of approximately 3.5 to 4.5 standard score points; effect sizes between $d = .59$ and $d = .99$). However, at delayed follow up, 11 months after the intervention had been completed, the advantage of the OL group had increased to 7.9 standard score points compared to the untreated control group ($d = 1.24$—a very large effect), and this group was now showing a larger gain than either the TC or COM groups (gains of 5.2 and 4.7 standard-score points, respectively). Furthermore, it appeared that the effects of the OL and COM interventions were at least partly accounted for by changes in a measure of vocabulary that had been taught in these interventions. The children in the OL intervention also showed statistically reliable improvements at the end of the intervention in a standardized test of vocabulary knowledge involving words that had not been taught in the intervention. This, together with the increased size of reading-comprehension advantage

at follow-up for this group, suggests that the intervention had resulted in some generalized improvements in these children's oral-language comprehension abilities.

The Clarke et al. (2010) study provides support for the idea that the language weaknesses that characterize poor comprehenders can be ameliorated by suitable teaching. It will be important to see such results replicated and preferably extended to interventions of longer duration. The children in this study were 8- to 9-year-olds who were in their fourth year of full-time education. A natural question is whether a similar oral-language-intervention program delivered earlier in development could prevent the development of such language- and reading-comprehension difficulties. Bowyer-Crane et al. (2008) compared the effects of a phonology-with-reading program (teaching letter-sound knowledge, phonological awareness, and early reading skills) and an OL program (involving vocabulary instruction, listening comprehension exercises, and narrative skills) in 4- to 5-year-old children with weak OL skills at school entry. The results from this randomized controlled trial showed clearly that the program was effective in boosting children's vocabulary and grammatical skills and that these effects were maintained 5 months after the trial had ended. However, at this point in development, these children's reading-comprehension skills were still at a very basic level, and there was no reliable difference in reading-comprehension skills between the groups. Nevertheless, the form of training used in this trial shows clear similarities to the OL program delivered by Clarke et al. to older children with reading-comprehension impairments. It seems a high priority for future studies to assess the extent to which early OL enrichment programs could improve children's OL and reading-comprehension skills. Current evidence suggests that this is a realistic possibility. We should also emphasize that many children experience difficulties with both word-recognition and language-comprehension skills, and such children may require interventions that address both of these problems (i.e., a combination of the two approaches to intervention that were evaluated by Bowyer-Crane et al., 2008).

# Recommended Reading

Carroll, J.M., Bowyer-Crane, C., Duff, F., Hulme, C., & Snowling, M.J. (2010). *Effective intervention for language and literacy in the early years.* Oxford, England: Wiley-Blackwell. An accessible account of a large-scale intervention study concerned with boosting children's early reading and language skills, written to be intelligible to teachers, practitioners, and policymakers.

Catts, H., Adlof, S., & Ellis-Weismer, S. (2006). (See References). Documents clearly the different language profiles of children with dyslexia and reading-comprehension impairment.

Clarke, P., Snowling, M., Truelove, E., & Hulme, C. (2010). (See References). Presents the results of the first randomized controlled trial to evaluate effective interventions for children with reading-comprehension impairment.

Hulme, C., & Snowling, M. (2009). (See References). Provides an overview of current understanding of different developmental disorders of language, learning, and cognition.

# Declaration of Conflicting Interests

The authors declared no potential conflicts of interest with respect to the research, authorship, and/or publication of this article.

# References

American Psychiatric Association. (1994). *Diagnostic and statistical manual of mental disorders.* (4th ed.) Washington, DC: Author.

Bowyer-Crane, C., Snowling, M.J., Duff, F.J., Fieldsend, E., Carroll, J., Miles, J.N.V., et al. (2008). Improving early language and literacy skills: Differential effects of an oral language versus a phonology with reading intervention. *Journal of Child Psychology & Psychiatry, 49,* 422–432.

Cain, K. (2010). *Reading development and difficulties.* Chichester, England: Wiley-Blackwell.

Catts, H., Adlof, S., & Ellis-Weismer, S. (2006). Language deficits in poor comprehenders: A case for the simple view of reading. *Journal of Speech-Language-Hearing Research, 49,* 278–293.

Clarke, P., Snowling, M., Truelove, E., & Hulme, C. (2010). Ameliorating children's reading comprehension difficulties: A randomised controlled trial. *Psychological Science, 21,* 1106–1116.

Gough, P.B., Hoover, W., & Petersen, C.L. (1996). Some observations on the simple view of reading. In C. Cornoldi & J. Oakhill (Eds.), *Reading comprehension difficulties.* (pp. 1–13). Mahwah, NJ: Erlbaum.

Gough, P.B., & Tunmer, W.E. (1986). Decoding, reading and reading disability. *Remedial and Special Education, 7,* 6–10.

Heckman, J.J. (2006). Skill formation and the economics of investing in disadvantaged children. *Science, 312,* 1900–1902.

Hulme, C., & Snowling, M. (2009). *Developmental disorders of language, learning and cognition.* Chichester, England: Wiley-Blackwell.

Juel, C., Griffith, P.L., & Gough, P.B. (1986). Acquisiton of literacy: A longitudinal study of children in first and second grade. *Journal of Educational Psychology, 78,* 243–255.

Keenan, J., Betjeman, R., & Olson, R. (2008). Reading comprehension tests vary in the skills they assess: Differential dependence on decoding and oral comprehension. *Scientific Studies of Reading, 12,* 281–300.

Keenan, J., Betjeman, R., Wadsworth, S., de Fries, J., & Olson, R. (2006). Genetic and environmental influences on reading and listening comprehension. *Journal of Research in Reading, 29,* 75–91.

Lervåg, A., & Aukrust, V.G. (2010). Vocabulary knowledge is a critical determinant of the difference in reading comprehension growth between first and second language learners. *Journal of Child Psychology & Psychiatry, 51,* 612–620.

Nation, K., Clarke, P., Marshall, C.M., & Durand, M. (2004). Hidden language impairments in children: Parallels between poor reading comprehension and specific language impairment? *Journal of Speech, Language, and Hearing Research, 47,* 199–211.

Nation, K., Cocksey, J., Taylor, J., & Bishop, D.V.M. (2010). A longitudinal investigation of early reading and language skills in children with poor reading comprehension. *Journal of Child Psychology & Psychiatry, 51,* 1031–1039.

Oakhill, J. (1984). Inferential and memory skills in children's comprehension of stories. *British Journal of Educational Psychology, 54,* 31–39.

Reading for Meaning Project (2010). *Reading for meaning.* Retrieved from http://readingformeaning.co.uk

Snowling, M.J., Stothard, S.E., Clarke, P., Bowyer-Crane, C., Harrington, A., Truelove, E., et al. (2009). *York Assessment of Reading for Comprehension.* Passage Reading. London, England: GL Publishers.

Stothard, S., & Hulme, C. (1995). A comparison of phonological skills in children with reading comprehension difficulties and children with decoding difficulties. *Journal of Child Psychology & Psychiatry, 36,* 399–408.

Vellutino, F.R., Fletcher, J.M., Snowling, M.J., & Scanlon, D.M. (2004). Specific reading disability (dyslexia): What have we learned in the past four decades? *Journal of Child Psychology & Psychiatry, 45,* 2–40.

Wechsler, D. (2005). *Wechsler Individual Achievement Test, 2nd Edition (WIAT II).* London, England: The Psychological Corp.

Yuill, N., & Oakhill, J. (1991). *Children's problems in text comprehension.* Cambridge, England: Cambridge University Press.

# Critical Thinking

1. Although reading comprehension has been labeled a "hidden disability," should teachers be able to detect a problem through homework assignments, quizzes, and tests?

2. If older children's reading comprehension is more dependent on language comprehension why is the deficit hard to address?

3. If some children have a problem with reading comprehension, how might building their vocabulary be a reliable treatment for oral-language comprehension?

**CHARLES HULME,** Department of Psychology, University of York, Room PS/B105, Heslington, York, YO10 5DD, UK
E-mail: ch1@york.ac.uk

# Recess—It's Indispensable!

The demise of recess in many elementary schools—and of outdoor play in general—is an issue of great concern to many members of the Play, Policy, and Practice Interest Forum. If there is any doubt that this is a problem, pick up publications as diverse as *Sports Illustrated, Pediatrics,* the *New York Times,* or your local newspaper to read about it.

Most of us remember recess as an important part of the school day. It was a time to be outdoors; to organize our own games; to play on the swings, slides, and other playground equipment; or just to hang out with friends.

In contrast, children today are likely to have 10 to 15 minutes of outdoor playtime during the school day, if they are lucky. No wonder there is an upswing in childhood obesity and an increase in childhood heart disease and type 2 diabetes. No wonder teachers are concerned about a generation of children who can't entertain themselves, have social difficulties, and are fidgety and off task in class.

## Cutting Back on Recess

In the late 1980s, some school systems began cutting back on recess to allow more instructional time. The trend accelerated with the passage of No Child Left Behind in 2001 and was particularly widespread in urban schools with high numbers of children from marginalized populations (Jarrett 2003; Roth et al. 2003; NCES 2006).

The arguments against recess involved both academics and safety issues. Some administrators believed their school's test scores would improve if children spent more time on school work. Some feared lawsuits from playground injuries.

A number of school systems have a recess policy; others allow the principals or teachers to determine whether the children go out to play. Officially having recess and *actually* having recess are two different issues. A recent study in *Pediatrics* (Barros, Silver, & Stein 2009), using a national data set of 11,000 children, found that 30 percent of third-graders had fewer than 15 minutes of recess a day. Recess time is often cut because of academic pressures or as punishment.

## Recess's Many Benefits

To make recommendations for policy changes, we, as members of the Play, Policy, and Practice Interest Forum, spent the past decade investigating what research says about the need for recess. On the one hand, we found no research to support

## How Many Children Have Recess?

How many children are deprived of recess every day? Although we don't know exactly, statistics reveal a troubling trend.

A 2005 National Center for Education Statistics (NCES 2006) survey found that

- 7 percent of first-graders and 8 percent of third-graders never had recess; and
- 14 percent of first-graders and 15 percent of third-graders had only 1 to15 minutes of recess a day.

According to official figures provided by school systems, since the enactment of No Child Left Behind,

- 20 percent of the school systems have decreased time for recess, averaging cuts of 50 minutes per week (Center on Education Policy 2008).

**We found no research to support administrators' assumptions that test scores required by No Child Left Behind could be improved by keeping children in the classroom all day.**

administrators' assumptions that test scores required by No Child Left Behind could be improved by keeping children in the classroom all day. On the other hand, there is considerable research to suggest that recess has many benefits for children in the cognitive, social-emotional, and physical domains. Jarrett (2002) gives a summary of many of the research studies that found the following cognitive, social-emotional, and physical benefits of recess:

### *Cognitive*

- Children are less fidgety and more on-task when they have recess, and children with ADHD (attention deficit/ hyperactivity syndrome) are among those who benefit most.

# The Demographics of Recess

A nationwide study on how first through fifth grade children spend their time at school found that on a randomly selected day, 21 percent of children did not have any recess (Roth et al. 2003). The study noted demographic disparities:

- 39 percent of African American students versus 15 percent of White students did not have recess;
- 44 percent of children living below the poverty line versus 17 percent of those above the poverty line were deprived of recess; and
- 25 percent of the children scoring below the mean on a standardized test versus 15 percent of those above the mean did not have recess.

An NCES survey (2006) also found disparities, with rural schools and affluent schools more likely to have recess. A 2003 survey of Georgia school systems (unpublished data collected by Jarrett and colleagues) found the same patterns but with 25 percent of kindergartners having no recess.

- Research on memory and attention shows that recall is improved when learning is spaced out rather than concentrated. Recess provides breaks during which the brain can "regroup."
- Brain research shows a relationship between physical activity and the development of brain connections.
- A school system that devoted a third of the day to nonacademic activities (art, music, physical activity) improved attitudes and fitness and slightly increased test scores, in spite of spending less time on academics.

## Social-Emotional

- On the playground, children exercise leadership, teach games to one another, take turns, and learn to resolve conflicts.
- In a free choice situation, children learn negotiation skills in order to keep the play going.
- On supervised playgrounds, particularly where children are taught games and conflict resolution skills, there is little fighting (see "Reconstructing Recess: One Principal's Story").
- Intervention programs during recess can successfully improve social skills.

# Reconstructing Recess: One Principal's Story

At Watsontown Elementary in central Pennsylvania, a small K-4 school where I am principal, the staff and I noticed conflicts, exclusion, and safety concerns on the playground during recess. We felt strongly that we needed to turn recess around.

We talked extensively and agreed that recess should be respectful, have safe play, include child choice, and encourage all children to participate. We also discussed the teachers' role at recess. We committed to simple, consistent rules—respect for self, others, the play environment, and the play equipment. Teachers brainstormed games that encourage responsibility, cooperation, and communication and made a list of the games to facilitate child choice.

We decided that before recess, children would choose from the list of cooperative games or old standbys-jump rope, hopscotch, four square). Children could also choose not to participate and instead play on their own. Teachers would review the rules and acceptable behaviors for the games before going to the playground ("What does it look like to tag someone?").

With the start of the new school year, we designated the second day Game Day for the staff to demonstrate the games, modeling the behaviors we wanted the children to use and allowing them to practice the skills in a safe environment. In a reflective writing activity at the end of Game Day, most children and teachers wrote about prosocial skills—inclusion, fair play, and teamwork.

Throughout the school year, teachers reinforced the concepts learned on Game Day. They helped children problem solve issues like what to do when teams had unequal skill levels and what happens if a child wants to jump rope but all the jump ropes are in use. Game Day didn't magically eliminate all of the playground concerns, but we now heard students supporting each other during recess.

Interested in reconstructing recess in your school? Here are some thoughts for teachers and administrators:

- Schedule recess every day for primary and elementary level children. Breaks from academics are important, and children need opportunities to practice positive social interactions.
- Agree on basic rules that apply throughout the school building and the day.
- Build a repertoire of games that encourage cooperation and responsibility and avoid conflicts.
- Teach the games using modeling and practice. Reinforce children's prosocial skills throughout the school year.
- Provide enough materials and equipment for several groups of children to play the same game. Help students make choices about which games to play.
- Provide teacher supervision during recess, and encourage the children during play.

—Susan Welteroth (swelteroth@wrsd.org)

## *Physical*

- Recess before rather than after lunch leads to healthier eating.
- Children who are active during the day are more active after school, whereas children who are sedentary during the day tend to remain sedentary after school (couch potato syndrome).

Children's activity levels are generally higher during recess than during physical education (PE). PE is not seen by the PE teachers or the children as a substitute for recess. Recess and PE serve different purposes. Research also suggests benefits for teachers, even when the teacher is required to supervise on the playground. Recess can help with classroom management:

- Teachers rated children's behavior as better in classes where children had at least 15 minutes of recess (Barros, Silver, & Stein 2009).
- Teachers get to know the children better when supervising them on the playground. This knowledge can be useful in developing curriculum and in preventing bullying.
- Time on the playground is a change of pace for the teacher as well as for the children.

## Children's Right to Play

We believe that recess is a right, not a privilege. Article 31 of the U.N. Convention on the Rights of the Child (www.unicef .org/crc) recognizes

> The right of the child to rest and leisure, to engage in play and recreational activities appropriate to the age of the child and to participate freely in cultural life and the arts.

We believe that recess, with its fun, movement, and opportunities to socialize through play, is a basic need and that policies against recess, whether made at the school system, school, or teacher level, discriminate against children. Depriving a child of recess as punishment is similar to depriving a child of lunch. It is not only unfair, it is also unhelpful. Just as hungry children cannot concentrate well, children deprived of breaks cannot concentrate well either. Sometimes the most disruptive children need recess the most.

## Stand up for Recess!

What can you do? Here are some steps you can take:

- Find out whether the schools in your community have recess, and if so, for how many minutes a day. Do *all* the children get recess?
- Check school playgrounds for safety. The National Program for Playground Safety (NPPS) has helpful online resources (www.playgroundsafety.org). Examine the needs for supervision. Generally, teachers supervise recess; but in some cases, other supervisors are hired.

## Critical Thinking

1. What's happening to recess in public schools today? Is it as common or less than it used to be, and why?
2. In what ways is recess good for children? What domains of development does it seem to benefit?

# Social Awareness + Emotional Skills = Successful Kids

New funding and congressional support are poised to bring the best social and emotional learning research into more classrooms nationwide.

TORI DEANGELIS

The sad truth is that most U.S. schools don't foster good mental health or strong connections with friends and nurturing adults. Data show that only 29 percent of sixth-through 12th-grade students report that their schools provide caring, encouraging environments. Another 30 percent of high school students say they engage in high-risk behaviors, such as substance use, sex, violence and even suicide attempts.

For decades, a dedicated group of prevention experts—many of them psychologists—has been trying to improve those statistics through an approach called social and emotional learning, or SEL. They believe that if schools teach youngsters to work well with others, regulate their emotions and constructively solve problems, students will be better equipped to deal with life's challenges, including academic ones.

"It's about creating an environment where a child can learn—because if a child isn't emotionally prepared to learn, he or she is not going to learn," says SEL researcher and program developer Marc Brackett, PhD, head of the Emotional Intelligence Unit at Yale University's Edward Zigler Center in Child Development and Social Policy.

Critics charge that SEL programs are too broad-based and that social and emotional learning shouldn't necessarily fall on teachers' shoulders. Instead, families should oversee their children's social, emotional and character development, they contend. Yet studies show the programs improve mental health and behavior, boost children's social competence, and create more positive school climates. Students who participated in SEL programs gained an average of 11 percentage points more on achievement tests than youngsters who didn't take part in the programs, according to a meta-analysis of 213 studies of SEL programs, in press at *Child Development*, by prevention experts Joseph A. Durlak, PhD, of Loyola University Chicago; Roger P. Weissberg, PhD, of the University of Illinois at Chicago; and colleagues.

"That's pretty remarkable given how difficult it is to alter achievement test scores," says Mark Greenberg, PhD, director of the Prevention Research Center at Pennsylvania State University and creator of one of the longest-running and most rigorously studied SEL programs, PATHS (Promoting Alternative Thinking Strategies).

Some studies also show major gains long after an SEL program has ended. In the Seattle Social Development Project—a longitudinal study of 808 elementary school children who received a comprehensive SEL intervention in the first through sixth grade starting in 1981—participants reported significantly lower lifetime rates of violence and heavy alcohol use at age 18 than no-intervention controls. In addition, intervention-group students were more likely to complete high school than controls—91 percent compared with 81 percent—and to have lower rates of major depression, post-traumatic stress disorder, anxiety and social phobia at ages 24 and 27. (See the *Archives of Pediatrics and Adolescent Medicine,* Vol. 153, No. 3; Vol. 156, No. 5; and Vol. 159, No. 1).

In a related vein, Greenberg and others are starting to show that the programs affect executive functioning, an ability some researchers think may be even more important than IQ.

"The ability to maintain attention, to shift your set and plan ahead—these are obviously important learning skills that our programs are significantly improving upon," Greenberg says.

Other researchers are starting to examine other untapped areas the programs may be affecting, including health, parenting and even the behavior of children whose parents underwent the original interventions. Researchers are also applying SEL programs abroad, with military families and with special-education populations.

## The Tenets of Social and Emotional Learning

Researchers have been studying a version of SEL since the 1970s, but it was first popularized in "Emotional Intelligence," the 1995 best-seller by psychologist Daniel Goleman, PhD. He argued that emotional intelligence can be taught and that schools should teach it systematically.

While SEL programs vary somewhat in design and target different ages, they all work to develop core competencies: self-awareness, social awareness, self-management, relationship skills and responsible decision-making. Instead of focusing on a single negative behavior—such as drug use, sexual risk-taking or aggression, for instance—SEL researchers take a broad-brush approach to tackling these problems. They believe all of these behaviors share common roots: a lack of social and emotional competence, often exacerbated by factors such as family disruption, violent neighborhoods and genetic and biological dispositions. Schools and families can counter these risks, SEL proponents say, by facilitating students' emotional and social skills and providing environments that both nurture and challenge children.

A look at the PATHS program shows how these programs work. Like many SEL programs, it uses easy-to-understand, teacher-led lessons and activities that help students learn to recognize feelings in themselves and others, manage their thoughts and emotions more effectively, and solve interpersonal problems. One activity, for instance, has youngsters construct posters resembling a three-color traffic signal. Each signal light represents a different aspect of constructive problem-solving: Red is "stop and calm down," yellow is "go slow and think," and green is "go ahead, try my plan." Children apply this guide to real-life problems, then evaluate how their solutions worked.

Active strategies like this are embedded in a comprehensive program that teachers share in 131 sequential lessons over a seven-year period, from kindergarten to sixth grade. Children don't just get didactic information but have many chances to practice these skills both in and out of the classroom, Greenberg explains.

"Comprehensive SEL programs create many opportunities for children to practice these skills in the challenging situations they face every day in the classroom and on the playground," he says. "They also build caring, safe school climates that involve everyone in the school."

An interesting synergy results when these programs are offered, Greenberg adds. When children are taught these skills, they learn how to foster their own well-being and become more resilient. That, in turn, builds a more positive classroom climate that better engages children in learning. And as they become more absorbed in learning, children are more likely to do better in school.

"Building emotional awareness, self-control and relationship skills are master skills," Greenberg says. "When we nurture them, children do better in all areas of their daily lives, including school."

The programs, however, are far from perfect, critics and proponents say. While a 2005 review shows that about 59 percent of schools use some kind of SEL programming, the quality varies widely, says Weissberg. In fact, the Collaborative for Academic, Social and Emotional Learning, or CASEL—a nonprofit organization founded by Goleman in 1994 dedicated to advancing the science and evidence base of SEL and promoting the quality of SEL programs—places only 22 of the nation's several hundred SEL programs (including Greenberg's and Hawkins') on its list of exemplary programs for being well-designed and evidence-based, among other criteria. Researchers also continue to debate whether universal or more targeted curricula are better, since SEL programs tend to have the greatest impact on troubled kids.

Meanwhile, educators are feeling an enormous pressure to have kids do well on standardized testing, even in tight economic times, says Weissberg. "So there are several barriers that make it a challenge to implement SEL programs with high quality and fidelity," he says.

## SEL Goes National

That said, more money is pouring into the field, thanks to the positive research findings on social and emotional learning. The NoVo Foundation, a philanthropy headed by Peter and Jennifer Buffett (Peter is investor Warren Buffett's son), has offered $10 million in grants: $3.4 million in research funds and $6.3 million in development funds for CASEL.

Potentially more far-reaching is the Academic, Social, and Emotional Learning Act (H.R. 4223), announced at a CASEL forum in Washington, D.C., in December. The bill, introduced by Rep. Dale Kildee (D-Mich.) and co-sponsored by Rep. Tim Ryan (D-Ohio) and Rep. Judy Biggert (R-Ill.), would authorize the U.S. Department of Education to establish a national SEL training center and provide grants to support evidence-based SEL programs, as well as evaluate their success.

"I don't think I could have imagined that our field would have come this far," says Weissberg, CASEL's president.

In an effort to make the best SEL programming available nationwide, CASEL leaders plan to collaborate with evidence-based SEL providers, work with model school districts, share research to inform federal legislation and state policy, and think realistically about how to implement these programs on a broad scale, says Weissberg. If the legislation passes, it should enhance these efforts, he adds.

The December CASEL forum underscored the field's growing clout and psychologists' central role in it, adds APA Chief Executive Officer Norman Anderson, PhD, who attended the meeting. There, psychologists and other SEL researchers and practitioners rubbed elbows with legislators, philanthropists, national media and even some Hollywood celebrities, including Goldie Hawn, who heads her own SEL-related organization.

"This group of experts is doing an outstanding job of moving the SEL model forward and making a real difference in the lives of our children," says Anderson. He is particularly pleased that research is starting to show a link between developing children's resilience and academic performance, he says.

"These efforts represent another bridge between the worlds of psychology and education," Anderson adds. "It's all very exciting."

## Critical Thinking

1. Assume you have a close friend who is having problems with a child who is acting out consistently in class with teachers and peers. Describe how you would review, critique, and present the data regarding SEL (Social and Emotional Leaning) programs to your friend.

2. Speculate as to whether SEL may differ in its effectiveness rates, depending on factors such as sex of participant, ethnicity, family history, and demographics.

**TORI DEANGELIS** is a writer in Syracuse, N.Y.

# Kindergartners Explore Spirituality

**"The fun thing about studying different beliefs is that . . . they are different."**

BEN MARDELL AND MONA M. ABO-ZENA

**Max:** You know who made flowers? God. Who made clouds? God. That's what my mom told me.

**Emily:** Just because your mom says he's real doesn't mean he is real.

**Robert:** Who made the first person on earth?

**Max:** God.

**Emily:** Gorillas. People evolved from gorillas and started to lose their hair to be more like people.

**Max:** God made the first person on Earth. The first people are Adam and Eve. I'm sure God is the one. Gorillas can't talk. They do nothing.

**Emily:** That's not true.

**Max:** It is true. Gorillas are not a person that has magic.

These kindergartners are sitting around the snack table, talking. Conversations like this are not uncommon in early childhood classrooms. Young children are actively working to make sense of the world, including what it means when people disagree about deeply held beliefs (many of which originate at home and reflect religious and spiritual values). Early childhood is a time when understandings of differences are formed (Derman-Sparks & Edwards 2010). Guided explorations about differences in beliefs are important because they help children develop healthy attitudes about spiritual plurality, and they cultivate meaningful home–school relations with diverse families.

This article is for early childhood teachers, administrators, and families interested in helping young children develop positive views about diverse spiritual beliefs and the people who embrace them. The article is based on a project in which Max, Emily, Robert, and their 15 classmates studied their own and others' understanding of creation, heaven, and the divine at the Eliot-Pearson Children's School, a lab school at Tufts University in Medford, Massachusetts. The Children's School is an inclusion model early childhood center serving 3-year-olds through second-graders. (At the time of the project, Ben was

the kindergarten room's lead teacher. Mona, then a doctoral student in child development, consulted on the project.)

The article is organized around five questions readers may have about the project:

- Why was this project undertaken?
- What did the project involve?
- What did the parents say?
- What did the teachers learn?
- What did the children learn?

Our answers explain why we explored this unusual—and we suspect in many places, taboo—topic, and why we believe teachers should recognize and support children's learning about spirituality, beliefs, and religion.

## Why Was This Project Undertaken?

The children's expressed interest led us to a study of beliefs. We were reluctant to undertake this project, unsure about opening up such a potentially controversial subject. This experience has led us to believe that in order to raise citizens who can navigate and contribute to our religiously diverse world, early childhood educators must create safe spaces for children to explore spirituality and differing beliefs (Baumgartner & Buchanan 2010).

In their play and conversations, the kindergartners demonstrated a strong interest in spiritual matters (for example, the conversation between Max, Emily, and Robert). While we noted this interest from the start of the year, we initially made no effort to integrate it into the curriculum. Midway through the year, several children asked directly to study God. The success of the ensuing God Study Group (four children who met for six weeks to pursue this interest) convinced us that it was possible to study beliefs with kindergartners.

It is not just our kindergarten students who are interested in spiritual matters. Many young children are particularly curious about beliefs, making frequent reference to topics with religious and spiritual implications (Coles 1990). Because early childhood is the genesis of knowledge about and dispositions toward differences, it is a good time for guided explorations of different beliefs that can help children develop healthy attitudes toward others and themselves.

---

**Many young children are particularly curious about beliefs, making frequent reference to topics with religious and spiritual implications.**

---

Curricula on religion are supported from multiple perspectives. From an academic perspective, religion is a central component of social studies. From an interfaith perspective, leaders from faith traditions have collaborated to find common ground to guide religiously inclusive school policies, practices, and curricula (Haynes, Thomas, & Ferguson 2007). From the social justice perspective, religion and religious pluralism are essential elements of an anti-bias approach. Hence the wisdom of the NAEYC Early Childhood Program Standards and Accreditation Criteria that call for the acknowledgment and discussion of different beliefs in early childhood settings (NAEYC 2007, criteria 1.A.02, 2.L.03, 7.A.02).

The National Council for the Social Studies explains, "Knowledge about religions is not only characteristic of an educated person, but is also absolutely necessary for understanding and living in a world of diversity" (Haynes, Thomas, & Ferguson 2007, 44). While the study of specific world religions generally occurs in middle and high school, developing the disposition of tolerance is a task for early childhood education. This is particularly important in the United States, the world's most religiously diverse nation (Eck 2002). To help our youngest citizens appreciate and understand one another, we should provide safe places for them to explore spiritual beliefs and differences.

## What Did the Project Involve?

During the final two months of the school year, our kindergarten curriculum focuses on one topic that all the children explore together (to view one such capstone project, see "An Example of a Developmentally Appropriate Kindergarten Study" on the CD-ROM that accompanies the third edition of *Developmentally Appropriate Practice* [Copple & Bredekamp 2009]). To guide this project, we use the tool of documentation to listen carefully to children's interests, ideas, and level of engagement to fashion developmentally appropriate activities (Katz & Chard 1989; Mardell 1999; Project Zero & Reggio Children 2000). Children generate questions, solve problems, and create collective products, participating in the "whole game of learning" (Perkins 2009).

The Beliefs Project began with children drawing pictures of their theories and questions (for example, Robert asked, "Why can you not see God? 'Cause God made something, but he doesn't have hands. It's just clear. So who made the first people on the earth? God?"). The children and teachers then discussed these theories and questions among ourselves, interviewed members of the school community and local experts (including a priest, imam, rabbi, and an atheist philosopher) about their beliefs, listened to and then discussed music with spiritual significance, and transformed the dramatic play area into some children's vision of heaven. The children shared what they had learned with their families and school community by each contributing a piece to a class puzzle and describing the piece in a short video.

---

**To help our youngest citizens appreciate and understand one another, we should provide safe places for them to explore spiritual beliefs and differences.**

---

To provide a detailed picture of our teaching practices, we focus on how the children turned the dramatic play area into heaven. The impetus to transform dramatic play had several sources. Play is a core resource for young children's learning (Carlsson-Paige 2008), and for the first few weeks of the Beliefs Project, we had been wondering how to access play to support the children's explorations. At the same time, looking over video and observation notes, we realized that two children with language delays had been having difficulty participating in conversations. These two children were wonderful and committed players, so dramatic play seemed an obvious way to help them engage in the inquiry. And all the children were interested in heaven. In their conversations, questions, and drawings, heaven appeared again and again.

So we invited the children to create their vision of heaven. The process took a week and involved intentionally choreographing individual, small group, and whole class activities. To begin, six children (including the two with language delays) chose to draw their ideas of heaven during exploration time. After a review of the diverse ideas about heaven that the class had encountered, the children drew and chatted for 40 minutes. This in-depth experience helped the children with language difficulties articulate their ideas. As one explained, "I'm making it beautiful. My friend told me how heaven looks."

Children then shared their ideas with their classmates:

**Larissa:** This is the stairs to get up, and here's a little slide, and you can lie down. And the curtains aren't finished.

**Caroline:** I think a heart would be the center of heaven.

**Emily:** I think heaven is a planet like Earth, but you can only go when you are dead. Some people think God is perfect, but if God is perfect, why are there wars? I think there is a good god and a bad god and they fight. And sometimes one wins and sometimes the other wins. I think heaven is nice because you should have what you want when you die. To get into heaven you climb in and slide down, like a playground. Stairs are narrow and hard to get up, so you have to be dead to go. If you're dead, you can slide up.

The next day another group convened. The teacher shared the drawings and comments from the previous day to launch plans for dramatic play. The children built on the playground idea, deciding to add swings. Perhaps because of an association with hearts, it was suggested that there be a lot of red. The group captured their ideas in a collective drawing, which they shared with the whole group to get feedback. The reaction was generally positive, and additional ideas were provided (for example, the need for clouds).

Work days followed. While children could come and go as they chose, the high level of engagement with the project was clear when four children asked to stay inside during recess to work on the dramatic play area. After three intensive days of construction, heaven was opened for play. It was a very popular destination.

---

**After three intensive days of construction, heaven was opened for play. It was a very popular destination.**

---

## What Did the Families Say?

The parents were critical allies during the Beliefs Project. They encouraged us to pursue this inquiry, shared conversations they were having with their children, and made pivotal suggestions about the project. This is not surprising. Spiritual questions—religious and nonreligious—occupy a significant part of many adults' thoughts. Families embraced the opportunity to engage in something so important to their children's education. Of course, smooth sailing through such an emotionally charged topic was not guaranteed. The positive outcome we enjoyed was the result of efforts to respect and include all the families' beliefs, and the overall culture of the school.

The teaching team invited families to participate in the project even before its inception. As we considered undertaking this inquiry, we sent out information about our intentions and invited feedback. While generally supportive, parents asked to be kept informed and expressed the desire that certain points of view be represented. During the project we issued weekly newsletters and kept a binder that charted daily activities. Parents were invited to join us in our conversations with a local priest, rabbi, imam, and philosopher, and we held several meetings to discuss the directions of the project.

At one of these meetings a family raised a concern that the curriculum's name (originally the God Project) was not inclusive; although all families have a belief system, not all of these include a belief in God or a higher being. We acknowledged this concern, and brought it to the children. They unanimously concluded that it would be important to rename the project (to the Beliefs Project) so that no one would feel left out.

Family involvement in the project reflected the level of parent involvement in the school generally and the positive regard for diversity. As one mother reflected, "Eliot-Pearson already has a whole culture of being able to talk about differences. . . . It was very comfortable for children, for parents, [and] for teachers to move into this kind of conversation, to push the frontier a little further. Because we were already so comfortable talking about [differences]."

Of course, it is conceivable that in other contexts families may be opposed to such a project. In such a situation, we recommend working to understand the nature of the opposition, explaining the goals of the project (to further a tolerance of different beliefs, not to teach specific beliefs), and explaining the importance of children participating in such experiences.

At a reunion of the families one year after the project was completed, parents indicated that they could not have imagined such public conversations about religious differences, because they had been raised at a time when such discussions were taboo. They were delighted their children were freed from this restriction. They marveled at young children's ability to engage in deep conversations about religion and beliefs. And they appreciated the potential long-term impact of the project.

## What Did the Teachers Learn?

We learned that young children can engage in authentic and civil discussions about beliefs. These kindergartners were curious about their classmates' beliefs. They listened attentively to the views of members of our extended community. They enjoyed trying to make sense of questions that have perplexed humanity from the beginning of time. And we learned that allowing for such conversations in the classroom can help build connections between home and school.

We now believe that early childhood educators need to be proactive and intentional in incorporating issues of religious diversity into classrooms. Here, our foremost advice is to listen. We suspect that conversations that touch on religious and spiritual matters occur in classrooms with more frequency than many adults think. Teachers can model interest and tolerance, provide information about the images and practices that children encounter (for example, the Madonna statue in the yard across from the school playground or why Younnis is going to be absent from school for Eid), and help clarify misconceptions about others' beliefs.

---

**Teachers can model interest and tolerance, provide information about the images and practices that children encounter, and help clarify misconceptions about others' beliefs.**

---

Just as teachers include experiences about cultural and racial diversity in formal curricula, teachers should consider bringing differences in beliefs into classroom conversations. The objective is to support children's explorations of their own questions and learn about the perspectives of others. Listening will alert teachers to the specific interests of their students.

We acknowledge that some teachers may face greater opposition, receive less support, and feel less comfortable in discussing beliefs with young children. Not everyone will feel prepared in undertaking curriculum units on beliefs. Nevertheless, we believe that these conversations should occur in all early childhood settings. As with other anti-bias topics, tolerance about differences in beliefs is an essential disposition for all children. Teachers should encourage children to ask questions about, discuss, and explore different beliefs whether they attend public or private, secular or religious schools. Parents, teachers, and administrators should discuss a range of developmentally appropriate ways to support open and curious attitudes toward different beliefs and the people who hold them.

---

**As with other anti-bias topics, tolerance about differences in beliefs is an essential disposition for all children.**

---

## What Did the Children Learn?

When children are deeply engaged in a topic, they learn in many directions at once (Project Zero & Reggio Children 2000). Participation in the Beliefs Project promoted the children's problem-solving and critical-thinking abilities. It provided authentic experiences in using books and technology to gain information, in discussing and presenting ideas in a group, and in using drawing and writing to express ideas. In Massachusetts, these are among the language arts curriculum standards for kindergarten (Massachusetts Department of Education 2001).

To conclude the project we helped the children create a video. Each child contributed a drawing of a puzzle piece with a verbal explanation of their thinking about beliefs. Some children discussed heaven while others focused on the big bang. Regardless of the topic, each child demonstrated a high level of commitment to producing quality work. The children drew several drafts, using peer feedback to improve their drawings, and embraced the challenge of explaining their beliefs. For example, one of the children who had difficulty with expressive language explained, "I believe in heaven and God lives in my heart. He acts for all of the children, and all of our prayers. And all the animals and all the earth. We have to go to God." Interestingly, despite this striking amount of verbal output, the child expressed dissatisfaction, saying she had not explained all she wanted to. I comforted her, noting that beliefs are something that people think and learn about for their entire lives.

The children also learned tolerance. At the conclusion of the project, we asked the children what they had learned. Larissa answered, "There are many different beliefs in this school and even more beliefs in the world." Caroline expressed her enjoyment of the study, explaining, "All of the ideas together, it looked nice for Dramatic Play Heaven. I just feel like I'm having a party of everyone's beliefs." Max picked up on this idea, saying, "It's something like Caroline's. It's like a big party of beliefs." Having disagreed sharply with Emily about the genesis of people several months earlier, Max now explained, "The fun thing about studying different beliefs is that they are different."

## References

Baumgartner, J.J., & T. Buchanan. 2010. Supporting each child's spirit. *Young Children* (65) 2: 90–95.

Carlsson-Paige, N. 2008. *Taking back childhood: Helping your kids thrive in a fast-paced, media-saturated, violence-filled world.* New York, NY: Penguin.

Coles, R. 1990. *The spiritual life of children.* Boston, MA: Houghton Mifflin.

Copple, C., & S. Bredekamp, eds. 2009. *Developmentally appropriate practice in early childhood programs serving children from birth through age 8.* 3rd ed. Washington, DC: NAEYC.

Derman-Sparks, L., & J.O. Edwards. 2010. *Anti-bias education for young children and ourselves.* Washington, DC: NAEYC.

Eck, D.L. 2002. *A new religious America: How a "Christian country" has become the world's most religiously diverse nation.* San Francisco, CA: HarperOne.

Haynes, C.C., O. Thomas, & J. Ferguson, eds. 2007. *Finding common ground: A First Amendment guide to religion and public education.* Nashville, TN: First Amendment Center.

Katz, L., & S. Chard. 1989. *Engaging children's minds: The project approach.* Norwood, NJ: Ablex.

Mardell, B. 1999. *From basketball to the Beatles: In search of compelling early childhood curriculum.* Portsmouth, NH: Heinemann.

Massachusetts Department of Education. 2001. English language arts curriculum frameworks. www.doe.mass/edu/frameworks/ela/0601.pdf

NAEYC. 2007. *NAEYC Early Childhood Program Standards and Accreditation Criteria: The mark of quality in early childhood education.* Rev. ed. Washinhton, DC: Author. www.naeyc.org/torch

Perkins, D. 2009. *Making learning whole: How seven principles of teaching can transform education.* San Francisco: Jossey-Bass.

Project Zero & Reggio Children. 2000. *Making learning visible: Children as individual and group learners.* Reggio Emilia, Italy: Reggio Children.

## Critical Thinking

1. How can discussions about spirituality between children help children understand differences between people and create a more "inclusive" school environment?

2. Given the experiences described in this article, what are some benefits that parents and teachers might find through having civil and constructive discussions about young children's beliefs?

---

**BEN MARDELL**, PhD, is a researcher at Project Zero at the Harvard Graduate School of Education and an associate professor of early childhood education at Lesley University, in Cambridge, Massachusetts. He has taught infants, toddlers, preschoolers, and kindergartners. bmardell@lesley.edu. **MONA M. ABO-ZENA**, PhD, is a research associate at the Eliot-Pearson Department of Child Development at Tufts University. She has more than 15 years of teaching, administrative, and board experience in public and religious schools.

---

# UNIT 3
# Social and Emotional Development

## Unit Selections

## Learning Outcomes

- Explain to parents and teachers the value of helping their children develop self-control.

- Explain how childhood self-control would influence later outcomes. Describe the processes or mechanisms that link the two.

- Argue that morality can be understood as both hard-wired and socially conditioned without contradiction.

- Reevaluate prevalent claims about cognitive abilities (or lack thereof) in infants. Explain to teachers and principals how their behavior may contribute to some children being marginalized, and describe to them what steps they could take to prevent and intervene in cases of peer rejection.

- Argue that children's education could be enhanced by including mindfulness or contemplative practices in the school day.

- Design a creative product—design a puppet show, or write a simple children's book, or write song lyrics—to help children understand how their behavior can lead to peer rejection and how they might change their behavior.

- Parents ask you if their child, a withdrawn, shy girl, is going to do well at child care. Explain to them what the research shows about temperament and child care.

- You're asked to give a talk to parents of young children about child care, and you soon learn that they all think development is purely "nurture." Describe specific processes involving stress hormones, brain functions, and other biological processes that help them understand the key role of nature in children's adaptation to child care.

- Evaluate and assess the extent to which genes and the environment influence the development and maintenance of antisocial behavior in children. Based on this article, support your arguments with evidence and information involving early biological factors and the neurobiological stress response systems (e.g., early physical adversity such as birth complications, temperament, lower resting stress levels, stronger negative response reactivity, and higher sensation-seeking behavior). Explain how social and environmental factors also can exacerbate or mediate these more biological factors.

- Summarize and recommend interventions that may help reduce antisocial behavior in children. Cite supportive evidence on the efficacy of the various interventions.

- Recommend possible changes in medical practice or training that would assist physicians and child specialists in better diagnosing and treating children with antisocial behavior, conduct disorder, or oppositional defiant disorder.

- Explain how culture is important in children's peer relationships.

- Describe how the impact of peer relationships on children's socioemotional development is mediated or partly explained by culture.

- Argue to a religious conservative, who believes that homosexuality is a choice, that there is a strong genetic and biological basis for sexual orientation.

- Recommend to teachers and caregivers of young children how they can help children develop empathy and prosocial behavior.

## Student Website

www.mhhe.com/cls

## Internet References

**Max Planck Institute for Psychological Research**
www.mpg.de/english/institutesProjectsFacilities/instituteChoice/psychologische_forschung
**National Child Care Information Center (NCCIC)**
www.nccic.org
**Serendip**
http://serendip.brynmawr.edu/serendip

One of the truisms about our species is that we are social animals. From birth, each person's life is a constellation of relationships, from family at home to friends in the neighborhood and school. This unit addresses how children's social and emotional development is influenced by important relationships with parents, peers, and teachers.

When John Donne in 1623 wrote, "No man is an island, entire of itself . . . any man's death diminishes me, because I am involved in mankind," he implied that all humans are connected to each other and that these connections make us who we are. Early in this century, sociologist C. H. Cooley highlighted the importance of relationships with the phrase "looking-glass self" to describe how people tend to see themselves as a function of how others perceive them. Personality theorist Alfred Adler, also writing in the early twentieth century, claimed that personal strength derived from the quality of one's connectedness to others: The stronger the relationships, the stronger the person. The notion that a person's self-concept arises from relations with others also has roots in developmental psychology. As Jean Piaget once wrote, "There is no such thing as isolated individuals; there are only relations." The articles in this unit respect these traditions by emphasizing the theme that a child's development occurs within the context of relationships.

Unfortunately, a variety of genetic and environmental factors may affect infants who will suffer negative outcomes in later childhood and even adulthood. In "The Role of Neurobiological Deficits in Childhood Antisocial Behavior" researchers discuss childhood depression and identify risk factors such as specific neurobiological deficits that combined with early adverse environments can contribute to antisocial behavior, conduct disorders and oppositional defiant disorders in early childhood and interventions that may be effective for these children. Similarly, the author of "Don't!: The Secret of Self-Control" writes about the research showing how children's ability to moderate and control themselves develops during early childhood.

Individual differences in children's temperaments and reactivity may also play a role in how they adjust to environments including child care. Noted researchers Phillips, Fox, and Gunnar review the evidence on child outcomes in the article, "Same Place, Different Experiences: Bringing Individual Differences to Research in Child Care."

A significant milestone of early childhood involves a child's ability to socialize, communicate and play effectively with peers. The

(c) Bananastock

articles, "Culture, Peer Interaction, and Socioemotional Development," and "Caring About Caring: What Adults Can Do to Promote Young Children's Prosocial Skills" point to the importance of encouraging children to engage in contemplative behaviors such as mindfulness, as well understanding how culture and healthy peer interaction shapes children's socioemotional well-being and how adults and teachers can serve as models of caring and prosocial behavior for children.

Another major influence in the landscape of childhood is friendship. When do childhood friendships begin? Friends become increasingly important during the elementary school years. If forming strong, secure attachments with family members is an important task of early childhood, then one of the major psychological achievements of middle childhood is a move toward the peer group.

Some parents will become alarmed when their son shows pronounced interest in girls' dolls or when their young daughter prefers to wear only boys' clothing and behaves like a tomboy. Should these parents worry? In "Is Your Child Gay?" author Jesse Bering reviews a few new studies that may shed light on how gender nonconforming play behavior in young children may be linked to later sexual orientation preferences in adults.

# Young Children Enforce Social Norms

Marco F. H. Schmidt and Michael Tomasello

Human societies are organized very differently from those of other primates. Most prominently, human societies structure many of their activities via cooperative institutional arrangements, which are created by "agreement" for a common purpose and in which individuals play well-defined roles with prespecified rights and obligations. These range from relatively simple institutions, such as marriage, to highly complex institutions, such as the governments of modern industrialized nations.

The glue of human societies and their institutions is social norms, which seem to be unique to humans. That is to say, what holds these cooperative social arrangements together is individual humans' tendency to do things the way that others in the group do them—indeed, in the way they are *expected* by others in the group to do them (Chudek & Henrich, 2011). Social norms do not derive their binding power from brute physical force but rather from the mutual expectations within the social group to which each individual, at least implicitly, *agrees* to bind himself or herself—so that they apply generally to all who so agree.

## Types of Social Norms

The prototypes of social norms are *moral norms*. As Nichols (2004) has argued, moral norms derive much of their normative influence on human behavior from the fact that, to some degree, they are in line with humans' natural aversion to harming others and natural attraction to helping others (see Warneken & Tomasello, 2009, for a review). Thus, with no other motivations in play, moral norms for helping others and against inflicting harm on others serve to reinforce already existing values. But what additional force is added by the norms?

That norms do indeed supply additional force is clear from the fact that people follow not only moral norms but also "arbitrary" *conventional norms* whose violation would involve no direct harm or victimization (Turiel, 1983)—norms concerning such things as the appropriate clothing for a funeral (but see Kelly, Stich, Haley, Eng, & Fessler, 2007, for a critique of the moral/conventional distinction). Our motivation to conform to conventional norms stems at least partly from not wanting to be disapproved of, or punished, by others. But it also stems partly from our desire to belong (to the group), and to conform and do things the "right" way. Preschool children already know the difference between a statistical norm (e.g., people don't wear blue jeans to bed) and a true social norm

(e.g., people don't wear blue jeans to funerals), and in new situations they want to know such things as "Where do we hang our coats?" and "Where should I sit?" (Kalish, 1998; Kalish & Cornelius, 2007).

There is a less-noted, specific type of conventional norm that works somewhat differently. Whereas moral norms and many conventional norms regulate already existing activities (typically in cooperative ways), *constitutive norms* to some degree actually create new social realities, typically in the form of "X counts as Y in context C" (Searle, 1995). For example, although individuals mate and have children in any case, the institution of marriage creates institutional roles with deontic powers. Thus, a father legitimated by the institution of marriage is empowered by society to make life-and-death decisions for his children. Police legitimated by the "consent of the governed"—a political notion advocated by the philosophers John Locke (1690/1988) and Jean-Jacques Rousseau (1762/1997)—are entitled to do all kinds of things that would not be tolerated if they were done by private individuals.

Particularly clear cases of constitutive norms are provided by rule games, in which violating a norm—for example, moving a pawn backward in a game of chess—is not just failing to follow a convention (though it is that) but is not playing the game "we" agreed upon at all. Wearing a tattered T-shirt to a funeral is reprehensible, but moving a pawn backward in the game of chess is simply not playing chess.

## Children's Understanding and Enforcement of Social Norms

The vast majority of work on social norms in children has focused on moral and, to a lesser degree, conventional norms and on the question of why young children respect and follow them. Piaget (1932) noted that children initially follow moral norms out of respect for the authority of adults and older children. However, in the same book, Piaget also reported studies of Swiss children's application and understanding of rules in games of marbles, arguing that regardless of whether the rules of marbles strike adults as "moral," they instantiate the fundamental process of rule acquisition and following: "The rules of the game of marbles are handed down, just like so-called moral realities, from one generation to another, and are preserved solely by the respect that is felt for them by individuals" (p. 2). However, as children become older (by about 7 to 12 years of age), their respect for the rules of the game is derived less from authority and more from the fact that they have autonomously agreed to abide by them; thus, there is a kind of reciprocity and mutual respect among players (this is what evolutionists often call *contingent reciprocity:* I agree to cooperate if everyone else does also).

Recently, we have been engaged in a line of research focused on children's understanding of the norms governing simple rule games. Our question is at what point young children stop thinking of games' rules as immutable dictates handed down from powerful authorities and begin thinking of them as something like agreements into which they have entered. To investigate this question, we have focused on a novel aspect of the ontogeny of social norms. Beginning at around 3 years of age, young children do not just follow social norms but actively enforce them on others—even from a third-party stance, in situations in which they themselves are not directly involved or affected. Although there are many prudential reasons for following social norms, it is not immediately clear why a 3-year-old child should feel compelled to actually enforce them on others. Such group-oriented behavior opens the possibility that young children are not merely driven by individualistic motives but that, from early on, they start to identify with their cultural group, which leads to prosocial motives for preserving the group's ways of doing things.

The first study was reported by Rakoczy, Warneken, and Tomasello (2008). In this study, 2- and 3-year-old children watched as a puppet announced that she would now "dax." But then she performed a different action than the one the children had previously seen an adult performing and calling "daxing." Many children objected in some way (whereas they did not object if the puppet performed the same action without calling it "daxing"); importantly, in doing so, the 3-year-olds reliably used normative language such as "It doesn't work like that. You have to do it like this." These utterances demonstrated that the children were not just objecting to the puppet's actions because they personally did not like them or because they objected to the puppet as an individual, but rather because what the puppet was doing not the way the action *should* be performed by anyone (a generic, normative assessment). And they were not just objecting to the fact that the puppet did not perform the action she said she would: Rakoczy, Brosche, Warneken, and Tomasello (2009) obtained the same results with a nonverbal indication of the game context (i.e., indication that an action X is appropriate when performed on this table, but not when performed on that table).

It is worth noting that the rule games involved in these studies were solitary activities; playing them incorrectly did not disrupt the game for any other players. So why did children object and correct the puppet? Why should children care about deviations from norms if no one is harmed by them? We do not know the answer to this question, but in two recent studies, children of about the same age behaved very similarly—they objected, using normative language—when a puppet violated a moral norm against harm (i.e., by destroying another person's picture; Vaish, Missana, & Tomasello, 2011) or a norm against infringements on property rights (Rossano, Rakoczy,

& Tomasello, 2011). Children's reactions to violations of rule games thus appear to be quite similar, both quantitatively and qualitatively, to their reactions to violations of moral norms that cause actual harm—which is a bit puzzling. Critically, however, children do differentiate these two types of norms: Schmidt, Rakoczy, and Tomasello (in press) found that whereas young children enforce moral norms equally on all violators, they enforce game norms only on members of their own cultural in-group (e.g., people who speak the same language)—presumably because only "we" fall within the scope of the norm and can be expected to respect it.

Another key question is where the generality of these norms comes from. Csibra and Gergely (2009) have hypothesized that natural pedagogy is an evolved cognitive system whereby children, when they recognize that they are being taught something, automatically jump to the conclusion that it is generic information about the way things work (instead of nongeneralizable information about specific things, e.g., personal preferences). In the studies concerning children's game rules, an adult always explicitly taught the children how the game was played. However, in a recent study by Schmidt, Rakoczy, and Tomasello (2011), there was no pedagogy (or adult normative language) involved. Nevertheless, when 3-year-old children saw a puppet interact with a novel artifact in a way that differed from the way they had just seen an adult interacting with it (she immediately recognized it and acted on it confidently), they again corrected the wayward puppet, again quite often using normative language, which they did not do if the adult had previously interacted with the artifact in only an exploratory way, as if it were novel for her. Young children thus do not need explicit instructions or communication from adults (which is indeed less common in traditional societies; Lancy, 1996), or any other kind of special marking from adults, to see an action as socially normative; they just need to see that adults apparently expect things to work a certain way (see Casler, Terziyan, & Greene, 2009, for observations of children protesting against third parties for using artifacts in nonconventional ways).

It is difficult to interpret these findings as being compatible with the idea that children see game rules and other constitutive norms as somehow essentialistic (i.e., unalterable and immutable) features of the external world. They apply them only in appropriate contexts and only to the appropriate social group (and can apply them without adult teaching). Another line of research has undermined the essentialistic interpretation even further. Rakoczy (2008) and Wyman, Rakoczy, and Tomasello (2009) looked at children's understanding of constitutive norms used in the special context of games of pretense. Three-year-old children again objected—in much the same way as in the other studies involving game rules—when a puppet used a wooden block as a pretend sandwich, because the child and an adult had previously designated this block as pretend soap ("No, you can't eat that. It's soap!"). When the same block was later designated as a sandwich in a different game, children objected if it was used as soap.

These studies demonstrate with special clarity that young children can, at least in pretense, understand that the way a game is played is, in a sense, an "agreement" that can be changed, not something written in stone. In addition, it is worth noting that this ability to socially designate a wooden block as a sandwich—and then treat it as such in subsequent actions—may be seen as a forerunner of humans' astounding ability to accord to otherwise unremarkable objects and people special cultural statuses (e.g., paper as money and persons as presidents) based only on "agreement" (Searle, 1995). Pretend play of this type may thus be seen as the cradle of humans' understanding of institutional reality (Rakoczy & Tomasello, 2007).

## Social Norms as Shared Intentionality

Everyone knows that children follow social norms, but they also, from about 3 years of age, enforce them. One could already argue from this basic fact that children do not view social norms as part of the essential structure of external reality, in which case they would not need enforcing by mere mortals. So it is possible that children are not really enforcing social norms after all but only mimicking their parents—but that merely pushes the question back to why the parents are enforcing them in the first place. Imitation has to stop somewhere, so it does not help us with the question of origins. Moreover, in the modern understanding of social learning, children imitate only what they in some sense understand (e.g., Tomasello, Kruger, & Ratner, 1993). If children see a parent enforcing a norm, and if they then want to do the "same thing" in a novel context, they must understand what the adult is objecting to—not a specific behavior but rather the violation of a norm—which implies some understanding of norms.

Instead, we think that the experimental findings suggest something like the following explanation. When children begin to identify with their cultural group—which more and more research is showing happens at a very young age, based on such things as linguistic accent and common clothing (e.g., Kinzler, Dupoux, & Spelke, 2007)—they understand that part of this group identification is that "we" do things in certain ways. Gilbert (1989) argued that when someone wants to be a member of a group, they, in essence, jointly accept the social norms that the members of the group commit themselves to, which naturally includes upholding the norms when others in the group violate them (see Gräfenhain, Behne, Carpenter, & Tomasello, 2009). And so, our proposal is that enforcing norms is an integral part of becoming a member of a cultural group, given individuals' evolved skills and motivations for shared intentionality and group identification (Tomasello, Carpenter, Call, Behne, & Moll, 2005; Tomasello, Melis, Tennie, Wyman, & Herrmann, in press). Later in development, these same skills and motivations enable children to participate more fully in, and perhaps even contribute to, the institutional reality of their culture.

The evolution of human cooperation has been made possible by people's tendency both to follow social norms and also to enforce them—and, indeed, to regulate individual behavior by internalizing group norms and applying them to the self in acts of guilt and shame (Boyd & Richerson, 2006). People may follow social norms for external reasons (e.g., to avoid sanctions), but people's enforcement of social norms suggests some kind of

prosocial motivation toward, or identification with, their group and its lifeways, and a motivation to preserve them—a kind of group-mindedness. The fact that young children enforce social norms suggests that they are already participating in this collective intentionality.

## Recommended Reading

Boyd, R., & Richerson, P. J. (2006). (See References). A theoretical account of how cultural evolution paved the way for the adaptiveness of social instincts.

Piaget, J. (1932). (See References). A historical classic that started the investigation of young children's understanding of social norms.

Rakoczy, H., Warneken, F., & Tomasello, M. (2008). (See References). A paper presenting the first studies to investigate young children's understanding of social norms (via norm enforcement), using the new methodology of spontaneous protest.

Searle, J. R. (1995). (See References). A philosophical account of the ontology of social facts and institutions such as social norms.

Tomasello, M., Carpenter, M., Call, J., Behne, T., & Moll, H. (2005). (See References). A theoretical account of how skills and motivations for shared intentionality manifest themselves during human development.

## References

Boyd, R., & Richerson, P. J. (2006). Culture and the evolution of the human social instincts. In N. Enfield & S. Levinson (Eds.), *Roots of human sociality: Culture, cognition, and interaction* (pp. 453–477). Oxford, England: Berg.

Casler, K., Terziyan, T., & Greene, K. (2009). Toddlers view artifact function normatively. *Cognitive Development, 24,* 240–247. doi:10.1016/j.cogdev.2009.03.005

Chudek, M., & Henrich, J. (2011). Culture–gene coevolution, norm-psychology and the emergence of human prosociality. *Trends in Cognitive Sciences, 15,* 218–226. doi:10.1016/j.tics.2011.03.003

Csibra, G., & Gergely, G. (2009). Natural pedagogy. *Trends in Cognitive Sciences, 13,* 148–153. doi:10.1016/j.tics.2009.01.005

Gilbert, M. (1989). *On social facts.* London, England: Routledge.

Gräfenhain, M., Behne, T., Carpenter, M., & Tomasello, M. (2009). Young children's understanding of joint commitments to act jointly. *Developmental Psychology, 45,* 1430–1443. doi:10.1037/a0016122

Kalish, C. W. (1998). Reasons and causes: Children's understanding of conformity to social rules and physical laws. *Child Development, 69,* 706–720.

Kalish, C. W., & Cornelius, R. (2007). What is to be done? Children's ascriptions of conventional obligations. *Child Development, 78,* 859–878.

Kelly, D., Stich, S., Haley, K. J., Eng, S. J., & Fessler, D. M. T. (2007). Harm, affect, and the moral/conventional distinction. *Mind & Language, 22,* 117–131. doi:10.1111/j.1468-0017.2007.00302.x

Kinzler, K. D., Dupoux, E., & Spelke, E. S. (2007). The native language of social cognition. *Proceedings of the National Academy of Sciences, USA, 104,* 12577–12580. doi:10.1073/pnas.0705345104

Lancy, D. F. (1996). *Playing on the mother-ground: Cultural routines for children's development.* New York, NY: Guilford Press.

Locke, J. (1988). *Two treatises of government* (3rd ed., P. Laslett, Ed.). Cambridge, England: Cambridge University Press. (Original work published 1690)

Nichols, S. (2004). *Sentimental rules: On the natural foundations of moral judgment.* Oxford, England: Oxford University Press.

Piaget, J. (1932). *The moral judgment of the child.* London, England: Routledge Kegan Paul.

Rakoczy, H. (2008). Taking fiction seriously: Young children understand the normative structure of joint pretence games. *Developmental Psychology, 44,* 1195–1201. doi:10.1037/0012-1649.44.4.1195

Rakoczy, H., Brosche, N., Warneken, F., & Tomasello, M. (2009). Young children's understanding of the context relativity of normative rules in conventional games. *British Journal of Developmental Psychology, 27,* 445–456.

Rakoczy, H., & Tomasello, M. (2007). The ontogeny of social ontology: Steps to shared intentionality and status functions. In S. L. Tsohatzidis (Ed.), *Intentional acts and institutional facts: Essays on John Searle's social ontology* (pp. 113–137). Berlin, Germany: Springer-Verlag.

Rakoczy, H., Warneken, F., & Tomasello, M. (2008). The sources of normativity: Young children's awareness of the normative structure of games. *Developmental Psychology, 44,* 875–881.

Rossano, F., Rakoczy, H., & Tomasello, M. (2011). Young children's understanding of violations of property rights. *Cognition, 121,* 219–227. doi:10.1016/j.cognition.2011.06.007

Rousseau, J. J. (1997). *The Social Contract and other later political writings* (V. Gourevitch, Ed.). Cambridge, England: Cambridge University Press. (Original work published 1762)

Schmidt, M. F. H., Rakoczy, H., & Tomasello, M. (2011). Young children attribute normativity to novel actions without pedagogy or normative language. *Developmental Science, 14,* 530–539. doi:10.1111/j.1467-7687.2010.01000.x

Schmidt, M. F. H., Rakoczy, H., & Tomasello, M. (in press). Young children enforce social norms selectively depending on the violator's group affiliation. *Cognition.*

Searle, J. R. (1995). *The construction of social reality.* New York, NY: Free Press.

Tomasello, M., Carpenter, M., Call, J., Behne, T., & Moll, H. (2005). Understanding and sharing intentions: The origins of cultural cognition. *Behavioral and Brain Sciences, 28,* 675–691. doi:10.1017/S0140525X05000129

Tomasello, M., Kruger, A. C., & Ratner, H. H. (1993). Cultural learning. *Behavioral and Brain Sciences, 16,* 495–552.

Tomasello, M., Melis, A. P., Tennie, C., Wyman, E., & Herrmann, E. (in press). Two key steps in the evolution of human cooperation: The interdependence hypothesis. *Current Anthropology.*

Turiel, E. (1983). *The development of social knowledge: Morality and convention.* Cambridge, England: Cambridge University Press.

Vaish, A., Missana, M., & Tomasello, M. (2011). Three-year-old children intervene in third-party moral transgressions. *British Journal of Developmental Psychology, 29,* 124–130. doi:10.1348/026151010X532888

Warneken, F., & Tomasello, M. (2009). Varieties of altruism in children and chimpanzees. *Trends in Cognitive Sciences, 13,* 397–402. doi:10.1016/j.tics.2009.06.008

Wyman, E., Rakoczy, H., & Tomasello, M. (2009). Normativity and context in young children's pretend play. *Cognitive Development, 24,* 146–155. doi:10.1016/j.cogdev.2009.01.003

# Critical Thinking

1. How does this article help you understand children's acquisition of social norms? Because this article takes an evolutionary perspective, how do both nature and nurture affect social development?

2. What is the importance of feeling like a member of a group? How do children develop a sense of collective intentionality?

3. Why would it be surprising that children at such young ages would start to think of social norms and rules as shared agreements rather than as being handed down from authority figures?

**Marco F. H. Schmidt**, Department of Developmental and Comparative Psychology, Max Planck Institute for Evolutionary Anthropology, Deutscher Platz 6, 04103 Leipzig, Germany
E-mail: marco_schmidt@eva.mpg.de

From *Current Directions in Psychological Science,* vol. 21, no. 4, 2012, pp. 232–236. Copyright © 2012 by the Association for Psychological Science. Reprinted by permission of Sage Publications via Rightslink.

# Don't!
## *The Secret of Self-Control*

Children who are able to pass the marshmallow test enjoy greater success as adults.

JONAH LEHRER

In the late nineteen-sixties, Carolyn Weisz, a four-year-old with long brown hair, was invited into a "game room" at the Bing Nursery School, on the campus of Stanford University. The room was little more than a large closet, containing a desk and a chair. Carolyn was asked to sit down in the chair and pick a treat from a tray of marshmallows, cookies, and pretzel sticks. Carolyn chose the marshmallow. Although she's now forty-four, Carolyn still has a weakness for those air-puffed balls of corn syrup and gelatine. "I know I shouldn't like them," she says. "But they're just so delicious!" A researcher then made Carolyn an offer: she could either eat one marshmallow right away or, if she was willing to wait while he stepped out for a few minutes, she could have two marshmallows when he returned. He said that if she rang a bell on the desk while he was away he would come running back, and she could eat one marshmallow but would forfeit the second. Then he left the room.

Although Carolyn has no direct memory of the experiment, and the scientists would not release any information about the subjects, she strongly suspects that she was able to delay gratification. "I've always been really good at waiting," Carolyn told me. "If you give me a challenge or a task, then I'm going to find a way to do it, even if it means not eating my favorite food." Her mother, Karen Sortino, is still more certain: "Even as a young kid, Carolyn was very patient. I'm sure she would have waited." But her brother Craig, who also took part in the experiment, displayed less fortitude. Craig, a year older than Carolyn, still remembers the torment of trying to wait. "At a certain point, it must have occurred to me that I was all by myself," he recalls. "And so I just started taking all the candy." According to Craig, he was also tested with little plastic toys—he could have a second one if he held out—and he broke into the desk, where he figured there would be additional toys. "I took everything I could," he says. "I cleaned them out. After that, I noticed the teachers encouraged me to not go into the experiment room anymore."

Footage of these experiments, which were conducted over several years, is poignant, as the kids struggle to delay gratification for just a little bit longer. Some cover their eyes with their hands or turn around so that they can't see the tray. Others start kicking the desk, or tug on their pigtails, or stroke the marshmallow as if it were a tiny stuffed animal. One child, a boy with neatly parted hair, looks carefully around the room to make sure that nobody can see him. Then he picks up an Oreo, delicately twists it apart, and licks off the white cream filling before returning the cookie to the tray, a satisfied look on his face.

Most of the children were like Craig. They struggled to resist the treat and held out for an average of less than three minutes. "A few kids ate the marshmallow right away," Walter Mischel, the Stanford professor of psychology in charge of the experiment, remembers. "They didn't even bother ringing the bell. Other kids would stare directly at the marshmallow and then ring the bell thirty seconds later." About thirty percent of the children, however, were like Carolyn. They successfully delayed gratification until the researcher returned, some fifteen minutes later. These kids wrestled with temptation but found a way to resist.

The initial goal of the experiment was to identify the mental processes that allowed some people to delay gratification while others simply surrendered. After publishing a few papers on the Bing studies in the early seventies, Mischel moved on to other areas of personality research. "There are only so many things you can do with kids trying not to eat marshmallows."

But occasionally Mischel would ask his three daughters, all of whom attended the Bing, about their friends from nursery school. "It was really just idle dinnertime conversation," he says. "I'd ask them, 'How's Jane? How's Eric? How are they doing in school?'" Mischel began to notice a link between the children's academic performance as teen-agers and their ability to wait for the second marshmallow. He asked his daughters to assess their friends academically on a scale of zero to five. Comparing these ratings with the original data set, he saw a correlation. "That's when I realized I had to do this seriously," he says. Starting in 1981, Mischel sent out a questionnaire to all the reachable parents, teachers, and academic advisers of the six hundred and fifty-three subjects who had participated in the marshmallow task, who were by then in high school. He asked about every trait he could think of, from their capacity to plan and think ahead to their ability to "cope well with problems" and get along with their peers. He also requested their S.A.T. scores.

Once Mischel began analyzing the results, he noticed that low delayers, the children who rang the bell quickly, seemed more likely to have behavioral problems, both in school and at home. They got lower S.A.T. scores. They struggled in stressful situations, often had trouble paying attention, and found it difficult to maintain friendships. The child who could wait fifteen minutes had an S.A.T. score that was, on average, two hundred and ten points higher than that of the kid who could wait only thirty seconds.

Carolyn Weisz is a textbook example of a high delayer. She attended Stanford as an undergraduate, and got her PhD. in social psychology at Princeton. She's now an associate psychology professor at the University of Puget Sound. Craig, meanwhile, moved to Los Angeles and has spent his career doing "all kinds of things" in the entertainment industry, mostly in production. He's currently helping to write and produce a film. "Sure, I wish I had been a more patient person," Craig says. "Looking back, there are definitely moments when it would have helped me make better career choices and stuff."

Mischel and his colleagues continued to track the subjects into their late thirties—Ozlem Ayduk, an assistant professor of psychology at the University of California at Berkeley, found that low-delaying adults have a significantly higher body-mass index and are more likely to have had problems with drugs—but it was frustrating to have to rely on self-reports. "There's often a gap between what people are willing to tell you and how they behave in the real world," he explains. And so, last year, Mischel, who is now a professor at Columbia, and a team of collaborators began asking the original Bing subjects to travel to Stanford for a few days of experiments in an fMRI machine. Carolyn says she will be participating in the scanning experiments later this summer; Craig completed a survey several years ago, but has yet to be invited to Palo Alto. The scientists are hoping to identify the particular brain regions that allow some people to delay gratification and control their temper. They're also conducting a variety of genetic tests, as they search for the hereditary characteristics that influence the ability to wait for a second marshmallow.

If Mischel and his team succeed, they will have outlined the neural circuitry of self-control. For decades, psychologists have focussed on raw intelligence as the most important variable when it comes to predicting success in life. Mischel argues that intelligence is largely at the mercy of self-control: even the smartest kids still need to do their homework. "What we're really measuring with the marshmallows isn't will power or self-control," Mischel says. "It's much more important than that. This task forces kids to find a way to make the situation work for them. They want the second marshmallow, but how can they get it? We can't control the world, but we can control how we think about it."

Walter Mischel is a slight, elegant man with a shaved head and a face of deep creases. He talks with a Brooklyn bluster and he tends to act out his sentences, so that when he describes the marshmallow task he takes on the body language of an impatient four-year-old. "If you want to know why some kids can wait and others can't, then you've got to think like they think," Mischel says.

Mischel was born in Vienna, in 1930. His father was a modestly successful businessman with a fondness for café society and Esperanto, while his mother spent many of her days lying on the couch with an ice pack on her forehead, trying to soothe her frail nerves. The family considered itself fully assimilated, but after the Nazi annexation of Austria, in 1938, Mischel remembers being taunted in school by the Hitler Youth and watching as his father, hobbled by childhood polio, was forced to limp through the streets in his pajamas. A few weeks after the takeover, while the family was burning evidence of their Jewish ancestry in the fireplace, Walter found a long-forgotten certificate of U.S. citizenship issued to his maternal grandfather decades earlier, thus saving his family.

The family settled in Brooklyn, where Mischel's parents opened up a five-and-dime. Mischel attended New York University, studying poetry under Delmore Schwartz and Allen Tate, and taking studio-art classes with Philip Guston. He also became fascinated by psychoanalysis and new measures of personality, such as the Rorschach test. "At the time, it seemed like a mental X-ray machine," he says. "You could solve a person by showing them a picture." Although he was pressured to join his uncle's umbrella business, he ended up pursuing a PhD. in clinical psychology at Ohio State.

But Mischel noticed that academic theories had limited application, and he was struck by the futility of most personality science. He still flinches at the naïveté of graduate students who based their diagnoses on a battery of meaningless tests. In 1955, Mischel was offered an opportunity to study the "spirit possession" ceremonies of the Orisha faith in Trinidad, and he leapt at the chance. Although his research was supposed to involve the use of Rorschach tests to explore the connections between the unconscious and the behavior of people when possessed, Mischel soon grew interested in a different project. He lived in a part of the island that was evenly split between people of East Indian and of African descent; he noticed that each group defined the other in broad stereotypes. "The East Indians would describe the Africans as impulsive hedonists, who were always living for the moment and never thought about the future," he says. "The Africans, meanwhile, would say that the East Indians didn't know how to live and would stuff money in their mattress and never enjoy themselves."

Mischel took young children from both ethnic groups and offered them a simple choice: they could have a miniature chocolate bar right away or, if they waited a few days, they could get a much bigger chocolate bar. Mischel's results failed to justify the stereotypes—other variables, such as whether or not the children lived with their father, turned out to be much more important—but they did get him interested in the question of delayed gratification. Why did some children wait and not others? What made waiting possible? Unlike the broad traits supposedly assessed by personality tests, self-control struck Mischel as potentially measurable.

In 1958, Mischel became an assistant professor in the Department of Social Relations at Harvard. One of his first tasks was to develop a survey course on "personality assessment," but Mischel quickly concluded that, while prevailing theories held personality traits to be broadly consistent, the available data didn't back up this assumption. Personality, at least as it was then conceived, couldn't be reliably assessed at all. A few years later, he was hired as a consultant on a personality assessment initiated by the Peace Corps. Early Peace Corps volunteers had sparked several embarrassing international incidents—one mailed a postcard on which she expressed disgust at the sanitary habits of her host country—so the Kennedy Administration wanted a screening process to eliminate people unsuited for foreign assignments. Volunteers were tested for standard personality traits, and Mischel compared the results with ratings of how well the volunteers performed in the field. He found no correlation; the time-consuming tests predicted nothing. At this point, Mischel realized that the problem wasn't the tests—it was their premise. Psychologists had spent decades searching for traits that exist independently of circumstance, but what if personality can't be separated from context? "It went against the way we'd been thinking about personality since the four humors and the ancient Greeks," he says.

While Mischel was beginning to dismantle the methods of his field, the Harvard psychology department was in tumult. In 1960, the personality psychologist Timothy Leary helped start the Harvard Psilocybin Project, which consisted mostly of self-experimentation. Mischel remembers graduate students' desks giving way to mattresses, and large packages from Ciba chemicals, in Switzerland, arriving in the mail. Mischel had nothing against hippies, but he wanted modern psychology to be rigorous and empirical. And so, in 1962, Walter Mischel moved to Palo Alto and went to work at Stanford.

There is something deeply contradictory about Walter Mischel—a psychologist who spent decades critiquing the validity of personality tests—inventing the marshmallow task, a simple test with impressive predictive power. Mischel, however, insists there is no contradiction. "I've always believed there are consistencies in a person that can be looked at," he says. "We just have to look in the right way." One of Mischel's classic studies documented the aggressive behavior of children in a variety of situations at a summer camp in New Hampshire. Most psychologists assumed that aggression was a stable trait, but Mischel found that children's responses depended on the details of the interaction. The same child might consistently lash out when teased by a peer, but readily submit to adult punishment. Another might react badly to a warning from a counsellor, but play well with his bunkmates. Aggression was best assessed in terms of what Mischel called "if-then patterns." If a certain child was teased by a peer, then he would be aggressive.

One of Mischel's favorite metaphors for this model of personality, known as interactionism, concerns a car making a screeching noise. How does a mechanic solve the problem? He begins by trying to identify the specific conditions that trigger the noise. Is there a screech when the car is accelerating, or when it's shifting gears, or turning at slow speeds? Unless the mechanic can give the screech a context, he'll never find the broken part. Mischel wanted psychologists to think like mechanics, and look at people's responses under particular conditions. The challenge was devising a test that accurately simulated something relevant to the behavior being predicted. The search for a meaningful test of personality led Mischel to revisit, in 1968, the protocol he'd used on young children in Trinidad nearly a decade earlier. The experiment seemed especially relevant now that he had three young daughters of his own. "Young kids are pure id," Mischel says. "They start off unable to wait for anything—whatever they want they need. But then, as I watched my own kids, I marvelled at how they gradually learned how to delay and how that made so many other things possible."

A few years earlier, in 1966, the Stanford psychology department had established the Bing Nursery School. The classrooms were designed as working laboratories, with large one-way mirrors that allowed researchers to observe the children. In February, Jennifer Winters, the assistant director of the school, showed me around the building. While the Bing is still an active center of research—the children quickly learn to ignore the students scribbling in notebooks—Winters isn't sure that Mischel's marshmallow task could be replicated today. "We recently tried to do a version of it, and the kids were very excited about having food in the game room," she says. "There are so many allergies and peculiar diets today that we don't do many things with food."

Mischel perfected his protocol by testing his daughters at the kitchen table. "When you're investigating will power in a four-year-old, little things make a big difference," he says. "How big should the marshmallows be? What kind of cookies work best?" After several months of patient tinkering, Mischel came up with an experimental design that closely simulated the difficulty of delayed gratification. In the spring of 1968, he conducted the first trials of his experiment at the Bing. "I knew we'd designed it well when a few kids wanted to quit as soon as we explained the conditions to them," he says. "They knew this was going to be very difficult."

At the time, psychologists assumed that children's ability to wait depended on how badly they wanted the marshmallow. But it soon became obvious that every child craved the extra treat. What, then, determined self-control? Mischel's conclusion, based on hundreds of hours of observation, was that the crucial skill was the "strategic allocation of attention." Instead of getting obsessed with the marshmallow—the "hot stimulus"—the patient children distracted themselves by covering their eyes, pretending to play hide-and-seek underneath the desk, or singing songs from "Sesame Street." Their desire wasn't defeated—it was merely forgotten. "If you're thinking about the marshmallow and how delicious it is, then you're going to eat it," Mischel says. "The key is to avoid thinking about it in the first place."

In adults, this skill is often referred to as metacognition, or thinking about thinking, and it's what allows people to outsmart their shortcomings. (When Odysseus had himself tied to the ship's mast, he was using some of the skills of metacognition: knowing he wouldn't be able to resist the Sirens' song, he made it impossible to give in.) Mischel's large data set from various studies allowed him to see that children with a more accurate understanding of the workings of self-control were better able to delay gratification. "What's interesting about four-year-olds is that they're just figuring out the rules of thinking," Mischel says. "The kids who couldn't delay would often have the rules backwards. They would think that the best way to resist the marshmallow is to stare right at it, to keep a close eye on the goal. But that's a terrible idea. If you do that, you're going to ring the bell before I leave the room."

According to Mischel, this view of will power also helps explain why the marshmallow task is such a powerfully predictive test. "If you can deal with hot emotions, then you can study for the S.A.T. instead of watching television," Mischel says. "And you can save more money for retirement. It's not just about marshmallows."

Subsequent work by Mischel and his colleagues found that these differences were observable in subjects as young as nineteen months. Looking at how toddlers responded when briefly separated from their mothers, they found that some immediately burst into tears, or clung to the door, but others were able to overcome their anxiety by distracting themselves, often by playing with toys. When the scientists set the same children the marshmallow task at the age of five, they found that the kids who had cried also struggled to resist the tempting treat.

The early appearance of the ability to delay suggests that it has a genetic origin, an example of personality at its most predetermined. Mischel resists such an easy conclusion. "In general, trying to separate nature and nurture makes about as much sense as trying to separate personality and situation," he says. "The two influences are completely interrelated." For instance, when Mischel gave delay-of-gratification tasks to children from low-income families in the Bronx, he noticed that their ability to delay was below average, at least compared with that of children in Palo Alto. "When you grow up poor, you might not practice delay as much," he says. "And if you don't practice then you'll never figure out how to distract yourself. You won't develop the best delay strategies, and those strategies won't become second nature." In other words, people learn how to use their mind just as they learn how to use a computer: through trial and error.

But Mischel has found a shortcut. When he and his colleagues taught children a simple set of mental tricks—such as pretending that the candy is only a picture, surrounded by an imaginary frame—he dramatically improved their self-control. The kids who hadn't been able to wait sixty seconds could now wait fifteen minutes. "All I've done is given them some tips from their mental user manual," Mischel says. "Once you realize that will power is just a matter of learning how to control your attention and thoughts, you can really begin to increase it."

Marc Berman, a lanky graduate student with an easy grin, speaks about his research with the infectious enthusiasm of a freshman taking his first philosophy class. Berman works in the lab of John Jonides, a psychologist and neuroscientist at the University of Michigan, who is in charge of the brain-scanning experiments on the original Bing subjects. He knows that testing forty-year-olds for self-control isn't a straightforward proposition. "We can't give these people marshmallows," Berman says. "They know they're part of a long-term study that looks at delay of gratification, so if you give them an obvious delay task they'll do their best to resist. You'll get a bunch of people who refuse to touch their marshmallow."

This meant that Jonides and his team had to find a way to measure will power indirectly. Operating on the premise that the ability to delay eating the marshmallow had depended on a child's ability to banish thoughts of it, they decided on a series of tasks that measure the ability of subjects to control the contents of working memory—the relatively limited amount of information we're able to consciously consider at any given moment. According to Jonides, this is how self-control "cashes out" in the real world: as an ability to direct the spotlight of attention so that our decisions aren't determined by the wrong thoughts.

Last summer, the scientists chose fifty-five subjects, equally split between high delayers and low delayers, and sent each one a laptop computer loaded with working-memory experiments. Two of the experiments were of particular interest. The first is a straightforward exercise known as the "suppression task." Subjects are given four random words, two printed in blue and two in red. After reading the words, they're told to forget the blue words and remember the red words. Then the scientists provide a stream of "probe words" and ask the subjects whether the probes are the words they were asked to remember. Though the task doesn't seem to involve delayed gratification, it tests the same basic mechanism. Interestingly, the scientists found that high delayers were significantly better at the suppression task: they were less likely to think that a word they'd been asked to forget was something they should remember.

In the second, known as the Go/No Go task, subjects are flashed a set of faces with various expressions. At first, they are told to press the space bar whenever they see a smile. This takes little effort, since smiling faces automatically trigger what's known as "approach behavior." After a few minutes, however, subjects are told to press the space bar when they see frowning faces. They are now being forced to act against an impulse. Results show that high delayers are more successful at not pressing the button in response to a smiling face.

When I first started talking to the scientists about these tasks last summer, they were clearly worried that they wouldn't find any behavioral differences between high and low delayers. It wasn't until early January that they had enough data to begin their analysis (not surprisingly, it took much longer to get the laptops back from the low delayers), but it soon became obvious that there were provocative differences between the two groups. A graph of the data shows that as the delay time of the four-year-olds decreases, the number of mistakes made by the adults sharply rises.

The big remaining question for the scientists is whether these behavioral differences are detectable in an fMRI machine. Although the scanning has just begun—Jonides and his team are still working out the kinks—the scientists sound confident. "These tasks have been studied so many times that we pretty much know where to look and what we're going to find," Jonides says. He rattles off a short list of relevant brain regions, which his lab has already identified as being responsible for working-memory exercises. For the most part, the regions are in the frontal cortex—the overhang of brain behind the eyes—and include the dorsolateral prefrontal cortex, the anterior prefrontal cortex, the anterior cingulate, and the right and left inferior frontal gyri. While these cortical folds have long been associated with self-control, they're also essential for working memory and directed attention. According to the scientists, that's not an accident. "These are powerful instincts telling us to reach for the marshmallow or press the space bar," Jonides says. "The only way to defeat them is to avoid them, and that means paying attention to something else. We call that will power, but it's got nothing to do with the will."

The behavioral and genetic aspects of the project are overseen by Yuichi Shoda, a professor of psychology at the University of Washington, who was one of Mischel's graduate students. He's been following these "marshmallow subjects" for more than thirty years: he knows everything about them from their academic records and their social graces to their ability to deal with frustration and stress. The prognosis for the genetic research remains uncertain. Although many studies have searched for the underpinnings of personality since the completion of the Human Genome Project, in 2003, many of the relevant genes remain in question. "We're incredibly complicated creatures," Shoda says. "Even the simplest aspects of personality are driven by dozens and dozens of different genes." The scientists have decided to focus on genes in the dopamine pathways, since those neurotransmitters are believed to regulate both motivation and attention. However, even if minor coding differences influence delay ability—and that's a likely possibility—Shoda doesn't expect to discover these differences: the sample size is simply too small.

In recent years, researchers have begun making house visits to many of the original subjects, including Carolyn Weisz, as they try to better understand the familial contexts that shape self-control. "They turned my kitchen into a lab," Carolyn told me. "They set up a little tent where they tested my oldest daughter on the delay task with some cookies. I remember thinking, I really hope she can wait."

While Mischel closely follows the steady accumulation of data from the laptops and the brain scans, he's most excited by what comes next. "I'm not interested in looking at the brain just so we can use a fancy machine," he says. "The real question is what can we do with this fMRI data that we couldn't do before?" Mischel is applying for an N.I.H. grant to investigate various mental illnesses, like obsessive-compulsive disorder and attention-deficit disorder, in terms of the ability to control and direct attention.

Mischel and his team hope to identify crucial neural circuits that cut across a wide variety of ailments. If there is such a circuit, then the same cognitive tricks that increase delay time in a four-year-old might help adults deal with their symptoms. Mischel is particularly excited by the example of the substantial subset of people who failed the marshmallow task as four-year-olds but ended up becoming high-delaying adults. "This is the group I'm most interested in," he says. "They have substantially improved their lives."

Mischel is also preparing a large-scale study involving hundreds of schoolchildren in Philadelphia, Seattle, and New York City to see if self-control skills can be taught. Although he previously showed that children did much better on the marshmallow task after being taught a few simple "mental transformations," such as pretending the marshmallow was a cloud, it remains unclear if these new skills persist over the long term. In other words, do the tricks work only during the experiment or do the children learn to apply them at home, when deciding between homework and television?

Angela Lee Duckworth, an assistant professor of psychology at the University of Pennsylvania, is leading the program. She first grew interested in the subject after working as a high-school math teacher. "For the most part, it was an incredibly frustrating experience," she says. "I gradually became convinced that trying to teach a teenager algebra when they don't have self-control is a pretty futile exercise." And so, at the age of thirty-two, Duckworth decided to become a psychologist. One of her main research projects looked at the relationship between self-control and grade-point average. She found that the ability to delay gratification—eighth graders were given a choice between a dollar right away or two dollars the following week—was a far better predictor of academic performance than I.Q. She said that her study shows that "intelligence is really important, but it's still not as important as self-control."

Last year, Duckworth and Mischel were approached by David Levin, the co-founder of KIPP, an organization of sixty-six public charter schools across the country. KIPP schools are known for their long workday—students are in class from 7:25 A.M. to 5 P.M.—and for dramatic improvement of inner-city students' test scores. (More than eighty percent of eighth graders at the KIPP academy in the South Bronx scored at or above grade level in reading and math, which was nearly twice the New York City average.) "The core feature of the KIPP approach is that character matters for success," Levin says. "Educators like to talk about character skills when kids are in kindergarten—we send young kids home with a report card about 'working well with others' or 'not talking out of turn.' But then, just when these skills start to matter, we stop trying to improve them. We just throw up our hands and complain."

Self-control is one of the fundamental "character strengths" emphasized by KIPP—the KIPP academy in Philadelphia, for instance, gives its students a shirt emblazoned with the slogan "Don't Eat the Marshmallow." Levin, however, remained unsure about how well the program was working—"We know how to teach math skills, but it's harder to measure character strengths," he says—so he contacted Duckworth and Mischel, promising them unfettered access to KIPP students. Levin also helped bring together additional schools willing to take part in the experiment, including Riverdale Country School, a private school in the Bronx; the Evergreen School for gifted children, in Shoreline, Washington; and the Mastery Charter Schools, in Philadelphia.

For the past few months, the researchers have been conducting pilot studies in the classroom as they try to figure out the most effective way to introduce complex psychological concepts to young children. Because the study will focus on students between the ages of four and eight, the classroom lessons will rely heavily on peer modelling, such as showing kindergartners a video of a child successfully distracting herself during the marshmallow task. The scientists have some encouraging preliminary results—after just a few sessions, students show significant improvements in the ability to deal with hot emotional states—but they are cautious about predicting the outcome of the long-term study. "When you do these large-scale educational studies, there are ninety-nine uninteresting reasons the study could fail," Duckworth says. "Maybe a teacher doesn't show the video, or maybe there's a field trip on the day of the testing. This is what keeps me up at night."

Mischel's main worry is that, even if his lesson plan proves to be effective, it might still be overwhelmed by variables the scientists can't control, such as the home environment. He knows that it's not enough just to teach kids mental tricks—the real challenge is turning those tricks into habits, and that requires years of diligent practice. "This is

where your parents are important," Mischel says. "Have they established rituals that force you to delay on a daily basis? Do they encourage you to wait? And do they make waiting worthwhile?" According to Mischel, even the most mundane routines of childhood—such as not snacking before dinner, or saving up your allowance, or holding out until Christmas morning—are really sly exercises in cognitive training: we're teaching ourselves how to think so that we can outsmart our desires. But Mischel isn't satisfied with such an informal approach. "We should give marshmallows to every kindergartner," he says. "We should say, 'You see this marshmallow? You don't have to eat it. You can wait. Here's how.'"

## Critical Thinking

1. When do children develop the capacity for self-control, and how do psychological and neurological development affect this capacity?

2. Does self-control in childhood predict later behavior and achievement? If so, in what ways?

3. Some of the most valuable insights about child development have resulted from simple experiments with common materials. What is the marshmallow test? If you were to conduct similar studies, how would you revise the procedure or materials?

4. In what ways did the marshmallow test measure not only children's self-control but their obedience to authority or reaction to novel situations?

# The Moral Life of Babies

Paul Bloom

Not long ago, a team of researchers watched a 1-year-old boy take justice into his own hands. The boy had just seen a puppet show in which one puppet played with a ball while interacting with two other puppets. The center puppet would slide the ball to the puppet on the right, who would pass it back. And the center puppet would slide the ball to the puppet on the left . . . who would run away with it. Then the two puppets on the ends were brought down from the stage and set before the toddler. Each was placed next to a pile of treats. At this point, the toddler was asked to take a treat away from one puppet. Like most children in this situation, the boy took it from the pile of the "naughty" one. But this punishment wasn't enough—he then leaned over and smacked the puppet in the head.

This incident occurred in one of several psychology studies that I have been involved with at the Infant Cognition Center at Yale University in collaboration with my colleague (and wife), Karen Wynn, who runs the lab, and a graduate student, Kiley Hamlin, who is the lead author of the studies. We are one of a handful of research teams around the world exploring the moral life of babies.

Like many scientists and humanists, I have long been fascinated by the capacities and inclinations of babies and children. The mental life of young humans not only is an interesting topic in its own right; it also raises—and can help answer—fundamental questions of philosophy and psychology, including how biological evolution and cultural experience conspire to shape human nature. In graduate school, I studied early language development and later moved on to fairly traditional topics in cognitive development, like how we come to understand the minds of other people—what they know, want and experience.

But the current work I'm involved in, on baby morality, might seem like a perverse and misguided next step. Why would anyone even entertain the thought of babies as moral beings? From Sigmund Freud to Jean Piaget to Lawrence Kohlberg, psychologists have long argued that we begin life as amoral animals. One important task of society, particularly of parents, is to turn babies into civilized beings—social creatures who can experience empathy, guilt and shame; who can override selfish impulses in the name of higher principles; and who will respond with outrage to unfairness and injustice. Many parents and educators would endorse a view of infants and toddlers close to that of a recent Onion headline: "New Study Reveals Most Children Unrepentant Sociopaths." If children enter the world already equipped with moral notions, why is it that we have to work so hard to humanize them?

A growing body of evidence, though, suggests that humans do have a rudimentary moral sense from the very start of life. With the help of well-designed experiments, you can see glimmers of moral thought, moral judgment and moral feeling even in the first year of life. Some sense of good and evil seems to be bred in the bone. Which is not to say that parents are wrong to concern themselves with moral development or that their interactions with their children are a waste of time. Socialization is critically important. But this is not because babies and young children lack a sense of right and wrong; it's because the sense of right and wrong that they naturally possess diverges in important ways from what we adults would want it to be.

## Smart Babies

Babies seem spastic in their actions, undisciplined in their attention. In 1762, Jean-Jacques Rousseau called the baby "a perfect idiot," and in 1890 William James famously described a baby's mental life as "one great blooming, buzzing confusion." A sympathetic parent might see the spark of consciousness in a baby's large eyes and eagerly accept the popular claim that babies are wonderful learners, but it is hard to avoid the impression that they begin as ignorant as bread loaves. Many developmental psychologists will tell you that the ignorance of human babies extends well into childhood. For many years the conventional view was that young humans take a surprisingly long time to learn basic facts about the physical world (like that objects continue to exist once they are out of sight) and basic facts about people (like that they have beliefs and desires and goals)—let alone how long it takes them to learn about morality.

I am admittedly biased, but I think one of the great discoveries in modern psychology is that this view of babies is mistaken.

A reason this view has persisted is that, for many years, scientists weren't sure how to go about studying the mental life of babies. It's a challenge to study the cognitive abilities of any creature that lacks language, but human babies present an additional difficulty, because, even compared to rats or birds, they are behaviorally limited: they can't run mazes or peck at levers. In the 1980s, however, psychologists interested in exploring how much babies know began making use of one of the few behaviors that young babies can control: the movement of their eyes. The eyes are a window to the baby's soul. As adults do, when babies see something that they find interesting or surprising, they tend to look at it longer than they would at something they find uninteresting or expected. And when given a choice between two things to look at, babies usually opt to look at the more pleasing thing. You can use "looking time," then, as a rough but reliable proxy for what captures babies' attention: what babies are surprised by or what babies like.

The studies in the 1980s that made use of this methodology were able to discover surprising things about what babies know about the nature and workings of physical objects—a baby's "naïve physics." Psychologists—most notably Elizabeth Spelke and Renée Baillargeon—conducted studies that essentially involved showing babies magic tricks, events that seemed to violate some law of the universe: you remove the supports from beneath a block and it floats in midair, unsupported; an object disappears and then reappears in another location; a box is placed behind a screen, the screen falls backward into empty space. Like adults, babies tend to linger on such scenes—they look longer at them than at scenes that are identical in all regards except that they don't violate physical laws. This suggests that babies have expectations about how objects should behave. A vast body of research now suggests that—contrary to what was taught for decades to legions of psychology undergraduates—babies think of objects largely as adults do, as connected masses that move as units, that are solid and subject to gravity and that move in continuous paths through space and time.

Other studies, starting with a 1992 paper by my wife, Karen, have found that babies can do rudimentary math with objects. The demonstration is simple. Show a baby an empty stage. Raise a screen to obscure part of the stage. In view of the baby, put a Mickey Mouse doll behind the screen. Then put another Mickey Mouse doll behind the screen. Now drop the screen. Adults expect two dolls—and so do 5-month-olds: if the screen drops to reveal one or three dolls, the babies look longer, in surprise, than they do if the screen drops to reveal two.

A second wave of studies used looking-time methods to explore what babies know about the minds of others—a baby's "naïve psychology." Psychologists had known for a while that even the youngest of babies treat people different from inanimate objects. Babies like to look at faces; they mimic them, they smile at them. They expect engagement: if a moving object becomes still, they merely lose interest; if a person's face becomes still, however, they become distressed.

But the new studies found that babies have an actual understanding of mental life: they have some grasp of how people think and why they act as they do. The studies showed that, though babies expect inanimate objects to move as the result of push-pull interactions, they expect people to move rationally in accordance with their beliefs and desires: babies show surprise when someone takes a roundabout path to something he wants. They expect someone who reaches for an object to reach for the same object later, even if its location has changed. And well before their 2nd birthdays, babies are sharp enough to know that other people can have false beliefs. The psychologists Kristine

Onishi and Renée Baillargeon have found that 15-month-olds expect that if a person sees an object in one box, and then the object is moved to another box when the person isn't looking, the person will later reach into the box where he first saw the object, not the box where it actually is. That is, toddlers have a mental model not merely of the world but of the world as understood by someone else.

These discoveries inevitably raise a question: If babies have such a rich understanding of objects and people so early in life, why do they seem so ignorant and helpless? Why don't they put their knowledge to more active use? One possible answer is that these capacities are the psychological equivalent of physical traits like testicles or ovaries, which are formed in infancy and then sit around, useless, for years and years. Another possibility is that babies do, in fact, use their knowledge from Day 1, not for action but for learning. One lesson from the study of artificial intelligence (and from cognitive science more generally) is that an empty head learns nothing: a system that is capable of rapidly absorbing information needs to have some prewired understanding of what to pay attention to and what generalizations to make. Babies might start off smart, then, because it enables them to get smarter.

# Nice Babies

Psychologists like myself who are interested in the cognitive capacities of babies and toddlers are now turning our attention to whether babies have a "naïve morality." But there is reason to proceed with caution. Morality, after all, is a different sort of affair than physics or psychology. The truths of physics and psychology are universal: objects obey the same physical laws everywhere; and people everywhere have minds, goals, desires and beliefs. But the existence of a universal moral code is a highly controversial claim; there is considerable evidence for wide variation from society to society.

In the journal *Science* a couple of months ago, the psychologist Joseph Henrich and several of his colleagues reported a cross-cultural study of 15 diverse populations and found that people's propensities to behave kindly to strangers and to punish unfairness are strongest in large-scale communities with market economies, where such norms are essential to the smooth functioning of trade. Henrich and his colleagues concluded that much of the morality that humans possess is a consequence of the culture in which they are raised, not their innate capacities.

At the same time, though, people everywhere have *some* sense of right and wrong. You won't find a society where people don't have some notion of fairness, don't put some value on loyalty and kindness, don't distinguish between acts of cruelty and innocent mistakes, don't categorize people as nasty or nice. These universals make evolutionary sense. Since natural selection works, at least in part, at a genetic level, there is a logic to being instinctively kind to our kin, whose survival and well-being promote the spread of our genes. More than that, it is often beneficial for humans to work together with other humans, which means that it would have been adaptive to evaluate the niceness and nastiness of other individuals. All this is reason to consider the innateness of at least basic moral concepts.

In addition, scientists know that certain compassionate feelings and impulses emerge early and apparently universally in human development. These are not moral concepts, exactly, but they seem closely related. One example is feeling pain at the pain of others. In his book "The Expression of the Emotions in Man and Animals," Charles Darwin, a keen observer of human nature, tells the story of how his first son, William, was fooled by his nurse into expressing sympathy at a very young age: "When a few days over 6 months old, his nurse pretended to cry, and I saw that his face instantly assumed a melancholy expression, with the corners of his mouth strongly depressed."

There seems to be something evolutionarily ancient to this empathetic response. If you want to cause a rat distress, you can expose it to the screams of other rats. Human babies, notably, cry more to the cries of other babies than to tape recordings of their *own* crying, suggesting that they are responding to their awareness of someone else's pain, not merely to a certain pitch of sound. Babies also seem to want to assuage the pain of others: once they have enough physical competence (starting at about 1 year old), they soothe others in distress by stroking and touching or by handing over a bottle or toy. There are individual differences, to be sure, in the intensity of response: some babies are great soothers; others don't care as much. But the basic impulse seems common to all. (Some other primates behave similarly: the primatologist Frans de Waal reports that chimpanzees "will approach a victim of attack, put an arm around her and gently pat her back or groom her." Monkeys, on the other hand, tend to shun victims of aggression.)

Some recent studies have explored the existence of behavior in toddlers that is "altruistic" in an even stronger sense—like when they give up their time and energy to help a stranger accomplish a difficult task. The psychologists Felix Warneken and Michael Tomasello have put toddlers in situations in which an adult is struggling to get something done, like opening a cabinet door with his hands full or trying to get to an object out of reach. The toddlers tend to spontaneously help, even without any prompting, encouragement or reward.

Is any of the above behavior recognizable as moral conduct? Not obviously so. Moral ideas seem to involve much more than mere compassion. Morality, for instance, is closely related to notions of praise and blame: we want to reward what we see as good and punish what we see as bad. Morality is also closely connected to the ideal of impartiality—if it's immoral for you to do something to me, then, all else being equal, it is immoral for me to do the same thing to you. In addition, moral principles are different from other types of rules or laws: they cannot, for instance, be overruled solely by virtue of authority. (Even a 4-year-old knows not only that unprovoked hitting is wrong but also that it would continue to be wrong even if a teacher said that it was O.K.) And we tend to associate morality with the possibility of free and rational choice; people *choose* to do good or evil. To hold someone responsible for an act means that we believe that he could have chosen to act otherwise.

Babies and toddlers might not know or exhibit any of these moral subtleties. Their sympathetic reactions and motivations—including their desire to alleviate the pain of others—may not be much different in kind from purely nonmoral reactions and motivations like growing hungry or wanting to void a full bladder. Even if that is true, though, it is hard to conceive of a moral system that didn't have, as a starting point, these empathetic capacities. As David Hume argued, mere rationality can't be the foundation of morality, since our most basic desires are neither rational nor irrational. " 'Tis not contrary to reason," he wrote, "to prefer the destruction of the whole world to the scratching of my finger." To have a genuinely moral system, in other words, some things first have to matter, and what we see in babies is the development of *mattering*.

## Moral-Baby Experiments

So what do babies really understand about morality? Our first experiments exploring this question were done in collaboration with a postdoctoral researcher named Valerie Kuhlmeier (who is now an associate professor of psychology at Queen's University in Ontario). Building on previous work by the psychologists David and Ann Premack, we began by investigating what babies think about two particular kinds of action: helping and hindering.

Our experiments involved having children watch animated movies of geometrical characters with faces. In one, a red ball would try to go up a hill. On some attempts, a yellow square got behind the ball and gently nudged it upward; in others, a green triangle got in front of it and pushed it down. We were interested in babies' expectations about the ball's attitudes—what would the baby expect the ball to make of the character who helped it and the one who hindered it? To find out, we then showed the babies additional movies in which the ball either approached the square or the triangle. When the ball approached the triangle (the hinderer), both 9- and 12-month-olds looked longer than they did when the ball approached the square (the helper). This was consistent with the interpretation that the former action surprised them; they expected the ball to approach the helper. A later study, using somewhat different stimuli, replicated the finding with 10-month-olds, but found that 6-month-olds seem to have no expectations at all. (This effect is robust only when the animated characters have faces; when they are simple faceless figures, it is apparently harder for babies to interpret what they are seeing as a social interaction.)

This experiment was designed to explore babies' expectations about social interactions, not their moral capacities per se. But if you look at the movies, it's clear that, at least to adult eyes, there is some latent moral content to the situation: the triangle is kind of a jerk; the square is a sweetheart. So we set out to investigate whether babies make the same judgments about the characters that adults do. Forget about how babies expect the ball to act toward the other characters; what do babies themselves think about the square and the triangle? Do they prefer the good guy and dislike the bad guy?

Here we began our more focused investigations into baby morality. For these studies, parents took their babies to the Infant Cognition Center, which is within one of the Yale psychology buildings. (The center is just a couple of blocks away from where Stanley Milgram did his famous experiments on obedience in the early 1960s, tricking New Haven residents into believing that they had severely harmed or even killed strangers with electrical shocks.) The parents were told about what was going to happen and filled out consent forms, which described the study, the risks to the baby (minimal) and the benefits to the baby (minimal, though it is a nice-enough experience). Parents often asked, reasonably enough, if they would learn how their baby does, and the answer was no. This sort of study provides no clinical or educational feedback about individual babies; the findings make sense only when computed as a group.

For the experiment proper, a parent will carry his or her baby into a small testing room. A typical experiment takes about 15 minutes. Usually, the parent sits on a chair, with the baby on his or her lap, though for some studies, the baby is strapped into a high chair with the parent standing behind. At this point, some of the babies are either sleeping or too fussy to continue; there will then be a short break for the baby to wake up or calm down, but on average this kind of study ends up losing about a quarter of the subjects. Just as critics describe much of experimental psychology as the study of the American college undergraduate who wants to make some extra money or needs to fulfill an Intro Psych requirement, there's some truth to the claim that this developmental work is a science of the interested and alert baby.

In one of our first studies of moral evaluation, we decided not to use two-dimensional animated movies but rather a three-dimensional display in which real geometrical objects, manipulated like puppets, acted out the helping/hindering situations: a yellow square would help the circle up the hill; a red triangle would push it down. After showing the babies the scene, the experimenter placed the helper and the hinderer on a tray and brought them to the child. In this instance, we opted to record not the babies' looking time but rather which character they reached for, on the theory that what a baby reaches for is a reliable indicator of what a baby wants. In the end, we found that 6- and 10-month-old infants overwhelmingly preferred the helpful individual to the hindering individual. This wasn't a subtle statistical trend; just about all the babies reached for the good guy.

(Experimental minutiae: What if babies simply like the color red or prefer squares or something like that? To control for this, half the babies got the yellow square as the helper; half got it as the hinderer. What about problems of unconscious cueing and unconscious bias? To avoid this, at the moment when the two characters were offered on the tray, the parent had his or her eyes closed, and the experimenter holding out the characters and recording the responses hadn't seen the puppet show, so he or she didn't know who was the good guy and who was the bad guy.)

One question that arose with these experiments was how to understand the babies' preference: did they act as they did because they were attracted to the helpful individual or because they were repelled by the hinderer or was it both? We explored this question in a further series of studies that introduced a neutral character, one that neither helps nor hinders. We found that,

given a choice, infants prefer a helpful character to a neutral one; and prefer a neutral character to one who hinders. This finding indicates that both inclinations are at work—babies are drawn to the nice guy and repelled by the mean guy. Again, these results were not subtle; babies almost always showed this pattern of response.

Does our research show that babies believe that the helpful character is *good* and the hindering character is *bad?* Not necessarily. All that we can safely infer from what the babies reached for is that babies prefer the good guy and show an aversion to the bad guy. But what's exciting here is that these preferences are based on how one individual treated another, on whether one individual was helping another individual achieve its goals or hindering it. This is preference of a very special sort; babies were responding to behaviors that adults would describe as nice or mean. When we showed these scenes to much older kids—18-month-olds—and asked them, "Who was nice? Who was good?" and "Who was mean? Who was bad?" they responded as adults would, identifying the helper as nice and the hinderer as mean.

To increase our confidence that the babies we studied were really responding to niceness and naughtiness, Karen Wynn and Kiley Hamlin, in a separate series of studies, created different sets of one-act morality plays to show the babies. In one, an individual struggled to open a box; the lid would be partly opened but then fall back down. Then, on alternating trials, one puppet would grab the lid and open it all the way, and another puppet would jump on the box and slam it shut. In another study (the one I mentioned at the beginning of this article), a puppet would play with a ball. The puppet would roll the ball to another puppet, who would roll it back, and the first puppet would roll the ball to a different puppet who would run away with it. In both studies, 5-month-olds preferred the good guy—the one who helped to open the box; the one who rolled the ball back—to the bad guy. This all suggests that the babies we studied have a general appreciation of good and bad behavior, one that spans a range of actions.

A further question that arises is whether babies possess more subtle moral capacities than preferring good and avoiding bad. Part and parcel of adult morality, for instance, is the idea that good acts should meet with a positive response and bad acts with a negative response—justice demands the good be rewarded and the bad punished. For our next studies, we turned our attention back to the older babies and toddlers and tried to explore whether the preferences that we were finding had anything to do with moral judgment in this mature sense. In collaboration with Neha Mahajan, a psychology graduate student at Yale, Hamlin, Wynn and I exposed 21-month-olds to the good guy/bad guy situations described above, and we gave them the opportunity to reward or punish either by giving a treat to, or taking a treat from, one of the characters. We found that when asked to give, they tended to choose the positive character; when asked to take, they tended to choose the negative one.

Dispensing justice like this is a more elaborate conceptual operation than merely preferring good to bad, but there are still-more-elaborate moral calculations that adults, at least, can easily make. For example: Which individual would you prefer—someone who rewarded good guys and punished bad guys or someone who punished good guys and rewarded bad guys? The same amount of rewarding and punishing is going on in both cases, but by adult lights, one individual is acting justly and the other isn't. Can babies see this, too?

To find out, we tested 8-month-olds by first showing them a character who acted as a helper (for instance, helping a puppet trying to open a box) and then presenting a scene in which this helper was the target of a good action by one puppet and a bad action by another puppet. Then we got the babies to choose between these two puppets. That is, they had to choose between a puppet who rewarded a good guy versus a puppet who punished a good guy. Likewise, we showed them a character who acted as a hinderer (for example, keeping a puppet from opening a box) and then had them choose between a puppet who rewarded the bad guy versus one who punished the bad guy.

The results were striking. When the target of the action was itself a good guy, babies preferred the puppet who was nice to it. This alone wasn't very surprising, given that the other studies found an overall preference among babies for those who act nicely. What was more interesting was what happened when they watched the bad guy being rewarded or punished. Here they chose the punisher. Despite their overall preference for good actors over bad, then, babies are drawn to bad actors when those actors are punishing bad behavior.

All of this research, taken together, supports a general picture of baby morality. It's even possible, as a thought experiment, to ask what it would be like to see the world in the moral terms that a baby does. Babies probably have no conscious access to moral notions, no idea why certain acts are good or bad. They respond on a gut level. Indeed, if you watch the older babies during the experiments, they don't act like impassive judges—they tend to smile and clap during good events and frown, shake their heads and look sad during the naughty events (remember the toddler who smacked the bad puppet). The babies' experiences might be cognitively empty but emotionally intense, replete with strong feelings and strong desires. But this shouldn't strike you as an altogether alien experience: while we adults possess the additional critical capacity of being able to consciously reason about morality, we're not otherwise that different from babies—our moral feelings are often instinctive. In fact, one discovery of contemporary research in social psychology and social neuroscience is the powerful emotional underpinning of what we once thought of as cool, untroubled, mature moral deliberation.

## Is This the Morality We're Looking For?

What do these findings about babies' moral notions tell us about adult morality? Some scholars think that the very existence of an innate moral sense has profound implications. In 1869, Alfred Russel Wallace, who along with Darwin discovered natural selection, wrote that certain human capacities—including "the higher moral faculties"—are richer than what you could expect from a product of biological evolution. He concluded that some sort of godly force must intervene to create these capacities. (Darwin was horrified at this suggestion, writing to Wallace, "I hope you have not murdered too completely your own and my child.")

A few years ago, in his book "What's So Great About Christianity," the social and cultural critic Dinesh D'Souza revived this argument. He conceded that evolution can explain our niceness in instances like kindness to kin, where the niceness has a clear genetic payoff, but he drew the line at "high altruism," acts of entirely disinterested kindness. For D'Souza, "there is no Darwinian rationale" for why you would give up your seat for an old lady on a bus, an act of nice-guyness that does nothing for your genes. And what about those who donate blood to strangers or sacrifice their lives for a worthy cause? D'Souza reasoned that these stirrings of conscience are best explained not by evolution or psychology but by "the voice of God within our souls."

The evolutionary psychologist has a quick response to this: To say that a biological trait evolves for a purpose doesn't mean that it always functions, in the here and now, for that purpose. Sexual arousal, for instance, presumably evolved because of its connection to making babies; but of course we can get aroused in all sorts of situations in which baby-making just isn't an option—for instance, while looking at pornography. Similarly, our impulse to help others has likely evolved because of the reproductive benefit that it gives us in certain contexts—and it's not a problem for this argument that some acts of niceness that people perform don't provide this sort of benefit. (And for what it's worth, giving up a bus seat for an old lady, although the motives might be psychologically pure, turns out to be a cold-bloodedly smart move from a Darwinian standpoint, an easy way to show off yourself as an attractively good person.)

The general argument that critics like Wallace and D'Souza put forward, however, still needs to be taken seriously. The morality of contemporary humans really does outstrip what evolution could possibly have endowed us with; moral actions are often of a sort that have no plausible relation to our reproductive success and don't appear to be accidental byproducts of evolved adaptations. Many of us care about strangers in faraway lands, sometimes to the extent that we give up resources that could be used for our friends and family; many of us care about the fates of nonhuman animals, so much so that we deprive ourselves of pleasures like rib-eye steak and veal scaloppine. We possess abstract moral notions of equality and freedom for all; we see racism and sexism as evil; we reject slavery and genocide; we try to love our enemies. Of course, our actions typically fall short, often far short, of our moral principles, but these principles do shape, in a substantial way, the world that we live in. It makes sense then to marvel at the extent of our moral insight and to reject the notion that it can be explained in the language of natural selection. If this higher morality or higher altruism were found in babies, the case for divine creation would get just a bit stronger.

But it is not present in babies. In fact, our initial moral sense appears to be biased toward our own kind. There's plenty of research showing that babies have within-group preferences: 3-month-olds prefer the faces of the race that is most familiar to them to those of other races; 11-month-olds prefer individuals who share their own taste in food and expect these individuals to be nicer than those with different tastes; 12-month-olds prefer to learn from someone who speaks their own language over someone who speaks a foreign language. And studies with young children have found that once they are segregated into different groups—even under the most arbitrary of schemes, like wearing different colored T-shirts—they eagerly favor their own groups in their attitudes and their actions.

The notion at the core of any mature morality is that of impartiality. If you are asked to justify your actions, and you say, "Because I wanted to," this is just an expression of selfish desire. But explanations like "It was my turn" or "It's my fair share" are potentially moral, because they imply that anyone else in the same situation could have done the same. This is the sort of argument that could be convincing to a neutral observer and is at the foundation of standards of justice and law. The philosopher Peter Singer has pointed out that this notion of impartiality can be found in religious and philosophical systems of morality, from the golden rule in Christianity to the teachings of Confucius to the political philosopher John Rawls's landmark theory of justice. This is an insight that emerges within communities of intelligent, deliberating and negotiating beings, and it can override our parochial impulses.

The aspect of morality that we truly marvel at—its generality and universality—is the product of culture, not of biology. There is no need to posit divine intervention. A fully developed morality is the product of cultural development, of the accumulation of rational insight and hard-earned innovations. The morality we start off with is primitive, not merely in the obvious sense that it's incomplete, but in the deeper sense that

when individuals and societies aspire toward an enlightened in which all beings capable of reason and suffering are on an equal footing, where all people are equal—they are fighting with what children have from the get-go. The biologist Richard Dawkins was right, then, when he said at the start of his book *The Selfish Gene,* "Be warned that if you wish, as I do, to build a society in which individuals cooperate generously and unselfishly toward a common good, you can expect little help from biological nature." Or as a character in the Kingsley Amis novel *One Fat Englishman* puts it, "It was no wonder that people were so horrible when they started life as children."

Morality, then, is a synthesis of the biological and the cultural, of the unlearned, the discovered and the invented. Babies possess certain moral foundations—the capacity and willingness to judge the actions of others, some sense of justice, gut responses to altruism and nastiness. Regardless of how smart we are, if we didn't start with this basic apparatus, we would be nothing more than amoral agents, ruthlessly driven to pursue our self-interest. But our capacities as babies are sharply limited. It is the insights of rational individuals that make a truly universal and unselfish morality something that our species can aspire to.

# Critical Thinking

1. Given the information in this article, would you conclude that babies have a moral life? What qualifications or reservations would you have?

2. In what ways could the various findings cited in this article be used to argue that morality is determined by "nature"? In what ways could they support the "naurture" argument?

**PAUL BLOOM** is a professor of psychology at Yale. His new book, *How Pleasure Works,* will be published next month.

# Same Place, Different Experiences: Bringing Individual Differences to Research in Child Care

Deborah A. Phillips, Nathan A. Fox, and Megan R. Gunnar

Research on child care has focused on how various features of care, notably the timing and amount of exposure, type and stability of care, and level of quality, affect the typical course of development (Lamb & Ahnert, 2006; Phillips & Lowenstein, in press; Phillips, McCartney, & Sussman, 2006). In this article, we argue that the next wave of child-care research needs to draw upon insights from research on temperament, and even newer evidence regarding stress reactivity, to explicate how individual differences interact with features of child care to produce distinct patterns of outcomes for different children.

During the infant day-care debate of the mid-1980s, temperament was repeatedly mentioned as an important moderating influence to be examined in future research (see Fein & Fox, 1988). Belsky (1988) noted the need to understand the characteristics of the "50 percent or more of the infants" who, in his review of the extant literature, established secure relationships with their mothers "despite" early exposure to child care. He and other commentators (Clarke-Stewart, 1988; Phillips, McCartney, Scarr, & Howes, 1987; Sroufe, 1988) pointed specifically to infant temperament as an especially promising variable to pursue to gain a more nuanced understanding of within-group differences in the effects of infant child care. Nevertheless, the contribution of temperament to the evolving portrait of child-care effects has remained a relatively neglected issue, perhaps because the driving questions for so much of this research over the past 20 years have been *whether* and *under what conditions* of care—not *for whom*—child care confers risk or protection. It is this neglect that we seek to remedy.

## Child-Care Risks and Benefits

At the outset, a brief summary of what current evidence tells us about *whether* and *under what conditions* child-care experiences affect early development is warranted insofar as this evidence sets the stage for our focus on the *for whom* question.

This evidence now indicates that early nonparental care environments sometimes pose risks to young children and sometimes confer benefits, but most often they play a less powerful—albeit significant and cumulative—role in the context of other potent influences, such as the quality of parental care (National Institute of Child Health and Human Development Early Child Care Research Network [NICHD ECCRN], 2006; Phillips et al., 2006). Efforts to explain these divergent effects have focused on identifying the conditions of care that affect children's social development because this is the behavioral domain for which mixed outcomes have been reported most frequently.

Extensive evidence indicates that higher *quality* of child care increases the odds of positive social skills and adjustment, while higher *amounts* of child care contribute to elevated (albeit non-clinical) levels of externalizing behavior, including aggression, noncompliance, risk taking, and impulsivity (NICHD ECCRN, 2006; Phillips & Lowenstein, in press; Phillips et al., 2006). Recent longitudinal findings from the NICHD Study of Early Child Care and Youth Development indicate that this pattern holds up through age 15 years (Belsky et al., 2007; NICHD ECCRN, 2005). Other attempts to discern the conditions under which child care elevates the odds of negative social behavior have pointed to the contribution of type of care and, specifically, time in center-based care (Belsky et al., 2007; NICHD ECCRN, 2005). Some have speculated that the proximal or active ingredient behind these effects is the social opportunities and challenges posed by peer groups (Fabes, Hanish, & Martin, 2003), and emerging evidence lends support to this possibility. As Crockenberg (2003) has noted, however, the relatively small effect sizes in these studies make it clear that only some children display heightened externalizing behavior in response to child care, thus highlighting the pressing question of who these children are. Unfortunately, these studies rarely examined the mediating role played by children's temperaments, and when they did, significant findings did not emerge. They also relied almost exclusively on parental and teacher reports of temperament, which limited their conclusions. This body of research is therefore unable to shed much light on the question of which children are most sensitive to variation in quality and quantity of child care.

## Why the *for Whom* Question?

We argue that this mixed pattern of evidence points to the need to go beyond examination of the type, quantity, and quality of care to understand how the day-to-day experiences of individual children in the same child-care settings might differ, thus leading to different outcomes for different children. Two interrelated strands of evidence are especially pertinent in this context. The first strand involves preliminary evidence that child-care influences vary with certain temperamental dispositions in young children (Fox, Henderson, Rubin, Calkins, & Schmidt, 2001; Watamura, Donzella, Alwin, & Gunnar, 2003), especially tendencies toward negative emotional reactivity, inhibition, and social reticence. The second strand implicates child-care experiences in the early development of physiological processes that govern the regulation of stress (Geoffroy, Cote, Parent, & Seguin, 2006; Vermeer & van IJzendoorn, 2006). Considered together, these two strands of research create an exciting opportunity to revisit how the field approaches questions of individual differences among infants and children in response to child care. They also carry the potential to bring evidence from child-care research to bear on pressing questions regarding how early social experiences get "under the skin" to affect the paths that children follow toward problematic or promising futures.

## Temperament and Child Care

It is now well established that individual differences in patterns of emotional reactivity to novelty early in infancy are associated with subsequent social outcomes (Fox, Henderson, Marshall, Nichols, & Ghera, 2005; Kagan, Snidman, & Arcus, 1998). Negative emotional reactivity in early infancy, characterized by high levels of crying and motor arousal during presentation of novel sensory stimuli, appears to be a precursor to behavioral inhibition and social reticence. Positive reactivity, characterized by high motor arousal in the absence of negative emotion, is associated with a pattern of behavioral exuberance that, if not tempered by strong regulatory control, can manifest itself in externalizing behaviors (Rothbart & Bates, 2006).

Efforts to understand the influence of rearing environments on the development of children with varying temperamental profiles have focused almost exclusively on the home environment and parenting (Degnan, Henderson, Fox, & Rubin, 2008; Hane, Cheah, Rubin, & Fox, 2008). Only recently have examinations of the influence of nonparental child care on children with varying temperaments begun to emerge, driven by questions about whether links between child care and developmental outcomes are more pronounced for children with particular temperamental profiles and whether child-care experiences play a role in the discontinuities that are often

seen in the expression of temperament over time. The answer that is emerging, in both cases, is yes.

Both the amount of child care and the quality of care have been found to affect children with different temperaments in different ways, with both positive and negative impacts being reported in the literature. With regard to the amount of care, greater exposure to child care has been associated with increased internalizing behavior for children characterized by their mothers as, or observed to be, fearful of novelty, but not for their unfearful peers (Crockenberg & Leerkes, 2005; De Shipper, Tavecchio, van IJzendoorn, & van Zeijl, 2004). Crockenberg and Leerkes (2005) further reported that long hours in child care led to more externalizing behavior for children observed to be more easily frustrated by limits and that this effect was restricted to children attending child-care centers, which raises the issue of peer influences that has become salient within the child-care literature more broadly. Others, however, have reported positive associations between exposure to child care and social behavior among children with more emotionally reactive temperaments. In one case, longer hours in care predicted fewer internalizing symptoms in 5-year-olds characterized as temperamentally positive in infancy (Almas, Phillips, & Fox, 2009); in another, exposure to child care with peers during the toddler years differentiated behaviorally inhibited children who became less inhibited over time from those who displayed greater stability in this temperamental style (Fox et al., 2001).

Variation in child-care quality also appears to have differing consequences for children with different temperamental profiles. Pluess and Belsky (2009) found that the teacher-rated social development of preschool- and kindergarten-age children who were portrayed by their mothers as temperamentally difficult during infancy was more susceptible to variation in the quality of child care—but not to variation in the amount of care—than was the case for children who were not difficult as infants. Results just emerging from a collaboration between Phillips and Fox indicate that toddlers characterized as high in temperamental fear at 4 months of age were, compared to their less reactive peers, more sensitive to variation in the quality of their child-care experiences defined in terms of both positive peer interactions (Almas et al., in press) and caregiver sensitivity-warmth and an overall positive emotional climate (Phillips et al., 2010). Almas and colleagues (in press) found that more positive peer interactions in child care at 24 months were associated with *less* wariness around unfamiliar peers in the lab at 36 months of age for these children, but not for their temperamentally more typical peers. Phillips and colleagues (2010) found that higher quality caregiving was uniquely associated with less isolation from peers in child care at age 24 months for the children characterized by negative reactivity as infants. Children characterized by positive reactivity were also less isolated from peers under conditions of higher quality care. This evidence is reminiscent of prior findings that the quality of peer interactions experienced by infants who were rated high in social fear was more positive among those in high-quality care and more negative among infants in low-quality care than was the case for their peers who were rated low in social fear (Volling & Feagans, 1995).

These findings clearly implicate child care as an important environment to consider in research on the developmental pathways followed by children with differing temperamental profiles. They also indicate that temperament contributes to individual differences in response to both the amount and quality of child care that children experience. In both cases, the results point particularly to children characterized by negative emotionality, inhibition, and social fear as a group who may be especially sensitive to variation in features of child care. At this point, however, the findings are mixed with regard to which dimensions of child care matter most for children at the more reactive ends of the temperament spectrum.

# The Regulation of Stress and Child Care

Turning to the second strand of research on child care, we call attention to the activity of the hypothalamic–pituitary–adrenal (HPA) system, which regulates physiological and behavioral responses to stress. Recent research clearly suggests that some children react to child care as a stressful experience. This evidence, in turn, is directly pertinent to efforts to understand which children, under what conditions, are most likely to respond this way and what behavioral processes these responses set in motion. We start with a brief summary of the role of cortisol as an influence on early development.

The HPA system produces cortisol, a steroid hormone that plays critical roles in adaptation to stressors (Gunnar & Quevedo, 2007). The impact of elevated levels of cortisol on neural development depends, in part, on the neural systems that are activated in response to given stressors. Research on animals shows that when cortisol is elevated in conjunction with events stimulating fear and anxiety, it supports the laying down of threat memories and affects plasticity in brain regions coordinating anxious, fearful behavior (Roozendaal, McEwen, & Chattarji, 2009). Cortisol's impact on the brain also reflects activity of corticotropin-releasing hormone (CRH). This neuropeptide is produced not only in the hypothalamus (where it regulates the cascade of events that ultimately increase cortisol production by the adrenal glands) but also in brain systems that support fear and anxiety (e.g., amygdala) and the orchestration of behavioral and sympathetic fight-flight responses.

Interactions between cortisol, CRH, and other neurochemical systems activated in response to perceived threat have been shown in animal studies to bias developing organisms toward heightened defensive rather than exploratory responses to novel or ambiguous situations, including social encounters (Joels & Baram, 2009). Thus, it is hypothesized that repeated or prolonged activation of the HPA axis and CRH in the context of adverse or threatening care experiences may increase the functioning of brain systems underlying fear and anxiety and impair the development of brain systems involved in memory and behavior regulation. Explicit links to enduring behavioral consequences, however, remain to be documented. These neurological, regulatory effects are expected to be more marked during periods of rapid brain development, such as the first years of life, when children are also adjusting to child care (Gunnar & Quevedo, 2007).

With respect to child care, several studies in both the United States and abroad indicate that children in child care exhibit higher cortisol levels (due largely to rising levels over the course of the day) than they do on days spent at home. Both meta-analyses (Geoffroy et al., 2006; Vermeer & van IJzendoorn, 2006) and recent data (Dettling, Gunnar, & Donzella, 1999; Gunnar, Kryzer, van Ryzin, & Phillips, 2010) suggest that this pattern is more notable in toddlers and younger preschoolers than in older preschoolers and school-aged children. It is also more pronounced among children in full-day care (Geoffroy et al., 2006; Vermeer & van IJzendoorn, 2006) and those in poorer quality care (Dettling, Parker, Lane, Sebanc, & Gunnar, 2000; Gunnar et al., 2010; Legendre, 2003; Sims, Guilfoyle, & Parry, 2006; Watamura, Kryzer, & Robertson, 2009). Intrusive, overcontrolling caregiver–child interactions (Gunnar et al., 2010), as well as daily schedules characterized by long periods of both provider-directed, structured activities and frequent full-group transitions (Sims et al., 2006), have been associated with larger rises in cortisol over the child-care day. Notably, these are also child-care conditions that are known to be associated with poorer socioemotional outcomes for young children. Unfortunately, to date, there are no long-term longitudinal studies linking variation in child-care quality with both behavioral and neurobiological responding among children in care. Moreover, there is some evidence that elevated cortisol levels at child care (relative to home) resolve themselves with age and exposure to care (Ouellet-Morin et al., 2010).

In an initial attempt to better understand concurrent relations between child-care quality, cortisol elevations, and children's behavior in child care, we (Gunnar et al.; 2010) recently examined preschool-aged children in family child-care settings. As in other studies, we found that cortisol levels were higher at child care than at home, rose from morning to afternoon at child care, and were particularly high by late afternoon at child care. Four of 10 children met criteria that indicate a significant stress response of the HPA axis. Cortisol elevations were associated with both child-care quality and children's behavior. Specifically, cortisol rose more over the day in family child-care homes in which children received more intrusive, overcontrolling care. For girls, anxious–vigilant behavior was associated with larger rises in cortisol; for boys, angry–aggressive behavior was associated with the rise in cortisol. A 6-month follow-up study addressed the question of the longer term consequences of these altered cortisol patterns associated with early child-care experience (Gunnar, Kryzer, van Ryzin, & Phillips, in press). The rise in cortisol at Time 1 was associated with higher levels of anxious—vigilant behavior in child care and with more internalizing symptoms at Time 2. However, these associations emerged only among children who, at Time 1, were observed (laboratory assessment) to display, and were rated by parent and caregivers as having, behaviorally inhibited temperaments.

This pattern of findings raises the possibility that children's temperaments play a role in their neurobiological and behavioral adaptation to child care. Not only have children with differing temperaments been found to react differently to variation in the amount and quality of child care, as reviewed earlier, but certain temperaments have been implicated in studies of cortisol responses among children in child care. Specifically, while not found consistently (Watamura, Sebanc, & Gunnar, 2002), there is a tendency for children who, according to observation or teacher or parent reports, display social fearfulness, negative emotional temperaments, and poorer self-control to show relatively larger rises in cortisol levels over the course of the day in child care than do their more temperamentally easy-going peers (Dettling et al., 1999; Dettling et al., 2000; Tout, de Haan, Kipp Campbell, & Gunnar, 1998; Watamura et al., 2003).

What might underlie the relation between temperament and stress reactivity in the context of child care? Our speculation leads us to the role of social evaluative threat in the activation of the HPA system. Social evaluative threat, which includes being rejected, ignored, or worried about making mistakes and being thought badly of, is a very potent trigger of fear and anxiety, and thus of stress, in adults and children (Dickerson & Kemeny, 2004; van Goozen, Fairchild, Snoek, & Harold, 2007). In that child-care environments confront young children with the challenge of negotiating relations with other children at a stage when peer skills are just developing, they may be more stressful for certain children. For children with more negative, inhibited temperaments, the experience of child care may provide more frequent opportunities for the activation of social fearfulness, which characterizes children with this temperamental disposition. For children who tend toward aggressive behavior, child care may pose experiences of social threat that arise from negative peer interactions.

Longer hours in care likely play a role insofar as the challenges of negotiating peer interactions, which are especially daunting for children with these more reactive temperaments, become even more taxing over the course of the child-care day. Quality of care adds to this equation insofar as the caregivers' ability to provide emotional support and buffer children from peer-related sources of stress (e.g., isolation, rejection, aggression) probably contributes to whether or not these children, in particular, experience child care as stressful. Speculation that these issues will be more salient in settings with larger groups of children (Belsky et al., 2007; Legendre, 2003) requires additional exploration, given that they appear to be operational in small family day-care settings, as well (Gunnar et al., 2010, in press). To come full circle, then, current evidence suggests that the features of child care that we have highlighted need to be examined in conjunction with children's temperaments and experiences of stress to best capture the processes that render child care either a positive or negative experience for young children.

# Implications for Child-Care Research

The evidence we have reviewed raises the possibility that the emergence and nature of both negative and positive social-emotional effects associated with child care depend on the interplay between children's individual differences, notably those associated with temperament and stress reactivity, and the circumstances of their child care, particularly with regard to the social challenges these settings pose to young children and how well the children are supported by the adults who care for them in their efforts to manage these challenges. This assertion is consistent with both the biological sensitivity to context theory (Boyce & Ellis, 2005) and with the differential susceptibility hypothesis (Belsky, 1997; Belsky & Pluess, 2009). While the differential susceptibility hypothesis focuses on genes and temperamental dispositions, and the biological sensitivity to context theory emphasizes physiological reactivity to stress as a trait that enhances sensitivity to context, they are both consistent with the argument that children at the extremes of the temperament spectrum will be more sensitive to variations in environmental conditions. Accordingly, children with more reactive temperaments would be hypothesized not only to experience more stress and negative outcomes than other children do when rearing conditions are poor but also to experience less stress and better outcomes when rearing conditions are especially supportive.

At the outset, we argued that emerging evidence at the intersection of stress reactivity, temperament, and child care holds the potential to advance understanding of the factors that converge to render child care a beneficial or risky context for young children. We further asserted that this question needs to be approached from an individual differences perspective, for which notions of biological sensitivity to context are especially pertinent. Guided by this general perspective, we call for four lines of research.

First, to make predictions about the effects of child care on children with different temperaments, there is a need for increased specificity to the measurement of temperament and with that, better description of which aspects of temperament are involved in shaping the trajectories of social and emotional development for children with varying child-care experiences. In this context, it is essential to have more refined information about the composition of the child-care peer group (with regard to temperamental and behavioral dispositions) and more refined observations of both how children with different temperaments negotiate peer interactions and how caregivers either support or fail to support these efforts. Further, it will be important to examine the possibility that high-quality caregiving entails somewhat different strategies for the withdrawn, inhibited child than it does for the approach-driven, exuberant child.

Second, longitudinal studies are needed to understand how children who begin care with differing temperamental dispositions change over time in child care as a function of their experiences with both child-care providers and other children. This will necessarily entail sampling children in different types of care, with differing peer demands and wide variation in the quality of caregiving. Further, this work needs to take the children's age and history of child-care experience into account.

Third, longitudinal studies that integrate assessments of temperament and stress reactivity (i.e., cortisol levels) are needed to advance understanding of how these two facets of development—one a biologically based disposition and the other a physiological reaction to environmental conditions—interact to influence children's social-emotional, regulatory, and cognitive responses to child care in the short and long term. Here again, specific observations of how children who vary in temperament and stress reactivity deploy coping strategies when confronted with challenging social encounters—and are facilitated or undermined by their caregivers—will be an important element of this work.

Finally, we urge efforts to examine the role that temperament, as well as other indicators of biological risk (e.g., special needs status), plays in conjunction with indicators of environmental risk, such as poverty and low parental education or literacy, in influencing the developmental impacts of child care. Such efforts would have huge payoffs (see, e.g., Corapci, 2008).

Our hope is that these new directions for research on child care, focused on questions of individual differences, will ultimately lead to greater understanding of the children for whom we should have the greatest concern and, accordingly, who we have the greatest potential to help, as they experience the challenges and opportunities posed by their early histories of exposure to child care.

# References

Almas, A., Phillips, D., & Fox, N. (2009). *The moderating role of temperamental reactivity in the associations between non-maternal childcare during toddlerhood and children's internalizing and externalizing behavior at 5 years of age.* Unpublished manuscript, University of Maryland.

Almas, A., Phillips, D., Henderson, H., Hane, A., Degnan, K., & Fox, N. (in press). The relations between infant negative reactivity, non-maternal childcare, and children's interactions with familiar and unfamiliar peers. *Social Development.*

Belsky, J. (1988). The "effects" of infant day care reconsidered. *Early Childhood Research Quarterly, 3,* 235–272.

Belsky, J. (1997). Variation in susceptibility to rearing influences: An evolutionary argument. *Psychological Inquiry, 8,* 182–186.

Belsky, J., & Pluess, M. (2009). Beyond diathesis stress: Differential susceptibility to environmental influences. *Psychological Bulletin, 135,* 885–908.

Belsky, J., Vandell, D. L., Burchinal, M., Clarke-Stewart, K. A., McCartney, K., Owen, M. T., et al. (2007). Are there long-term effects of early child care? *Child Development, 78,* 681–701.

Boyce, W. T., & Ellis, B. J. (2005). Biological sensitivity to context: I. An evolutionary developmental theory of the origins and functions of stress reactivity. *Development and Psychopathology, 17,* 271–301.

Clarke-Stewart, K. A. (1988). "The 'effects' of infant day care reconsidered" reconsidered. *Early Childhood Research Quarterly, 3,* 293–318.

Corapci, F. (2008). The role of child temperament on Head Start preschoolers' social competence in the context of cumulative risk. *Journal of Applied Developmental Psychology, 29,* 1–16.

Crockenberg, S. C. (2003). Rescuing the baby from the bathwater: How gender and temperament influence how child care affects child development. *Child Development, 74,* 1034–1038.

Crockenberg, S. C., & Leerkes, E. M. (2005). Infant temperament moderates associations between childcare type and quantity and externalizing and internalizing behaviors at 2½ years. *Infant Behavior and Development, 28,* 20–35.

Degnan, K. A., Henderson, H. A., Fox, N. A., & Rubin, K. H. (2008). Predicting social wariness in middle childhood: The moderating roles of childcare history, maternal personality, and maternal behavior. *Social Development, 17,* 471–487.

De Shipper, J. C., Tavecchio, L. W. C., van IJzendoorn, M. H., & van Zeijl, J. (2004). Goodness-of-fit in center day care: Relations of temperament, stability, and quality of care with the child's adjustment. *Early Childhood Research Quarterly, 19,* 257–272.

Dettling, A. C., Gunnar, M. R., & Donzella, B. (1999). Cortisol levels of young children in full-day childcare centers: Relations with age and temperament. *Psychoneuroendocrinology, 24,* 519–536.

Dettling, A., Parker, S. W., Lane, S., Sebanc, A., & Gunnar, M. R. (2000). Quality of care and temperament determine whether cortisol levels rise over the day for children in full-day child care. *Psychoneuroendocrinology, 25,* 819–836.

Dickerson, S. S., & Kemeny, M. E. (2004). Acute stressors and cortisol responses: A theoretical integration and synthesis of laboratory research. *Psychological Bulletin, 130,* 355–391.

Fabes, R. A., Hanish, L. D., & Martin, C. L. (2003). Children at play: The role of peers in understanding the effects of child care. *Child Development, 74,* 1039–1043.

Fein, G., & Fox, N. (Guest Eds.). (1988). Special Issue: Infant day care. *Early Childhood Research Quarterly, 3*(3).

Fox, N. A., Henderson, H. A., Marshall, P. J., Nichols, K. E., & Ghera, M. M. (2005). Behavioral inhibition: Linking biology and behavior within a developmental framework. *Annual Review of Psychology, 56,* 235–262.

Fox, N. A., Henderson, H. A., Rubin, K. H., Calkins, S. D., & Schmidt, L. A. (2001). Continuity and discontinuity of behavioral inhibition and exuberance: Psychophysiological and behavioral influences across the first four years of life. *Child Development, 72,* 1–21.

Geoffroy, M.-C., Cote, S. M., Parent, S., & Seguin, J. R. (2006). Daycare attendance, stress, and mental health. *Canadian Journal of Psychiatry, 51,* 607–615.

Gunnar, M. R., Kryzer, E., van Ryzin, M. J., & Phillips, D. A. (2010). The rise in cortisol in family day care: Associations with aspects of care quality, child behavior, and child sex. *Child Development, 81,* 853–870.

Gunnar, M. R., Kryzer, E., van Ryzin, M. J., & Phillips, D. A. (in press). The import of the cortisol rise at child care differs as a function of behavioral inhibition. *Developmental Psychology.*

Gunnar, M. R., & Quevedo, L. (2007). The neurobiology of stress and development. *Annual Review of Psychology, 58,* 145–173.

Hane, A. A., Cheah, C., Rubin, K. H., & Fox, N. A. (2008). The role of maternal behavior in the relation between shyness and social reticence in early childhood and social withdrawal in middle childhood. *Social Development, 17,* 795–811.

Joels, M., & Baram, T. Z. (2009). The neurosymphony of stress. *Nature Review Neuroscience, 10,* 459–466.

Kagan, J., Snidman, N., & Arcus, D. (1998). Childhood derivates of high and low reactivity in infancy. *Child Development, 69,* 1483–1493.

Lamb, M. E., & Ahnert, L. (2006). Nonparental child cae: Context, concepts, correlates, and consequences. In W. Damon & R. M. Lerner (Series Eds.) & K. A. Renninger & I. E. Sigel (Vol. Eds.), *Handbook of child psychology: Vol. 4. Child psychology in practice* (6th ed., pp. 950–1016). Hoboken, NJ: Wiley.

Legendre, A. (2003). Environmental features influencing toddlers' bioemotional reactions in day care centers. *Environment and Behavior, 35,* 523–549.

National Institute of Child Health and Human Development Early Child Care Research Network. (2005). Early child care and children's development in the primary grades: Results from the NICHD Study of Early Child Care. *American Educational Research Journal, 43,* 537–570.

National Institute of Child Health and Human Development Early Child Care Research Network. (2006). *Child care and child development. Results from the NICHD Study of Early Child Care and Youth Development.* New York: Guildford.

Ouellet-Morin, I., Tremblay, R. E., Boivin, M., Meaney, M., Kramer, M., & Cote, S. M. (2010). Diurnal cortisol secretion at home and in child care: A prospective study of 2-year old toddlers. *Journal of Child Psychology and Psychiatry, 51,* 295–303.

Phillips, D., Crowell, N., Sussman, A. L., Fox, N., Hane, A., Gunnar, M., et al. (2010). *Child care and children's temperaments: A story of moderation.* Manuscript submitted for publication.

Phillips, D., & Lowenstein, A. (in press). Structure and goals of preschool educational settings. *Annual Review of Psychology.*

Phillips, D., McCartney, K., Scarr, S., & Howes, C. (1987). Selective review of infant day care research: A cause for concern. *Zero to Three, 7,* 18–21.

Phillips, D., McCartney, K., & Sussman, A. (2006). Child care and early development, In K. McCartney & D. Phillips (Eds.), *Handbook of Early Childhood Development* (pp. 471–489). Malden, MA: Blackwell.

Pluess, M., & Belsky, J. (2009). Differential susceptibility to rearing experience: The case of childcare. *Journal of Child Psychology and Psychiatry, 50,* 396–404.

Roozendaal, B., McEwen, B. S., & Chattarji, S. (2009). Stress, memory and the amygdale. *Natural Review of Neuroscience, 10,* 423–433.

Rothbart, M. K., & Bates, J. E. (2006). Temperament. In W. Damon & R. Lerner (Series Eds.) & N. Eisenberg (Vol. Ed.), *Handbook of child psychology: Vol. 3. Social, emotional, and personality development* (pp. 99–166). Hoboken, NJ: Wiley.

Sims, M., Guilfoyle, A., & Parry, T. S. (2006). Children's cortisol levels and quality of child care provision. *Child: Care, Health, and Development, 32,* 453–466.

Sroufe, L. A. (1988). A developmental perspective on day care. *Early Childhood Research Quarterly, 3,* 283–292.

Tout, K., de Haan, M., Kipp Campbell, E. K., & Gunnar, M. R. (1998). Social behavior correlates of cortisol activity in child care: Gender differences and time of day effects. *Child Development, 69,* 1247–1262.

van Goozen, S. H., Fairchild, G., Snoek, H., & Harold, G. T. (2007). The evidence for neurobiological model of childhood antisocial behavior. *Psychological Bulletin, 133,* 149–182.

Vermeer, H. J., & van IJzendoorn, M. H. (2006). Children's elevated cortisol levels at daycare: A review and meta-analysis. *Early Childhood Research Quarterly, 21,* 390–401.

Volling, B., & Feagans, L. (1995). Infant day care and children's social competence. *Infant Behavior and Development, 18,* 177–188.

Watamura, S. E., Donzella, B., Alwin, J., & Gunnar, M. R. (2003). Morning to afternoon increases in cortical concentrations for infants and toddlers at child care: Age differences and behavioral correlates. *Child Development, 74,* 1006–1020.

Watamura, S. E., Kryzer, E. M., & Robertson, S. S. (2009). Cortisol patterns at home and child care: Afternoon differences and evening recovery in children attending very high quality full-day center-based child care. *Journal of Applied Developmental Psychology, 30,* 475–485.

Watamura, S. E., Sebanc, A. M., & Gunnar, M. R. (2002). Rising cortisol at childcare: Relations with nap, rest, and temperament. *Developmental Psychobiology, 40,* 33–42.

## Critical Thinking

1. How does this article help us move beyond the traditional approaches to studying how child care affects children? How does this article help you appreciate the need to study individual differences between children?

2. Why are children's temperament and reactivity to stress so important for shaping how they respond to, and are affected by, child care?

The authors wish to thank Alisa Almas for her assistance with the manuscript.

# The Role of Neurobiological Deficits in Childhood Antisocial Behavior

Stephanie H. M. van Goozen, Graeme Fairchild, and Gordon T. Harold

Antisocial behavior is a significant social and clinical concern. Every year, more than 1.6 million people are killed as a result of violence, and many more suffer from physical or mental health problems stemming from violence (World Health Organization, 2002). Antisocial behavior committed by youths is an issue of particular concern. A recent survey showed that citizens of European nations see themselves as having "significant" difficulties with antisocial behavior, and that the problem is above all associated with people under 25 years of age ("Bad behaviour," 2006).

The term *antisocial behavior* refers to the fact that people who are on the receiving end of the behavior are disadvantaged by it, and that social norms and values are violated. Not only aggression but also activities such as theft, vandalism, lying, truancy, running away from home, and oppositional behaviors are involved.

Most normally developing children will occasionally exhibit negative and disobedient behavior toward adults and engage in lying, fighting, and bullying other children. When antisocial behavior forms a pattern that goes beyond the "normal" realm and starts to have adverse effects on the child's functioning, psychiatrists tend to make a diagnosis of conduct disorder (CD) or oppositional defiant disorder (ODD; American Psychiatric Association, 1994). These disorders are relatively common in children, with estimated prevalences ranging from 5 to 10%. The extent to which these disorders can be treated via therapy is limited, and, as a result, these children are at risk for a host of negative outcomes in adolescence and adulthood, including dropping out of school, criminality unemployment, dependence on welfare, and substance abuse (Hill & Maughan, 2001).

There is a growing consensus that both child-specific (i.e., genetic, temperamental) and social (e.g., early adversity) factors contribute to the development and maintenance of antisocial behavior, although most research has focused on identifying specific contextual factors that impinge on the developing child. For example, negative life events, family stress, and parental relationship problems have been associated with antisocial-behavior problems in children. However, there is increasing evidence that factors organic to individual children exacerbate the risk of antisocial behavior to those who live with social adversity. Here, we review evidence relating to the role of neurobiological factors in accounting for the link between early adversity and childhood antisocial behavior and propose that consideration of biological factors underlying this stress-distress link significantly advances understanding of the mechanisms explaining individual differences in the etiology of antisocial behavior.

Research suggests that neurobiological deficits related to the functioning of the stress systems in children with CD are linked to antisocial behavior. We argue that familial factors (e.g., genetic influences, early adversity) are linked to negative outcomes through the mediating and transactional interplay with neurobiological deficits (see Figure 1) and propose that stress hyporeactivity is an index of persistent and serious antisocial behavior.

## Stress-Response Systems

There are clear indications that stress plays an important role in explaining individual differences in antisocial behavior. The systems involved in the regulation of stress are the neuroendocrine hypothalamic-pituitary-adrenal (HPA) axis and the psychophysiological autonomic nervous system (ANS). Cortisol is studied in relation to HPA-axis activation, and heart rate (HR) and skin-conductance (SC) responses are used as markers of ANS (re)activity.

The starting point of our approach is that antisocial individuals are less sensitive to stress. This can be deduced from the fact that antisocial individuals engage in risky or dangerous behavior more often than other people do and seem less deterred by its possible negative consequences. There are two explanations for the proposed relationship between lower stress sensitivity and antisocial behavior. One theory claims that antisocial individuals are fearless (Raine, 1996). A lack of fear leads to antisocial behavior because individuals are less sensitive to the negative consequences of their own or other people's behavior in general and to the receipt of punishment in particular. The implications for treatment are clear: Antisocial individuals will have problems learning the association between behavior and punishment, such

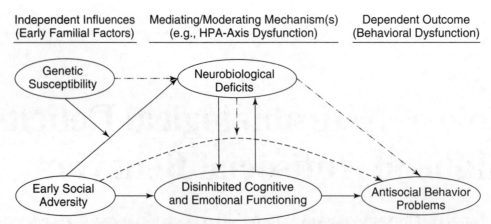

Independent Influences (Early Familial Factors) | Mediating/Moderating Mechanism(s) (e.g., HPA-Axis Dysfunction) | Dependent Outcome (Behavioral Dysfunction)

**Figure 1** Theoretical model relating early social adversity to later antisocial behavior problems. It is hypothesized that this relationship is explained by the underlying mediating and moderating role of neurobiological factors. The dashed rolled lines emanating from genetic susceptibility to neurobiological deficits and from neurobiological deficits to antisocial behavior problems represent an indirect (or mediating) pathway between these factors. The bold line emanating from genetic susceptibility to the pathway linking early social adversity to neurobiological deficits, and the dashed-dotted line from neurobiological deficits to the pathway linking early social adversity to antisocial behavior problems, represent proposed moderating influences from each source variable (i.e., genetic susceptibility and neurobiological deficits). A moderating influence is the equivalent of statistical interaction between two theoretical constructs. Bold and dashed-dotted lines in all other instances represent direct and indirect pathways linking primary theoretical constructs. For a full exposition of this model, see van Goosen, Fairchild, Snoek, and Harold (2007).

that pointing out the negative consequences of behavior, or punishing unacceptable behavior, is likely to have little or no effect.

The second explanation focuses on stress thresholds and sensation-seeking behavior (Zuckerman, 1979), and argues that antisocial individuals have elevated thresholds for stress. They are more easily bored and less easily put off by situations that normal people find stressful or dangerous.

What evidence is there that dysfunctional stress systems play a role in antisocial behavior? Several studies (e.g., Virkkumen, 1985) have found that antisocial adults have low resting levels of cortisol, SC, and HR. There is also evidence of inverse relationships between these physiological variables and the severity of the behavioral problems shown. Studies investigating the relation between biological stress parameters and antisocial behavior have also been performed in children (e.g., van Goozen et al., 1998), and the predicted (inverse) relations have been found.

Stress variables can also predict antisocial behavior over time. Raine, Venables, and Mednick (1997) measured HR in more than 1,700 three-year-old children. Aggressive behavior was assessed at age 11. Raine et al. found that low resting HR at age 3 predicted aggressive behavior at age 11. In a study of criminals' sons (who are at risk of becoming delinquent), Brenman et al. (1997) found that boys who did not become delinquent had higher HR and SC than did boys who became delinquent. The authors concluded that the boys in the former group were biologically protected by their heightened autonomic responsivity.

Studies of youths who engage in antisocial behavior show that they, like antisocial adults, have less reactive stress systems than do youths who do not engage in antisocial behavior. The question is whether the same applies to children with serious antisocial behavior who have been diagnosed with CD or ODD.

## Stress Studies in CD Children

Most studies collect stress data under resting conditions rather than during stress exposure. Antisocial individuals might be different from normal individuals in two respects: A low resting stress level could result in failing to avoid, or even approaching, stressful situations; and low stress reactivity implies that one is more fearless and cares less about possible negative consequences.

Our studies use a paradigm in which psychosocial stress is evoked by exposing children to frustration, provocation, and competition (e.g., van Goozen et al., 1998). The participant competes against a fictitious videotaped "opponent" who behaves in an antagonistic manner. The participant and opponent perform computerized tasks on which they can earn points. The participant is told that the person who earns the most points will receive an attractive prize. Some tasks are impossible to complete, which induces frustration. HR and SC are measured continuously, and cortisol is collected repeatedly in saliva.

CD children show lower HR, SC, and cortisol reactivity to stress than do normal children. Although CD children appear to be less affected at a biological level, they react more angrily and aggressively to provocation than do non-CD children and report feeling quite upset. It is known that CD children are impulsive, have hostile appraisal patterns, and engage in conflictual situations. It is striking that this pattern of appraisal and behavior is not accompanied by contextually appropriate somatic changes.

Genetic factors likely play a role in the functioning of the HPA axis and ANS. There is also evidence that stressful events—by which we mean serious stressors like neglect and traumatization—play an important role in "programming" the stress systems, particularly the HPA axis. This evidence comes mainly from nonhuman animal studies, but the neurobiological consequences of the types of severe stress that can be manipulated in animal studies also occur in humans.

# Early Experience and Family Adversity

Physical and biological problems during important phases in development (e.g., birth complications, stress or illness during pregnancy), together with early adversity (e.g., malnutrition, neglect, abuse), contribute importantly to the development of personality and psychopathology. There is increasing evidence that interactions between biological and environmental factors affect the developing brain (Huizink, Mulder, & Buitelaar, 2004).

Nonhuman animal studies show that stressors in early life can have permanent effects on the functioning of the HPA axis, resulting in altered basal and stress-reactivity levels. For example, Liu et al. (1997) varied the amount of licking and grooming behavior in mothers of newborn rats. In adulthood, offspring who had been exposed to normal maternal care were more capable of handling stress than were rats that had received less care. The former also expressed more stress-hormone receptors in the hippocampus, an area important for stress regulation, than did rats that had received less care. Thus, maternal behavior had a direct and lasting effect on the development of the stress systems of the offspring.

Such conclusions are based on data from nonhuman animals, and for obvious reasons it is difficult to conduct similar studies on humans. However, evidence from a handful of studies involving institutionalized children suggests that the processes at work are similar (Carlson & Earls, 1997; Gunnar, Morison, Chisolm, & Schuder, 2001).

Antisocial children are more likely to come from adverse rearing environments involving atypical caregiver–child interactions (Rutter & Silberg, 2002). It is known that CD children are more likely to experience compromised pre- or perinatal development due to maternal smoking, poor nutrition, or exposure to alcohol and/or drugs. It is possible that these factors have affected such children's stress-response systems and resulted in children with a difficult temperament.

# Stress Hyporeactivity as a Mediating Factor

We have suggested that physiological hyporeactivity may reflect an inability to generate visceral signals to guide behavior and, in particular, to regulate anger and reactive aggression (van Goozen, Fairchild, Snoek, & Harold, 2007). Evidence from nonhuman animals indicates that abolishing the hormonal response to stress may impair processing of social signals and lead to abnormal patterns of aggression (Haller, Halász, Mikics, & Kruk, 2004). These studies also showed that abnormal aggressive behavior can be prevented by mimicking the hormonal response normally seen during aggressive encounters. These findings have clear parallels with abnormal aggression in humans, in the sense that the behavior is not only excessive but also often risky, badly judged, and callous.

We have proposed an integrative theoretical model linking genetic factors, early adversity, cognitive and neurobiological regulatory mechanisms, and childhood antisocial behavior (van Goozen et al., 2007; see Figure 1). Interactions between genetic predispositions and the environment in which they are expressed appear to be crucial in the etiology of antisocial-behavior problems. A genetic predisposition toward antisocial behavior may be expressed in adverse rearing environments in which the child receives harsh or inconsistent discipline or is exposed to high levels of interparental conflict or marital breakdown (Moffitt, 2005). It is likely that the origin of antisocial behavior in young children lies in this combination of a difficult temperament and a harsh environment in which there is ineffective socialization: A difficult child elicits harsh, inconsistent, and negative socialization behaviors, as a result of which a difficult temperament develops into antisocial behavior (Lykken, 1995). Conversely, the effects of a genetic predisposition may be minimized if the child is raised in an environment in which the parents express warmth or adopt a consistent, authoritative parenting style.

Some children are born with a more easygoing temperament than others. In cases of "hard-to-manage" children, a child's genotype can evoke negative behavior from the environment because genetic influences lead the individual to create, seek out, or otherwise end up in environments that match the genotype (Rutter & Silberg, 2002). These active, evocative gene–environment processes are extremely important in understanding the development and continuity of antisocial behavior (Moffitt, 2005). Social factors occurring independently of the child's genetic makeup or temperament can serve as contributory factors (Harold, Aitken, & Shelton, 2008).

We noted above that early brain development is vulnerable to the effects of environmental stress (Huizink et al., 2004), and that CD children are likely to have been exposed to early stress. A down-regulation of the stress-response system in the face of chronic stress in early life would be an adaptive mechanism, avoiding chronic arousal and excessive energy expenditure that could ultimately result in serious pathophysiological consequences. Given what we know about the background of CD children, it is plausible that these processes have occurred.

We propose that physiological hyporeactivity is a mediating and/or moderating factor for persistent and severe antisocial behavior and that the effects of variations in genetic makeup and early adversity on childhood antisocial behavior occur via this deficit. The primary pathway by which familial factors are linked to antisocial outcome is the reciprocal interplay with neurobiological deficits and resulting disinhibited cognitive (e.g., impulsivity, hostile bias) and emotional (e.g., increased anger) processing, with the latter serving as the psychological gateway through which neurobiological deficits find their expression in antisocial behavior.

# Conclusion

Antisocial behavior in children can be persistent and difficult to treat. Although behavioral interventions have been shown to be effective in milder forms of problem behavior, they have limited effectiveness in more seriously disturbed children (Hill & Maughan, 2001).

At present, we do not know what causes the pattern of neuro-biological impairments observed in antisocial children, although it is clear that genetic factors are involved (Caspi et al., 2002). An important line of research suggests that psychosocial adversity affects brain development. Knowing that many CD children have problematic backgrounds, it seems possible that exposure to severe stress has had an effect on the development of their stress systems. Longitudinal research in high-risk children is needed to shed more light on this issue.

Future interventions and treatments should benefit from a neurobiological approach: Neurobiological assessment of high-risk children could indicate whether their deficits are such that interventions involving "empathy induction" or "learning from punishment," for example, are unlikely to work. In such cases, pharmacological interventions could be considered as a treatment option. An important line of future research is to establish whether CD children with attenuated stress (re)activity would be more effectively treated by using pharmacological therapies that reinstate normal HPA-axis functioning.

Current interventions for childhood antisocial behavior have limited success because we lack knowledge of the cognitive–emotional problems of these children and their neurobiological bases. We also fail to assess the environmental risk factors that affect individual neurodevelopment. Furthermore, available treatment options do not target the individual's specific neurobiological vulnerabilities. It seems prudent to identify subgroups of children in whom different causal processes initiate and maintain behavioral problems. This should result in a better match between patient and treatment.

A final point is that the understandable tendency to focus on persistence of antisocial behavior runs the risk of overlooking the fact that a substantial proportion of antisocial children do not grow up to be antisocial adults (with prevalence rates for antisocial children who persist into adulthood ranging from 35 to 75%). Neurobiological factors could also account for this: Promising data from a handful of studies show that neurobiological factors differ between children who persist in and desist from antisocial behavior (Brennan et al., 1997; van de Wiel, van Goozen, Matthys, Snoek, & van Engeland, 2004). Expanding on this research base is essential if we are to reach a more adequate understanding of the causes, course, and consequences of childhood antisocial behavior and, most importantly, devise effective ways of reducing the negative consequences for society.

## Recommended Reading

Hill, J., & Maughan, B. (2001). *Conduct disorders in childhood and adolescence.* Cambridge, UK: Cambridge University Press. A clearly written and comprehensive review for readers who wish to expand their knowledge on conduct disorders in youngsters.

Moffitt, T.E. (2005). The new look of behavioral genetics in developmental psychopathology: Gene–environment interplay in antisocial behaviors. *Psychological Bulletin, 131,* 533–554. Explains and discusses the gene–environment interplay in antisocial behavior in more detail.

van Goozen, S.H.M., Fairchild, G., Snoek, H., & Harold, G.T. (2007). The evidence for a neurobiological model of childhood antisocial behavior. *Psychological Bulletin, 133,* 149–182. Discusses the neurobiological basis of antisocial behavior in greater detail than the current paper.

## References

American Psychiatric Association. (1994). *Diagnostic and statistical manual of mental disorders* (4th ed.). Washington, DC: Author.

Bad behaviour 'worst in Europe'. (2006). BBC News. Downloaded April 30, 2008, from http://news.bbc.co.uk/l/hi/uk/4751315.stm

Brennan, P.A., Raine, A., Schulsinger, F., Kirkegaard-Sorensen, L., Knop, J., Hutchings, B., et al. (1997). Psychophysiological protective factors for male subjects at high risk for criminal behavior. *American Journal of Psychiatry, 154,* 853–855.

Carlson, M., & Earls, F. (1997). Psychological and neuroendocrinological sequelae of early social deprivation in institutionalized children in Romania. *Annals of the New York Academy of Sciences, 807,* 419–428.

Caspi, A., McClay J., Moffitt, T.E., Mill, J., Martin, J., Craig, I.W., et al. (2002). Role of the genotype in the cycle of violence in maltreated children. *Science, 297,* 851–854.

Gunnar, M.R., Morison, S.J., Chisholm, K., & Schuder, M. (2001). Salivary cortisol levels in children adopted from Romanian orphanages. *Development and Psychopathology, 13,* 611–628.

Harold, G.T, Aitken, J.J., & Shelton, K.H. (2008). Inter-parental conflict and children's academic attainment: A longitudinal analysis. *Journal of Child Psychology and Psychiatry, 48,* 1223–1232.

Haller, J., Halász, J., Mikics, E., & Kruk, M.R. (2004). Chronic glucocorticoid deficiency-induced abnormal aggression, autonomic hypoarousal, and social deficit in rats. *Journal of Neuroendocrinology, 16,* 550–557.

Hill, J., & Maughan, B. (2001). *Conduct disorders in childhood and adolescence.* Cambridge, UK: Cambridge University Press.

Huizink, A.C., Mulder, E.J.H., & Buitelaar, J.K. (2004). Prenatal stress and risk for psychopathology: Specific effects or induction of general susceptibility. *Psychological Bulletin, 130,* 115–142.

Liu, D., Diorio, J., Tannenbaum, B., Caldji, C., Francis, D., Freedman, A., et al. (1997). Maternal care, hippocampal glucocorticoid receptors, and hypothalamic-pituitary-adrenal responses to stress. *Science, 277,* 1659–1662.

Lykken, D.T (1995). *The antisocial personalities.* Hillsdale, NJ: Erlbaum.

Moffitt, T.E. (2005). The new look of behavioral genetics in developmental psychopathology: Gene–environment interplay in antisocial behaviors. *Psychological Bulletin, 131,* 533–554.

Raine, A. (1996). Autonomic nervous system activity and violence. In D.M. Stoff & R.B. Cairns (Eds.), *Aggression and violence: Genetic, neurobiological and biological perspectives* (pp. 145–168). Mahwah, NJ: Erlbaum.

Raine, A., Venables, P.H., & Mednick, S.A. (1997). Low resting heart rate at age 3 years predisposes to aggression at age 11 years: Evidence from the Mauritius Child Health Project. *Journal of the American Academy of Child and Adolescent Psychiatry, 36,* 1457–1464.

Rutter, M., & Silberg, J. (2002). Gene–environment interplay in relation to emotional and behavioral disturbance. *Annual Review of Psychology, 53,* 463–490.

van de Wiel, N.M.H., van Goozen, S.H.M., Matthys, W., Snoek, H., & van Engeland, H. (2004). Cortisol and treatment effect in children with disruptive behavior disorders: A preliminary study. *Journal of the American Academy of Child and Adolescent Psychiatry, 43,* 1011–1018.

van Goozen, S.H.M., Fairchild, G., Snoek, H., & Harold, G.T. (2007). The evidence for a neurobiological model of childhood antisocial behaviour. *Psychological Bulletin, 133,* 149–182.

van Goozen, S.H.M., Matthys, W., Cohen-Kettenis P.T, Gispen-de Wied, C., Wiegant, V.M., & van Engeland, H. (1998). Salivary cortisol and cardiovascular activity during stress in oppositional-defiant disorder boys and normal controls. *Biological Psychiatry, 43,* 531–539.

Virkkunen, M. (1985). Urinary free cortisol secretion in habitually violent offenders. *Acta Psychiatrica Scandinavica, 72,* 40–44.

World Health Organization (2002). *World report on violence and health.* E.G. Krug, L.L. Dahlman, J.A. Mercy, A.B. Zwi, & R. Lozano (Eds.). Geneva, Switzerland: Author.

Zuckerman, M. (1979). *Sensation seeking: Beyond the optimum level of arousal.* Hillsdale, NJ: Erlbaum.

# Critical Thinking

1. Several highly visible cases of tragic school violence across the country have been traced to incidences of antisocial behavior in school. According to this article, what factors might have contributed toward making some children antisocial?

2. Suppose you are the parent of a young child who has been diagnosed with conduct disorder (CD) or oppositional defiant disorder (ODD). Based on this article, does this mean that your child will grow up to be an antisocial adult? What interventions (both behavioral and pharmacological) might be available to you for your child and how effective might these be?

3. Imagine you are a director or principal in a school with preschoolers or young children. Over the past year, the number of young children being diagnosed with possible conduct disorders in your school has doubled. Given the information in this article, what specific steps would you take to assist these children and families that would involve your teachers, the parents, and the surrounding medical community?

Address correspondence to **Stephanie H.M. van Goozen,** School of Psychology Cardiff University, Tower Building, Park Place, Cardiff CF10 3AT, United Kingdom; e-mail: vangoozens@cardiff.ac.uk.

From *Current Directions in Psychological Science*, March, 2008, pp. 224–228. Copyright © 2008 by the Association for Psychological Science. Reprinted by permission of Sage Publications via Rightslink.

# Is Your Child Gay?

If your son likes sissy stuff or your daughter shuns feminine frocks, he or she is more likely to buck the heterosexual norm. But predicting sexual preference is still an inexact science.

JESSE BERING

We all know the stereotypes: an unusually light, delicate, effeminate air in a little boy's step, an interest in dolls, makeup, princesses and dresses, and a strong distaste for rough play with other boys. In little girls, there is the outwardly boyish stance, perhaps a penchant for tools, a square-jawed readiness for physical tussles with boys, and an aversion to all the perfumed, delicate trappings of femininity.

These behavioral patterns are feared, loathed and often spoken of directly as harbingers of adult homosexuality. It is only relatively recently, however, that developmental scientists have conducted controlled studies to identify the earliest and most reliable signs of adult homosexuality. In looking carefully at the childhoods of gay adults, researchers are finding an intriguing set of behavioral indicators that homosexuals seem to have in common. Curiously enough, the age-old homophobic fears of many parents reflect some genuine predictive currency.

J. Michael Bailey and Kenneth J. Zucker, both psychologists, published a seminal paper on childhood markers of homosexuality in 1995. Bailey and Zucker examined sex-typed behavior—that long, now scientifically canonical list of innate sex differences in the behaviors of young males versus young females. In innumerable studies, scientists have documented that these sex differences are largely impervious to learning. They are also found in every culture examined. Of course, there are exceptions to the rule; it is only when comparing the aggregate data that sex differences leap into the stratosphere of statistical significance.

The most salient differences are in the domain of play. Boys engage in what developmental psychologists refer to as "rough-and-tumble play." Girls prefer the company of dolls to a knee in the ribs. Toy interests are another key sex difference, with boys gravitating toward toy machine guns and monster trucks and girls orienting toward baby dolls and hyperfeminized figurines. Young children of both sexes enjoy pretend play, but the roles within the fantasy context are gender-segregated by age two. Girls enact the role of, say, cooing mothers, ballerinas or fairy princesses, and boys prefer to be soldiers and superheroes. Not surprisingly, therefore, boys naturally select other boys for playmates, and girls would much rather play with other girls.

So on the basis of some earlier, shakier research, along with a good dose of common sense, Bailey and Zucker hypothesized that homosexuals would show an inverted pattern of sex-typed childhood behaviors—little boys preferring girls as playmates and becoming infatuated with their mother's makeup kit; little girls strangely enamored of field hockey or professional wrestling—that sort of thing. Empirically, the authors explain, there are two ways to investigate this hypothesis, with either a prospective or retrospective study. Using the prospective method, young children displaying sex-atypical patterns are followed into adolescence and early adulthood so that their sexual orientation can be assessed at maturity.

This method is not terribly practical for several reasons. Given that a small proportion of the population is homosexual, prospective studies require a large number of children. This approach also takes a long time, around 16 years. Finally, not a lot of parents are likely to volunteer their children. Right or wrong, this is a sensitive topic, and usually it is only children who present significant sex-atypical behaviors who are brought into clinics and whose cases are made available to researchers.

## Rough-and-Tumble Girls

For example, in a 2008 study psychologist Kelley Drummond and her colleagues interviewed 25 adult women who were referred by their parents for assessment at a mental health clinic when they were between three and 12 years old. At the time, all these girls had several diagnostic indicators of gender identity disorder. They might have strongly preferred male playmates, insisted on wearing boys' clothing, favored rough-and-tumble play, stated that they would eventually grow a penis or refused to urinate in a sitting position. Although only 12 percent of these women grew up to be gender dysphoric (the uncomfortable sense that your biological sex does not match your gender), the odds of these women reporting a bisexual or homosexual orientation were up to 23 times higher than would occur in a general sample of young women. Not all tomboys become lesbians, of course, but these data suggest that lesbians often have a history of cross-sex-typed behaviors.

And the same holds for gay men. Bailey and Zucker, who conducted a retrospective study in which adults answered questions about their past, revealed that 89 percent of randomly sampled gay men recalled cross-sex-typed childhood behaviors exceeding the heterosexual median.

Critics have argued that participants' memories may be distorted to fit with societal expectations and stereotypes. But in a clever study published in 2008 in *Developmental Psychology*, evidence from childhood home videos validated this retrospective method. People blindly coded child targets on the latter's sex-typical behaviors, as shown on the screen. The authors found that "those targets who, as adults, identified themselves as homosexual were judged to be gender nonconforming as children."

Numerous studies have since replicated this general pattern, revealing a strong link between childhood deviations from gender role norms and adult sexual orientation. There is also evidence of a "dosage effect": the more gender-nonconforming characteristics there are in childhood, the more likely it is that a homosexual or bisexual orientation will be present in adulthood.

Not all little boys who like to wear dresses grow up to be gay, nor do all little girls who despise dresses become lesbians. Many will be straight, and some, let's not forget, will be transsexuals. I was rather androgynous, showing a mosaic pattern of sex-typical and atypical behaviors. In spite of my parents' preferred theory that I was simply a young Casanova, Zucker and Bailey's findings may account for that old Polaroid snapshot in which 11 of the 13 other children at my seventh birthday party are little girls. But I wasn't an overly effeminate child, was never bullied as a "sissy" and, by the time I was 10, was indistinguishably as annoying, uncouth and wired as my close male peers.

## On the Monkey Bars

In fact, by age 13, I was deeply socialized into masculine norms. I took to middle school wrestling as a rather scrawny 80-pound eighth grader, and in so doing, ironically became all too conscious of my homosexual orientation.

Cross-cultural data show that prehomosexual boys are more attracted to solitary sports such as swimming, cycling and tennis than they are to rougher contact sports such as football and soccer; they are also less likely to be childhood bullies. In any event, I distinctly recall being with the girls on the monkey bars during recess in second grade while the boys were in the field playing football and looking over at them, thinking to myself how that was rather strange. I wondered why anyone would want to act that way.

Researchers readily concede that there are quite likely multiple—and no doubt extremely complicated—developmental routes to adult homosexuality. Heritable, biological factors interact with environmental experiences to produce sexual orientation. Because the data often reveal very early emerging traits in prehomosexuals, children who show pronounced sex-atypical behaviors may have more of a genetic loading to their homosexuality, whereas gay adults who were sex-typical

as children might trace their homosexuality more directly to particular childhood experiences.

Then we arrive at the most important question of all. Why do parents worry so much about whether their child may or may not be gay? All else being equal, I suspect we would be hard-pressed to find parents who would actually prefer their offspring to be homosexual. Evolutionarily, parental homophobia is a no-brainer: gay sons and lesbian daughters are not likely to reproduce (unless they get creative).

But bear this in mind, parents, there are other ways for your child to contribute to your overall genetic success than humdrum sexual reproduction. I don't know how much money or residual fame is trickling down to, say, k. d. lang, Elton John and Rachel Maddow's close relatives, but I can only imagine that these straight kin are far better off in terms of their own reproductive opportunities than they would be without a homosexual dangling so magnificently on their family trees. So cultivate your little prehomosexual's native talents, and your ultimate genetic payoff could, strangely enough, be even larger with one very special gay child than it would be if 10 mediocre straight offspring leaped from your loins.

If researchers eventually perfect the forecasting of adult sexual orientation in children, would parents want to know? I can say as a once prehomosexual pipsqueak that some preparation on the part of others would have made it easier on me, rather than constantly fearing rejection or worrying about some careless slipup leading to my "exposure." It would have at least avoided all those awkward, incessant questions during my teenage years about why I wasn't dating a nice pretty girl (or questions from the nice pretty girl about why I was dating her and rejecting her advances).

And another thing: it must be pretty hard to look into your prehomosexual toddler's limpid eyes, brush away the cookie crumbs from her cheek and toss her out on the streets for being gay.

## Critical Thinking

1. According to Bailey and Zucker, how can you tell if a young child is gay?

2. Suppose you are a parent and you observe your child exhibiting sex-atypical behavior. How do you react to your child, and why?

3. Does the article's author have a personal bias? Do his personal anecdotes influence your interpretation of the findings or understanding of children's sexuality?

4. What role might environmental experiences play in the development of sexual orientation?

5. Do the research findings in this article suggest a strong genetic link to homosexuality? Why or why not?

Excerpted from *Why Is the Penis Shaped Like That? . . . And Other Reflections on Being Human*, by **JESSE BERING**, by arrangement with Scientific American/Farrar, Straus and Giroux, LLC (North America), Transworld Ltd (UK), Jorge Zahara Editora Ltda (Brazil). Copyright © 2012 by Jesse Bering.

# Caring about Caring: What Adults Can Do to Promote Young Children's Prosocial Skills

Marilou Hyson and Jackie L. Taylor

*"I worry about how the children treat one another every day. There are those moments when they struggle to be kind, and when they make fun of someone else."*

—Amanda, Pre-K Teacher

*"[Some children] have a tough time fitting in. Children who . . . physically lash out at other children, hit, punch. I have a large number [of children] who need help."*

—Rachel, Teacher

*"I feel . . . responsible for the quality of the interactions children experience. Sometimes children make fun of one another or bully each other."*

—Maria, Pre-K Teacher

As reflected in these teachers' comments, many early childhood educators are seriously concerned about bullying and aggression. Children's negative social behaviors also dominate the media and are the focus of much current research. Recent studies result in some progress in understanding the early origins and harmful effects of physical and relational aggression (Crick et al. 2006) and designing interventions to reduce its occurrence (Ostrov et al. 2009). It is equally important to nurture positive alternatives—children's *prosocial* feelings and behavior toward others.

Nancy Eisenberg, a leading researcher in the area of prosocial behavior, and her coauthors describe prosocial behavior as "voluntary behavior intended to benefit another" (Eisenberg, Fabes, & Spinrad 2006, 646). This article draws extensively on their excellent literature review. The second author of this article (Taylor) conducted a survey and face-to-face interviews about prosocial development with early childhood teachers and directors in the spring of 2010. In the interviews, early childhood educators used terms such as *empathy, sharing, compassion, helping others, compromise, respect for others,* and *hugging other children* to describe prosocial behavior in young children

(Taylor 2010). Prosocial behaviors might also include cooperating, including others in play, giving a compliment, and comforting a child who is upset (Honig 2004; Ramaswamy & Bergin 2009).

One word, *voluntary,* is especially important in Eisenberg's definition of prosocial behavior. If children are forced to "be nice and share" or told to "say you're sorry," then their behavior is not voluntary and cannot be considered prosocial. The research we share in this article highlights many ways that children's prosocial development can be actively promoted without being forced.

## A Preview

With Eisenberg's definition in mind, we summarize the research on young children's prosocial development and behavior. In doing so, we emphasize studies and literature reviews published within the past 10 years, especially those with implications for how early childhood educators might intentionally promote prosocial skills among preschool and kindergarten children.

It is important to know that much of the prosocial research has been done with parents and children at home, not with teachers and children in center-based or family child care settings. Also, most of the research is correlational: thus it cannot show definitively that certain experiences *cause* children to be more prosocial or that children's prosocial skills *cause* them to develop other desirable competencies. However, we are confident of our conclusions here because in this review we have relied not just on the results of small individual studies but also on evidence from a number of different types of studies.

**A recent study of Head Start children showed that those who scored higher on assessments of prosocial competence were, later on in the year, assessed to be among the most "cognitively ready" for school.**

The scope of this short review is intentionally limited. We will be able to touch only briefly on research on prosocial development in infants and toddlers, in children with disabilities, and among culturally diverse children within and beyond the United States. Many of the general references listed at the end of this article will help readers pursue these and other topics in more depth.

# Key Questions

Our discussion of the research is organized around three questions: (1) Why is prosocial development so important—that is, why care about caring? (2) How do children develop prosocial skills—that is, are prosocial children born or made? and (3) What can early childhood professionals do to promote children's prosocial development?

## Why Care about Caring?

Early childhood educators want to help children become kind, generous, and empathic. Starting early is important, because early prosocial tendencies often continue into later years. Children who are more prosocial when they begin school continue to be more prosocial in the primary grades (Eisenberg, Fabes, & Spinrad 2006). And this pattern seems to continue: one study that followed children from preschool into early adulthood found that children who were observed to spontaneously share toys more often than their classmates showed more prosocial skill 19 years later (Eisenberg et al. 1999).

Children's prosocial competence also predicts their strengths in other areas, correlating with academic as well as social-emotional skills. For example, a recent study of Head Start children showed that those who scored higher on assessments of prosocial competence were, later on in the year, assessed to be among the most "cognitively ready" for school (Bierman et al. 2009). Another study showed that first-graders with low-income backgrounds who were more helpful to others had greater literacy skills in third grade (Miles & Stipek 2006). So there are many compelling reasons to care about caring.

## Prosocial Children: Are they Born or Made?

---

**"I have students who are 'natural' helpers. These are the students who clean up without being asked, help a friend clean up spilled milk, or give someone a toy without having to be asked. I am not sure why some children have a predisposition toward prosocial behavior and some seem to struggle."**

—Amanda, Pre-K Teacher

---

Although research has identified early signs of empathy and prosocial behavior among infants and toddlers, it takes a sensitive observer to notice these signs (see, for example, Quann & Wien 2006; McMullen et al. 2009; Gillespie & Hunter 2010). By their first birthday, many children show what Hoffman (2000) calls "empathic distress"—for example, crying when they see other children cry, or looking sad when caregivers look unhappy. Around 14 months, many toddlers spontaneously try to help if someone seems unhappy. Usually this involves the toddler doing something that would be comforting to the toddler, not necessarily what would comfort the other person. By 18 months, toddlers will even help a stranger in a research laboratory, picking up an object if they notice that the adult seems unable to do so (Warneken & Tomasello 2006).

During the preschool years, more signs of empathy, helpfulness, and concern for others usually appear, and preschoolers become more aware of and intentional about their prosocial actions (Eisenberg, Fabes, & Spinrad 2006). School-age children often behave more prosocially than they did as preschoolers, in part because of their growing ability to understand others' thoughts and feelings and to regulate their own distress and impulsive behavior.

Most children begin early in life to act in ways that show empathy and prosocial tendencies. Yet it is obvious that—at any age—some children are more helpful, concerned, and caring than others. Are such children simply born more prosocial than their peers?

Just as there are genetic influences on children's general sociability and empathy (Knafo et al. 2008), there may also be genetic influences on prosocial tendencies, as seen in studies of identical twins later raised in different families (Knafo & Plomin 2006). However, researchers agree that these influences are small in comparison with the strong influence of children's environments, especially when it comes to children's actual behaviors, not just their general feelings of empathy. The researchers' findings contrast with the common belief—reflected by a number of teachers interviewed in Taylor's study and shown in this article—that differences in prosocial tendencies are essentially genetic or "natural."

## What Can Early Childhood Professionals Do to Promote Children's Prosocial Development?

Adults are the most important features of young children's environments (see Pianta 1997; Shonkoff & Phillips 2000). In various ways, adults may encourage or discourage children's development of prosocial behavior. Across the grades, including preschool, classroom observations reveal how seldom children behave in prosocial ways and how seldom teachers explicitly encourage, reinforce, or discuss expectations for prosocial behavior (Spinrad & Eisenberg 2009). Even in some infant classrooms, observers may find active discouragement of prosocial interactions and relationships, as seen in one center (McMullen 2010) where staff always "taught" babies one by one, in isolation from others, and where staff moved a baby away from another when the two had contentedly been playing side by side.

Basing our discussion on relevant research, in the next section of the review we describe five areas in which early childhood professionals' actions can promote prosocial development.

# Promoting Children's Prosocial Development

Educators can promote prosocial development by building secure relationships, creating classroom community, modeling prosocial behavior, establishing prosocial expectations, and supporting families.

## 1. Building Secure Relationships

When teachers intentionally create secure relationships in early childhood programs, children benefit socially, emotionally, and academically (Howes & Ritchie 2002; Hamre & Pianta 2001; Palermo et al. 2007). Now we have evidence of the specific benefit of these relationships for children's prosocial development.

**"Some [children] have much more prosocial families [who are nurturing], and in a classroom they are more caring with peers."**

—Jermayn, Pre-K Teacher

Secure relationships begin at home but extend into early childhood program settings as well. Differences in children's attachment histories (that is, whether they have previously developed secure or insecure relationships within their family) may help explain why some children enter an early childhood program with more well-developed prosocial skills than others. There is good evidence that young children who have warm relationships and secure attachments to their parents are more likely to be empathic and prosocial (Kestenbaum, Farber, & Sroufe 1989; Zhou et al. 2002; Campbell & von Stauffenberg 2008), probably because children are more likely to notice and copy the behavior of adults to whom they feel a close connection.

Turning from parents to teachers, whether or not a child's parental attachment has been secure, when teachers have warm, secure relationships with individual children, those children show more empathy and behave more positively toward others in the classroom and as reported by mothers (Pianta & Stuhlman 2004; Spinrad & Eisenberg 2009).

Teachers can nurture warm relationships in many small ways: responding sensitively to children's everyday needs, interacting in emotionally supportive ways, listening and conversing with sincere attention. Sharing these small moments has been called "banking time" (Driscoll & Pianta 2010)—that is, investing brief, positive moments with individual children, especially those who are often overlooked or viewed negatively (Hyson 2004, 2008).

## 2. Creating a Classroom Community

A core value of developmentally appropriate practice is to create a caring community of learners (Copple & Bredekamp 2009). Just as warm teacher-child relationships predict children's prosocial skills, being a member of a close-knit learning community—in a classroom or family child care home—can also support children's prosocial development.

**Humans are social creatures, and even subtle changes in children's social environments can make them more aware of their connection to the group.**

Humans are social creatures, and even subtle changes in children's social environments can make them more aware of their connection to the group. In a recent experimental study (Over & Carpenter 2009), 18-month-olds were much more likely to spontaneously help a stranger in need after they were shown photographs of people together with others than after viewing photographs of individuals alone. Teachers can help create this affiliative atmosphere in many ways, such as posting class photographs, talking about group projects, and reminding children that they are all members of a caring group of friends.

Young children are actually more likely to use prosocial behavior when they are with other children than with adults (Eisenberg, Fabes, & Spinrad 2006). Teachers can tap into this tendency by creating many opportunities for children to work and play together. As they do so, however, teachers need to scaffold children's emerging prosocial skills; for example, teachers can give a child words with which to offer help to a classmate or suggest ways that two children can extend their pretend play in a mutually interesting direction.

Friendships are especially important as contexts for prosocial development. Children who have more "supportive friendships" in preschool have been found to be more prosocial (Sebanc 2003). Wanting to play with their friends, young children may feel motivated to behave prosocially, because other children may not want to play with them unless they cooperate, help solve problems, and engage in flexible give-and-take.

There is some evidence that children who spend time with very prosocial classmates are likely to become more prosocial themselves; over time, they come to adopt the more helpful, caring norms of their peers (Eisenberg, Fabes, & Spinrad 2006). However, it is often the case that the less-prosocial children tend to spend their time with one another, thus having fewer opportunities to learn from more-prosocial classmates.

These findings should encourage teachers to identify everyday opportunities and plan strategies that will give children time, space, and support to become fully engaged members of their learning communities (see in particular Whitin 2001; Honig 2004; Jones 2005; Copple & Bredekamp 2009). As part of this effort, teachers can intentionally counteract the separation of less-prosocial children from the more prosocial by pairing and mixing up children for various activities (Bodrova & Leong 2007), creating more ways for children to experience others' prosocial and empathic behavior.

## 3. Modeling Prosocial Behavior

**"I have found that most of my students respond very well to the use of puppet activities. The use of a puppet makes a huge difference. If they can talk through the problem with a puppet, they build up to talking it over with a peer."**

—Amanda, Pre-K Teacher

Adults' demonstration or modeling has been found to influence children's prosocial development in study after study (Eisenberg, Fabes, & Spinrad 2006). Many of these studies have used laboratory experiments to examine influences on children's generosity. For example, when children observe an adult behave in a generous way, they are very likely to imitate that behavior, not just immediately but even after considerable time has passed—as summarized by Eisenberg and Fabes (1998).

If an adult is warm, nurturing, and responsive, children are especially likely to notice and imitate aspects of their behavior, including prosocial actions (Hyson 2004). Thus, teachers who have those characteristics have a good chance of prompting children's empathic, helpful, caring, generous behavior by demonstrating that behavior themselves. Opportunities present themselves every day: helping a child put on a new jacket that buttons differently; expressing loving concern when a child's parent has been ill; and offering some materials that will help a child finish a project. To highlight this modeling, teachers can comment on what they are doing and why ("Oh, Carla, I see that you're having trouble with that. How about if I help you? It makes me happy to help children out when they need it."). Teachers can also promote these skills by modeling kindness and consideration in their interactions with colleagues and families.

## 4. Establishing Prosocial Expectations

**"I think how I address prosocial behavior plays a large role in how the children interact with one another and what they learn in the classroom."**

—Amanda, Pre-K Teacher

Important as adult relationships and modeling are, it is not enough to set up a nurturing environment for prosocial development, or even just to be prosocial ourselves. Children are more likely to develop empathy and prosocial skills if adults make it clear that they *expect* (but do not *force*) them to do so. Polite requests for children to be helpful and generous are effective and often necessary prompts for prosocial behavior (Eisenberg, Fabes, & Spinrad 2006). Sometimes adults may

think that they should be more subtle, but children—especially toddlers—may need clear prompts or cues. For example, in a laboratory study, Brownell, Svetlova, and Nichols (2009) found that 25-month-old children would share voluntarily, but to elicit this prosocial behavior the adult needed to offer an explicit cue about what she liked or wanted ("I like crackers!" "I need a cracker!"). Note that this differs from an adult either remaining silent and waiting for the child to think of sharing the snack or, at the other extreme, telling the child that he or she must share the crackers.

**It is important to point out that there are large cultural differences and that adults in some cultures emphasize prosocial skills far more than others.**

Researchers find that when parents are very clear about the kind of behavior they expect—and what they do *not* wish to see—children indeed become more helpful and caring than when expectations are less clearly defined (Eisenberg, Fabes, & Spinrad 2006). An especially strong influence on prosocial development is adults' use of the discipline strategy *induction*—pointing out the reasons for rules or the effect of one's behavior on others. For example, Marta's mother explains how her daughter's friend Sarah is feeling because of Marta's hurtful comments. As summarized by Eisenberg and her coauthors (2006), research indicates that induction strategies are most likely to be effective when they are presented at the child's developmental level, clear and consistent, and delivered by someone with whom the child has a close, warm relationship—which could potentially include both parents and teachers.

Adults differ a great deal in how clearly they communicate prosocial expectations to children. Although a full discussion of cross-cultural research on prosocial development is not our intention in this article, it is important to point out that there are large cultural differences and that adults in some cultures emphasize prosocial skills far more than others (Levine, Norenzayan, & Philbrick 2001; Eisenberg, Fabes, & Spinrad 2006; Trommsdorff, Friedlmeier, & Mayer 2007). In many cultures, including most non-Western cultures, children are often expected to do real work that helps the family, care for brothers and sisters, share even their beloved possessions with younger children, and generally be more cooperative members of the community. Teachers may notice differences between children's behaviors that emerge from families' culturally influenced prosocial expectations and may see these behaviors reflected in children's pretend play and interactions with peers. When a class includes children who are growing up within such cultures, other children may have a chance to learn more cooperative and caring ways of relating to their peers.

## 5. Supporting Families

In prosocial development, as in other aspects of children's lives, families are the first and most influential teachers. There are several areas where early childhood educators might support families in this role. Whatever their culture, many families do interact with their children in ways that are likely to encourage children to become more empathic, generous, and helpful. However, other families may, without realizing it, undermine prosocial development by relying on practices that are unlikely to produce these desired results. For example, many parents believe that children will become more prosocial if they are given treats or other rewards for "being nice." Research indicates just the opposite, however (Eisenberg, Fabes, & Spinrad 2006; Warneken & Tomasello 2008). Although such rewards may produce short-term results, they actually backfire in the long term. Children may become *less* generous when the expected rewards stop coming their way.

> **Research indicates that if parents help children learn to cope with their own negative feelings, their children become better able to tune in to and help others who are distressed.**

While respecting families' home practices, early childhood professionals might share information about the risk of rewarding children for sharing or being kind, and help families think of other ways to encourage these prosocial behaviors. For example, research indicates that if parents help children learn to cope with their own negative feelings, their children become better able to tune in to and help others who are distressed. Further, when parents talk with children about their own feelings, listen to their children when they are upset, and "coach" their children about how to express emotions, their children are likely to develop more prosocial skills (see, for example, Garner, Dunsmore, & Southam-Gerrow 2008). Research points out a few cautions about these conversations, however. First, one study (Trommsdorff 1995) suggests that when a mother becomes *overly* involved in discussing her child's distress or other highly emotional issues, the child may become so focused on her or his own negative feelings that it is difficult to regulate those emotions in order to empathize with others. And second, there is evidence that children often try to avoid conversations about their prior experiences with negative emotions, especially if mothers do not use an accepting, supportive, child-centered approach during the conversation (Waters et al. 2010).

Besides helping families have productive conversations, early childhood educators can also support families during other situations that can create risks for children's prosocial development. For example, data from a study of families living in poverty (Ryan, Kalil, & Leininger 2009) shows that those mothers who had less of a social safety net (that is, fewer available sources of social support) had children who were less prosocial, with more behavior problems, perhaps because of their mothers' stress levels. Through family and community outreach, early childhood programs may be in a good position to help families strengthen their social networks, thereby benefiting many aspects of parents' lives, including but not limited to their ability to strengthen their children's prosocial skills.

Families' child care challenges may also affect their children's prosocial development. Using data from the NICHD (National Institute for Child Health and Human Development) Study of Early Child Care and Youth Development, Morrissey (2009) suggests that when families use multiple child care arrangements, their children, especially younger toddlers, show less prosocial behavior than those who are in a more stable child care setting. It is possible that multiple caregiving arrangements lessen opportunities for children to develop the secure caregiver relationships that predict prosocial skill development. Although early childhood educators usually cannot control the factors that lead to individual families' child care decisions, they can advocate for policies and resources that help families access consistent, high-quality child care arrangements that will support prosocial skills as well as other competencies.

## Conclusion—Taking Action for Caring

The research reviewed in this article clearly demonstrates that the prosocial domain is a critical component of children's development. The research shows how specific early experiences may help children gain essential prosocial skills. We hope the evidence will encourage teachers, researchers, and policy makers to be at least as intentional in this domain as they are in early literacy and mathematics. The suggestions that follow, the examples of prosocial curricula and resources, and the checklist of recommended teaching practices may jump-start this process.

### Program-Level Actions.

A good starting point for an intentional approach to prosocial development is to examine and enhance the overall quality of the early childhood program. Children who attend higher quality family child care and center-based programs seem to show more empathy and positive behavior toward other children (Spinrad & Eisenberg 2009; Romano, Kohen, & Findlay 2010). This is not surprising, as many of the features associated with overall program quality are also likely to support the development of prosocial skills. Such features include professionally prepared staff who are grounded in early childhood development and pedagogy; a program environment that encourages children to work and play together; discipline strategies that encourage collaborative problem-solving; an emphasis on teachers' knowledge of holistic child development; and supports for close adult-child and peer relationships.

As suggested earlier, teachers can reexamine everyday routines and activities to see if the prosocial potential of the activities is being fully tapped (see "Research into Action"). In addition, teachers can implement various specialized curricula and other resources (see "Examples of Curricula and Other Resources for Supporting Prosocial Development") that target

# Examples of Curricula and Other Resources for Supporting Prosocial Development

*A Blueprint for the Promotion of Prosocial Behavior in Early Childhood* [including the Bingham Early Childhood Prosocial Curriculum], by Elda Chesebrough, Patricia King, Thomas P. Gullotta, and Martin Bloom. 2005. New York: Springer.

Center on the Social and Emotional Foundations for Early Learning (CSEFEL). **http://csefel.vanderbilt .edu**

Children's Kindness Network. **www.ckn-usa.org** (See especially Moozie's Kindness Curriculum, 2004.)

The Devereux Early Childhood Initiative. **www.devereux.org/site/PageServer? pagename=deci_index**

The Incredible Years: Parents, Teachers, and Children Social Skills Training series. **www.incredibleyears .com**

*Second Step: Social-Emotional Skills for Early Learning,* by Committee for Children. 2011. **www .cfchildren.org/programs/ssp/early-learning**

*Skillstreaming in Early Childhood: Teaching Prosocial Skills to the Preschool and Kindergarten Child,* by Ellen McGinnis and Arnold P. Goldstein. 1990. Champaign, IL: Research Press.

"Teaching Parents to Teach Children to be Prosocial," by Linda K. Elksnin and Nick Elksnin. 2000. **www .ldonline.org/article/Teaching_Parents_to_ Teach_Their_Children_to_be_Prosocial**

*Teaching Tolerance,* a project publication of the Southern Poverty Law Center. **www.tolerance.org**

positive social behavior and character education. A few cautions, however: such materials should be used to strengthen—but not replace—an across-the-board emphasis on prosocial development. And when deciding to adopt any curriculum or other resource, early childhood professionals should think about whether the resource is consistent with the research on prosocial development as well as whether there is evidence that the resource has been effective with children whose cultural or developmental characteristics are similar to those with whom the resource will be used.

## Research actions.

Thought-provoking as it is, the existing prosocial research is still more focused on looking at children at home with their families rather than in early childhood program environments. In the future, researchers must focus their work more closely on early childhood settings. Such research should analyze the effects of variations in classroom practices, teacher-child interactions, and teacher professional development on children's prosocial outcomes. Researchers also need to look more closely at early childhood programs' ability to support prosocial behavior among *all* children—children who differ in

# Research into Action: A Checklist of Everyday Strategies to Promote Prosocial Development

Early childhood program staff can intentionally implement these and other research-based strategies, using them in ways that respond to children's culture and other individual characteristics. Many of the references in this article may help guide implementation.

- Is each child—especially any child who may be struggling with behavioral challenges—involved in frequent, friendly, individual interactions with teachers? (Even a few minutes a day helps to build a secure relationship, the foundation for prosocial competence.)
- Are classroom jobs used to build prosocial skills and a sense of community? (Invite a few children to pitch in and help open boxes that have been delivered, or ask a child for help in rearranging the books so that others can find them more easily.)
- Does the physical environment promote cooperation and community participation? (Set up interest areas and materials to invite small groups to work together, share supplies, and interact.)
- Are photos displayed that show children working and playing together, and that show children as members of their class and of their families?
- Do adults model prosocial behavior by showing empathy and kindness to coworkers as well as to children by using respectful language such as *thank you* and *please*?
- Do teachers specifically, sincerely acknowledge children's prosocial behavior? ("I see that the two of you have started cleaning up the art area together. That's real cooperation!")
- Do teachers explain the reasons behind rules and help children understand the effects of their behavior on others? This kind of inductive discipline seems to encourage children to be kind and helpful.
- Do classroom rules include positive, prosocial expectations—the *dos,* not just the *don'ts*? ("We are kind to our friends.")
- Do teachers scaffold children's efforts to be helpful and kind by giving them words to use or offering suggestions about what to do? ("Polly, I think Adriana looks worried about getting a turn with that doll. What if you say 'It's OK, you will have it in just a few minutes'? Or maybe you can say, 'Adriana, how about if we play together?'")
- Do teachers prompt children to help them learn prosocial behavior? ("Mary, would you show our new friend where to put the blocks when everyone is finished playing with them?")
- Do families receive practical, culturally relevant tips during home visits or at parent meetings to encourage prosocial behavior at home? (Avoid rewards for niceness. Instead, set clear expectations and foster warm relationships.)

culture and language as well as those children who have disabilities and developmental delays (Dunlap & Powell 2009).

## Policy actions.

Finally, policy makers must focus attention on education standards and public policies that make prosocial competence a priority for early childhood education programs. Prosocial behavior is as important as, and also contributes to, outcomes in other developmental domains. Social and emotional outcomes are not always well represented in state early learning guidelines (Scott-Little, Kagan, & Frelow 2006), and specific prosocial indicators are even less evident. As states revise or expand these guidelines, early childhood professionals can point policy makers toward research that supports a more prominent role for prosocial outcomes.

---

**Children who attend higher quality family child care and center-based programs seem to show more empathy and positive behavior toward other children.**

---

With these actions by educators, researchers, and policy makers, the early childhood field will demonstrate with a clear, unified voice that it "cares about caring."

# References

Bierman, K.L., M.M. Torres, C.E. Domitrovich, J.A. Welsh, & S.D. Gest. 2009. "Behavioral and Cognitive Readiness for School: Cross-Domain Associations for Children Attending Head Start." *Social Development* 18 (2): 305–23.

Bodrova, E., & D.J. Leong. 2007. *Tools of the Mind: The Vygotskian Approach to Early Childhood Education.* 2nd ed. Columbus, OH: Merrill/Prentice Hall.

Brownell, C.A., M. Svetlova, & S. Nichols. 2009. "To Share or Not to Share: When Do Toddlers Respond to Another's Needs?" *Infancy* 14 (1): 117–30.

Campbell, S., & C. von Stauffenberg. 2008. "Child Characteristics and Family Processes That Predict Behavioral Readiness for School." In *Disparities in School Readiness: How Do Families Contribute to Transitions in School?* The Penn State University Family Issues Symposia Series, eds. A. Booth & A. Crouter, 225–58. New York: Taylor & Francis Group/Lawrence Erlbaum Associates.

Copple, C., & S. Bredekamp, eds. 2009. *Developmentally Appropriate Practice in Early Childhood Programs Serving Children from Birth through Age 8.* 3rd ed. Washington, DC: NAEYC.

Crick, N.R., J.M. Ostrov, J.E. Burr, C. Cullerton-Sen, E.A. Jansen-Yeh, & P. Ralston. 2006. "A Longitudinal Study of Relational and Physical Aggression in Preschool." *Journal of Applied Developmental Psychology* 27 (3): 254–68.

Driscoll, K.C., & R.C. Pianta. 2010. "Banking Time in Head Start: Early Efficacy of an Intervention Designed to Promote Supportive Teacher-Child Relationships." *Early Education and Development* 21 (1): 38–64.

Dunlap, G., & D. Powell. 2009. "Promoting Social Behavior of Young Children in Group Settings: A Summary of Research." Roadmap to Effective Intervention Practices #3. Tampa: University of South Florida, Technical Assistance Center on Social Emotional Intervention for Young Children. www.challengingbehavior.org/do/resources/documents/roadmap_3.pdf.

Eisenberg, N., & R.A. Fabes. 1998. "Prosocial Development." In *Handbook of Child Psychology, Vol. 3, Social, Emotional, and Personality Development.* 5th ed., eds. W. Damon & N. Eisenberg, 701–78. New York: John Wiley & Sons.

Eisenberg, N., R.A. Fabes, & T.L. Spinrad. 2006. "Prosocial Development." In *Handbook of Child Psychology, Vol.3, Social, Emotional, and Personality Development.* 6th ed., eds. W. Damon & R. Lerner, 647–702. Hoboken, NJ: John Wiley & Sons.

Eisenberg, N., I.K. Guthrie, B.C. Murphy, S.A. Shepard, A. Cumberland, & G. Carlo. 1999. "Consistency and Development of Prosocial Dispositions: A Longitudinal Study." *Child Development* 70 (6): 1360–372.

Garner, P.W., J.C. Dunsmore, & M. Southam-Gerrow. 2008. "Mother-Child Conversations about Emotions: Linkages to Child Aggression and Prosocial Behavior." *Social Development* 17: 259–77.

Gillespie, L.G., & A. Hunter. 2010. "Believe, Watch, Act! Promoting Prosocial Behavior in Infants and Toddlers." Rocking and Rolling: Supporting Infants, Toddlers, and Their Families. *Young Children* 65 (1): 42–43. www.naeyc.org/files/yc/file/201001/RocknRollWeb0110.pdf

Hamre, B.K., & R.C. Pianta. 2001. "Early Teacher–Child Relationships and the Trajectory of Children's School Outcomes through Eighth Grade." *Child Development* 72 (2): 625–38.

Hoffman, M.L. 2000. *Empathy and Moral Development: Implications for Caring and Justice.* New York: Cambridge University Press.

Honig, A. 2004. "How Teachers and Caregivers Can Help Children Become More Prosocial." In *A Blueprint for the Promotion of Pro-Social Behavior in Early Childhood,* eds. E. Chesebrough, P. King, T.P. Gullotta, & M. Bloom, 51–92. Issues in Children's and Families' Lives series. New York: Kluwer/Plenum.

Howes, C., & S. Ritchie. 2002. *A Matter of Trust: Connecting Teachers and Learners in the Early Childhood Classroom.* New York: Teachers College Press.

Hyson, M. 2004. *The Emotional Development of Young Children: Building an Emotion-Centered Curriculum.* New York: Teachers College Press.

Hyson, M. 2008. *Enthusiastic and Engaged Learners: Approaches to Learning in the Early Childhood Classroom.* New York: Teachers College Press; Washington, DC: NAEYC.

Jones, N. 2005. "Big Jobs: Planning for Competence." *Young Children* 60 (2): 86–93.

Kestenbaum, R., E.A. Farber, & L.A. Sroufe. 1989. "Individual Differences in Empathy among Preschoolers: Relation to Attachment History." *New Directions for Child Development* (44): 51–64.

Knafo, A., & R. Plomin. 2006. "Prosocial Behavior from Early to Middle Childhood: Genetic and Environmental Influences on Stability and Change." *Developmental Psychology* 42 (5): 771–86.

Knafo, A., C. Zahn-Waxler, C. Van Hulle, J.L. Robinson, & S.H. Rhee. 2008. "The Developmental Origins of a Disposition toward Empathy: Genetic and Environmental Contributions." *Emotion* 8 (6): 737–52.

Levine, R.V., A. Norenzayan, & K. Philbrick. 2001. "Cross-Cultural Differences in Helping Strangers." *Journal of Cross-Cultural Psychology* 32: 543–60.

McMullen, M.B. 2010 "Confronting the Baby Blues: A Social Constructivist Reflects on Time Spent in a Behaviorist Infant Classroom." *Early Childhood Research & Practice* 12 (1). http://ecrp.uiuc.edu/v12n1/mcmullen.html.

McMullen, M.B., J. Addleman, A.M. Fulford, S. Mooney, S. Moore, S. Sisk, & J. Zachariah. 2009. "Learning to Be *Me* while Coming to Understand *We*: Encouraging Prosocial Babies in Group Settings." *Young Children* 64 (4): 20–28. www.naeyc.org/yc/pastissues.

Miles, S.B., & D. Stipek, 2006. "Contemporaneous and Longitudinal Associations between Social Behavior and Literacy Achievement in a Sample of Low-Income Elementary School Children." *Child Development* 77: 103–17.

Morrissey, T.W. 2009. "Multiple Child-Care Arrangements and Young Children's Behavioral Outcomes." *Child Development* 80 (1): 59–76.

Ostrov, J.M., G.M. Massetti, K. Stauffacher, S.A. Godleski, K.C. Hart, K.M. Karch, A.D. Mullins, & E.E. Ries. 2009. "An Intervention for Relational and Physical Aggression in Early Childhood: A Preliminary Study." *Early Childhood Research Quarterly* 24 (1): 15–28.

Over, H., & M. Carpenter. 2009. "Eighteen-Month-Old Infants Show Increased Helping Following Priming with Affiliation." *Psychological Science* 20 (10): 1189–93. www.eva.mpg.de/psycho/pdf/Publications_2009_PDF/Over_Carpenter_2009.pdf.

Palermo, F., L.D. Hanish, C.L. Martin, R.A. Fabes, & M. Reiser. 2007. "Preschoolers' Academic Readiness: What Role Does the Teacher-Child Relationship Play?" *Early Childhood Research Quarterly* 22 (4): 407–22.

Pianta, R.C. 1997. "Adult-Child Relationship Processes and Early Schooling." *Early Education and Development* 8 (1): 11–26.

Pianta, R.C., & M. Stuhlman. 2004. "Teacher-Child Relationships and Children's Success in the First Years of School." *School Psychology Review* 33 (3): 444–58.

Quann, V., & C. Wien. 2006. "The Visible Empathy of Infants and Toddlers." *Young Children* 61 (4): 22–29.

Ramaswamy, V., & C. Bergin. 2009. "Do Reinforcement and Induction Increase Prosocial Behavior? Results of a Teacher-Based Intervention in Preschools." *Journal of Research in Childhood Education* 23 (4): 527–38.

Romano, E., D.E. Kohen, & L.C. Findlay. 2010. "Associations among Child Care, Family, and Behavior Outcomes in a Nation-Wide Sample of Preschool-Aged Children." *International Journal of Behavioral Development* 34 (5): 427–40.

Ryan, R.M., A. Kalil, & L. Leininger. 2009. "Low-Income Mothers' Private Safety Nets and Children's Socioemotional Well-Being." *Journal of Marriage and Family* 71 (2): 278–97.

Scott-Little, C., S.L. Kagan, & V. Frelow. 2006. "Conceptualization of Readiness and the Content of Early Learning Standards: The Intersection of Policy and Research?" *Early Childhood Research Quarterly* 21: 153–73.

Sebanc, A. 2003. "The Friendship Features of Preschool Children: Links with Prosocial Behavior and Aggression." *Social Development* 12 (2): 249–68.

Shonkoff, J.P., & D.A. Phillips, eds. 2000. *From Neurons to Neighborhoods: The Science of Early Childhood Development.* Report of the National Research Council. Washington, DC: National Academies Press. www.nap.edu/catalog.php?record_id=9824.

Spinrad, T.L., & N. Eisenberg. 2009. "Empathy, Prosocial Behavior, and Positive Development in the Schools." In *Handbook of Positive Psychology in Schools*, eds. R. Gilman, E.S. Huebner, & M.J. Furlong, 119–29. New York: Routledge/Taylor & Francis Group.

Taylor, J.L. 2010. Prosocial Development Survey and Interviews with ECE Teachers and Directors. Unpublished research.

Trommsdorff, G. 1995. "Person–Context Relations as Developmental Conditions for Empathy and Prosocial Action: A Cross-Cultural Analysis." In *Development of Person–Context Relations*, eds. T.A. Kinderman & J. Valsiner, 113–46. Hillsdale, NJ: Lawrence Erlbaum.

Trommsdorff, G., W. Friedlmeier, & B. Mayer. 2007. "Sympathy, Distress, and Prosocial Behavior of Preschool Children in Four Cultures." *International Journal of Behavioral Development* 31 (3): 284–93.

Warneken, F., & M. Tomasello. 2006. "Altruistic Helping in Human Infants and Young Chimpanzees." *Science* 31: 1301–03.

Warneken, F., & M. Tomasello. 2008. "Extrinsic Rewards Undermine Altruistic Tendencies in 20-Month-Olds." *Developmental Psychology* 44 (6): 1785–88.

Waters, S., E. Virmani, R.A. Thompson, S. Meyer, A. Raikes, & R. Jochem. 2010. "Emotion Regulation and Attachment: Unpacking Two Constructs and Their Association." *Journal of Psychopathology and Behavior Assessment* 32: 37–47.

Whitin, P. 2001. "Kindness in a Jar." *Young Children* 56 (5): 18–22.

Zhou, Q., N. Eisenberg, S. Losoya, R.A. Fabes, M. Reiser, I.K. Guthrie, et al. 2002. "The Relations of Parental Warmth and Positive Expressiveness to Children's Empathy-Related Responding and Social Functioning: A Longitudinal Study." *Child Development* 73: 893–915.

# Critical Thinking

1. Compare and contrast ways that children themselves and early childhood professionals can promote children's prosocial behaviors.

2. Hyson and Taylor state that educators can promote prosocial development in five ways. What are they, and what are some other ways that educators could promote prosocial development within the classroom?

3. Why do less-prosocial children tend to spend time with one another, and how might this affect their prosocial development?

---

**MARILOU HYSON**, PhD, is a US and international early childhood consultant based in Stock-bridge, Massachusetts. A former editor in chief of *Early Childhood Research Quarterly* and former NAEYC associate executive director, she has published several books on emotional development and children's approaches to learning. marilou. hyson@gmail.com. **JACKIE L. TAYLOR**, MS, is program director of the Texas AEYC in Austin, home of the T.E.A.C.H. Early Childhood TEXAS Project. Jackie is a 2009 Head Start Fellow and serves on the State Early Childhood Career Development System Advisory Committee. She has provided training and consulting on children's prosocial behavior to early childhood programs for over 18 years. jackietaylor@texasaeyc.org.

This Research in Review article was edited by journal research editor Mary McMullen, PhD, professor of early childhood education at Indiana University in Bloomington.

The authors wish to thank the teachers and directors in the Central Texas area who participated in the surveys and interviews. For copies of survey information, please contact Jackie Taylor at jackietaylor@ texasaeyc.org.

---

# Culture, Peer Interaction, and Socioemotional Development

## Xinyin Chen

Developmental research has indicated that peer interaction plays an important role in children's socioemotional functioning and adjustment (Hartup, 1992; Rubin, Bukowski, & Parker, 2006). Peer interaction provides opportunities for children to learn social and problem-solving skills from each other and to understand rules and standards for appropriate behaviors in different settings. Moreover, social relationships established through interaction are a major source of feelings of security and belonging, which are associated with socioemotional development in various domains (see Rubin et al., 2006, for a review). On the other hand, peer interaction is likely to be shaped by cultural norms and values in the society or community. As argued by Hinde (1987), different levels of social experiences are embedded within an all-reaching cultural system. Consistent with this argument, cross-cultural research has indicated that, in part, culture determines the nature, function, and features of children's peer interaction (e.g., Farver, Kim, & Lee, 1995; Schneider, Smith, Poisson, & Kwan, 1997).

Given this background, my colleagues and I have suggested an initial idea about the role of peer interaction in bridging culture and socioemotional development (e.g., Chen, Chung, & Hsiao, 2009). In this article, I elaborate on this idea and attempt to frame it with a relatively systematic contextual-developmental perspective. According to this perspective, social interaction in various settings is an important context that serves to mediate the links between cultural values and individual development. The social evaluation and regulation processes in peer interaction play a crucial role in building and facilitating the links. Specifically, during interaction, peers evaluate individual behaviors in ways that are consistent with the norms and values endorsed in the peer world. Moreover, peers react to these behaviors accordingly and express particular attitudes (e.g., acceptance, rejection) toward children who display the behaviors. Social evaluations and reactions, in turn, may regulate children's behaviors and ultimately their developmental patterns. In the following sections, I focus on the main aspects of this perspective, including (a) culture and social evaluations, (b) the regulatory function of peer interaction, and (c) the active role of children in the social processes. The article concludes with a discussion of general issues, implications, and future directions.

## Culture and Social Evaluations in Peer Interaction

Different societies and communities may place different values on children's social behaviors and characteristics such as independence, obedience, and emotion expression (e.g., Hofstede, 2001; Kleinman, 1986; Safdar et al., 2009; Schwartz, 1994, 2009). These values, in turn, provide a basis for social evaluations and reactions in peer interaction. According to Chen and French (2008), two major dimensions of socioemotional functioning, social initiative and self-control, are reflected in most of these values. Whereas social initiative, which refers to the tendency to initiate and maintain social participation, as often indicated by reactivity in challenging situations, is relatively more valued in Western self-oriented societies (e.g., Asendorpf, 1993; Chen et al., 1998; Smetana, 2002), self-control, the ability to modulate behavioral and emotional reactivity in social interaction, is more emphasized in group-oriented or collectivistic societies (e.g., Greenfield, Suzuki, & Rothstein-Fisch, 2006; Ho, 1986; Schwartz, 1994). Consistent with this pattern, Chen et al. (1998) found that child reactivity, which might impede spontaneous social engagement and participation, was positively associated with maternal acceptance and support in China, but with maternal disappointment, disapproval, and punishment orientation Canada; Chen et al. (2003) found that Chinese parents expected their children to maintain a higher level of control than Canadian parents expected from theirs; Schwartz (1994) found that individuals in group-oriented nations attributed greater importance to values of self-discipline and compliance; and Keller et al. (2004) reported that in Western cultures, self-regulation or control is viewed as conflicting with the child's autonomy and freedom, whereas in group-oriented cultures, it is viewed as a duty, expressing social maturity and competence. Cultural values regarding the two dimensions may affect the attitudes of children in different societies toward social behaviors, such as prosocial-cooperative behavior (active social participation with effective control), aggression-disruption (high social initiative and low control), and shyness (low social initiative and adequate control to constrain behaviors and emotions toward self).

There is cumulative evidence indicating cross-cultural differences in children's and adolescents' judgments and evaluations of social behaviors. In Western societies, for example, prosocial-cooperative behavior is often seen as a personal decision based on such factors as how much one likes the target person(s) (Eisenberg, Fabes, & Spinrad, 2006). In societies that value group harmony, however, children view prosocial-cooperative behavior as more obligatory. According to Miller (1994), whereas individuals in Western societies attempt to maintain a balance between prosocial concerns and individual freedom of choice, individuals in group-oriented societies view responsiveness to the needs of others to be a fundamental commitment. Indeed, it has been found that, relative to their American counterparts, youth in some Asian and Latino societies tend to hold a higher standard of social responsibility and are more concerned about prosocial-cooperative behaviors in social interaction (e.g., Miller, 1994; Schneider, Fonzi, Tomada, & Tani, 2000).

Cole and her colleagues (e.g., Cole, Bruschi, & Tamang, 2002) have studied how Brahman and Tamang school-age children in rural Nepal judge and react to anger and aggression. Brahmans are high-caste Hindus who value caste hierarchy and dominance. In contrast, Tamangs, with a background of Tibetan Buddhism, value social equality, compassion, and modesty. Accordingly, Brahman children are more likely to endorse anger and aggressive behaviors than are Tamang children. Killen and Brenick (2011) have found that Korean children view aggressive behavior as more negative, and peer exclusion of aggressive children as more legitimate, than do U.S. children. Although aggression is generally discouraged in North America, aggressive behavior may be associated with social support and approval in certain peer groups (e.g., Rodkin, Farmer, Pearl, & van Acker, 2000). In cultures such as that of the Yanoamo Indians, in which aggressive and violent behaviors are considered socially acceptable or even desirable, aggressive children, especially boys, may be regarded as "stars" and "heroes" by their peers (Chagnon, 1983). In some central and southern Italian communities, aggressive behavior may also be perceived by children as indicating social competence (Casiglia, Lo Coco, & Zappulla, 1998). Aggressive behavior is thus associated with less negative peer evaluation in these cultures than in cultures that strictly prohibit aggression.

Cultural differences may be particularly evident in social evaluations of children's shy-inhibited behavior. In the literature (see Rubin, Coplan, & Bowker, 2009), the display of shy-inhibited behavior is thought to derive from internal anxiety and a lack of self-confidence in challenging social situations. Shy-inhibited children are believed to be socially incompetent and immature in Western, particularly North American, societies that value assertiveness, expressiveness, and competitiveness. Shyness is viewed as less problematic and deviant in some Asian and European cultures such as China, Indonesia, Korea, and Sweden (Eisenberg, Pidada, & Liew, 2001; Farver et al., 1995; Kerr, Lambert, & Bem, 1996). In traditional Chinese culture, for example, shy-inhibited behavior is considered an indication of accomplishment and maturity; shy, wary, and inhibited children are perceived as well-behaved and understanding (e.g., Chen, 2010).

Such cultural differences are highlighted by a study of peer attitudes toward children in China and Canada who displayed shy and inhibited behaviors (Chen, DeSouza, Chen, & Wang 2006). Observing peer interaction in free-play settings in groups of 4-year-olds, the researchers found that when shy children in Canada attempted to initiate social interaction, peers were likely to make negative responses such as overt refusal, disagreement, and intentional ignoring of the initiation. In contrast, peers in China tended to respond to such attempts at social interaction in a more positive manner by controlling their negative actions and by showing approval and support. The passive, wary, and low-power initiative behaviors that were often displayed by shy children were perceived by peers in Canada as incompetent but were perceived by peers in China as appropriate or even desirable, indicating cautiousness, courteousness, and a desire for social engagement. In addition, whereas in Canada, peers were more likely to make negative or high-power voluntary initiations with shy children than with nonshy children (e.g., using direct demands such as "Gimme that" or verbal teasing), in China, there were no differences in voluntary initiations that peers made to shy and nonshy children. Taken together, these results suggest that in their interactions with children who display shy behavior, peers in Canada are generally antagonistic, forceful, and unreceptive, whereas peers in China tend to be more supportive and cooperative.

Cultural values are also reflected in general peer attitudes such as acceptance and rejection. Although research findings are not highly consistent, the existing evidence indicates that shy children seem to experience fewer problems with peer acceptance in societies where assertiveness and autonomy are not valued or encouraged. Eisenberg et al. (2001), for example, found that shyness in third-grade Indonesian children was negatively associated with peer nominations of dislike. The point is further illustrated by the cross-cultural differences in relations between shyness and peer attitudes in Chinese and Canadian children and by the effects of social changes that have occurred in China over the past two decades. When my colleagues and I conducted several studies with elementary school children in the early 1990s, we consistently found that shyness was associated with peer rejection (negative sociometric nominations) in Canada but with peer acceptance (positive sociometric nominations) in China (e.g., Chen, Rubin, & Li, 1995). However, as China has shifted toward a competitive, market-oriented society, with an accompanying introduction of more individualistic values, children's shyness has increasingly been associated with peer rejection (Chang et al., 2005; Chen, Cen, Li, & He, 2005; Hart et al., 2000).

# The Regulatory Function of Culturally Directed Peer Interaction in Socioemotional Development

While culture provides guidance for social judgments and evaluations in peer interaction and imparts meanings to behaviors, peer interaction, through the evaluation and reaction processes, may regulate children's behaviors and their developmental patterns. As indicated by Duval and Silvia (2002), social interaction situations are likely to elicit one's attention to external demands, which constitutes an important condition for the regulation of behaviors. Continuous feedback from others during interaction may enhance children's awareness of social expectations and the differences between their behavior and those expectations, leading them to adjust their behavior.

From the contextual-developmental perspective, the regulatory function of peer interaction is an integral part of the mediating process through which culture influences individual development. The process may occur gradually as children attempt to maintain or modify their behaviors or behavioral styles during peer interactions to accord with culturally directed social evaluations. In North America, for example, the negative peer feedback that shy children receive creates heightened pressure on them to alter their behaviors. Those with adequate social-cognitive and self-control abilities may regulate their behaviors to improve their peer status (e.g., Rubin, Coplan, Fox, & Calkins, 1995); those who fail to do so may experience frustrations, distress, and other negative emotions such as loneliness and depression (e.g., Rubin et al., 2009), which, in turn, reinforces the negative social evaluation of shy behaviors. In China, on the other hand, the peer approval and support that shy children receive inform them that their wary and restrained behaviors are regarded as acceptable and appropriate (e.g., Chen et al., 2006). The favorable experience is conducive to the development of self-confidence, which helps shy children display their competencies in social interactions and other areas such as school performance (Chen, Chen, Li, & Wang, 2009). As noted, however, since assertiveness and self-direction are more valued recently in urban China, children may attempt to adjust their behaviors according to the new expectations (Chen, Cen, et al., 2005).

The need for intimate affect and mutual support within friendship, a sense of belonging to the group, and overall peer acceptance in larger settings such as classroom (Sullivan, 1953) is the main motivational force that directs children to participate in peer interactions, to attend to peers' social evaluations, and to maintain or modify their behaviors according to peer standards. Close relationships with peers and overall peer acceptance have been found to be associated with a sense of well-being (Rubin et al., 2006), whereas a lack of intimate friendships or the experience of peer rejection or isolation has been found to be associated with social dissatisfaction, negative self-regard, and other symptoms of psychological problems (e.g., Berndt, 2002; Hartup, 1992). Children's motivation to obtain peer affiliation and integration, as reflected in their attempt to understand others' attitudes and expectations and to maintain their behaviors accordingly, constitutes an important basis for the regulatory function of peer interaction.

A number of factors, at both the individual and the group levels, may affect the regulatory function of peer interaction. Among them, children's sensitivity to social evaluations has received some attention in developmental research. Social-evaluative sensitivity, which is largely an individual-level process that occurs in the group context, includes both cognitive and affective aspects, such as attention to evaluations of peers, understanding of social cues, and concern about social relationships. Research has indicated that sensitivity to social evaluations may (a) promote behaviors that are expected and encouraged by peers, (b) hinder behaviors that jeopardize relationships, and (c) motivate children to be attuned to social environments and actively resolve problems in interactions (Henirch, Blatt, Kuperminc, Zohar, & Leadbeater, 2001; Rudolph & Conley, 2005).

There are substantial individual and gender differences in how children attend to social evaluations due to past experiences and social-cognitive abilities (Dodge, Coie, & Lynam, 2006; Maccoby, 1998; Rudolph & Conley, 2005). Cultural values such as those of self-orientation versus group orientation may also affect children's social-evaluative sensitivity. In cultures in which how one is viewed by others is regarded as more important than how one views oneself, children may be especially inclined to attend to others' perceptions of them. Indeed, children and adolescents in East Asian societies such as Japan have been found to display higher levels of social-evaluative concern (e.g., concern about "losing face") than do children in North America (e.g., Cohen & Hoshino-Browne, 2005; Dong, Yang, & Ollendick, 1994). This cross-cultural difference may explain, in part, the findings that East Asian children tend to conform to social and cultural expectations and display rule-abiding behaviors more than do their North American counterparts (Ho, 1986; Stevenson, 1991).

## The Active Role of Children

By focusing on peer interaction processes, the contextual-developmental perspective inevitably emphasizes the active role of children in development. This role may be reflected in children's sensitivity and response (e.g., compliance, resistance) to social influence. Moreover, children may play an active role through their participation in adopting existing cultures and constructing new cultures for social evaluations and other activities in the group (Corsaro & Nelson, 2003). Brown (1990), for example, found that children and adolescents in the United States formed a variety of natural or informal peer groups out of common interests, such as "jocks," "populars," "partiers," "brains," and "burnouts," each with its own distinct group norm. Similarly, Chen, Chang, He, and Liu (2005) found that Chinese children often spontaneously formed groups based on their academic attitudes and prosocial-antisocial orientations. Peer cultures developed by children provide a basis for group functioning and at the same time guidance for children to engage in mutual evaluations in interaction and to maintain their behaviors according to group norms (Chen, Chang, et al., 2005).

The construction of new cultures may be most likely to take place in peer activities of children with different backgrounds (Chen & Chen, 2010; Tamis-LeMonda et al., 2008). International and domestic migrations have made exposure to different beliefs and lifestyles a part of the experience of most children and adolescents today. Moreover, communication and exchange across nations in the globalization process have created a constantly changing context with diverse values for youth in most societies. The varied backgrounds of children are a resource for their construction of new cultural systems that incorporate different, and perhaps complementary, values and behavioral norms such as responsibility, achievement, and independence (Fuligni, 1998). Social competence that children develop based on mixed and integrated cultural values may allow them to function effectively and flexibly in various circumstances.

# General Issues, Implications, and Future Directions

Cross-cultural research has indicated considerable variations in socioemotional functioning among children in different societies (e.g., Whiting & Edwards, 1988). To explain the variations, researchers often focus on the analysis of cultural backgrounds in terms of collectivistic versus individualistic, independent versus interdependent, or other categories. Relatively little is known about the processes through which cultural beliefs and values are involved in human development. In the developmental field, theorists and researchers have long been interested in the socialization role of adults, especially parents and educators, in transmitting cultural values to the young generation (e.g., Goodnow, 1997; LeVine et al., 1994). Sociocultural theory (Vygotsky, 1978), for example, emphasizes children's internalization of external symbolic systems through guided learning in which adults or experienced members of the society assist children in solving problems (Cole, 1996; Rogoff, 2003). Nevertheless, the processes of cultural influence on development, particularly in socioemotional areas, may be more complicated than internalization of cultural systems or learning from senior members of the society. Unlike symbolic systems or tools for solving cognitive tasks, many cultural norms and values that serve to maintain interpersonal harmony and group functioning, such as self-control in resource-limited situations and helping others, may not have inherent benefit per se and thus may not be readily appreciated by children. Maintaining behaviors according to certain cultural standards may even require personal sacrifice, which may not occur without motivation for peer affiliation and acceptance. Moreover, adult influence becomes more indirect, distal, and perhaps inadequate as children develop greater autonomy with age and engage in more social activities outside the home and classroom. Social psychologists (e.g., Abrams & Hogg, 2004; Tajfel, 1981) have suggested the role of group norms in the formation and change of individual attitudes and behaviors. However, group norm influence is discussed mainly within the self-system in terms of *perceived* membership of social groups, group identification, self-categorization, and in-group favoritism, with little attention to the context of social interaction.

The contextual-developmental perspective highlights the role of peer interaction as a context in mediating the links between culture and socioemotional development. According to this perspective, cultural norms and values provide a basis for social evaluations in peer interaction, which, in turn, serve to regulate individual behavior. Children play an active role in development through constructing new cultures to direct social evaluations and other peer activities. Thus, the meditational processes occur mainly at the group level, including the establishment of group norms, acceptance-based peer evaluations, and peer regulation of children's behaviors. Individual characteristics such as sensitivity to social expectations may affect the processes through constraining or facilitating group influence. Culture may be involved in the processes in several main manners. First, norms and values with respect to specific behaviors such as cooperation, aggression, and shyness may direct social evaluation of these behaviors. Second, self-oriented versus group-oriented cultural systems may affect children's social-evaluative sensitivity. Third, the extent to which culture allows and encourages children to maintain, adopt, and transform existing values in the society and to develop new values may promote or undermine the active role of children in development. It should be noted that the term *mediation* is used in a broad sense in this article to refer to social processes in the influence of mainstream cultures of the society, as well as values and subcultures of peer groups.

Social evaluation and regulation may be common in peer interaction from middle childhood to adolescence. From the developmental perspective, however, the social interaction processes may vary qualitatively and quantitatively across developmental stages. There are different internal and external demands for peer affiliation and the display of autonomous actions in different developmental periods. With increasing age, social interaction becomes more extensive and complicated as children are more interested in, and capable of, exploring different lifestyles with peers (Brown, 1990). As children develop their social-cognitive abilities, they become more competent in understanding social evaluations, integrating various values for peer activities, and regulating their behaviors. A high level of peer interaction and mature social-cognitive abilities in the later years may facilitate the impact of sophisticated and diverse cultures on individual functioning.

In Western societies, increase in peer interaction from childhood to early adolescence is believed to arise from the desire for support in attaining personal autonomy and independence from the family (Rubin et al., 2006). Children are encouraged to pursue personal interest and gradually develop self-identity and individuality through peer activities (Brown, 1990). As children seek independence, they may start to feel the tension from the constraint of the peer group and attempt to maintain a balance between the pursuit of self-interest and peer restriction. In contrast, in group-oriented cultures that value commitment to social relationships, children are encouraged to establish strong social affiliation, identify with the group, and assume responsibility for the group (Sharabany, 2006). In this context, the development of social responsibility is a major indication of competence (e.g., Miller, 1994). Thus, children across cultures may become more active and capable in peer interaction with age, but the increasingly active and capable role of children may be expressed differently to achieve different developmental goals (e.g., personal autonomy vs. social responsibility).

Another issue concerning the mediating role of peer interaction is how culture affects the social processes by specifying the function and structure of peer relationships. In Western cultures, for example, support from friends is a major mechanism through which children develop a positive sense of self-worth (Sullivan, 1953). This function is less salient in non-Western cultures (e.g., French, Pidada, & Victor, 2005). In many Asian and Latino group-oriented cultures, instrumental aid in children's friendships (e.g., sharing money, protecting friends from harm, mutual assistance in learning) appears to be more important than self-validation (Gonzalez, Moreno, & Schneider, 2004; Way, 2006). Furthermore, in larger peer settings, Western children tend to engage in more sociodramatic activities than do children in other societies such as Korea, India, Kenya, and Mexico (e.g., Edwards, 2000; Farver & Shin, 1997). According to Farver et al. (1995), social interaction in playful and sociodramatic activities in Western societies may facilitate the development of self-confidence and assertiveness, whereas in some other societies, social interaction in task-oriented activities may help children develop cooperation and self-control that are prized by their culture. Thus, cultural values of specific functions and forms of peer relationships and activities help children organize their interactions in ways that promote the development of related behaviors. By emphasizing particular features of peer relationships, culture also enhances the relevance of socially valued characteristics to peer evaluations, as well as children's sensitivity to evaluations with regard to these characteristics.

The contextual-developmental perspective has implications for research and practical work. The emphasis of the perspective on the cultural aspect of social interaction suggests that it is important to explore cultural norms and values underlying children's social interaction in order to understand its nature and significance. At the same time, this emphasis indicates that researchers should investigate the relation between culture and human development in a social interaction context; research that treats culture as a personal characteristic without social context (e.g., research that relies mainly on self-report data from a "culture" questionnaire) is likely to provide limited information toward an understanding of cultural involvement in children's socioemotional functioning. Finally, the contextual-developmental perspective makes clear that it is important for parents, educators, and professionals to consider the social interaction context in developing culturally effective and appropriate remediation programs for children who display socio-emotional problems.

In this article, I have focused mainly on the processes in which peer interaction serves to mediate the links between cultural values and socioemotional development. Missing is a discussion of specific cultures or cultural aspects. I have used broad categories like group-oriented versus self-oriented values mainly to illustrate how culture affects the development of individual functioning, such as social initiative and self-control, through peer evaluation and regulation. Researchers have discussed a number of cultural aspects or values such as those concerning emotional expression and suppression (e.g., Kleinman, 1986; Rothbaum & Trommsdorff, 2006; Safdar et al., 2009). However, most such discussions, especially those focusing on broad categories, have been criticized for their over-simplistic categorization of cultures and their inadequacy to explain the substantial heterogeneity within cultures and massive differences between cultures that are assumed to be extreme (e.g., collectivist vs.

individualist; Miller, 2002). An important question concerning the contextual-developmental perspective is what specific cultural values are mediated mainly through peer interaction and what specific cultural values are mediated mainly by other socialization agents such as parents and teachers (e.g., filial piety in Chinese culture). Another question is whether the peer interaction processes differ in mediating different cultural values. These issues should be explored in future research.

Finally, the contextual-developmental perspective on the role of peer interaction in human development is largely speculative. Although there is some evidence for the influence of cultural values on social attitudes in peer interaction and for the links between peer evaluations and individual behaviors (e.g., Chen et al., 2006), the general framework remains to be tested in empirical research. Moreover, many issues in the framework, such as how peer interaction and other socialization processes affect each other in their joint contributions to development, need to be further clarified and examined. Therefore, it is crucial to engage in continuous exploration of culture and human development.

# References

Abrams, D., & Hogg, M. A. (2004). Metatheory: Lessons from social identity research. *Personality and Social Psychology Review, 8,* 98–106.

Asendorpf, J. B. (1993). Abnormal shyness in children. *Journal of Child Psychology and Psychiatry, 34,* 1069–1081.

Berndt, T. J. (2002). Friendship quality and social development. *Current Directions in Psychological Science, 11,* 7–10.

Brown, B. B. (1990). Peer groups and peer cultures. In S. S. Feldman & G. R. Elliott (Eds.), *At the threshold: The developing adolescent* (pp. 171–196). Cambridge, MA: Harvard University Press.

Casiglia, A. C., Lo Coco, A., & Zappulla, C. (1998). Aspects of social reputation and peer relationships in Italian children: A cross-cultural perspective. *Developmental Psychology, 34,* 723–730.

Chagnon, N. A. (1983). *Yanomamo: The fierce people.* New York: Holt, Rinehart & Winston.

Chang, L., Lei, L., Li, K. K., Liu, H., Guo, B., Wang, Y., et al. (2005). Peer acceptance and self-perceptions of verbal and behavioural aggression and withdrawal. *International Journal of Behavioral Development, 29,* 49–57.

Chen, X. (2010). Socioemotional development in Chinese children. In M. H. Bond (Ed.), *Handbook of Chinese psychology* (pp. 37–52). Oxford, UK: Oxford University Press.

Chen, X., Cen, G., Li, D., & He, Y. (2005). Social functioning and adjustment in Chinese children: The imprint of historical time. *Child Development, 76,* 182–195.

Chen, X., Chang, L., He, Y., & Liu, H. (2005). The peer group as a context: Moderating effects on relations between maternal parenting and social and school adjustment in Chinese children. *Child Development, 76,* 417–434.

Chen, X., & Chen, H. (2010). Children's social functioning and adjustment in the changing Chinese society. In R. K. Silbereisen & X. Chen (Eds.), *Social change and human development: Concepts and results* (pp. 209–226). London: Sage.

Chen, X., Chen, H., Li, D., & Wang, L. (2009). Early childhood behavioral inhibition and social and school adjustment in

Chinese children: A five-year longitudinal study. *Child Development, 80,* 1692–1704.

Chen, X., Chung, J., & Hsiao, C. (2009). Peer interactions, relationships and groups from a cross-cultural perspective. In K. H. Rubin, W. Bukowski, & B. Laursen (Eds.), *Handbook of peer interactions, relationships, and groups* (pp. 432–151). New York: Guilford.

Chen, X., DeSouza, A., Chen, H., & Wang, L. (2006). Reticent behavior and experiences in peer interactions in Canadian and Chinese children. *Developmental Psychology, 42,* 656–665.

Chen, X., & French, D. (2008). Children's social competence in cultural context. *Annual Review of Psychology, 59,* 591–616.

Chen, X., Hastings, P., Rubin, K. H., Chen, H., Cen, G., & Stewart, S. L. (1998). Childrearing attitudes and behavioral inhibition in Chinese and Canadian toddlers: A cross-cultural study. *Developmental Psychology, 34,* 677–686.

Chen, X., Rubin, K. H., & Li, Z. (1995). Social functioning and adjustment in Chinese children: A longitudinal study. *Developmental Psychology, 31,* 531–539.

Chen, X., Rubin, K. H., Liu, M., Chen, H., Wang, L., Li, D., et al. (2003). Compliance in Chinese and Canadian toddlers. *International Journal of Behavioral Development, 27,* 428–436.

Cohen, D., & Hoshino-Browne, E. (2005). Insider and outsider perspectives on the self and social world. In R. M. Sorrentino, D. Cohen, J. M. Olson, & M. P. Zanna (Eds.), *Culture and social behavior: The tenth Ontario symposium* (pp. 49–76). Mahwah, NJ: Erlbaum.

Cole, M. (1996). *Cultural psychology.* Cambridge, MA: Harvard University Press.

Cole, P. M., Bruschi, C., & Tamang, B. L. (2002). Cultural differences in children's emotional reactions to difficult situations. *Child Development, 73 ,* 983–996.

Corsaro, W. A., & Nelson, E. (2003). Children's collective activities and peer culture in early literacy in American and Italian preschools. *Sociology of Education, 76,* 209–227.

Dodge, K. A., Coie, J. D., & Lynam, D. (2006). Aggression and antisocial behavior in youth. In N. Eisenberg (Ed.), *Handbook of child psychology: Vol. 3. Social, emotional, and personality development* (pp. 719–88). New York: Wiley.

Dong, Q., Yang, B., & Ollendick, T. H. (1994). Fears in Chinese children and adolescents and their relations to anxiety and depression. *Journal of Child Psychology and Psychiatry, 35,* 351–363.

Duval, T. S., & Silvia, P. J. (2002). Self-awareness, probability of improvement, and the self-serving bias. *Journal of Personality and Social Psychology, 82,* 49–61.

Edwards, C. P. (2000). Children's play in cross-cultural perspective: A new look at the Six Culture Study. *Cross-Cultural Research, 34,* 318–338.

Eisenberg, N., Fabes, R. A., & Spinrad, T. L. (2006). Prosocial development. In N. Eisenberg (Ed.), *Handbook of child psychology: Vol. 3. Social, emotional, and personality development* (pp. 646–718). New York: Wiley.

Eisenberg, N., Pidada, S., & Liew, J. (2001). The relations of regulation and negative emotionality to Indonesian children's social functioning. *Child Development, 72,* 1747–1763.

Farver, J. M., Kim, Y. K., & Lee, Y. (1995). Cultural differences in Korean- and Anglo-American preschoolers' social interaction and play behaviors. *Child Development, 66,* 1088–1099.

Farver, J. M., & Shin, Y. L. (1997). Social pretend play in Korea- and Anglo-American preschoolers. *Child Development, 68,* 544–556.

French, D. C., Pidada, S., & Victor, A. (2005). Friendships of Indonesian and United States youth. *International Journal of Behavioral Development, 29,* 304–313.

Fuligni, A. J. (1998). The adjustment of children from immigrant families. *Current Directions in Psychological Science, 7,* 99–103.

Gonzalez, Y., Moreno, D. S., & Schneider, B. H. (2004). Friendship expectations of early adolescents in Cuba and Canada. *Journal of Cross-Cultural Psychology, 35,* 436–445.

Goodnow, J. J. (1997). Parenting and the transmission and internalization of values: From social-cultural perspectives to within-family analyses. In J. E. Grusec & L. Kuczynski (Eds.), *Handbook of parenting and the transmission of values* (pp. 333–361). New York: Wiley.

Greenfield, P. M., Suzuki, L. K., & Rothstein-Fisch, C. (2006). Cultural pathways through human development. In K. A. Renninger & I. E. Sigel (Eds.), *Handbook of child psychology: Vol. 4. Child psychology in practice* (pp. 655–699). New York: Wiley.

Hart, C. H., Yang, C., Nelson, L. J., Robinson, C. C., Olson, J. A., Nelson, D. A., et al. (2000). Peer acceptance in early childhood and subtypes of socially withdrawn behaviour in China, Russia and the United States. *International Journal of Behavioral Development, 24,* 73–81.

Hartup, W. W. (1992). Social relationships and their developmental significance. *American Psychologist, 44,* 120–126.

Henirch, C. C., Blatt, S. J., Kuperminc, G. P., Zohar, A., & Leadbeater, B. J. (2001). Levels of interpersonal concerns and social functioning in early adolescent boys and girls. *Journal of Personality Assessment, 76,* 48–67.

Hinde, R. A. (1987). *Individuals, relationships and culture.* Cambridge, UK: Cambridge University Press.

Ho, D. Y. F. (1986). Chinese pattern of socialization: A critical review. In M. H. Bond (Ed.), *The psychology of the Chinese people* (pp. 1–37). New York: Oxford University Press.

Hofstede, G. (2001). *Culture's consequences: Comparing values, behaviors, institutions, and organizations across nations* (2nd ed.). Thousand Oaks, CA: Sage.

Keller, H., Yovsi, R., Borke, J., Kartner, J., Jensen, H., & Papaligoura, Z. (2004). Developmental consequences of early parenting experiences: Self-recognition and self-regulation in three cultural communities. *Child Development, 75,* 1745–1760.

Kerr, M., Lambert, W. W., & Bem, D. J. (1996). Life course sequelae of childhood shyness in Sweden: Comparison with the United States. *Developmental Psychology, 32,* 1100–1105.

Killen, M., & Brenick, A. (2011). Morality, exclusion, and culture. In X. Chen & K. H. Rubin (Eds.), *Socioemotional development in cultural context* (pp. 239–262). New York: Guilford.

Kleinman, A. (1986). *Social origins in distress and disease.* New Haven, CT: Yale University Press.

LeVine, R. A., Dixon, S., LeVine, S., Richman, A., Leiderman, P. H., Keefer, C. H., et al. (1994). *Child care and culture: Lessons from Africa.* New York: Cambridge University Press.

Maccoby, E. E. (1998). *The two sexes: Growing up apart, coming together.* Cambridge, MA: Harvard University Press.

Miller, J. G. (1994). Cultural diversity in the morality of caring: Individually oriented versus duty-based interpersonal moral codes. *Cross-Cultural Research, 28,* 3–39.

Miller, J. G. (2002). Bring culture to basic psychological theory—Beyond individualism and collectivism: Comment on Oyserman et al. (2002). *Psychological Bulletin, 128,* 97–109.

Rodkin, P. C., Farmer, T. W., Pearl, R., & van Acker, R. (2000). Heterogeneity of popular boys: Antisocial and prosocial configurations. *Developmental Psychology, 36,* 14–24.

Rogoff, B. (2003). *The cultural nature of human development.* New York: Oxford University Press.

Rothbaum, F., & Trommsdorff, G. (2006). Do roots and wings complement or oppose one another: The socialization of relatedness and autonomy in cultural context. In J. Grusec & P. Hastings (Eds.), *Handbook of socialization: Theory and research* (pp. 461–489). New York: Guilford.

Rubin, K. H., Bukowski, W., & Parker, J. G. (2006). Peer interactions, relationships, and groups. In N. Eisenberg (Ed.), *Handbook of child psychology: Vol. 3. Social, emotional, and personality development* (pp. 571–645). New York: Wiley.

Rubin, K. H., Coplan, R., & Bowker, J. (2009). Social withdrawal in childhood. *Annual Review of Psychology, 60,* 141–171.

Rubin, K. H., Coplan, R. J., Fox, N. A., & Calkins, S. (1995). Emotionality, emotion regulation, and preschoolers' social adaptation. *Development and Psychopathology, 7,* 49–62.

Rudolph, K. D., & Conley, C. S. (2005). The socioemotional costs and benefits of social-evaluative concerns: Do girls care too much? *Journal of Personality, 73,* 115–137.

Safdar, S., Friedlmeier, W., Matsumoto, D., Yoo, S. H., Kwantes, C. T., & Kakai, H. (2009). Variations of emotional display rules within and across cultures: A comparison between Canada, USA, and Japan. *Canadian Journal of Behavioural Science, 41,* 1–10.

Schneider, B. H., Fonzi, A., Tomada, G., & Tani, F. (2000). A cross-national comparison of children's behavior with their friends in situations of potential conflict. *Journal of Cross-Cultural Psychology, 31,* 259–266.

Schneider, B. H., Smith, A., Poisson, S. E., & Kwan, A. B. (1997). Cultural dimensions of children's peer relations. In S. Duck (Ed.), *Handbook of personal relationships: Theory, research and interventions* (2nd ed., pp. 121–146). Hoboken, NJ: Wiley.

Schwartz, S. H. (1994). Beyond individualism/collectivism: New cultural dimensions of values. In U. Kim, H. C. Triandis, C. Kâğitçibaşi, S. C. Choi, & G. Yoon (Eds.), *Individualism and collectivism: Theory, method, and applications* (pp. 85–119). Thousand Oaks, CA: Sage.

Schwartz, S. H. (2009). Culture matters: National value cultures, sources and consequences. In C. Y. Chiu, Y. Y. Hong, S. Shavitt, & R. S. Wyer Jr. (Eds.), *Understanding culture: Theory, research and application* (pp. 127–150). New York: Psychology Press.

Sharabany, R. (2006). The cultural context of children and adolescents: Peer relationships and intimate friendships among Arab and Jewish children in Israel. In X. Chen, D. French, & B. Schneider (Eds.), *Peer relationships in cultural context* (pp. 452–478). New York: Cambridge University Press.

Smetana, J. (2002). Culture, autonomy, and personal jurisdiction. In R. Kail & H. Reese (Eds.), *Advances in child development and behavior* (Vol. 29, pp. 52–87). New York: Academic Press.

Stevenson, H. W. (1991). The development of prosocial behavior in large-scale collective societies: China and Japan. In R. A. Hinde & J. Groebel (Eds.), *Cooperation and prosocial behaviour* (pp. 89–105). Cambridge, UK: Cambridge University Press.

Sullivan, H. S. (1953). *The interpersonal theory of psychiatry.* New York: Norton.

Tajfel, H. (1981). *Human groups and social categories.* Cambridge, UK: Cambridge University Press.

Tamis-LeMonda, C. S., Way, N., Hughes, D., Yoshikawa, H., Kalman, R. K., & Niwa, E. (2008). Parents' goals for children: The dynamic co-existence of collectivism and individualism in cultures and individuals. *Social Development, 17,* 183–209.

Vygotsky, L. S. (1978). *Mind in society: The development of higher psychological processes.* Cambridge, MA: Harvard University Press.

Way, N. (2006). The cultural practice of close friendships among urban adolescents in the United States. In X. Chen, D. French, & B. Schneider (Eds.), *Peer relationships in cultural context* (pp. 403–425). New York: Cambridge University Press.

Whiting, B. B., & Edwards, C. P. (1988). *Children of different worlds.* Cambridge, MA: Harvard University Press.

# Critical Thinking

1. According to Chen and French, what are the two major dimensions of socioemotional functioning? Discuss how they provide a basis for social evaluations and reactions in peer interaction.

2. The article states that "cultural differences may be particularly evident in social evaluations of children's shy-inhibited behavior." Discuss why this may be.

3. What are the consequences, as indicated by research, of sensitivity to social evaluations?

4. What role do peer cultures, developed by children, play in guiding children's social behaviors? How does the establishment of these peer cultures indicate children's active roles in their own development?

Correspondence concerning this article should be addressed to **Xinyin Chen**, Applied Psychology-Human Development Division, Graduate School of Education, University of Pennsylvania, 3700 Walnut St., Philadelphia, PA 19104; e-mail: xinyin@gse.upenn.edu.

©2011 The Author
Child Development Perspectives © 2011 The Society for Research in Child Development DOI: 10.1111/j.1750-8606.2011.00187.x

# UNIT 4

# Parenting and Family Issues

## Unit Selections

## Learning Outcomes

- The first article presents evidence that growing up with gay or lesbian parents does not hurt children psychologically. Explain why many Americans still think this is not a healthy family situation, and describe how you would use scientific evidence to respond to them.

- Given that gay and lesbian families face discrimination or prejudice in subtle or overt ways, explain how it may seem all the more impressive that their children do not appear to suffer psychologically compared to children of heterosexual parents.

- Because the research on children in gay and lesbian families is fairly recent, many questions remain. Design a study to analyze some aspects of children's development that have not yet been measured in children or in certain family types that have not yet been studied adequately.

- Describe in detail the habituation procedure that the researchers used to measure infants' internal working models.

- Explain to parents who might not understand psychological experiments and research why a baby's looking time at visual stimuli like "non-responsive" ovals could in fact reveal what is going on inside the baby's head.

- Assess and summarize the research on the effects of divorce on children's adjustment in terms of child's age, sex of child, ethnicity, family income, and interparental conflict. Given these outcomes, what recommendations would you make to parents who are considering divorce but want to reduce the negative effects on their children?

- Evaluate and discuss the effects of genetics versus environment on children's adjustment to divorce in terms of interparental conflict, parenting practices, parents' psychological well-being and adjustment, and genetic factors.

- Compare and contrast the differential effects of divorce versus remarriage on children's short- and long-term adjustment. Analyze and identify any common themes or factors that may explain and integrate children's outcomes across both family transitions.

- Propose additional changes or modifications in divorce law, awarding of custody, and child support and enforcement that would best serve the interests of affected children. Justify your proposed changes with research evidence.

- Account for historical trends in societal and cultural attitudes toward divorce. Discuss the role of religion, government, legal issues, economics, and politics.

- Explain how cultural values and beliefs about parenting influence how parents discipline their children in the United States and in East Asian countries.

- Describe how parental control is a kind of family dynamic that is important for children's good outcomes, but too little or too much control can lead to developmental problems.
- Identify the factors that explain within-family differences in parent–child relations, such as similarity between parents and children, developmental histories, equity and exchange, and family structure and composition.
- Define "universalism" as it functions in the field of psychology and offer evidence that challenges universalist
- assumptions.
- Differentiate between mechanisms and effects in understanding psychological phenomena.
- Design a lesson plan for a lecture to social workers and therapists who are just beginning to work with culturally diverse families.
- Describe how siblings' lives seem similar and yet different in families with different cultural backgrounds.
- Describe how being a child of an undocumented immigrant affects the child's development.
- Design a presentation to community government leaders and school officials to describe what kinds of policies would help children of undocumented immigrants.

# Student Website

www.mhhe.com/cls

# Internet References

**The National Association for Child Development (NACD)**
> www.nacd.org

**National Council on Family Relations**
> www.ncfr.com

**Parenting and Families**
> www.cyfc.umn.edu

**Parentsplace.com: Single Parenting**
> www.parentsplaceonline.org/resource-library/single-parenting

**National Stepfamily Resource Center**
> www.stepfam.org

Few people today realize that the potential freedom to choose parenthood—deciding whether to become a parent, deciding when to have children, or deciding how many children to have—is a development due to the advent of reliable methods of contraception and other recent sociocultural changes. Moreover, unlike any other significant job to which we may aspire, few, if any, of us will receive any formal training or information about the lifelong responsibility of parenting. For most of us, our behavior is generally based on our own conscious and subconscious recollections of how we were parented as well as on our observations of the parenting practices of others around us. In fact, our society often behaves as if the mere act of producing a baby automatically confers upon the parents an innate parenting ability, furthermore, that a family's parenting practices should remain private and not be subjected to scrutiny or criticism by outsiders.

Given this climate, it is not surprising that misconceptions about many parenting practices persist. Only within the last 40 years or so have researchers turned their lenses on the scientific study of the family. Social, historical, cultural, and economic forces also have dramatically changed the face of the American family today. In fact, the vast majority of parents never take courses or learn of the research on parenting. This unit helps present some of the research on the many complex factors related to successful parenting.

One of the most fundamental achievements of infancy is for the baby to develop a strong attachment to a parent or primary adult caregiver. Recent data by researchers Johnson, Dweck, and Chen in "Evidence of Infants' Internal Working Models of Attachment" show that infants are capable of developing abstract mental attachment representations in forging an attachment bond.

Between 43 percent and 50 percent of first marriages will end in divorce in the United States. Researcher Jennifer Lansford summarizes the wealth of data on the effects of divorce on children's development in "Parental Divorce and Children's Adjustment" and makes recommendations that might improve children's adjustment to divorce in the areas of child custody and child support policies and enforcement.

"Spare the rod or spoil the child" is an oft-heard retort used to justify spanking children for misbehaving. Even today, a majority of parents in the United States admit to relying on spanking as a form of discipline for their children, and many do not view spanking as inappropriate. Researchers are beginning to accumulate evidence of the negative consequences of spanking for children. The authors of "The Case Against Spanking" present evidence showing that parents' use of physical discipline can pose risks to children.

Research on lesbian and gay parents demonstrates that children's adjustment and development are not negatively affected by having same-sex parents. In fact, the studies show that children from same-sex parents are equally likely to thrive as children from heterosexual parents. What matters more is the quality of the parenting relationships as described in Patterson's article, "Children of Lesbian and Gay Parents." This important data is being used to assist judges when awarding custody and helping to develop sound family policies.

The majority of children in the United States will grow up with siblings in their families. In "Sibling Experiences in Diverse Family Contexts" provide important information on the powerful role that siblings have on each others' development and the complex

© Ingram Publishing

interplay these family relationships have in different cultures and family structures.

Very few parents in America or anywhere else on the planet ever take courses in parenting or child development. So how do parents learn to parent? Do we learn to parent from the way our parents treated us as children? Do parents control or discipline their children differently depending on different cultural norms? What forms of discipline or parental control and guidance are least effective or most effective? Researchers answer some of these questions in "The Role of Parental Control in Children's Development in Western and East Asian Countries."

Increasingly, as conditions in other foreign countries worsen or as parents seek to better the living conditions for their families, some parents are resorting to more extreme measures by immigrating illegally to the United States and often birthing children in the United States. What consequences await these children whose parents move illegally across borders? In "The Effects of Parental Undocumented Status on the Developmental Contexts of Young Children in Immigrant Families," the authors describe how children of undocumented parents are affected by the complex legal, public policy and economic factors that surround these families' lives.

# Why Fathers Really Matter

JUDITH SHULEVITZ

Motherhood begins as a tempestuously physical experience but quickly becomes a political one. Once a woman's pregnancy goes public, the storm moves outside. Don't pile on the pounds! Your child will be obese. Don't eat too little, or your baby will be born too small. For heaven's sake, don't drink alcohol. Oh, please: you can sip some wine now and again. And no matter how many contradictory things the experts say, don't panic. Stress hormones wreak havoc on a baby's budding nervous system.

All this advice rains down on expectant mothers for the obvious reason that mothers carry babies and create the environments in which they grow. What if it turned out, though, that expectant fathers molded babies, too, and not just by way of genes?

Biology is making it clearer by the day that a man's health and well-being have a measurable impact on his future children's health and happiness. This is not because a strong, resilient man has a greater likelihood of being a fabulous dad—or not only for that reason—or because he's probably got good genes. Whether a man's genes are good or bad (and whatever "good" and "bad" mean in this context), his children's bodies and minds will reflect lifestyle choices he has made over the years, even if he made those choices long before he ever imagined himself strapping on a Baby Bjorn.

Doctors have been telling men for years that smoking, drinking and recreational drugs can lower the quality of their sperm. What doctors should probably add is that the health of unborn children can be affected by what and how much men eat; the toxins they absorb; the traumas they endure; their poverty or powerlessness; and their age at the time of conception. In other words, what a man needs to know is that his life experience leaves biological traces on his children. Even more astonishingly, those children may pass those traces along to their children.

Before I began reading up on fathers and their influence on future generations, I had a high-school-biology-level understanding of how a man passes his traits on to his child. His sperm and the mother's egg smash into each other, his sperm tosses in one set of chromosomes, the egg tosses in another, and a child's genetic future is set for life. Physical features: check. Character: check. Cognitive style: check. But the pathways of inheritance, I've learned, are subtler and more varied than that. Genes matter, and culture matters, and how fathers behave matters, too.

Lately scientists have become obsessed with a means of inheritance that isn't genetic but isn't nongenetic either. It's epigenetic. "Epi," in Greek, means "above" or "beyond." Think of epigenetics as the way our bodies modify their genetic makeup. Epigenetics describes how genes are turned on or off, in part through compounds that hitch on top of DNA—or else jump off it—determining whether it makes the proteins that tell our bodies what to do.

In the past decade or so, the study of epigenetics has become so popular it's practically a fad. Psychologists and sociologists particularly like it because gene expression or suppression is to some degree dictated by the environment and plays at least as large a role as genes do in the development of a person's temperament, body shape and predisposition to disease. I've become obsessed with epigenetics because it strikes me as both game-changing and terrifying. Our genes can be switched on or off by three environmental factors, among other things: what we ingest (food, drink, air, toxins); what we experience (stress, trauma); and how long we live.

Epigenetics means that our physical and mental tendencies were not set in stone during the Pleistocene age, as evolutionary psychology sometimes seems to claim. Rather, they're shaped by the life we lead and the world we live in right now. Epigenetics proves that we are the products of history, public as well as private, in parts of us that are so intimately ours that few people ever imagined that history could reach them. (One person who did imagine it is the French 18th-century naturalist Jean-Baptiste Lamarck, who believed that acquired traits could be inherited. Twentieth-century Darwinian genetics dismissed Lamarckism as laughable, but because of epigenetics, Lamarckism is staging a comeback.)

The best-known example of the power of nutrition to affect the genes of fathers and sons comes from a corner of northern Sweden called Overkalix. Until the 20th century, Overkalix was cut off from the rest of the world, unreachable by road, train or even, in wintertime, boat, because the frozen Baltic Sea could not be crossed. Thus, when there were bad harvests in Overkalix, the children starved, and when there were good harvests, they stuffed themselves.

More than a decade ago, three Swedish researchers dug up records from Overkalix going back to 1799 in order to correlate its children's health data with records of regional harvests and other documents showing when food was and wasn't available. What the researchers learned was extremely odd. They found that when boys ate badly during the years right before puberty, between the ages of 9 and 12, their sons, as adults, had lower than normal rates of heart disease. When boys ate all too well during that period, their grandsons had higher rates of diabetes.

When the study appeared in 2002, a British geneticist published an essay speculating that how much a boy ate in pre-puberty could permanently reprogram the epigenetic switches that would govern the manufacture of sperm a few years later. And then, in a process so intricate that no one agrees yet how it happens but probably has something to do with the germline (the reproductive cells that are handed down to children, and to children's children), those reprogrammed switches are transferred to his sons and his sons' sons.

A decade later, animal studies confirm that a male mammal's nutritional past has a surprisingly strong effect on his offspring. Male rats that are starved before they're mated produce offspring with less blood sugar and altered levels of corticosterone (which protects against stress) and insulin-like growth factor 1 (which helps babies develop).

Southeast Asian men who chew betel nuts, a snack that contains a chemical affecting metabolic functioning, are more likely to have children with weight problems and heart disease. Animal studies have shown that the effects of betel nut consumption by a male may extend to his grandchildren.

Environmental toxins leave even more florid traces on grandchildren and great-grandchildren. Vinclozin, a fungicide that used to be sprayed all over America (it's less common now), is what's known as an endocrine disrupter; it blocks the production of testosterone. Male rats whose mothers receive a fat dose of vinclozin late in their pregnancy are highly likely to be born with defective testicles and reduced fertility. These problems seem to reappear in up to four generations of male rats after the mother is poisoned.

That food and poison change us is not all that surprising, even if it is surprising how far down the change goes. What is unexpected are the psychological dimensions of epigenetics. To learn more about these, I visited the Mount Sinai Medical Center laboratory of Dr. Eric Nestler, a psychiatrist who did a discomfiting study on male mice and what he calls "social defeat." His researchers put small normal field mice in cages with big, nasty retired breeders, and let the big mice attack the smaller mice for about five minutes a day. If a mean mouse and a little mouse were pried apart by means of a screen, the torturer would claw at the screen, trying to get at his victim. All this subjected the field mouse to "a horrendous level of stress," Dr. Nestler told me. This process was repeated for 10 days, with a different tormentor placed in each cage every day. By the time the torture stopped, about two-thirds of the field mice exhibited permanent and quantifiable symptoms of the mouse equivalents of depression, anxiety and post-traumatic stress disorder. The researchers then bred these unhappy mice with normal females. When their pups grew up, they tended to over-react to social stress, becoming so anxious and depressed that they wouldn't even drink sugar water. They avoided other mice as much as they could.

Dr. Nestler is not sure exactly how the mouse fathers' trauma communicates itself to their offspring. It may be via sperm, or it may be through some more complicated dance of nature and nurture that involves sperm but also other factors. When instead of letting the "defeated" mice mate, Dr. Nestler's researchers killed them, harvested their sperm and impregnated the female mice through artificial means, the offspring were largely normal. Perhaps the sperm was harvested at the wrong stage in the process, says Dr. Nestler. Or maybe the female mouse picked up some signal when she had sex with the dysfunctional male mouse, some telltale pheromone or squeak, that made her body withhold nutrition and care from his pups. Females have been known to not invest in the spawn of non-optimal males, an outcome that makes perfect evolutionary sense—why waste resources on a loser?

When it comes to the epigenetics of aging, however, there is little question that the chemical insults and social setbacks of everyday life distill themselves in sperm. A woman is born with all the eggs she'll ever carry. By the time a man turns 40, on the other hand, his gonad cells will have divided 610 times to make spermatozoa. By the time he's in his 50s, that number goes up to 840. Each time those cells copy themselves, mistakes may appear in the DNA chain. Some researchers now think that a percentage of those mistakes reflects not just random mutations but experience-based epigenetic markings that insinuate themselves from sperm to fetus and influence brain development. Another theory holds that aging gonad cells are more error-prone because the parts of the DNA that should have spotted and repaired any mistakes have been epigenetically tamped down. In any case, we now know that the children of older fathers show more signs of schizophrenia, autism and bipolar disorder than children of younger ones.

In a meta-analysis of a population study of more than a million people published last year, Christina Hultman of the Karolinska Institute of Sweden concluded that children of men older than 50 were 2.2 times as likely to have autism as children of 29-year-olds, even after the study had factored out mothers' ages and known risk factors for autism. By the time the men passed 55, the risk doubled to 4.4 times that of 29-year-olds. Can the aging of the parent population explain the apparent spike in autism cases? A study published last month in *Nature* that used whole-genome sequencing on 78 Icelandic families made the strongest case to date that as fathers age, mutations in their sperm spike dramatically. Some of the mutations found by the researchers in Reykjavik have been linked to autism and schizophrenia in children.

In his Washington Heights laboratory at the New York State Psychiatric Institute, Jay Gingrich, a professor of psychobiology, compares the pups of young male mice (3 months old or so) to those of old male mice (12 to 14 months old). The differences between the pups, he told me, weren't "earth-shattering"—they weighed about the same and there weren't big gaps in their early development. But discrepancies appeared when the mice grew up. The adult offspring of the older fathers had less adventuresome personalities; they also reacted to loud noises in unusual ways that paralleled reactions evinced by schizophrenics who heard similar sounds.

Still, Dr. Gingrich said, "the differences were subtle" until he decided to pool the data on their behavior and graph it on a bell curve. A "vast majority" of the children of the older mice were "completely normal," he said, which meant their score fell under the upside-down parabola of the curve. The real differences came at the tails or skinny ends of the bell curve. There was about a sixfold increase in likelihood that one of the "abnormal outliers," mice with cognitive or behavioral handicaps, "would come from an older father." Conversely, the super-high-performing mice were about six times more likely to come from a younger father. "I'm an inherently skeptical person," Dr. Gingrich told me, but he was impressed by these results.

One unanswered question about autism and schizophrenia is how they crop up in generation after generation; after all, wildly dysfunctional individuals don't usually flourish romantically. "I think we're going to have to consider that advanced paternal age, with its epigenetic effects, may be a way of explaining the mysteries of schizophrenia and autism, insofar as the rates of these disorders have maintained themselves—and autism may be going up," Dr. Gingrich said. "From a cruel Darwinian perspective, it's not clear how much success these folks have at procreating, or how else these genes maintain themselves in the population."

When you're an older mother, you get used to the sidelong glances of sonogram technicians, the extra battery of medical tests, the fear that your baby has Down syndrome, the real or imagined hints from younger mothers that you're having children so late because you care more about professional advancement than family. But as the research on paternal inheritance piles up, the needle of doubt may swing at least partway to fathers. "We're living through a paradigm shift," said Dolores Malaspina, a professor of psychiatry at New York University who has done pioneering work on older fathers and schizophrenia.

Older mothers no longer need to shoulder all the blame: "It's the aging man who damages the offspring."

Aging, though, is only one of the vicissitudes of life that assault a man's reproductive vitality. Think of epigenetics as having ushered in a new age of sexual equality, in which both sexes have to worry about threats to which women once felt uniquely exposed. Dr. Malaspina remembers that before she went to medical school, she worked in a chemical plant making radioactive drugs. The women who worked there came under constant, invasive scrutiny, lest the toxic workplace contaminate their eggs. But maybe, Dr. Malaspina points out, the plant managers should have spared some concern for the men, whose germlines were just as susceptible to poisoning as the women's, and maybe even more so. The well-being of the children used to be the sole responsibility of their mothers. Now fathers have to be held accountable, too. Having twice endured the self-scrutiny and second-guessing that goes along with being pregnant, I wish them luck.

## Critical Thinking

1. What biological and genetic processes in fathers may affect their offspring?

2. How might these effects be passed on over multiple generations?

3. Why should we be concerned about how fathers' age and health may affect their reproductive health?

JUDITH SHULEVITZ is the science editor for *The New Republic*.

# Children of Lesbian and Gay Parents

Does parental sexual orientation affect child development, and if so, how? Studies using convenience samples, studies using samples drawn from known populations, and studies based on samples that are representative of larger populations all converge on similar conclusions. More than two decades of research has failed to reveal important differences in the adjustment or development of children or adolescents reared by same-sex couples compared to those reared by other-sex couples. Results of the research suggest that qualities of family relationships are more tightly linked with child outcomes than is parental sexual orientation.

CHARLOTTE J. PATTERSON

D oes parental sexual orientation affect child development, and if so, how? This question has often been raised in the context of legal and policy proceedings relevant to children, such as those involving adoption, child custody, or visitation. Divergent views have been offered by professionals from the fields of psychology, sociology, medicine, and law (Patterson, Fulcher, & Wainright, 2002). While this question has most often been raised in legal and policy contexts, it is also relevant to theoretical issues. For example, does healthy human development require that a child grow up with parents of each gender? And if not, what would that mean for our theoretical understanding of parent–child relations? (Patterson & Hastings, in press). In this article, I describe some research designed to address these questions.

## Early Research

Research on children with lesbian and gay parents began with studies focused on cases in which children had been born in the context of a heterosexual marriage. After parental separation and divorce, many children in these families lived with divorced lesbian mothers. A number of researchers compared development among children of divorced lesbian mothers with that among children of divorced heterosexual mothers and found few significant differences (Patterson, 1997; Stacey & Biblarz, 2001).

These studies were valuable in addressing concerns of judges who were required to decide divorce and child custody cases, but they left many questions unanswered. In particular, because the children who participated in this research had been born into homes with married mothers and fathers, it was not obvious how to understand the reasons for their healthy development. The possibility that children's early exposure to apparently heterosexual male and female role models had contributed to healthy development could not be ruled out.

When lesbian or gay parents rear infants and children from birth, do their offspring grow up in typical ways and show healthy development? To address this question, it was important to study children who had never lived with heterosexual parents. In the 1990s, a number of investigators began research of this kind.

An early example was the Bay Area Families Study, in which I studied a group of 4- to 9-year-old children who had been born to or adopted early in life by lesbian mothers (Patterson, 1996, 1997). Data were collected during home visits. Results from in-home interviews and also from questionnaires showed that children had regular contact with a wide range of adults of both genders, both within and outside of their families. The children's self-concepts and preferences for same-gender playmates and activities were much like those of other children their ages. Moreover, standardized measures of social competence and of behavior problems, such as those from the Child Behavior Checklist (CBCL), showed that they scored within the range of normal variation for a representative sample of same-aged American children. It was clear from this study and others like it that it was quite possible for lesbian mothers to rear healthy children.

## Studies Based on Samples Drawn from Known Populations

Interpretation of the results from the Bay Area Families Study was, however, affected by its sampling procedures. The study had been based on a convenience sample that had been assembled by word of mouth. It was therefore impossible to rule out the possibility that families who participated in the research were especially well adjusted. Would a more representative sample yield different results?

To find out, Ray Chan, Barbara Raboy, and I conducted research in collaboration with the Sperm Bank of California

(Chan, Raboy, & Patterson, 1998; Fulcher, Sutfin, Chan, Scheib, & Patterson, 2005). Over the more than 15 years of its existence, the Sperm Bank of California's clientele had included many lesbian as well as heterosexual women. For research purposes, this clientele was a finite population from which our sample could be drawn. The Sperm Bank of California also allowed a sample in which, both for lesbian and for heterosexual groups, one parent was biologically related to the child and one was not.

We invited all clients who had conceived children using the resources of the Sperm Bank of California and who had children 5 years old or older to participate in our research. The resulting sample was composed of 80 families, 55 headed by lesbian and 25 headed by heterosexual parents. Materials were mailed to participating families, with instructions to complete them privately and return them in self-addressed stamped envelopes we provided.

Results replicated and expanded upon those from earlier research. Children of lesbian and heterosexual parents showed similar, relatively high levels of social competence, as well as similar, relatively low levels of behavior problems on the parent form of the CBCL. We also asked the children's teachers to provide evaluations of children's adjustment on the Teacher Report Form of the CBCL, and their reports agreed with those of parents. Parental sexual orientation was not related to children's adaptation. Quite apart from parental sexual orientation, however, and consistent with findings from years of research on children of heterosexual parents, when parent–child relationships were marked by warmth and affection, children were more likely to be developing well. Thus, in this sample drawn from a known population, measures of children's adjustment were unrelated to parental sexual orientation (Chan et al., 1998; Fulcher et al., 2005).

Even as they provided information about children born to lesbian mothers, however, these new results also raised additional questions. Women who conceive children at sperm banks are generally both well educated and financially comfortable. It was possible that these relatively privileged women were able to protect children from many forms of discrimination. What if a more diverse group of families were to be studied? In addition, the children in this sample averaged 7 years of age, and some concerns focus on older children and adolescents. What if an older group of youngsters were to be studied? Would problems masked by youth and privilege in earlier studies emerge in an older, more diverse sample?

# Studies Based on Representative Samples

An opportunity to address these questions was presented by the availability of data from the National Longitudinal Study of Adolescent Health (Add Health). The Add Health study involved a large, ethnically diverse, and essentially representative sample of American adolescents and their parents. Data for our research were drawn from surveys and interviews completed by more than 12,000 adolescents and their parents at home and from surveys completed by adolescents at school.

Parents were not queried directly about their sexual orientation but were asked if they were involved in a "marriage, or marriage-like relationship." If parents acknowledged such a relationship, they were also asked the gender of their partner. Thus, we identified a group of 44 12- to 18-year-olds who lived with parents involved in marriage or marriage-like relationships with same-sex partners. We compared them with a matched group of adolescents living with other-sex couples. Data from the archives of the Add Health study allowed us to address many questions about adolescent development.

Consistent with earlier findings, results of this work revealed few differences in adjustment between adolescents living with same-sex parents and those living with opposite-sex parents (Wainright, Russell, & Patterson, 2004; Wainright & Patterson, 2006). There were no significant differences between teenagers living with same-sex parents and those living with other-sex parents on self-reported assessments of psychological well-being, such as self-esteem and anxiety; measures of school outcomes, such as grade point averages and trouble in school; or measures of family relationships, such as parental warmth and care from adults and peers. Adolescents in the two groups were equally likely to say that they had been involved in a romantic relationship in the last 18 months, and they were equally likely to report having engaged in sexual intercourse. The only statistically reliable difference between the two groups—that those with same-sex parents felt a greater sense of connection to people at school—favored the youngsters living with same-sex couples. There were no significant differences in self-reported substance use, delinquency, or peer victimization between those reared by same- or other-sex couples (Wainright & Patterson, 2006).

Although the gender of parents' partners was not an important predictor of adolescent well-being, other aspects of family relationships were significantly associated with teenagers' adjustment. Consistent with other findings about adolescent development, the qualities of family relationships rather than the gender of parents' partners were consistently related to adolescent outcomes. Parents who reported having close relationships with their offspring had adolescents who reported more favorable adjustment. Not only is it possible for children and adolescents who are parented by same-sex couples to develop in healthy directions, but—even when studied in an extremely diverse, representative sample of American adolescents—they generally do.

These findings have been supported by results from many other studies, both in the United States and abroad. Susan Golombok and her colleagues have reported similar results with a near-representative sample of children in the United Kingdom (Golombok et al., 2003). Others, both in Europe and in the United States, have described similar findings (e.g., Brewaeys, Ponjaert, Van Hall, & Golombok, 1997).

The fact that children of lesbian mothers generally develop in healthy ways should not be taken to suggest that they encounter no challenges. Many investigators have remarked upon the fact that children of lesbian and gay parents may encounter anti-gay sentiments in their daily lives. For example, in a study of

10-year-old children born to lesbian mothers, Gartrell, Deck, Rodas, Peyser, and Banks (2005) reported that a substantial minority had encountered anti-gay sentiments among their peers. Those who had had such encounters were likely to report having felt angry, upset, or sad about these experiences. Children of lesbian and gay parents may be exposed to prejudice against their parents in some settings, and this may be painful for them, but evidence for the idea that such encounters affect children's overall adjustment is lacking.

# Conclusions

Does parental sexual orientation have an important impact on child or adolescent development? Results of recent research provide no evidence that it does. In fact, the findings suggest that parental sexual orientation is less important than the qualities of family relationships. More important to youth than the gender of their parent's partner is the quality of daily interaction and the strength of relationships with the parents they have.

One possible approach to findings like the ones described above might be to shrug them off by reiterating the familiar adage that "one cannot prove the null hypothesis." To respond in this way, however, is to miss the central point of these studies. Whether or not any measurable impact of parental sexual orientation on children's development is ever demonstrated, the main conclusions from research to date remain clear: Whatever correlations between child outcomes and parental sexual orientation may exist, they are less important than those between child outcomes and the qualities of family relationships.

Although research to date has made important contributions, many issues relevant to children of lesbian and gay parents remain in need of study. Relatively few studies have examined the development of children adopted by lesbian or gay parents or of children born to gay fathers; further research in both areas would be welcome (Patterson, 2004). Some notable longitudinal studies have been reported, and they have found children of same-sex couples to be in good mental health. Greater understanding of family relationships and transitions over time would, however, be helpful, and longitudinal studies would be valuable. Future research could also benefit from the use of a variety of methodologies.

Meanwhile, the clarity of findings in this area has been acknowledged by a number of major professional organizations. For instance, the governing body of the American Psychological Association (APA) voted unanimously in favor of a statement that said, "Research has shown that the adjustment, development, and psychological well-being of children is unrelated to parental sexual orientation and that children of lesbian and gay parents are as likely as those of heterosexual parents to flourish" (APA, 2004). The American Bar Association, the American Medical Association, the American Academy of Pediatrics, the American Psychiatric Association, and other mainstream professional groups have issued similar statements.

The findings from research on children of lesbian and gay parents have been used to inform legal and public policy debates across the country (Patterson et al., 2002). The research literature on this subject has been cited in amicus briefs filed by the APA in cases dealing with adoption, child custody, and also in cases related to the legality of marriages between same-sex partners. Psychologists serving as expert witnesses have presented findings on these issues in many different courts (Patterson et al., 2002). Through these and other avenues, results of research on lesbian and gay parents and their children are finding their way into public discourse.

The findings are also beginning to address theoretical questions about critical issues in parenting. The importance of gender in parenting is one such issue. When children fare well in two-parent lesbian-mother or gay-father families, this suggests that the gender of one's parents cannot be a critical factor in child development. Results of research on children of lesbian and gay parents cast doubt upon the traditional assumption that gender is important in parenting. Our data suggest that it is the quality of parenting rather than the gender of parents that is significant for youngsters' development.

Research on children of lesbian and gay parents is thus located at the intersection of a number of classic and contemporary concerns. Studies of lesbian- and gay-parented families allow researchers to address theoretical questions that had previously remained difficult or impossible to answer. They also address oft-debated legal questions of fact about development of children with lesbian and gay parents. Thus, research on children of lesbian and gay parents contributes to public debate and legal decision making, as well as to theoretical understanding of human development.

# References

American Psychological Association (2004). Resolution on sexual orientation, parents, and children. Retrieved September 25, 2006, from www.apa.org/pi/lgbc/policy/parentschildren.pdf

Brewaeys, A., Ponjaert, I., Van Hall, E.V., & Golombok, S. (1997). Donor insemination: Child development and family functioning in lesbian mother families. *Human Reproduction, 12,* 1349–1359.

Chan, R.W., Raboy, B., & Patterson, C.J. (1998). Psychosocial adjustment among children conceived via donor insemination by lesbian and heterosexual mothers. *Child Development, 69,* 443–457.

Fulcher, M., Sutfin, E.L., Chan, R.W., Scheib, J.E., & Patterson, C.J. (2005). Lesbian mothers and their children: Findings from the Contemporary Families Study. In A. Omoto & H. Kurtzman (Eds.), *Recent research on sexual orientation, mental health, and substance abuse* (pp. 281–299). Washington, DC: American Psychological Association.

Gartrell, N., Deck., A., Rodas, C., Peyser, H., & Banks, A. (2005). The National Lesbian Family Study: 4. Interviews with the 10-year-old children. *American Journal of Orthopsychiatry, 75,* 518–524.

Golombok, S., Perry, B., Burston, A., Murray, C., Mooney-Somers, J., Stevens, M., & Golding, J. (2003). Children with lesbian parents: A community study. *Developmental Psychology, 39,* 20–33.

Patterson, C.J. (1996). Lesbian mothers and their children: Findings from the Bay Area Families Study. In J. Laird & R.J. Green (Eds.), *Lesbians and gays in couples and families: A handbook for therapists* (pp. 420–437). San Francisco: Jossey-Bass.

Patterson, C.J. (1997). Children of lesbian and gay parents. In T. Ollendick & R. Prinz (Eds.), *Advances in clinical child psychology* (Vol. 19, pp. 235–282). New York: Plenum Press.

Patterson, C.J. (2004). Gay fathers. In M.E. Lamb (Ed.), *The role of the father in child development* (4th ed., pp. 397–416). New York: Wiley.

Patterson, C.J., Fulcher, M., & Wainright, J. (2002). Children of lesbian and gay parents: Research, law, and policy. In B.L. Bottoms, M.B. Kovera, & B.D. McAuliff (Eds.), *Children, social science and the law* (pp. 176–199). New York: Cambridge University Press.

Patterson, C.J., & Hastings, P. (in press). Socialization in context of family diversity. In J. Grusec & P. Hastings (Eds.), *Handbook of socialization.* New York: Guilford Press.

Stacey, J., & Biblarz, T.J. (2001). (How) Does sexual orientation of parents matter? *American Sociological Review, 65,* 159–183.

Wainright, J.L., & Patterson, C.J. (2006). Delinquency, victimization, and substance use among adolescents with female same-sex parents. *Journal of Family Psychology, 20,* 526–530.

Wainright, J.L., Russell, S.T., & Patterson, C.J. (2004). Psychosocial adjustment and school outcomes of adolescents with same-sex parents. *Child Development, 75,* 1886–1898.

## Critical Thinking

1. How does growing up with gay or lesbian parents influence how children turn out academically, emotionally, sexually, or in other ways—do such children turn out "different"? Is there any empirical, scientific basis for thinking that such families are not healthy for children?

2. In terms of how children develop, how does the quality of family relationships matter in comparison to the sexual orientation of the parents?

Address correspondence to **CHARLOTTE J. PATTERSON,** Department of Psychology, P.O. Box 400400, University of Virginia, Charlottesville, VA 22904; e-mail: cjp@virginia.edu.

From *Current Directions in Psychological Science*, October 2006, pp. 241–244. Copyright © 2006 by the Association for Psychological Science. Reprinted by permission of Sage Publications via Rightslink.

# Evidence of Infants' Internal Working Models of Attachment

Susan C. Johnson, Carol S. Dweck, and Frances S. Chen

Nearly half a century ago, psychiatrist John Bowlby proposed that the instinctual behavioral system that underpins an infant's attachment to his or her mother is accompanied by "internal working models" of the social world—models based on the infant's own experience with his or her caregiver (Bowlby, 1958, 1969/1982). These mental models were thought to mediate, in part, the ability of an infant to use the caregiver as a buffer against the stresses of life, as well as the later development of important self-regulatory and social skills.

Hundreds of studies now testify to the impact of caregivers' behavior on infants' behavior and development: Infants who most easily seek and accept support from their parents are considered secure in their attachments and are more likely to have received sensitive and responsive caregiving than insecure infants; over time, they display a variety of socioemotional advantages over insecure infants (Cassidy & Shaver, 1999). Research has also shown that, at least in older children and adults, individual differences in the security of attachment are indeed related to the individual's representations of social relations (Bretherton & Munholland, 1999). Yet no study has ever directly assessed internal working models of attachment in infancy. In the present study, we sought to do so.

## Method

Using a visual habituation technique, we tested expectations of caregivers' responsiveness in 10 securely and 11 insecurely attached 12- to 16-month-old infants (mean age = 403 days; 13 females). Attachment security was measured in the lab using the Strange Situation (Ainsworth, Blehar, Waters, & Wall, 1978).

Following Bowlby (1958, 1969/1982) and Ainsworth (Ainsworth et al., 1978), we predicted that different experiences with their own primary caregivers would lead infants to construct different internal working models, including different expectations of caregivers' responsiveness. Thus, we expected that secure infants, compared with insecure infants, would look longer at a display of an unresponsive caregiver (relatively unexpected) relative to a display of a responsive caregiver (relatively expected).

Given recent demonstrations of the abstractness and generality of infants' reasoning about agents (Gergely, Nádasdy, Csibra, & Bíró, 1995; Johnson, 2003; Kuhlmeier, Wynn, & Bloom, 2003), we chose to test infants' expectations with displays of animated geometric characters, rather than actual people. Infants were habituated to a video of two animated ellipses enacting a separation event. The large "mother" and small "child" appeared together at the bottom of a steep incline, and then the mother traveled halfway up the incline to a small plateau. As the mother came to rest there, the child below began to cry, an event depicted by a slight pulsation and bouncing and an actual human infant cry. The animation then paused, allowing the participant to look at the scene as long as he or she desired. Once the participant looked away, the sequence was repeated until his or her visual attention to the event declined to half of its initial amount, as measured by the duration of the participant's looks. When an infant reached this criterion of habituation, each of two test outcomes was shown twice. Each test outcome opened with the mother still positioned halfway up the incline, as the child continued to cry. In the *responsive* outcome, the mother returned to the child. In the *unresponsive* outcome, the mother continued up the slope, away from the child. The order in which the outcomes were presented was counterbalanced. Interest in each outcome was measured by looking time.

The Strange Situation sessions of all 21 infants were blind-coded by the third author after training at the Institute of Child Development's Attachment Workshop. A second blind coder, the first author, scored 10 randomly selected sessions. The coders' agreement was 90%, and kappa was .83.

The visual looking times of all infants were coded on-line by an observer blind to attachment status and test event. A second blind observer, also on-line, coded the looking times of 13 of the infants, achieving 93% agreement and a kappa of .82.

## Results

Mean looking times for the last three trials of habituation and each outcome were calculated for each infant (see Figure 1). Securely attached infants looked for 5.9 s (SD = 4.1) at the last three habituation events, 10.2 s (SD = 8.9) at the unresponsive-caregiver outcome, and 7.3 s (SD = 7.0) at the responsive-caregiver outcome. The comparable times in insecurely attached infants were 5.4 s (SD = 2.9), 6.6 s (SD = 3.5), and 8.0 s

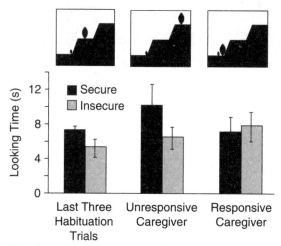

**Figure 1** Mean looking times (in seconds) to habituation and test events among secure and insecure infants. Standard error bars are shown. Each illustration depicts the final scene in the video corresponding to the graph below. The large oval represents the "mother," and the small oval represents the "child."

($SD = 5.4$). Preliminary analyses showed no effect of gender or order of presentation on looking times in the outcome trials.

A mixed analysis of variance with attachment status (secure, insecure) and outcome (responsive, unresponsive) as variables revealed no differences between secure and insecure infants in the overall amount of time that they looked at the test displays, $F(1, 19) = 0.31$, n.s., and no differences between the overall looking times (secure and insecure infants combined) to responsive versus unresponsive outcomes, $F(1, 19) = 0.48$, n.s. However, as predicted, infants' relative interest in the two outcomes did vary by group. Secure infants looked relatively longer at the unresponsive outcome than the responsive outcome compared with the insecure infants, $F(1, 19) = 4.76$, $p = .042$.[1] These results constitute direct positive evidence that infants' own personal attachment experiences are reflected in abstract mental representations of social interactions.

The current method opens a new window onto the nature of internal working models of attachment. In addition, these representations can now be traced as they emerge, well before existing behavioral measures of attachment can be employed. The literature on attachment has shown the profound impact of early experience. The method used in the present study provides a means of looking into the mind upon which that experience has left its imprint.

# Note

1. Results of additional analyses converged. One-tailed, pairwise comparisons revealed a significant effect of outcome within the secure group, $t(9) = 1.99$, $p < .04$, but not the

insecure group. Also, 7 of the 10 secure infants looked longer at the unresponsive than at the responsive outcome, whereas 7 of the 11 insecure infants showed the opposite result, $p < .07$, Mann-Whitney test. The looking behaviors of the two subtypes of insecure infants (6 avoidant, 5 resistant) did not differ.

# References

Ainsworth, M.D.S., Blehar, M.C., Waters, E., & Wall, S. (1978). *Patterns of attachment: A psychological study of the strange situation.* Hillsdale, NJ: Erlbaum.

Bowlby, J. (1958). The nature of the child's ties to his mother. *International Journal of Psychoanalysis, 39,* 350.

Bowlby, J. (1982). *Attachment and loss: Vol. 1. Attachment.* New York: Basic Books. (Original work published 1969)

Bretherton, I., & Munholland, K.A. (1999). Internal working models revisited. In J. Cassidy & P.R. Shaver (Eds.), *Handbook of attachment: Theory, research, and clinical applications* (pp. 89–111). New York: Guilford Press.

Cassidy, J., & Shaver, P.R. (Eds.). (1999). *Handbook of attachment: Theory, research, and clinical applications.* New York: Guilford Press.

Gergely, G., Nádasdy, Z., Csibra, G., & Bíró, S. (1995). Taking the intentional stance at 12 months of age. *Cognition, 56,* 165–193.

Johnson, S.C. (2003). Detecting agents. *Philosophical Transactions of the Royal Society B, 358,* 549–559.

Kuhlmeier, V.A., Wynn, K., & Bloom, P. (2003). Attribution of dispositional states by 12-month-olds. *Psychological Science, 14,* 402–408.

# Critical Thinking

1. What is the evidence from this experiment for the notion that infants, in fact, possess internal working models of attachment?

2. What were the key differences between securely attached and insecurely attached infants' responses to the visual stimuli?

3. What are some ways that you would modify the experiment if you were to replicate it?

SUSAN C. JOHNSON, CAROL S. DWECK, and FRANCES S. CHEN Stanford University.

Address correspondence to Susan C. Johnson, Department of Psychology, Jordan Hall, Bldg. 420, Stanford University, Stanford, CA 94305; e-mail: scj@psych.stanford.edu.

**Acknowledgments**—We thank C. Lai, P. Romera, C. Titchenal, and L. Weitzel for assistance.

# Parental Divorce and Children's Adjustment

JENNIFER E. LANSFORD

In the United States, between 43% and 50% of first marriages end in divorce (U.S. Census Bureau, 2004), and 50% of American children will experience their parents' divorce (National Center for Health Statistics, 2008). Given the large number of families affected by divorce each year, parents, clinicians, and policymakers alike are concerned with understanding how experiencing parental divorce affects children's adjustment. Indeed, many parents considering divorce ask whether they should stay together for the sake of their children.

Key questions in the research literature have focused on whether divorce per se affects children's adjustment and, if so, why and how. The literature has at times portrayed two extreme positions on whether divorce affects children's adjustment (Cherlin, 1999). The first extreme position holds that the long-term effects of divorce on children are quite debilitating and that children carry a lasting negative burden years after the divorce in terms of mental health and interpersonal relationships (e.g., Glenn, 2001; Popenoe, 1993, 2003; Wallerstein, Lewis, & Blakeslee, 2000). This work has drawn criticism for methodological (e.g., reliance on small samples of clinical populations) and ideological reasons. For example, Coontz (1992) points out that many condemnations of divorce and nontraditional families stem from misguided perceptions of family life in previous decades and that myths about family life in the past reflected reality for only a small subset of middle-class European Americans. At the opposite extreme is the position that divorce has no measurable long-term effects on children (e.g., Harris, 1998). This extreme has been criticized because it appears to conflict with hundreds of empirical studies to the contrary.

Between these two extremes, most researchers have come to the conclusion that divorce has some negative effects on children's adjustment but that these effects may be small in magnitude and not universal. For example, in a meta-analysis of 92 studies conducted in the 1950s through 1980s, Amato and Keith (1991b) reported that 70% of studies found lower well-being for children whose parents had divorced than for children whose parents had not divorced; the median effect size was .14 of a standard deviation. Conduct problems and father–child relationship outcomes showed the largest effect sizes, and psychological adjustment and self-concept outcomes showed the smallest effect sizes (Amato & Keith, 1991b). Amato (2001) updated the meta-analysis using 67 studies published in the 1990s. Although 88% of the effects suggested lower well-being for children whose parents divorced than for children whose parents did not divorce, only 42% of the effects were significant (Amato, 2001). There has been considerable debate in the literature regarding the extent to which these effects are attributable to divorce per se or to correlated factors such as exposure to interparental conflict.

The main purpose of this review is to provide an overview of the nuances represented in the patterns of findings regarding links between parental divorce and children's short-term and long-term adjustment. First, I consider how divorce is related to several different aspects of children's adjustment. Second, I examine the timing of divorce, demographic characteristics, children's adjustment prior to the divorce, and stigmatization as moderators of the links between divorce and children's adjustment. Third, I examine income, interparental conflict, parenting, and parents' well-being as mediators of relations between divorce and children's adjustment. Fourth, I describe the caveats and limitations of the research literature. Finally, I consider the notable policies related to grounds for divorce, child support, and child custody in light of how they might affect children's adjustment to their parents' divorce.

## Indicators of Children's Adjustment

Although findings regarding whether and how parental divorce is related to children's adjustment are not always clear in the literature, there is agreement among most researchers that children experiencing parental divorce are at risk for a variety of negative developmental outcomes (see Cherlin, 1999, for a review). However, the magnitude of these effects appears to depend on the indicators of adjustment under consideration, and some studies find no differences on particular outcomes between children whose parents divorce and those whose parents stay together (Ruschena, Prior, Sanson, & Smart, 2005). Externalizing behaviors, internalizing problems, academic achievement, and quality of social relationships are frequently included indicators of adjustment in the divorce literature. Studies that have examined these indicators of adjustment at discrete time points provide some evidence that children whose parents have divorced have more externalizing and internalizing problems, lower academic achievement, and more problematic social relationships than do children whose parents have not divorced (e.g., Cherlin et al., 1991; Emery, Waldron, Kitzmann, & Aaron, 1999).

Meta-analyses have revealed that divorce has larger effects on relationships with nonresidential fathers and externalizing behaviors than it does on internalizing problems or academic achievement (Amato, 2001; Amato & Keith, 1991b). In the earlier meta-analysis (Amato & Keith, 1991b), divorce was found to have larger effects on academic achievement than on internalizing problems, but in the later meta-analysis (Amato, 2001), divorce was found to have larger effects on internalizing problems than on academic achievement. In these meta-analyses, effect sizes depended on the methodological sophistication of the studies under consideration. More methodologically sophisticated studies (e.g., those with multiple-item scales and control variables) showed smaller effect sizes than did less methodologically sophisticated studies. Methodologically unsophisticated studies may overestimate the effects of divorce on children. For example, if socioeconomic status is not controlled, children who have experienced divorce and are living with a single mother may show worse adjustment than do children who are living with two parents in part because of the confounding effect of having fewer economic resources in single-mother families.

A problem with relying on indicators of adjustment measured at a single point in time is that these indicators are likely to look worse if they are assessed in close temporal proximity to the time of the divorce, but they show improvement over time because the short-term effects of divorce tend to look worse than the long-term effects. The examination of developmental trajectories of adjustment has several advantages over the examination of adjustment at discrete points in time. The examination of trajectories makes it possible to track change over time from before the divorce occurs to some period following the divorce. The inclusion of predivorce adjustment

in these models is important because of evidence that children whose parents eventually divorce show poorer adjustment prior to the divorce than do children whose parents do not divorce (e.g., Cherlin, Chase-Lansdale, & McRae, 1998; Doherty & Needle, 1991). Links between parental divorce and children's adjustment are often attenuated or eliminated by controlling for predivorce adjustment. For example, Sun and Li (2001) used longitudinal data from a nationally representative sample and found that differences in academic achievement between children whose parents divorced and children whose parents stayed together could be accounted for almost entirely by children's academic achievement and family functioning prior to the divorce.

Although one can control for prior adjustment in analyses predicting subsequent adjustment at a discrete point in time, such analyses do not allow for an examination of how these effects continue to develop over time. Children often have more short-term adjustment difficulties immediately after their parents' divorce, but these difficulties may lessen in severity or disappear following an initial adjustment period (Chase-Lansdale & Hetherington, 1990). Studying trajectories of adjustment that extend from before the parents' divorce to a period well after the divorce will provide a more complete picture of children's long-term adjustment.

To overcome the limitations of cross-sectional approaches, Cherlin et al. (1998) followed a large sample of children born in 1958 in Great Britain prospectively from childhood to the age of 33. Prior to their parents' divorce, individuals whose parents eventually divorced had more internalizing and externalizing problems than did individuals whose parents did not divorce. However, divorce itself also contributed to higher levels of long-term internalizing and externalizing problems into adulthood. It is important to note that their findings suggested that some of the effects of divorce during childhood may not manifest themselves shortly after the divorce and that they may not become apparent until adolescence or adulthood. The gap between groups of individuals whose parents had and had not divorced widened over the course of several years from childhood to adulthood. Cherlin et al. (1998) suggested that parental divorce may curtail educational achievement or disrupt social relationships in ways that are not apparent until children try to enter the labor market, marry, or have children of their own.

In a sample of American children followed from before kindergarten through Grade 10, Malone et al. (2004) used latent change score models to examine trajectories of teacher-rated externalizing behavior over time. Parental divorce was unrelated to girls' externalizing behavior trajectories, regardless of the timing of divorce. Parental divorce was related to boys' externalizing trajectories differently depending on the timing of the divorce. In particular, parental divorce during elementary school was related to an increase in boys' externalizing behaviors that began in the year of the divorce and persisted for years afterward. Parental divorce during middle school was related to an increase in boys' externalizing behaviors in the year of the divorce that declined below baseline levels in the year following the divorce and persisted into subsequent years.

Several studies also address whether parental divorce during childhood relates to long-term effects on adults' own romantic relationships and their relationships with their parents later in life. Intergenerational studies suggest that parental divorce doubles the risk that one's own marriage will end in divorce, in part because individuals whose parents have divorced are less likely to view marriage as a lifelong commitment (Amato & DeBoer, 2001); the risk is exacerbated if both spouses experienced their parents' divorce (Hetherington & Elmore, 2004). There is also evidence that intergenerational transmission of divorce is mediated by interpersonal skill deficits (e.g., communication patterns not conducive to supporting a long-term intimate relationship) that make it more difficult for individuals whose parents have divorced to sustain their own intimate relationships (Amato, 1996). In addition to being at greater risk for difficulties in romantic relationships, adults whose parents divorced have lower quality relationships with their parents (particularly fathers) during adulthood, on average (Lye, 1996). However, these associations depend on the parents' marital quality prior to the divorce, the gender of the parent, and the gender of the adult child (Booth & Amato, 1994; Orbuch, Thornton, & Cancio, 2000).

To summarize, research suggests that children whose parents have divorced have higher levels of externalizing behaviors and internalizing problems, lower academic achievement, and more problems in social relationships than do children whose parents have not divorced. But, the magnitude of these effects is attenuated after controlling for children's adjustment prior to the divorce and other potential confounds. Furthermore, even though children whose parents divorce have worse adjustment on average than do children whose parents stay together, most children whose parents divorce do not have long-term negative outcomes. For example, in their longitudinal study of a representative sample of 17,414 individuals in Great Britain who were followed from ages 7 to 23, Chase-Lansdale, Cherlin, and Kiernan (1995) reported that the likelihood of scoring in the clinical range on the Malaise Inventory, which measures a wide range of adult emotional disorders, was 11% for young adults who had experienced their parents' divorce and 8% for young adults who had not experienced their parents' divorce. Nevertheless, analyses using data from this sample after they were followed to age 33 led Cherlin et al. (1998) to conclude that the adjustment gap between individuals who had and had not experienced parental divorce widened over time and that although part of the effect of parental divorce could be attributed to factors prior to the divorce, experiencing parental divorce during childhood was related to worse mental health when the offspring were in their 20s and 30s.

Hetherington and Kelly (2002) concluded that 25% of individuals whose parents divorce have serious long-term social, emotional, or psychological problems in adulthood in comparison with 10% of individuals whose parents have stayed together; still, this means that 75% of individuals whose parents divorce do not have serious long-term impairment during adulthood. Even studies that do find long-term effects of divorce generally report that the effect sizes are small. For example, Allison and Furstenberg (1989) used longitudinal data from a nationally representative sample and concluded that although divorce was related to behavior problems, psychological distress, and low academic achievement, the effect sizes for divorce were smaller than those found for gender differences (but larger than those found for several other demographic variables). Amato (2003) concluded that about 10% of children whose parents divorce grow up to have poorer psychological well-being than would have been predicted if their parents had stayed together, 18% of children whose parents divorce have more marital discord as adults than do children whose parents stayed together, and 35% of children whose parents divorce have worse relationships with their fathers than do children whose parents stayed together. Laumann-Billings and Emery (2000) caution that researchers and clinicians may reach different conclusions regarding the long-term effects of divorce because researchers often study psychological or behavioral problems, whereas clinicians often are faced with clients' subjective impressions of their psychological distress (which may not be manifest in psychological or behavioral disorders). Taken together, these findings indicate that the majority of children whose parents divorce do not have long-term adjustment problems, but the risk of externalizing behaviors, internalizing problems, poorer academic achievement, and problematic social relationships is greater for children whose parents divorce than for those whose parents stay together. Different children may manifest adjustment problems in different ways. Future research should adopt a more person-centered approach to investigate whether, for example, those children whose grades are dropping are the same children whose internalizing or externalizing problems are increasing following their parents' divorce.

# Moderators of Links between Divorce and Children's Adjustment

Despite the research suggesting that divorce is related to children's adjustment, there is considerable evidence that these effects do not operate in the same way for all children. Links between divorce and children's adjustment are moderated by several factors, including children's age at the time of their parents' divorce, children's age at the time of the study, the length of time since the divorce, children's demographic characteristics (gender, race/ethnicity), children's adjustment prior to the divorce, and stigmatization of divorce (by location or historical period).

## Children's Age at Divorce, Age at the Time of the Study, and Length of Time since Divorce

Studies have shown mixed results with respect to how the timing of divorce affects children's adjustment (see Hetherington, Bridges, & Insabella, 1998). Hetherington (1989) suggests that, in comparison with older children, young children may be less capable of realistically assessing the causes and consequences of divorce, may feel more anxious about abandonment, may be more likely to blame themselves, and may be less able to take advantage of resources outside the family to cope with the divorce. All of these factors may contribute to findings that young children experience more problems after their parents divorce than do children who are older when the divorce occurs (Allison & Furstenberg, 1989). Note that this conclusion applies specifically to divorce; other findings suggest that adjusting to parents' remarriage may be harder for adolescents than for younger children (Hetherington, Stanley-Hagan, & Anderson, 1989). It may be that divorce has effects on particular outcomes that are salient during the developmental period during which the divorce occurs. For example, academic achievement, identity development, and emerging romantic relationships may be affected by divorce that occurs during adolescence because these domains of functioning are developmentally salient then.

A methodological problem is that in many studies, children's reported age reflects their age at the time of the study rather than their age at the time of their parents' divorce. Amato (2001) noted this lack of availability of children's age at the time of the divorce as a limitation in his meta-analysis. The most common approach is to study children in a particular developmental stage (e.g., early childhood, middle childhood, adolescence) and compare the adjustment of children whose parents have divorced

with the adjustment of children whose parents have not divorced. A drawback of this strategy is that the length of time between the parents' divorce and the time of the assessment will vary considerably across the sample. Lansford et al. (2006) addressed this limitation by using the time of parental divorce as an anchor point and modeling trajectories of adjustment over a period from 1 year prior to the divorce to 3 years after the divorce. This approach makes it possible to compare children at comparable points of time in relation to their parents' divorce. Lansford et al. (2006) also analyzed a matched group of children whose parents did not divorce. Results suggested that parental divorce occurring from kindergarten to Grade 5 exerted more adverse effects on internalizing and externalizing problems than did parental divorce occurring from Grades 6 to 10, whereas parental divorce occurring from Grades 6 to 10 exerted more adverse effects on grades.

## Children's Demographic Characteristics

Researchers have attempted to understand how children's demographic characteristics (primarily gender and race) may moderate the link between parental divorce and children's adjustment. Early research findings suggested that parental divorce was related to more adjustment difficulties for boys than girls but that parents' remarriage was related to more adjustment difficulties for girls than for boys (see Hetherington, Cox, & Cox, 1985). However, recent findings have been more mixed; there is no consistent pattern regarding whether divorce has more adverse effects on girls or boys. Some studies report that boys have more adjustment problems following parental divorce than do girls (Morrison & Cherlin, 1995; Shaw, Emery, & Tuer, 1993). Other studies report that girls have more adjustment problems following parental divorce than do boys (Allison & Furstenberg, 1989). Still other studies report no gender differences (e.g., Amato & Cheadle, 2005; Sun & Li, 2002). There is also evidence that the particular outcomes affected by parental divorce may differ by gender. For example, early childbearing has been found to be associated with parental divorce for girls, and more unemployment has been found to be associated with parental divorce for boys (McLanahan, 1999). In their meta-analysis, Amato and Keith (1991b) found no gender differences except that boys whose parents divorced had a harder time adjusting socially than did girls.

It has been proposed that parental divorce may have a less negative effect on African American children than on European American children (Jeynes, 2002). Specifically, researchers have suggested that because African American children tend to experience less of a decrease in household income following parents' divorce and there is a greater norm for single parenthood in the African American community (Cherlin, 1998; Laosa, 1988), these factors may mitigate the effects of divorce on African American youth. Research assessing these effects has produced mixed results, but a meta-analysis of 37 studies investigating links between parental divorce and adults' well-being found that effect sizes were smaller for African Americans than for European Americans (Amato & Keith, 1991a), which is consistent with the hypothesis that divorce would have a less negative effect on African American children than for European American children.

## Children's Adjustment Prior to the Divorce

Some evidence suggests that children whose parents eventually divorce already have more adjustment problems many years before the divorce (Cherlin et al., 1998). Genetic or other environmental factors may be contributing to these adjustment problems, and the children's adjustment may have appeared to be just as problematic even if the parents had not divorced. Chase-Lansdale et al. (1995) found a steeper increase in adjustment problems after parental divorce for children who were well-adjusted prior to the divorce than for children with predivorce adjustment problems (or for children whose parents did not divorce). However, the long-term adjustment of children with predivorce adjustment problems was worse than it was for children who were better adjusted prior to the divorce (Chase-Lansdale et al., 1995). Controlling for children's adjustment prior to their parents' divorce greatly reduces differences between children whose parents divorce and those whose parents stay together (Cherlin et al., 1991).

Children with positive attributes such as attractiveness, easy temperament, and social competence are also more resilient following their parents' divorce (Hetherington et al., 1989). In part, this may be because children with such attributes are more likely to have strong support networks outside the family (e.g., from teachers or peers) and to evoke positive responses from others. In an epidemiological sample of 648 children who were initially assessed when they were 1–10 years old and assessed again 8 years later, Kasen, Cohen, Brook, and Hartmark (1996) found significant interactions between temperament assessed in the first 10 years of life and family structure in the prediction of subsequent adjustment. In particular, the risk of oppositional defiant disorder was exacerbated for children who had early affective problems and were living with a single mother or in a stepfamily; the authors speculated that the stress of adjusting to new living arrangements may have overwhelmed the coping capacities of these already vulnerable children.

On the other hand, Kasen et al. (1996) also found that the risk of overanxiety disorder was reduced for children (especially boys) who were socially immature early in life and were living with a single mother; the authors speculated that needing to play more "adult" roles in a single-parent family may have enhanced the social skills of previously immature children. Thus, children's adjustment can moderate the effects of divorce on subsequent adjustment.

## Stigmatization

At a societal level, stigmatization has been considered as a potential moderator of the link between parents' divorce and children's adjustment. Divorce would be expected to have more detrimental effects for children in societal contexts in which family forms other than two-parent biological families are stigmatized than it would in societies that are more accepting of diverse family forms. There is some empirical support for this perspective. For example, Amato and Keith's (1991b) meta-analysis revealed smaller effect sizes for some outcomes in more recent studies than in studies from earlier decades, suggesting that the effects of divorce became less pronounced over time from the 1950s to the 1980s. Amato and Keith also reported that studies conducted outside the United States on average found more problems with conduct, psychological adjustment, and both mother–child and father–child relationships than did studies conducted in the United States. One explanation for these findings is that divorce is less stigmatized in the United States than in many other countries (Amato & Keith, 1991b). On the other hand, Amato (2001) found that although the adjustment of children whose parents had and had not divorced became increasingly similar over time from the 1950s to the 1980s, the gap between these two groups began to increase again in the 1990s (Reifman, Villa, Amans, Rethinam, & Telesca, 2001, reached a similar conclusion). It is not clear that stigmatization increased again over this same time period.

# Mediators of Links between Divorce and Children's Adjustment

Most researchers no longer simply compare the adjustment of children whose parents have and have not divorced. Instead, researchers have adopted more complex models of how divorce may be related to children's adjustment and now investigate moderators as described previously or analyze their data to understand the mechanisms through which divorce might affect children's adjustment. Several scholars have argued that processes occurring in all types of families are more important than family structure in relation to the well-being of children and adolescents (e.g., Dunn, Deater-Deckard, Pickering, & O'Connor, 1998; Lansford, Ceballo, Abbey, & Stewart, 2001). Taking family process and other mediating variables into account attenuates the association between the experience of parental divorce and children's adjustment (e.g., Amato & Keith, 1991b; Mechanic & Hansell, 1989). It is also important to keep in mind that divorce can be conceptualized more as a process than as a discrete event, with the family processes leading up to and following the divorce being an integral part of the divorce itself.

## Income

In a review of five theoretical perspectives on why marital transitions may be related to children's adjustment, Hetherington et al. (1998) found some support for an economic disadvantage perspective suggesting that a drop in household income often accompanies divorce and mediates the link between parents' divorce and children's adjustment. Twenty-eight percent of single mothers and 11% of single fathers live in poverty in comparison with 8% of two-parent families (Grall, 2007). Following their parents' divorce, children most often live with single mothers who do not have the same financial resources they did prior to the divorce, especially if they are not receiving regular child-support payments from nonresidential fathers. This sometimes necessitates a change for the worse in housing, neighborhoods, and schools. These economic hardships and their sequelae can lead to behavioral and emotional problems in children. For example, Guidubaldi, Cleminshaw, Perry, and McLoughlin (1983) surveyed children whose parents had and had not divorced and found differences between them on 27 out of 34 outcomes before controlling for income, but only found 13 differences between them after controlling for income, suggesting that income plays an important role but does not account for all of the effect of divorce on children's adjustment. Furthermore, children's adjustment often worsens rather than improves following remarriage and its accompanying increase in economic resources (Hetherington et al., 1989). Taken together, these findings suggest that income is important, but there is more contributing to children's adjustment problems following divorce than a decrease in household income.

## Interparental Conflict

Interparental conflict has received substantial empirical attention. There is consistent evidence that high levels of interparental conflict have negative and long-lasting implications for children's adjustment (Davies & Cummings, 1994; Grych & Fincham, 1990). Amato (1993) and Hetherington et al. (1998) found more support for a parental conflict perspective on why divorce is related to children's adjustment than for any other theoretical perspective that has been proposed to account for this link. Averaging across measures in their review, children in high-conflict, intact families scored .32 standard deviation below children in low-conflict, intact families and .12 standard deviation below children in divorced families on measures of adjustment, suggesting that exposure to high levels of conflict was more detrimental to children than was parental divorce (Hetherington et al., 1998). To illustrate, using data from the National Survey of Families and Households, Vandewater and Lansford (1998) found that when interparental conflict and family structure (married and never divorced vs. divorced and not remarried) were considered simultaneously after controlling for family demographic covariates and children's prior adjustment, high interparental conflict was related to more externalizing behaviors, internalizing problems, and trouble with peers, but family structure was not significantly related to child outcomes. The finding that children whose parents divorce look worse before the divorce than do comparable children whose parents do not divorce is also consistent with this perspective; worse adjustment prior to the divorce could be accounted for, in part, by exposure to interparental conflict.

If divorce leads to a reduction in children's exposure to interparental conflict, one might expect that their adjustment would improve. Indeed, this issue is at the heart of parents' question of whether they should stay in a conflicted marriage for the sake of the children. In an important longitudinal investigation of this issue, Amato, Loomis, and Booth (1995) found that children's problems decrease when parents in a high-conflict marriage divorce (which encompassed 30%–49% of divorces), whereas children's problems increase when parents in a low-conflict marriage divorce. Booth and Amato (2001) examined correlates of divorce for low-conflict couples and found that factors such as less integration in the community, having fewer friends, not owning a home, and having more positive attitudes toward divorce were related to an increased likelihood of divorce; the authors suggest that because these factors may be less salient to children than conflict between their parents, the divorce may come as more of an unwelcome and unexpected shock, accounting for the more negative effects of divorce on children from low-conflict families than those seen in children from high-conflict families.

Researchers have moved beyond monolithic characterizations of conflict into descriptions of particular types of conflict and specific aspects of interparental conflict that may be especially detrimental to children. Overt conflict may be physical or verbal and includes behaviors and emotions such as belligerence, contempt, derision, screaming, insulting, slapping, threatening, and hitting; exposure to overt conflict has been linked to children's externalizing problems (Buehler et al., 1998). Covert conflict may include passive-aggressive techniques such as trying to get the child to side with one parent, using the child to get information about the other parent, having the child carry messages to the other parent, and denigrating the other parent in the presence of the child; covert conflict has been linked more to internalizing problems than to externalizing problems (Buehler et al., 1998). Amato and Afifi (2006) found that the feeling of being caught between parents even into young adulthood was associated with high-conflict marriages but not with divorce and that it was related to more internalizing problems and worse parent–child relationships. Thus, children whose parents divorce may have better long-term adjustment than do children whose parents remain in high-conflict marriages if divorce enables children to escape from exposure to conflict and feelings of being caught between their parents.

## Parenting

Another mechanism that has been proposed many times in the literature as an explanation for the links between parental divorce and children's adjustment is the disruption in parenting practices that may occur following divorce. Divorce can make it more difficult for parents to monitor and supervise children effectively (Buchanan, Maccoby, & Dornbusch, 1996; McLanahan & Sandefur, 1994), to discipline consistently (Hetherington, Cox, & Cox, 1979), and to provide warmth and affection (Forehand, Thomas, Wierson, & Brody, 1990; Hetherington & Stanley-Hagan, 1999). After divorce, parent–child conflict often increases, and family cohesion decreases (Short, 2002).

As with studies of children's adjustment showing that children whose parents eventually divorce have significantly more predivorce adjustment problems than do children whose parents do not divorce, parents who eventually divorce have been found to have more problematic parenting practices as long as 8–12 years before the divorce than do parents who do not divorce (Amato & Booth, 1996; Shaw et al., 1993). Parenting problems contribute to children's adjustment problems in all types of family structures. Several studies provide evidence that controlling for the quality of parenting attenuates the link between parental divorce and children's adjustment (Amato, 1986; Amato & Gilbreth, 1999; Simons, Whitbeck, Beaman, & Conger, 1994; Tschann, Johnson, & Wallerstein, 1989; Videon, 2002). For example, in a study of mothers and their sons in Grades 1–3, Martinez and Forgatch (2002) found that mothers' encouragement of academic skills mediated the relation between marital

transitions and boys' academic achievement and that a more general indicator of effective parenting mediated the link between marital transitions and externalizing and internalizing problems.

Some studies have investigated whether contact with the noncustodial parent and the quality of this relationship also mediate the link between parental divorce and children's adjustment. In a meta-analysis of 63 studies, Amato and Gilbreth (1999) found that improved child adjustment (academic achievement and fewer externalizing and internalizing problems) was unrelated to frequency of contact with nonresident fathers but was associated with nonresident fathers' payment of child support, authoritative parenting, and feelings of father–child closeness.

## Parents' Well-Being

Yet another possible mediator of the link between parental divorce and children's adjustment is parents' well-being. Marital conflict and divorce increase parents' depression, anxiety, and stress, which decrease parents' ability to parent well and may in turn negatively affect children's adjustment. Mothers' history of delinquent behavior has also been found to account for much of the link between parental divorce and children's externalizing behaviors (Emery et al., 1999). These relations are complicated. Through assortative mating, parents with problems such as depression, substance use, or antisocial behavior are at risk of selecting spouses with similar problems (Maes et al., 1998). These parental risk factors increase marital conflict and divorce (Merikangas, 1984). Children may share some of these parental characteristics genetically or through shared environmental experiences.

## Caveats

Because children cannot be randomly assigned to family structure groups, studies of links between parents' divorce and children's adjustment are necessarily correlational. Despite researchers' attempts to control for potential confounds, it is possible that uncontrolled variables account for associations between divorce and adjustment. Two large bodies of research that present important caveats for understanding links between parental divorce and children's adjustment are studies of children's adjustment in stepfamilies and studies of genetic effects.

### Remarriage and Stepfamilies

Much of the literature comparing the adjustment of children whose parents have or have not divorced is complicated by the fact that children are often exposed not only to one marital transition (i.e., their biological parents' divorce) but to multiple marital transitions (e.g., the initial divorce plus subsequent remarriages and divorces). If these multiple transitions are not taken into account, children's adjustment to divorce may be confounded with children's adjustment to remarriage and possibly multiple divorces. The present review focuses on parental divorce rather than stepfamilies, but several excellent reviews provide nuanced information about children's adjustment following their parents' remarriage (e.g., Dunn, 2002; Hetherington & Clingempeel, 1992; Hetherington et al., 1999).

## Genetic Effects

Recent research has attempted to estimate the relative contributions of genes and environments in accounting for the likelihood that parents will divorce and the adjustment of their children following the divorce (Neiderhiser, Reiss, & Hetherington, 2007). Lykken (2002) presents evidence that a monozygotic twin has a 250% increase in risk of divorcing if his or her cotwin has divorced. Furthermore, divorce is more concordant between monozygotic than dizygotic twins (McGue & Lykken, 1992). These findings support the role of genetics as a risk factor for divorce, but Jocklin, McGue, and Lykken (1996) further specified the personality mechanisms through which this effect occurs. That is, they found between 30% and 42% of the heritability of divorce to be associated with the heritability of the personality characteristics of positive emotionality, negative emotionality, and less constraint, which were, in turn, associated with divorce (Jocklin et al., 1996).

Research also has begun to examine genotype–environment interactions to understand under what environmental conditions genes may express themselves. An important question is whether the genetic contributions to divorce also account for the poorer adjustment of children whose parents have divorced or whether experiencing parental divorce contributes above and beyond the genetic risks. In a longitudinal study of 398 biological and adoptive families, O'Connor, Caspi, DeFries, and Plomin (2000) found that children who experienced their biological parents' divorce by the age of 12 had higher levels of behavior problems and substance use and lower levels of achievement and social adjustment than did children whose biological parents did not divorce. Children who experienced their adoptive parents' divorce by the age of 12 also had higher levels of behavior problems and substance use than did children who did not experience their adoptive parents' divorce, but these two groups of adopted children did not differ on achievement or social adjustment. These findings suggest the importance of gene–environment interactions in contributing to achievement and social adjustment and suggest the importance of the environment in accounting for links between parental divorce and children's behavior problems and substance use (O'Connor et al., 2000).

Using a high-risk sample in Australia, D'Onofrio et al. (2005) compared the offspring of adult twins on externalizing, internalizing, and substance-use problems and concluded that environmental (rather than genetic) effects of divorce accounted for the higher rates of problems among the group that experienced their parents' divorce. In a further elaboration of the process involved in genetic versus environmental effects, D'Onofrio et al. (2006) found that the experience of divorce was related to earlier age of first intercourse and more emotional and educational problems, whereas earlier use of drugs and likelihood of cohabitation were predicted by genetic and other selection factors. Using a children of twins design with a population-based American sample, D'Onofrio et al. (2007) found that genetic and other selection factors, rather than divorce per se, accounted for differences in internalizing problems, whereas substance use was not accounted for by genetic factors. The reasons for the discrepancies between the findings from these studies are not clear. However, although the precise nature of which genetic or environmental factors contribute to distinct developmental outcomes is not clear from the research to date, it is apparent that genetic and environmental contributions both shape whether individuals will eventually divorce and, if they do, how their children may adjust to the divorce.

## Divorce Laws and Policies

The questions of whether family structure per se affects children's adjustment and, if so, why and how it does so are important in informing policy because one can adjust policy to influence different proximal mechanisms that may affect children's adjustment. At one level, answers to questions related to whether and how divorce affects children's adjustment also influence how hard it should be for parents to divorce in the first place (e.g., determining if it is better to stay in a conflicted marriage for the sake of the children). States differ in terms of requirements related to waiting periods, counseling, the length of separation needed prior to divorce, and other factors that affect how hard it is to get a divorce in a given state. Despite shifts in rates immediately after a new policy is implemented, the difficulty of divorcing and rates of divorce are for the most part unrelated after this initial phase (Wolfers, 2003), so policies are unlikely to influence how many parents divorce over the long run.

At another level, understanding children's adjustment following divorce is important for implementing policies that can help children once their parents have decided to divorce. For example, if divorce increases children's risk for externalizing behaviors because it results in more limited financial resources available to children and, in turn, the risks of dangerous neighborhoods associated with lower SES, then a reasonable policy response would be to make noncustodial parents more responsible for child-support payments. Similarly, state policies may minimize or exacerbate interparental conflict, with implications for children's adjustment. Key policy issues related to children's adjustment involve the divorce process (e.g., grounds for divorce), custody decisions, and financial support of children. Each category of policies is reviewed below.

## Grounds for Divorce

The primary distinction of importance related to grounds for divorce involves whether fault is considered in the divorce proceedings. If fault is considered, then divorce is granted only if one spouse is determined to be "guilty" (of adultery, physically or sexually abusing the spouse or a child, abandoning the home for at least a year, or other serious offenses) and the other spouse is determined to be "innocent" (Nakonezny, Shull, & Rodgers, 1995). The consent of the "innocent" spouse is needed to grant the divorce, and divorce is not granted if both spouses are "guilty." In theory, the innocent spouse is awarded alimony, child support, and property in a fault-based divorce. If fault is not considered, both spouses do not need to provide consent, and alimony, child support, and property are no longer awarded according to fault but according to needs and the ability to pay.

No-fault grounds for divorce were enacted in all 50 states between the 1950s and 1980s, and all 50 states now allow no-fault divorces. However, only 15 states have entirely eliminated fault-based divorces (Grounds for Divorce, n.d.). In the other 35 states, one may choose between a no-fault divorce and a fault-based divorce. The most common reasons for selecting a fault-based divorce are to avoid a longer waiting period often required for a no-fault divorce or to obtain a larger share of the marital assets or more alimony. A main concern related to children's adjustment is that proving guilt and innocence in a fault-based divorce tends to perpetuate acrimony and conflict between the parents, which may lead to worse outcomes for their children.

## Child Custody Policies

Child custody policies include several guidelines that determine with whom the child lives following divorce, how time is divided in joint custody situations, and visitation rights. The most frequently applied custody guideline is the "best interests of the child" standard, which takes into account the parents' preferences, the child's preferences, the interactions between parents and children, children's adjustment, and all family members' mental and physical health (see Kelly, 1994). Recently, the approximation rule has been proposed as an alternative to the best interests of the child standard because of concerns that the latter does not provide enough concrete guidance and leaves too many factors to be evaluated at the discretion of individual judges (American Law Institute, 2002). The approximation rule holds that custody should be awarded to each parent to approximate the amount of time each spent in providing care for the children during the marriage. Opinions range from support of the approximation rule as an improvement over the best interests of the child standard (Emery, Otto, & O'Donohue, 2005) to criticisms that the approximation rule would lead to biases against fathers and be less sensitive to the needs of individual families than is the best interests of the child standard (Warshak, 2007). Regardless of the custody standard applied, custody disputes that are handled through mediation rather than litigation have been found to be related to more involvement of the non-residential parent in the child's life, without increasing interparental conflict (Emery, Laumann-Billings, Waldron, Sbarra, & Dillon, 2001; Emery, Sbarra, & Grover, 2005).

A distinction is made between legal custody, which involves making decisions regarding the child, and physical custody, which involves daily living arrangements. The most common arrangement following divorce is for parents to share joint legal custody but for mothers to have sole physical custody. Several studies have investigated whether children's adjustment is related to custody arrangements following their parents' divorce. Using data from a large national sample, Downey and Powell (1995) found few differences between the adjustment of children whose fathers had custody following divorce and those whose mothers had custody. For the few outcomes in which differences did emerge, children appeared somewhat better adjusted in paternal custody families if income was left uncontrolled, but after controlling for income, children appeared somewhat better adjusted in maternal custody families (Downey & Powell, 1995).

Major benefits of joint custody include the access to financial resources and other resources that a second parent can provide and the more frequent and meaningful contact that is possible between both parents and the child (Bender, 1994). The major concerns raised with respect to joint custody are that it may prolong children's exposure to conflict between parents with acrimonious relationships and reduce stability that is needed for children's positive adjustment (Johnston, 1995; Twaite & Luchow, 1996). In a meta-analysis of 33 studies comparing joint physical or legal custody with sole maternal custody, Bauserman

(2002) concluded that children in joint custody (either physical or legal) had fewer externalizing and internalizing problems and better academic achievement and social relationships than did children in sole maternal custody. Parents with joint custody reported having less past and current conflict than did parents with sole custody, but the findings regarding better adjustment of children in joint custody held after controlling for interparental conflict. Nevertheless, caution is warranted, because there are a wide array of factors affecting the selection of joint versus sole custody that can plausibly explain differences in adjustment for children in these different custody situations. An additional methodological concern is that only 11 of the 33 studies included in Bauserman's meta-analysis were published—21 were unpublished dissertations, and 1 was another unpublished manuscript. Therefore, the majority of the studies included in the meta-analyses have not passed the rigor of peer review. The finding that joint physical and joint legal custody were equally associated with better child adjustment is consistent with the finding from Amato and Gilbreth's (1999) meta-analysis that there was little relation between children's adjustment and the frequency with which they had contact with their father. Amato and Gilbreth (1999) found that the quality of children's relationship with their father is a more important predictor of children's adjustment than is frequency of contact. If joint physical or legal custody promotes more positive father–child relationships, this might account for the more positive adjustment of children in joint custody reported by Bauserman (2002).

## Child-Support Policies and Enforcement

Child-support policies involve a diverse set of factors related to ensuring that noncustodial parents provide financial support for their children. States vary in their statutory criteria for child support: whether the state can take a percentage of the noncustodial parent's wages, formulas for child support, discretion to have payment made directly to the court, and long-arm statutes. Historically, public assistance played an important role in the economic status of divorced mothers and children (see Garfinkel, Melli, & Robertson, 1994, for a review). Guidelines of "reasonableness" were used by states to determine noncustodial parents' responsibility to pay child support. Local judges used budgets submitted by custodial parents in conjunction with the ability of the noncustodial parent to pay (based on income and other factors), but awards differed considerably from court to court, and the child-support awards were generally too small to pay for a fair share of rearing the children (Garfinkel et al., 1994).

Federal legislation in 1984, 1988, and 1996 provided numerical formulas to guide decisions about child-support awards, authorized states to withhold the noncustodial parent's wages to make child-support payments, and implemented other changes to make it easier for custodial parents to obtain a support award and for courts to enforce those awards (see Roberts, 1994). For example, some states will not issue driver's licenses, vehicle registrations, or state-issued permits to individuals who are behind in child-support payments. Nevertheless, only 57% of custodial parents have a child-support award, and only 47% of those receive full payments (Grall, 2007). Whether custodial parents receive payments is still highly dependent on noncustodial parents' motivation and ability to pay (Thomas & Sawhill, 2005).

In addition to policies specifically focused on child-support payments, policies related to alimony and distribution and maintenance of property also affect the financial resources available to children following divorce. Long-term alimony is no longer as common as it was in the past, except in situations with extenuating circumstances (e.g., a spouse has health problems that prohibit work; Katz, 1994). More common is short-term alimony or rehabilitative alimony, which is provided for a limited period of time during which the spouse receiving alimony (usually the wife) goes to school or gains other skills to enable her to return to the workforce (Katz, 1994). In determining how property is divided following divorce, both monetary and nonmonetary factors are typically considered. Over time, the nonmonetary contributions of parents who stay home with children and the economic needs of children have been given greater consideration in changing statutory laws affecting the distribution of assets following divorce. To the extent that they affect the financial resources available to children, policies involving child support, alimony, and distribution of property following divorce can be important for children's postdivorce adjustment.

## Summary

In contrast to the necessity of correlational studies on effects of divorce itself, it is possible to collect experimental data to examine the effects of policies related to divorce. This will be an important direction for future research. Some data could come from natural experiments (e.g., comparing children in states with a particular policy of interest to children in states with a different policy). Other data could come from true experiments in which some children are randomly assigned to interventions being evaluated and other children are randomly assigned to the state's status quo (evaluations along these lines have been conducted in relation to different methods of determining child-support payments, such as in New York's Child Assistance Program; Hamilton, Burstein, & Long, 1998). Policy evaluations have the potential to lead to recommendations for a set of standards that could improve children's adjustment following their parents' divorce by making the divorce process less acrimonious and the decisions regarding finances and custody as conducive to children's well-being as possible.

## Summary and Conclusions

In this article, I reviewed the research literature on links between parental divorce and children's adjustment. First, I considered evidence regarding how divorce is related to children's externalizing behaviors, internalizing problems, academic achievement, and social relationships. Research suggests that children whose parents have divorced have higher levels of externalizing behaviors and internalizing problems, lower academic achievement, and more problems in social relationships than do children whose parents have not divorced. However, even though children whose parents divorce have worse adjustment on average than do children whose parents do not divorce, most children whose parents divorce do not have long-term negative outcomes.

Second, I examined children's age at the time of the divorce, age at the time of the study, length of time since the divorce, demographic characteristics, children's adjustment prior to the divorce, and stigmatization as moderators of the links between divorce and children's adjustment. There is evidence that, for behavioral outcomes, children who are younger at the time of their parents' divorce may be more at risk than are children who are older at the time of the divorce, but for academic outcomes and social relationships (particularly with romantic partners), adolescents whose parents divorce may be at greater risk than are younger children. The evidence is inconclusive regarding whether girls or boys are more affected by divorce, but there is some evidence that European American children are more negatively affected by divorce than are African American children. Children who have adjustment difficulties prior to divorce are more negatively affected by divorce than are children who are functioning well before the divorce. In cultural and historical contexts in which divorce is stigmatized, children may show worse adjustment following divorce than they do in contexts where divorce is not stigmatized.

Third, I examined income, interparental conflict, parenting, and parents' well-being, as mediators of relations between divorce and children's adjustment. All four of these mediators attenuate the link between parental divorce and children's adjustment difficulties. Interparental conflict has received the most empirical support as an important mediator.

Fourth, I noted the caveats of the research literature. This review focused on the relation between divorce and children's adjustment, but stepfamily formation and subsequent divorces are often part of the experience of children whose biological parents divorce. Recent work using adoption and twin designs demonstrates the importance of both genetics and environments (and their interaction) in predicting the likelihood of divorce and children's adjustment following parental divorce.

Fifth, I considered notable policies related to grounds for divorce, child custody, and child support in light of how they might affect children's adjustment to their parents' divorce. Policies that reduce interparental conflict and provide economic security to children have the potential to benefit children's adjustment. Evaluating whether particular policies are related to children's adjustment following their parents' divorce has the potential to inform future policymaking.

It is important to end this review by emphasizing that not all children experience similar trajectories before or after experiencing their parents' divorce. Thus, trajectories of adjustment that may be typical of many children may not be exhibited by an individual child. Furthermore, what initially appear to be effects of divorce are likely to be a complex combination of parent, child, and contextual factors that precede and follow the divorce in conjunction with the divorce itself.

## References

Allison, P.D., & Furstenberg, F.F., Jr. (1989). How marital dissolution affects children: Variations by age and sex. *Developmental Psychology, 25,* 540–549.

Amato, P.R. (1986). Marital conflict, the parent–child relationship, and child self-esteem. *Family Relations, 35,* 403–410.

Amato, P.R. (1993). Children's adjustment to divorce: Theories, hypotheses, and empirical support. *Journal of Marriage and the Family, 55,* 23–38.

Amato, P.R. (1996). Explaining the intergenerational transmission of divorce. *Journal of Marriage and the Family, 58,* 628–640.

Amato, P.R. (2001). Children of divorce in the 1990s: An update of the Amato and Keith (1991) meta-analysis. *Journal of Family Psychology, 15,* 355–370.

Amato, P.R. (2003). Reconciling divergent perspectives: Judith Wallerstein, quantitative family research, and children of divorce. *Family Relations, 52,* 332–339.

Amato, P.R., & Afifi, T.D. (2006). Feeling caught between parents: Adult children's relations with parents and subjective well-being. *Journal of Marriage and the Family, 68,* 222–235.

Amato, P.R., & Booth, A. (1996). A prospective study of divorce and parent–child relationships. *Journal of Marriage and the Family, 58,* 356–365.

Amato, P.R., & Cheadle, J. (2005). The long reach of divorce: Divorce and child well-being across three generations. *Journal of Marriage and the Family, 67,* 191–206.

Amato, P.R., & DeBoer, D.D. (2001). The transmission of marital instability across generations: Relationship skills or commitment to marriage? *Journal of Marriage and the Family, 63,* 1038–1051.

Amato, P.R., & Gilbreth, J.G. (1999). Nonresident fathers and children's well-being: A meta-analysis. *Journal of Marriage and the Family, 61,* 557–573.

Amato, P.R., & Keith, B. (1991a). Parental divorce and adult well-being: A meta-analysis. *Journal of Marriage and the Family, 53,* 43–58.

Amato, P.R., & Keith, B. (1991b). Parental divorce and the well-being of children: A meta-analysis. *Psychological Bulletin, 110,* 26–46.

Amato, P.R., Loomis, L.S., & Booth, A. (1995). Parental divorce, marital conflict, and offspring well-being during early adulthood. *Social Forces, 73,* 895–915.

American Law Institute. (2002). *Principles of the law of family dissolution: Analysis and recommendations.* Newark, NJ: Matthew Bender.

Bauserman, R. (2002). Child adjustment in joint-custody versus sole-custody arrangements: A meta-analytic review. *Journal of Family Psychology, 16,* 91–102.

Bender, W.N. (1994). Joint custody: The option of choice. *Journal of Divorce and Remarriage, 21,* 115–131.

Booth, A., & Amato, P.R. (1994). Parental marital quality, parental divorce, and relations with parents. *Journal of Marriage and the Family, 56,* 21–34.

Booth, A., & Amato, P.R. (2001). Parental predivorce relations and offspring postdivorce well-being. *Journal of Marriage and the Family, 63,* 197–212.

Buchanan, C.M., Maccoby, E.E., & Dornbusch, S.M. (1996). *Adolescents after divorce.* Cambridge, MA: Harvard University Press.

Buehler, C., Krishnakumar, A., Stone, G., Anthony, C., Pemberton, S., Gerard, J., & Barber, B.K. (1998). Interparental conflict styles and youth problem behaviors: A two-sample replication study. *Journal of Marriage and the Family, 60,* 119–132.

Chase-Lansdale, P.L., Cherlin, A.J., & Kiernan, K.K. (1995). The long-term effects of parental divorce on the mental health of young adults: A developmental perspective. *Child Development, 66,* 1614–1634.

Chase-Lansdale, P.L., & Hetherington, E.M. (1990). The impact of divorce on life-span development: Short and long term effects. In P.B. Baltes, D.L. Featherman, & R.M. Lerner (Eds.), *Life-span development and behavior* (pp. 105–150). Hillsdale, NJ: Erlbaum.

Cherlin, A.J. (1998). Marriage and marital dissolution among Black Americans. *Journal of Comparative Family Studies, 29,* 147–158.

Cherlin, A.J. (1999). Going to extremes: Family structure, children's well-being, and social science. *Demography, 36,* 421–428.

Cherlin, A.J., Chase-Lansdale, P.L., & McRae, C. (1998). Effects of parental divorce on mental health throughout the life course. *American Sociological Review, 63,* 239–249.

Cherlin, A.J., Furstenberg, F.F., Chase-Lansdale, P.L., Kiernan, K.E., Robins, P.K., Morrison, D.R., & Teitler, J.O. (1991). Longitudinal studies of effects of divorce on children in Great Britain and the United States. *Science, 252,* 1386–1389.

Coontz, S. (1992). *The way we never were: American families and the nostalgia trap.* New York: Basic Books.

Davies, P.T., & Cummings, E.M. (1994). Marital conflict and child adjustment: An emotional security hypothesis. *Psychological Bulletin, 116,* 387–411.

Doherty, W.J., & Needle, R.H. (1991). Psychological adjustment and substance use among adolescents before and after parental divorce. *Child Development, 62,* 328–337.

D'Onofrio, B.M., Turkheimer, E., Emery, R.E., Maes, H.H., Silberg, J., & Eaves, L.J. (2007). A children of twins study of parental divorce and offspring psychopathology. *Journal of Child Psychology and Psychiatry, 48,* 667–675.

D'Onofrio, B.M., Turkheimer, E., Emery, R.E., Slutske, W.S., Heath, A.C., Madden, P.A., & Martin, N.G. (2005). A genetically informed study of marital instability and its association with offspring psychopathology. *Journal of Abnormal Psychology, 114,* 570–586.

D'Onofrio, B.M., Turkheimer, E., Emery, R.E., Slutske, W.S., Heath, A.C., Madden, P.A., & Martin, N.G. (2006). A genetically informed study of the processes underlying the association between parental marital instability and offspring adjustment. *Developmental Psychology, 42,* 486–499.

Downey, D., & Powell, B. (1995). Do children in single-parent households fare better living with same-sex parents? *Journal of Marriage and the Family, 55,* 55–71.

Dunn, J. (2002). The adjustment of children in stepfamilies: Lessons from community studies. *Child and Adolescent Mental Health, 7,* 154–161.

Dunn, J., Deater-Deckard, K., Pickering, K., & O'Connor, T.G. (1998). Children's adjustment and prosocial behaviour in step-, single-parent, and non-stepfamily settings: Findings from a community study. *Journal of Child Psychology and Psychiatry, 39,* 1083–1095.

Emery, R.E., Laumann-Billings, L., Waldron, M.C., Sbarra, D.A., & Dillon, P. (2001). Child custody mediation and litigation: Custody, contact, and coparenting 12 years after initial dispute resolution. *Journal of Consulting and Clinical Psychology, 69,* 323–332.

Emery, R.E., Otto, R.K., & O'Donohue, W.T. (2005). A critical assessment of child custody evaluations: Limited science and a flawed system. *Psychological Science in the Public Interest, 6,* 1–29.

Emery, R.E., Sbarra, D., & Grover, T. (2005). Divorce mediation: Research and reflections. *Family Court Review, 43,* 22–37.

Emery, R.E., Waldron, M., Kitzmann, K.M., & Aaron, J. (1999). Delinquent behavior, future divorce or nonmarital childbearing, and externalizing behavior among offspring: A 14-year prospective study. *Journal of Family Psychology, 13,* 568–579.

Forehand, R., Thomas, A.M., Wierson, M., & Brody, G. (1990). Role of maternal functioning and parenting skills in adolescent functioning following parental divorce. *Journal of Abnormal Psychology, 99,* 278–283.

Garfinkel, I., Melli, M.S., & Robertson, J.G. (1994). Child support orders: A perspective on reform. *Future of Children, 4,* 84–100.

Glenn, N. (2001). Is the current concern about American marriage warranted? *Virginia Journal of Social Policy and the Law, 5*–47.

Grall, T.S. (2007). *Custodial mothers and fathers and their child support: 2005.* Washington, DC: U.S. Bureau of the Census.

Grounds for Divorce. (n.d.). Retrieved March 1, 2008, from www.divorcelawinfo.com/Pages/grounds.html

Grych, J.H., & Fincham, F.D. (1990). Marital conflict and children's adjustment: A cognitive-contextual framework. *Psychological Bulletin, 108,* 267–290.

Guidubaldi, J., Cleminshaw, H.K., Perry, J.D., & McLoughlin, C.S. (1983). The impact of parental divorce on children: Report of the nationwide NASP study. *School Psychology Review, 12,* 300–323.

Hamilton, W.L., Burstein, N.R., & Long, D. (1998). *Using incentives in welfare reform: The New York State Child Assistance Program.* Cambridge, MA: Abt Associates.

Harris, J.R. (1998). *The nurture assumption: Why children turn out the way they do.* New York: Free Press.

Hetherington, E.M. (1989). Coping with family transitions: Winners, losers, and survivors. *Child Development, 60,* 1–14.

Hetherington, E.M., Bridges, M., & Insabella, G.M. (1998). What matters? What does not? Five perspectives on the association between marital transitions and children's adjustment. *American Psychologist, 53,* 167–184.

Hetherington, E.M., & Clingempeel, W.G. (1992). Coping with marital transitions: A family systems perspective. *Monographs of the Society for Research in Child Development, 57* (2–3, Serial No. 227).

Hetherington, E.M., Cox, M., & Cox, R. (1979). Stress and coping in divorce: A focus on women. In J.E. Gullahorn (Ed.), *Psychology and women: In transition* (pp. 95–128). Washington, DC: V. H. Winston & Sons.

Hetherington, E.M., Cox, M., & Cox, R. (1985). Long-term effects of divorce and remarriage on the adjustment of children. *Journal of the American Academy of Child Psychiatry, 24,* 518–530.

Hetherington, E.M., & Elmore, A.M. (2004). The intergenerational transmission of couple instability. In P.L. Chase-Lansdale, K. Kiernan, & R.J. Friedman (Eds.), *Human development across lives and generations: The potential for change* (pp. 171–203). New York: Cambridge University Press.

Hetherington, E.M., Henderson, S.H., Reiss, D., Anderson, E.R., Bridges, M., Chan, R.W., et al. (1999). Adolescent siblings in stepfamilies: Family functioning and adolescent adjustment. *Monographs of the Society for Research in Child Development, 64* (4).

Hetherington, E.M., & Kelly, J. (2002). *For better or worse.* New York: Norton.

Hetherington, E.M., & Stanley-Hagan, M. (1999). The adjustment of children with divorced parents: A risk and resiliency perspective. *Journal of Child Psychology and Psychiatry, 40,* 129–140.

Hetherington, E.M., Stanley-Hagan, M., & Anderson, E.R. (1989). Marital transitions: A child's perspective. *American Psychologist, 44,* 303–312.

Jeynes, W. (2002). *Divorce, family structure, and the academic success of children.* New York: Haworth Press.

Jocklin, V., McGue, M., & Lykken, D.T. (1996). Personality and divorce: A genetic analysis. *Journal of Personality and Social Psychology, 71,* 288–299.

Johnston, J.R. (1995). Research update: Children's adjustment in sole custody compared to joint custody families and principles for custody decision making. *Family and Conciliation Courts Review, 33,* 415–425.

Kasen, S., Cohen, P., Brook, J.S., & Hartmark, C. (1996). A multiple-risk interaction model: Effects of temperament and divorce on psychiatric disorders in children. *Journal of Abnormal Child Psychology, 24,* 121–150.

Katz, S.N. (1994). Historical perspective and current trends in the legal process of divorce. *Future of Children, 4,* 44–62.

Kelly, J.B. (1994). The determination of child custody. *Future of Children, 4,* 121–142.

Lansford, J.E., Ceballo, R., Abbey, A., & Stewart, A.J. (2001). Does family structure matter? A comparison of adoptive, two parent biological, single mother, stepfather, and stepmother households. *Journal of Marriage and the Family, 63,* 840–851.

Lansford, J.E., Malone, P.S., Castellino, D.R., Dodge, K.A., Pettit, G.S., & Bates, J.E. (2006). Trajectories of internalizing, externalizing, and grades for children who have and have not experienced their parents' divorce. *Journal of Family Psychology, 20,* 292–301.

Laosa, L.M. (1988). Ethnicity and single parenting in the United States. In E.M. Hetherington & J.D. Arasteh (Eds.), *Impact of divorce, single parenting, and stepparenting on children* (pp. 23–49). Hillsdale, NJ: Erlbaum.

Laumann-Billings, L., & Emery, R.E. (2000). Distress among young adults from divorced families. *Journal of Family Psychology, 14,* 671–687.

Lye, D.N. (1996). Adult child–parent relationships. *Annual Review of Sociology, 22,* 79–102.

Lykken, D.T. (2002). How relationships begin and end: A genetic perspective. In A.L. Vangelisti, H.T. Reis, & M.A. Fitzpatrick (Eds.), *Stability and change in relationships* (pp. 83–102). New York: Cambridge University Press.

Maes, H.H.M., Neale, M.C., Kendler, K.S., Hewitt, J.K., Silberg, J.L., Foley, D.L., et al. (1998). Assortative mating for major psychiatric diagnoses in two population-based samples. *Psychological Medicine, 28,* 1389–1401.

Malone, P.S., Lansford, J.E., Castellino, D.R., Berlin, L.J., Dodge, K.A., Bates, J.E., & Pettit, G.S. (2004). Divorce and child behavior problems: Applying latent change score models to life event data. *Structural Equation Modeling, 11,* 401–423.

Martinez, C.R., Jr., & Forgatch, M.S. (2002). Adjusting to change: Linking family structure transitions with parenting and boys' adjustment. *Journal of Family Psychology, 16,* 107–117.

McGue, M., & Lykken, D.T. (1992). Genetic influence on risk of divorce. *Psychological Science, 3,* 368–373.

McLanahan, S.S. (1999). Father absence and the welfare of children. In E.M. Hetherington (Ed.), *Coping with divorce, single parenting, and remarriage: A risk and resiliency perspective* (pp. 117–145). Hillsdale, NJ: Erlbaum.

McLanahan, S., & Sandefur, G. (1994). *Growing up with a single parent.* Cambridge, MA: Harvard University Press.

Mechanic, D., & Hansell, S. (1989). Divorce, family conflict, and adolescents' well-being. *Journal of Health and Social Behavior, 30,* 105–116.

Merikangas, K.R. (1984). Divorce and assortative mating among depressed patients. *American Journal of Psychiatry, 141,* 74–76.

Morrison, D.R., & Cherlin, A.J. (1995). The divorce process and young children's well-being: A prospective analysis. *Journal of Marriage and the Family, 57,* 800–812.

Nakonezny, P.A., Shull, R.D., & Rodgers, J.L. (1995). The effect of no-fault divorce law on the divorce rate across the 50 states and its relation to income, education, and religiosity. *Journal of Marriage and the Family, 57,* 477–488.

National Center for Health Statistics. (2008). Marriage and divorce. Retrieved March 3, 2008, from www.cdc.gov/nchs/fastats/divorce.htm

Neiderhiser, J.M., Reiss, D., & Hetherington, E.M. (2007). The nonshared environment in adolescent development (NEAD) project: A longitudinal family study of twins and siblings from adolescence to young adulthood. *Twin Research and Human Genetics, 10,* 74–83.

O'Connor, T.G., Caspi, A., DeFries, J.C., & Plomin, R. (2000). Are associations between parental divorce and children's adjustment genetically mediated? An adoption study. *Developmental Psychology, 36,* 429–437.

Orbuch, T.L., Thornton, A., & Cancio, J. (2000). The impact of marital quality, divorce, and remarriage on the relationships between parents and their children. *Marriage and Family Review, 29,* 221–246.

Popenoe, D. (1993). American family decline, 1960–1990: A review and appraisal. *Journal of Marriage and the Family, 55,* 527–542.

Popenoe, D. (2003). Can the nuclear family be revived? In M. Coleman & L. Ganong (Eds.), *Points and counterpoints: Controversial relationship and family issues in the 21st century* (pp. 218–221). Los Angeles: Roxbury Publishing.

Reifman, A., Villa, L.C., Amans, J.A., Rethinam, V., & Telesca, T.Y. (2001). Children of divorce in the 1990s: A meta-analysis. *Journal of Divorce and Remarriage, 36,* 27–36.

Roberts, P.G. (1994). Child support orders: Problems with enforcement. *Future of Children, 4,* 101–120.

Ruschena, E., Prior, M., Sanson, A., & Smart, D. (2005). A longitudinal study of adolescent adjustment following family transitions. *Journal of Child Psychology and Psychiatry, 46,* 353–363.

Shaw, D.S., Emery, R.E., & Tuer, M.D. (1993). Parental functioning and children's adjustment in families of divorce: A prospective study. *Journal of Abnormal Child Psychology, 21,* 119–134.

Short, J.L. (2002). The effects of parental divorce during childhood on college students. *Journal of Divorce and Remarriage, 38,* 143–156.

Simons, R.L., Whitbeck, L.B., Beaman, J., & Conger, R.D. (1994). The impact of mothers' parenting, involvement by nonresidential fathers, and parental conflict on the adjustment of adolescent children. *Journal of Marriage and the Family, 56,* 356–374.

Sun, Y., & Li, Y. (2001). Marital disruption, parental investment, and children's academic achievement: A prospective analysis. *Journal of Family Issues, 22,* 27–62.

Sun, Y., & Li, Y. (2002). Children's well-being during parents' marital disruption process: A pooled time-series analysis. *Journal of Marriage and the Family, 64,* 472–488.

Thomas, A., & Sawhill, I. (2005). For love and money? The impact of family structure on family income. *Future of Children, 15,* 57–74.

Tschann, J.M., Johnson, J.R., & Wallerstein, J.S. (1989). Family processes and children's functioning during divorce. *Journal of Marriage and the Family, 51,* 431–444.

Twaite, J.A., & Luchow, A.K. (1996). Custodial arrangements and parental conflict following divorce: The impact on children's adjustment. *Journal of Psychiatry and Law, 24,* 53–75.

U.S. Census Bureau. (2004). Detailed tables: Number, timing and duration of marriages and divorces, 2004. Washington, DC: Author. Retrieved March 3, 2008, from www.census.gov/population/www/socdemo/marr-div/2004detailed_tables.html

Vandewater, E.A., & Lansford, J.E. (1998). Influences of family structure and parental conflict on children's well-being. *Family Relations, 47,* 323–330.

Videon, T.M. (2002). The effects of parent-adolescent relationships and parental separation on adolescent well-being. *Journal of Marriage and the Family, 64,* 489–503.

Wallerstein, J.S., Lewis, J.M., & Blakeslee, S. (2000). *The unexpected legacy of divorce: A 25 year landmark study.* New York: Hyperion.

Warshak, R.A. (2007). The approximation rule, child development research, and children's best interests after divorce. *Child Development Perspectives, 1,* 119–125.

Wolfers, J. (2003). Did unilateral divorce laws raise divorce rates? A reconciliation and new results. National Bureau of Economic Research Working Paper No. 10014. Retrieved March 1, 2008, from www.nber.org/papers/w10014

# Critical Thinking

1. A significant number of children in the United States will experience the divorce of their parents. Think of a child or children who have experienced their parents' divorce. Explain how divorce impacts children at different ages and by gender. Describe factors that can ameliorate the negative effects of divorce.

2. If your parents divorced, at what age were you, how did it make you feel, and explain how you coped with the divorce. Did your parents' divorce influence your feelings about marriage and divorce? If you were married with children and felt the need to get a divorce and you have children, explain what you could do to reduce the negative impact to your children.

3. Find out whether you live in a state that still permits determining fault as grounds for a divorce. Evaluate the pros and cons of proceeding with a divorce based on fault in terms of benefits and negative consequences on both parents and children involved in this type of legal divorce proceeding. Given the research data, explain how you would counsel parents contemplating a fault-based divorce?

4. Critique the legal and public policy positions regarding the determination of child custody, child-support, and alimony in light of the research regarding child outcomes.

5. Your best friend is considering remarriage and has full custody of a fifth grade son and a daughter who is a sophomore in high school. She has been a single mother who is struggling with a part-time job for two years and had a turbulent and difficult first marriage to a husband who is now largely absent. She has asked for your advice on what to expect in terms of her children's reactions if she remarries. Based on the research in this article, how would you counsel and advise her?

6. Do you think attitudes about divorce are changing in the United States? Explain and cite data. Contrast U.S. attitudes toward divorce with other countries and speculate on how these societal- or culturally-based attitudes may affect children's adjustment to divorce.

# The Role of Parental Control in Children's Development in Western and East Asian Countries

Eva M. Pomerantz and Qian Wang

There is a wealth of evidence from Western countries, such as the United States, that when parents exert control over children by intruding, pressuring, or dominating them in terms of their thoughts, feelings, and behavior, children suffer psychologically (for a review, see Pomerantz & Thompson, 2008). In contrast, when parents support children's autonomy by allowing them freedom of choice, supporting their initiative, and adopting their perspective, children in the West benefit. Initially, the assumption was that such effects are universal. However, beginning in the 1990s, it was suggested that several aspects of the culture in East Asian countries, such as China, make children more accepting of parental control so that the negative effects are not as strong as they are in Western countries (e.g., Chao, 1994; Iyengar & Lepper, 1999). Because control is considered one of the most influential dimensions of parenting (Maccoby & Martin, 1983), there has been much debate over the effects of parental control in East Asian (vs. Western) countries. As a consequence, there is now a sizable body of research, conducted mainly in the United States and China, from which it is possible to gain significant insights about similarities and differences in the effects of parental control in Western and East Asian countries.

## Parental Control

In theory and research on parenting, the term "control" is often used to refer to parental intrusiveness, pressure, or domination, with the inverse being parental support of autonomy (Grolnick & Pomerantz, 2009). The focus of much research has been psychological control, or parents' regulation of children's feelings and thoughts (e.g., Barber, Stolz, & Olsen, 2005). Psychological control is frequently contrasted with behavioral control, defined as parents' regulation of what children do. Behavioral control commonly includes parental guidance, monitoring, and rule setting. As such, it does not necessarily entail intrusiveness, pressure,

or domination; indeed, behavioral control has positive, rather than negative, effects on children's psychological development (Grolnick & Pomerantz, 2009). The debate about the effects of parental control in the West and East Asia has centered on control in the intrusive sense, with little attention to distinguishing between its targets—that is, whether parents are attempting to regulate children's psychology or behavior (Wang, Pomerantz, & Chen, 2007). We follow suit here, by focusing on parental control that is intruding, pressuring, or dominating, regardless of whether parents are attempting to regulate children's psychology or behavior.

## Universalist Perspectives

Much of the research so far has been guided by the idea that parental control undermines children's sense of autonomy, thereby interfering with their psychological development (e.g., Barber et al., 2005). In the context of self-determination theory, Deci and Ryan (1985) argue that there is a universal need for autonomy and that satisfaction of this need is essential to optimal psychological functioning. These investigators make the case that controlling environments detract from feelings of autonomy, regardless of culture. Thus, when parents exert control over children, for instance by making decisions for them about personal issues (e.g., who to be friends with), children suffer, as they feel they do not have control over their lives. Such a universalist perspective is also evident in parental acceptance–rejection theory, which holds that parental control may negatively influence children by conveying rejection—for example, when parents withdraw love because children have not met their expectations, children may feel that parents no longer care about them. Parental acceptance–rejection theory postulates that children's feelings of being rejected (vs. accepted) by parents play a role in their development regardless of culture, because relatedness is universally important (e.g., Rohner, Khaleque, & Cournoyer, 2004).

# Culture-Specific Perspectives

The major principle behind culture-specific perspectives is that Western and East Asian countries have distinct cultures that shape the effects of parental control on children's development leading the effects to be less negative in East Asian contexts. Iyengar and Lepper (1999), for instance, contend that when East Asian parents exert control over children by making decisions for them about personal issues, it does not have detrimental effects; taking on their parents' decisions as their own provides children with an opportunity to harmonize with parents, something that in East Asia is prioritized over autonomy, given the heightened cultural orientation toward interdependence. In a somewhat different vein, because East Asian notions about parents' role in children's development—such as the Chinese concept of *guan*, which means to govern as well as to care for—involve parental control with the ultimate aim of supporting children, parental control may not be experienced as rejecting by children (Chao, 1994). As parental control is more common in East Asia than in the West (e.g., Wang et al., 2007), it has also been suggested that East Asian parents may exert control more deliberately and calmly, with less negative affect, because control does not violate, and is even part of, "good parenting" (e.g., Grusec, Rudy, & Martini, 1997).

# Empirical Evidence

The culture-specific perspectives arose in part in response to a series of findings from the 1990s showing that authoritarian (vs. authoritative) parenting has a greater negative effect on American children of European heritage than it does on American children of Asian heritage in terms of academic functioning (e.g., grades) but not necessarily in terms of emotional functioning (e.g., depressive symptoms; e.g., Steinberg, Lamborn, Darling, Mounts, & Dornbusch, 1994). Unfortunately, conclusions about the dissimilarity of the effects of parental control in Western and East Asian countries cannot be made from such data, because authoritarian parenting is an amalgamation of multiple dimensions of parenting including control, structure, and acceptance. Thus, it is unclear if it is parental control that drives the difference (or absence of difference) in the effects of authoritarian parenting; it could be one of the other dimensions or the interaction between two or more of the dimensions.

The research on the effects of authoritarian parenting on children of European and Asian heritage in the United States was followed by research on the effects specifically of parental control in Western and East Asian countries. Hasebe, Nucci, and Nucci (2004) found that parents making decisions for children about personal issues was associated with dampened emotional functioning among American and Japanese high-school children. Similarly, Barber et al. (2005) documented positive associations between parental psychological control and adolescents' depression and delinquency in a variety of countries including the United States, Germany, China, and India. Because these studies used concurrent designs in which parental control and children's psychological functioning were examined at a single point in time, the findings cannot provide insight into whether parental control precedes dampened psychological functioning among children similarly in Western and East Asian contexts; determining whether it does is critical in drawing conclusions about the role of parental control in children's psychological development in the two regions.

Research following children over time in the United States and China sheds light on this issue. The more parents make decisions for children about personal issues as children enter adolescence, the more children's emotional functioning suffers 2 years later, adjusting for their earlier functioning; notably, the size of the effects in the United States and China do not differ (Qin, Pomerantz, & Wang, 2009). A comparable pattern is evident for psychological control (Wang et al., 2007): During early adolescence, such control predicts children's dampened emotional functioning 6 months later, taking into account children's earlier emotional functioning, similarly in the United States and China. Conversely, parental support of children's autonomy (e.g., encouraging them to express their opinions) predicts better subsequent emotional functioning among children in both countries, albeit with a stronger effect for positive, but not negative, emotional functioning in the United States. Parental support of children's autonomy also predicts children's enhanced grades over time similarly in the two countries, but its effect on children's motivation (e.g., investment in school) is stronger in the United States.

# Moderating Contexts

Although parental control appears to interfere with children's psychological functioning similarly in the West and East Asia, there may be some contexts in which it may do so to a greater extent in Western countries. Because the identification of such contexts represents a second step in elucidating whether the effects of parental control differ in the two regions, there is limited evidence on this issue. However, the existing evidence is suggestive of several circumstances under which the effects of parental control are stronger in the West. First, almost all of the research has been conducted in areas that are in or near urban centers. Given that such areas in East Asia have been increasingly exposed to Western values in the past few decades, it is unclear to what extent the findings are generalizable to rural areas. Indeed, parental control may play a stronger undermining role in urban areas than in rural areas, given that children, particularly boys, in urban China feel less of a sense of obligation to parents (Fuligni & Zhang, 2004) and are also more averse to conflict with parents than are their counterparts in rural areas (Zhang & Fuligni, 2006). Stronger effects of parental control in urban (versus rural) areas may also exist in the

West, however, given cultural variability by geographical area in the West (e.g., Plaut, Markus, & Lachman, 2002).

Second, differences in the strength of the effects of parental control in Western and East Asian countries may exist, as reflected in the extent to which parents decrease their control as children mature. Perhaps because of the West's heightened orientation toward independence and its less hierarchical structure (Triandis, 1994), American parents decrease their control (i.e., refraining from making decisions for their children about personal issues) more than do Chinese parents as children progress through the early adolescent years (Qin et al., 2009). As Western children expect this decrease in parental control more than East Asian children do (Feldman & Rosenthal, 1991), their psychological functioning may be influenced more by the extent to which their parents "loosen the reins" during these years. As shown in Figure 1, when American parents relinquish control by making fewer decisions for children about personal issues as children enter adolescence, children have better emotional functioning; although such a trend is also evident in China, it is substantially weaker (Qin et al., 2009). It is possible that Chinese children benefit more from a decline in parental control in later adolescence, when it may be more normative. Unfortunately, similarities and differences in how Western and East Asian children move through development have not been comprehensively documented.

Third, the effects of parental control over children's academic learning may be stronger in the West than in East Asia. In Confucian teaching, which is central in East Asian culture, learning is viewed as a moral endeavor in which individuals take on the lifelong task of constantly improving themselves (Li, 2005). Access to education is also more limited, but has greater financial impact, in East Asia (Pomerantz, Ng, & Wang, 2008). Given the moral and practical importance of children's learning, East Asian children may be particularly accepting of parental control when it comes to academics. Although the effects of parental control in the academic area have not been compared to the effects in other areas, there is some suggestive evidence. When European American children believe their mothers have made decisions for them about an academic task, they spend less time and perform more poorly on the task than they do when they make the decisions themselves; however, the reverse is true of Asian American children (Iyengar & Lepper, 1999). Research conducted in China, however, suggests this is the case only when children feel they have positive relationships with their mothers (Bao & Lam, 2008); it may be that children's sense of connectedness to their parents allows children to internalize parents' goals.

Fourth, parental control may take many forms, but the major focus of the comparative research has been on parents making decisions for children about personal issues and their exertion of psychological control over children. These forms of control may be at the extreme end of the continuum. It is possible that less extreme forms, such as

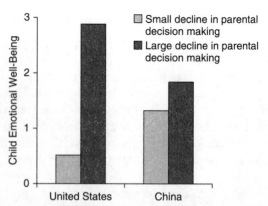

**Figure 1** The effects of change over time in parental decision making on child emotional well-being during early adolescence in the United States and China (adapted from Qin, Pomerantz, & Wang, 2009). In the United States, the larger the decline in parental (vs. child) decision making about personal issues as children progressed through the seventh and eighth grades (adjusting for such decision making at the beginning of seventh grade), the better children's emotional well-being at the end of eighth grade (adjusting for such well-being at the beginning of seventh grade). In China, there was a similar pattern, but it was significantly smaller.

providing assistance when children do not request it or hovering over children as they work on something, are more open to interpretation by children in terms of the extent to which they are seen to violate their autonomy or convey rejection. Consequently, culture may play a greater part in how such forms of control are interpreted, leading Western children to hold more negative views of less extreme forms of control than do East Asian children and thus to suffer more when their parents use them. For example, because the West is oriented more toward independence than is East Asia, Western children may see parents' hovering as children complete their homework as more of a violation of their autonomy than might their East Asian counterparts, who may instead interpret such behavior as an expression of parents' love.

## Underlying Mechanisms

Fully elucidating the effects of parental control in Western and East Asian countries involves identifying not only the circumstances that may lead to differences in the strength of effects but also the mechanisms underlying the effects. It is necessary to consider the possibility that similar effects reflect different processes. Given different cultural orientations toward independence and interdependence, for example, dampened feelings of autonomy may account for the negative effects of parental control to a greater extent among children in the West, whereas heightened feelings of rejection may account for them to a greater extent among children in East Asia. Under circumstances when there are differences in the effects, the differences need to be unpacked: For example, do they reflect differences in children's interpretation of parental control? In this vein, Chao's (1994) suggestion that parental control has less negative effects among East Asian (vs. Western) children because they view parents' attempts to regulate them as an act of love should be examined. And if differences in how children interpret parental control underlie differences in its effects, is this due, at least in part, to differences in how parents exert control—for instance, in the extent to which parents accompany control with negative affect, as suggested by Grusec et al. (1997)?

## Conclusions

In line with universalist perspectives, when parents exert control over children by intruding, pressuring, or dominating them, children suffer, whether they live in the West or East Asia. This undermining role, however, may not be uniform; its strength may differ in the two regions in some contexts. The negative effects of parental control are stronger in the West than in East Asia when parents fail to decrease it as children enter adolescence; parental control may also have stronger effects in the West when it is exerted over academics than in other areas of children's lives. These potential contextual forces, as well as others such as the extremity of control, need more direct investigation—something that may be accomplished as the focus moves away from asking *whether* the effects of parental control are stronger in the West than in East Asia to asking *when* they may be stronger, and *why*. Despite these lingering issues, the findings to date are consistent with self-determination theory's (Deci & Ryan, 1985) notion that there is a universal need for autonomy whose fulfillment may be undermined by controlling environments. Hence, recommendations that parents limit their intrusiveness in children's lives are likely to be useful both in the West and in East Asia.

## Recommended Readings

Chao, R.K. (1994). (See References). One of the first papers to suggest why parental control may not have as negative effects in East Asia as it does in the West.

Greenfield, P.M., Keller, H., Fuligni, A.J., & Maynard, A. (2003). Cultural pathways through universal development. *Annual Review of Psychology, 54,* 461–490. This paper provides a full discussion of issues of culture in children's development, including that of the differential effects of parental control.

Grolnick, W.S. (2003). *The psychology of parental control: How well-meant parenting backfires.* Mahwah, NJ: Erlbaum. A clearly written, user-friendly, and relatively comprehensive review for readers who wish to expand their knowledge of the effects of parental control.

Lansford, J.E., Chang, L., Dodge, K.A., Malone, P.A., Oburu, P., Palmerus, K., et al. (2005). Physical discipline and children's adjustment: Cultural normativeness as a moderator. *Child Development, 76,* 1234–1246. An innovative study that illustrates original research about the differential effects of parents' physical discipline in multiple countries.

Wang, Q., Pomerantz, E.M., & Chen, H. (2007). (See References). A representative study that illustrates original research about the differential effects of parental control in the United States and China.

## References

Bao, X.-H., & Lam, S.-F. (2008). Who makes the choice? Rethinking the role of autonomy and relatedness in Chinese children's motivation. *Child Development, 79,* 269–283.

Barber, B.K., Stolz, H.E., & Olsen, J.A. (2005). *Parental support, psychological control, and behavioral control: Assessing relevance across time, culture, and method* (Monographs of the Society for Research in Child Development, Serial No. 282, Vol. 70, No. 2). Boston: Blackwell.

Chao, R.K. (1994). Beyond parental control and authoritarian parenting style: Understanding Chinese parenting through the cultural notion of training. *Child Development, 65,* 1111–1119.

Deci, E.L., & Ryan, R.M. (1985). *Intrinsic motivation and self-determination in human behavior.* New York: Plenum.

Feldman, S.S., & Rosenthal, D.A. (1991). Age expectations of behavioural autonomy in Hong Kong, Australian and American Youth: The influence of family variables and adolescents' values. *International Journal of Psychology, 26,* 1–23.

Fuligni, A.J., & Zhang, W. (2004). Attitudes toward family obligation among adolescents in contemporary urban and rural China. *Child Development, 75,* 180–192.

Grolnick, W.S., & Pomerantz, E.M. (2009). Issues and challenges in studying parental control: Toward a new conceptualization. *Child Development Perspectives, 2,* 165–171.

Grusec, J.E., Rudy, D., & Martini, T. (1997). Parenting cognitions and child outcomes: An overview and implications for children's internalization of values. In J.E. Grusec & L. Kuczynski (Eds.), *Parenting and children's internalization of values: A handbook of contemporary theory* (pp. 259–282). Hoboken, NJ: Wiley.

Hasebe, Y., Nucci, L., & Nucci, M.S. (2004). Parental control of the personal domain and adolescent symptoms of psychopathology: A cross-national study in the United States and Japan. *Child Development, 75,* 815–828.

Iyengar, S.S., & Lepper, M.R. (1999). Rethinking the value of choice: A cultural perspective on intrinsic motivation. *Journal of Personality and Social Psychology, 76,* 349–366.

Li, J. (2005). Mind or virtue: Western and Chinese beliefs about learning. *Current Directions in Psychological Science, 14,* 190–194.

Maccoby, E.E., & Martin, J. (1983). Socialization in the context of the family: Parent child interaction. In E.M. Hetherington (Ed.), *Handbook of child psychology: Vol. 4. Socialization, personality, and social development* (4th ed., pp. 1–101). New York: Wiley.

Plaut, V.C., Markus, H.R., & Lachman, M.E. (2002). Place matters: Consensual features and regional variation in American well-being and self. *Journal of Personality and Social Psychology, 83,* 160–184.

Pomerantz, E.M., Ng, F.F., & Wang, Q. (2008). Culture, parenting, and motivation: The case of East Asia and the United States. In M.L. Maehr, S.A. Karabenick, & T.C. Urdan (Eds.), *Advances in motivation and achievement: Social psychological perspectives* (Vol. 15, pp. 209–240). Bingley, England: Emerald Group Publishing.

Pomerantz, E.M., & Thompson, R.A. (2008). Parents' role in children's personality development: The psychological resource principle. In O.P. John, R.W. Robins, & L.A. Pervin (Eds.), *Handbook of personality: Theory and research* (Vol. 3, pp. 351–374). New York: Guilford.

Qin, L., Pomerantz, E.M., & Wang, Q. (2009). Are gains in decision-making autonomy during early adolescence beneficial for emotional functioning? The case of the United States and China. *Child Development, 80,* 1705–1721.

Rohner, R.P., Khaleque, A., & Cournoyer, D.E. (2004). Cross-national perspectives on parental acceptance-rejection theory. *Marriage and Family Review, 35,* 85–105.

Steinberg, L., Lamborn, S.D., Darling, N., Mounts, N.S., & Dornbusch, S. (1994). Over-time changes in adjustment and competence among adolescents from authoritative, authoritarian, indulgent, and neglectful homes. *Child Development, 65,* 754–770.

Triandis, H.C. (1994). *Culture and social behavior.* New York: McGraw-Hill.

Wang, Q., Pomerantz, E.M., & Chen, H. (2007). The role of parents' control in early adolescents' psychological functioning: A longitudinal investigation in the United States and China. *Child Development, 78,* 1592–1610.

Zhang, W., & Fuligni, A.J. (2006). Authority, autonomy, and family relationships among adolescents in urban and rural China. *Journal of Research on Adolescence, 16,* 527–537.

# Critical Thinking

1. How would you expect children to respond to parental control in India? What would be the best way to find out?

2. What were the "contextual factors" that were at work in this article? What are some other contextual factors that might play a part in determining the effects of parental control?

Address correspondence to **Eva M. Pomerantz,** Department of Psychology, University of Illinois at Urbana-Champaign, 603 East Daniel Street, Champaign, IL 61820; e-mail: pomerntz@illinois.edu.

**Acknowledgments**—Writing of this article was supported by National Institute of Mental Health Grant R01 MH57505. We are grateful for the constructive comments on an earlier version of this article provided by Duane Kimme, Peggy Miller, Florrie Fei-Yin Ng, and members of the Center for Parent-Child Studies at the University of Illinois, Urbana-Champaign.

# The Case Against Spanking

*Physical discipline is slowly declining as some studies reveal lasting harms for children*

BRENDAN L. SMITH

A growing body of research has shown that spanking and other forms of physical discipline can pose serious risks to children, but many parents aren't hearing the message. "It's a very controversial area even though the research is extremely telling and very clear and consistent about the negative effects on children," says Sandra Graham-Bermann, PhD, a psychology professor and principal investigator for the Child Violence and Trauma Laboratory at the University of Michigan. "People get frustrated and hit their kids. Maybe they don't see there are other options."

Many studies have shown that physical punishment—including spanking, hitting and other means of causing pain—can lead to increased aggression, antisocial behavior, physical injury and mental health problems for children. Americans' acceptance of physical punishment has declined since the 1960s, yet surveys show that two-thirds of Americans still approve of parents spanking their kids.

But spanking doesn't work, says Alan Kazdin, PhD, a Yale University psychology professor and director of the Yale Parenting Center and Child Conduct Clinic. "You cannot punish out these behaviors that you do not want," says Kazdin, who served as APA president in 2008. "There is no need for corporal punishment based on the research. We are not giving up an effective technique. We are saying this is a horrible thing that does not work."

## Evidence of Harm

On the international front, physical discipline is increasingly being viewed as a violation of children's human rights. The United Nations Committee on the Rights of the Child issued a directive in 2006 calling physical punishment "legalized violence against children" that should be eliminated in all settings through "legislative, administrative, social and educational measures." The treaty that established the committee has been supported by 192 countries, with only the United States and Somalia failing to ratify it.

Around the world, 30 countries have banned physical punishment of children in all settings, including the home. The legal bans typically have been used as public education tools, rather than attempts to criminalize behavior by parents who spank their children, says Elizabeth Gershoff, PhD, a leading researcher on physical punishment at the University of Texas at Austin.

"Physical punishment doesn't work to get kids to comply, so parents think they have to keep escalating it. That is why it is so dangerous," she says.

After reviewing decades of research, Gershoff wrote the Report on Physical Punishment in the United States: *What Research Tells Us About Its Effects on Children*, published in 2008 in conjunction with Phoenix Children's Hospital. The report recommends that parents and caregivers make every effort to avoid physical punishment and calls for the banning of physical discipline in all U.S. schools. The report has been endorsed by dozens of organizations, including the American Academy of Pediatrics, American Medical Association and Psychologists for Social Responsibility.

After three years of work on the APA Task Force on Physical Punishment of Children, Gershoff and Graham-Bermann wrote a report in 2008 summarizing the task force's recommendations. That report recommends that "parents and caregivers reduce and potentially eliminate their use of any physical punishment as a disciplinary method." The report calls on psychologists and other professionals to "indicate to parents that physical punishment is not an appropriate, or even a consistently effective, method of discipline."

"We have the opportunity here to take a strong stand in favor of protecting children," says Graham-Bermann, who chaired the task force.

APA's Committee on Children, Youth and Families (CYF) and the Board for the Advancement of Psychology in the Public Interest unanimously approved a proposed resolution last year based on the task force recommendations. It states that APA supports "parents' use of non-physical methods of disciplining children" and opposes "the use of severe or injurious physical punishment of any child." APA also should support additional research and a public education campaign on "the effectiveness and outcomes associated with corporal punishment and nonphysical methods of discipline," the proposed resolution states. After obtaining feedback from other APA boards and committees in the spring of 2012, APA's Council of Representatives will consider adopting the resolution as APA policy.

Preston Britner, PhD, a child developmental psychologist and professor at the University of Connecticut, helped draft the proposed resolution as co-chair of CYF. "It addresses the concerns about physical punishment and a growing body of research on alternatives to physical punishment, along with the idea that psychology and psychologists have much to contribute to the development of those alternative strategies," he says.

More than three decades have passed since APA approved a resolution in 1975 opposing corporal punishment in schools and other institutions, but it didn't address physical discipline in the home. That resolution stated that corporal punishment can "instill hostility, rage and a sense of powerlessness without reducing the undesirable behavior."

# Research Findings

Physical punishment can work momentarily to stop problematic behavior because children are afraid of being hit, but it doesn't work in the long term and can make children more aggressive, Graham-Bermann says.

A study published last year in *Child Abuse and Neglect* revealed an intergenerational cycle of violence in homes where physical punishment was used. Researchers interviewed parents and children age 3 to 7 from more than 100 families. Children who were physically punished were more likely to endorse hitting as a means of resolving their conflicts with peers and siblings. Parents who had experienced frequent physical punishment during their childhood were more likely to believe it was acceptable, and they frequently spanked their children. Their children, in turn, often believed spanking was an appropriate disciplinary method.

The negative effects of physical punishment may not become apparent for some time, Gershoff says. "A child doesn't get spanked and then run out and rob a store," she says. "There are indirect changes in how the child thinks about things and feels about things."

As in many areas of science, some researchers disagree about the validity of the studies on physical punishment. Robert Larzelere, PhD, an Oklahoma State University professor who studies parental discipline, was a member of the APA task force who issued his own minority report because he disagreed with the scientific basis of the task force recommendations. While he agrees that parents should reduce their use of physical punishment, he says most of the cited studies are correlational and don't show a causal link between physical punishment and long-term negative effects for children.

"The studies do not discriminate well between non-abusive and overly severe types of corporal punishment," Larzelere says. "You get worse outcomes from corporal punishment than from alternative disciplinary techniques only when it is used more severely or as the primary discipline tactic."

In a meta-analysis of 26 studies, Larzelere and a colleague found that an approach they described as "conditional spanking" led to greater reductions in child defiance or anti-social behavior than 10 of 13 alternative discipline techniques, including reasoning, removal of privileges and time out (*Clinical Child and Family Psychology Review*, 2005). Larzelere defines conditional spanking as a disciplinary technique for 2- to 6-year-old children in which parents use two open-handed swats on the buttocks only after the child has defied milder discipline such as time out.

Gershoff says all of the studies on physical punishment have some shortcomings. "Unfortunately, all research on parent discipline is going to be correlational because we can't randomly assign kids to parents for an experiment. But I don't think we have to disregard all research that has been done," she says. "I can just about count on one hand the studies that have found anything positive about physical punishment and hundreds that have been negative."

# Teaching New Skills

If parents aren't supposed to hit their kids, what nonviolent techniques can help with discipline? The Parent Management Training program headed by Kazdin at Yale is grounded in research on applied behavioral analysis. The program teaches parents to use positive reinforcement and effusive praise to reward children for good behavior.

Kazdin also uses a technique that may sound like insanity to most parents: Telling toddlers to practice throwing a tantrum. Parents ask their children to have a pretend tantrum without one undesirable element, such as hitting or kicking. Gradually, as children practice controlling tantrums when they aren't angry, their real tantrums lessen, Kazdin says.

Remaining calm during a child's tantrums is the best approach, coupled with time outs when needed and a consistent discipline plan that rewards good behavior, Graham-Bermann says. APA offers the Adults & Children Together Against Violence program, which provides parenting skills classes through a nationwide research-based program called Parents Raising Safe Kids. The course teaches parents how to avoid violence through anger management, positive child discipline and conflict resolution.

Parents should talk with their children about appropriate means of resolving conflicts, Gershoff says. Building a trusting relationship can help children believe that discipline isn't arbitrary or done out of anger.

"Part of the problem is good discipline isn't quick or easy," she says. "Even the best of us parents don't always have that kind of patience."

# Critical Thinking

1. Why do you think some parents spank their children? What factors, ranging from parents' personalities and children-rearing beliefs to children's qualities, may lead to more or less spanking?

2. There is ample research suggesting that spanking has negative effects on children, but many parents nevertheless spank their children. Is this a problem? Should parents' child-rearing and disciplinary practices be informed or shaped by what social science has learned? Why might parents' behavior not be affected by social science findings?

3. Aside from social science, are there moral, ethical, or religious reasons why parents should, or should not, spank their children?

**BRENDAN L. SMITH** is a writer in Washington, D.C.

# Sibling Experiences in Diverse Family Contexts

SHIRLEY MCGUIRE AND LILLY SHANAHAN

In the United States, siblings are children's most constant social companions and provide a proximal and long-lasting context for development (Cicirelli, 1995; McHale & Crouter, 1996). The field of sibling research has grown considerably in recent years, showing that siblings can advance one another's social, emotional, and cognitive development in the context of their relationship (Brody, 2004; Dunn, 2007). We use the ecological perspective (e.g., Bronfenbrenner & Morris, 1998) to examine sibling experiences in family environments that are diverse in terms of their structure and ethnicity. We emphasize that micro-level sibling experiences and their meaning in children's development are embedded in macrocontexts; that is, sibling experiences are intricately linked with family context and cultural values across and within societies (see also Weisner, 1993).

## Sibling Experiences Are Embedded in Layers of Ecological Context

Sibling experiences have been studied using a variety of conceptual models, including behavior genetics, socialization and social learning theory, risk and resilience perspectives, and, broadly speaking, family and developmental systems models. Here, we use the broad umbrella of the ecological perspective on development (e.g., Bronfenbrenner & Morris, 1998) because it subsumes elements of many of these perspectives, has been commonly used in sibling research (e.g., East, Weisner, & Reyes, 2006; McHale & Crouter, 1996) and highlights the role of context in children's development. Indeed, the ecological perspective describes multiple embedded layers of context, ranging from microsystems (e.g., daily settings and relationships) to mesosystems (e.g., connections among microsystems such as the school–home interface) and macrosystems (e.g., societal and cultural beliefs). Ecological layers that are close to the individual both shape and are shaped by more distant, macrosystemic layers.

The importance of the macrosystem for understanding sibling experiences has been illustrated in cross-cultural research (Cicirelli, 1994; Nuckolls, 1993; Zukow, 1989). Families in the United States hold some expectations about sibling experiences, such as equal or fair parental treatment of siblings (Kowal & Kramer, 1997), but overall, siblings in U.S. society, compared with siblings in some non-Western societies, may have fewer clearly defined roles, such as caregiving, or economic obligations. In fact, U.S. siblings bear few legal rights and responsibilities for one another (Dwyer, 2006). This lack of legally prescribed sibling roles, and the overall diversity within U.S. society, may mean that within-society subcultures and contexts play an integral role in shaping the sibling experience and its influence on child development. In the next section, we review sibling experiences in families that vary by ethnicity and family structure (Fields, 2003a, 2003b; McLoyd, Cauce, Takeuchi, & Wilson, 2000; Parke, 2004) and discuss emerging family contexts in additional macrolevel niches (Weisner, 1993).

## Siblings in Ethnically and Structurally Diverse Family Contexts

Sibling research has focused almost exclusively on sibling processes in maritally intact European American families and has only recently explored sibling experiences in diverse family structures. Newer studies of African American and Mexican American siblings provide insight into sibling dynamics in other ecological niches in the United States. We begin by reviewing research conducted on school-age and teenage siblings in primarily two-parent European American families.

### *European American Families*

Sibling relationship research using two-parent, maritally intact European American families has been reviewed in detail elsewhere, along with studies of families of primarily European background in the United Kingdom and Canada (e.g., Brody, 1998, 2004; Dunn, 1996, 2007; Noller, 2005). Here, we outline three main lines of research that have been conducted on siblings in these family contexts. The first has examined the role of structural characteristics of the sibling dyad, including birth order, sex constellation, age gap, and genetic relatedness in children's development. With respect to birth order, parents tend to expect firstborns to conform to parental rules and expectations more than they do for laterborns (e.g., Sulloway, 1996). Mixed-sex sibling constellations provide opportunities for sex-typed treatment by parents, as illustrated by the finding that younger brothers with older sisters spent significantly less time doing housework than did younger sisters with older brothers (e.g., McHale, Crouter, & Whiteman, 2003). Regarding age gap, younger siblings with close-in-age older siblings may have increased access to older peers, who may, in turn, provide socialization for antisocial behaviors (e.g., Snyder, Bank, & Burraston, 2005). Genetic relatedness of the sibling dyad appears to contribute to relationship quality, with monozygotic twins experiencing closer, more trusting, and less hostile relationships compared with dizygotic twins and full siblings (McGuire, Segal, Gill, Whitlow, & Clausen, 2010; Reiss, Neiderhiser, Hetherington, & Plomin, 2000).

A second line of research has investigated relationship dynamics. At the dyadic level, similarities among siblings in terms of age and sex may foster both sibling differentiation (i.e., sibling differences in terms of personality and activity involvement; e.g., Feinberg & Hetherington, 2000; Shanahan, Kim, McHale, & Crouter, 2007) and social learning (e.g., sibling similarities in antisocial or empathic behaviors; Slomkowski, Rende, Conger, Simons, & Conger, 2001; Whiteman, McHale, & Crouter, 2007). Furthermore, sibling collusion (i.e., coercive sibling interactions) may contribute to the development of antisocial and risky sexual behaviors (Bullock & Dishion, 2002). Longitudinal studies reveal both stability and mean-level changes in sibling relationship quality across childhood and adolescence (e.g., Kim, McHale, Osgood, & Crouter, 2006; see Dunn, Slomkowski, & Beardsall, 1994, for British sample). At the family-systemic level, research on parents' differential treatment of siblings has shown that having a less positive or more negative relationship with parents than one's sibling does is linked with lower self-esteem and higher levels of internalizing and externalizing behaviors (e.g., McGuire, Dunn, & Plomin, 1995; McGuire, 2001; Shanahan, McHale, Crouter, & Osgood, 2008; see Jenkins, Rasbash, & O'Connor, 2003, for Canadian sample).

A third line of research has examined sibling experiences in a variety of ecological contexts within the European American community. For instance, sibling relationship processes in families with a disabled child differ from those in families with non-disabled children. Although parents tend to treat a child with a disability more "favorably" than they do the other children in the family, such differential treatment does not necessarily translate into sibling conflict and poor adjustment for the non-disabled children (McHale & Pawletko, 1992). A sibling's disability may "legitimize" differential treatment in the eyes of the nondisabled sibling (McHale & Pawletko, 1992), and siblings who appraise differential treatment as fair may have positive sibling relationships and adjustment despite being treated non-preferentially (Kowal & Kramer, 1997).

The importance of family context for understanding sibling dynamics has been further explored using studies of European American families from varying family structures, including divorced families and stepfamilies. One finding is that sibling relationships influence, and are influenced by, the conflict and ambivalence typically found in disrupted families. For example, conflict between parents tends to have a spillover effect, increasing sibling hostility and emotional distance (e.g., Hetherington & Clingempeel, 1992; Hetherington, Henderson, & Reiss, 1999). Siblings often experience decreases in mutual engagement following divorce and during the beginning stages of remarriage. Sibling hostility typically increases when a stepfamily is constituted but declines as children get older and spend more time together.

Siblings may also serve a buffering role during their parents' marital transitions, possibly compensating for a lack of parental availability and warmth. But studies on families of European background in the United States, the United Kingdom, and Canada suggest that both spillover and compensation processes may depend on the dyad sex constellation, dyad type (e.g., full siblings, half-siblings, or stepsiblings), and macrolevel influences (Anderson, 1999; Anderson & Rice, 1992; Dunn et al., 1999). For example, females provide more comfort to siblings, particularly to sisters, than do males (e.g., Gass, Jenkins, & Dunn, 2007; Kempton, Armistead, Wierson, & Forehand, 1991). Furthermore, unlike the pattern in the United States, in a U.K. sample, sibling relationship qualities in stepfamilies did not differ from those in nondivorced families, possibly because families in the United Kingdom receive greater government assistance during marital transitions, alleviating parental and child stress (Deater-Deckard, Dunn, & Lussier, 2002; Dunn et al., 1999). Thus, taking macrolevel economic and cultural factors into account when examining sibling experiences across family structures may help in understanding the specific processes that trigger conflict spillover or compensation in the sibling relationship (Conger & Conger, 1996; Larson & Almeida, 1999).

Finally, other intricacies of sibling life in divorced and remarried families still need to be documented, including the effects of visitation arrangements, the differential involvement of biological parents in siblings' and stepsiblings' lives, the relationship between the newly formed families after divorce, the implications of romantic attraction between genetically unrelated stepsiblings, and the redefining of sibling relationships after the dissolution of a second marriage (e.g., Bernstein, 1997; Drapeau, Simard, & Beaudry, 2000; Hetherington et al., 1999; Kaplan, Ade-Ridder, & Hennon, 1991). In addition, some of the issues discussed in this section may also apply to siblings from never-married families, another understudied (but growing) family structure (Fields, 2003b).

## African American Families

Recent research on African American families has examined sibling experiences in two-parent and single-parent family structures. These studies have begun to provide insight into sibling processes that may transcend ecological niches or that are specific to some family contexts. For instance, cluster analyses using sibling warmth and hostility measures revealed different sibling relationship types in two separate samples of two-parent families, one consisting of African American families from working- and middle-class backgrounds (McHale, Whiteman, Kim, & Crouter, 2007) and the other of European American families from similar economic circumstances (McGuire, McHale, & Updegraff, 1996). In both studies, researchers crossed measures of sibling negativity and positivity and found three types of relationships: a "high-negativity" group, a "high-warmth" group, and an "emotionally distant" group. In addition, high sibling negativity was associated with children's depression and risky behavior, and positive parent–child relationships were linked with high sibling positivity in the African American families (McHale et al., 2007), as well as in European American families in another study (Kim, McHale, Crouter, & Osgood, 2007).

Researchers have also identified important factors that may influence sibling dynamics specifically in African American families (McHale et al., 2007). For example, maternal experiences with racism were linked with sibling negativity, parental spirituality was linked with higher sibling warmth, and lower ethnic identity in the children was linked with sibling emotional distance.

Many African American siblings are raised by single mothers (Fields, 2003b), and studying these families can help test links among sibling experiences, family stress, economic hardship, and children's development. For example, in a study involving rural African American single-mother families, older siblings had both direct and indirect influences on their younger siblings. Older siblings' competence was directly linked with younger siblings' self-regulation and, indirectly via its positive link, to maternal psychological functioning and, in turn, quality of parenting (Brody, Kim, Murry, & Brown, 2003). Furthermore, as sibling support increased, sibling similarity in externalizing behaviors also increased (Brody, Kim, Murry, & Brown, 2005). This finding is consistent with some previous work on European American siblings suggesting that antisocial siblings with a supportive relationship may become "partners in crime" and socialize each other in delinquent behavior (Rowe & Gulley, 1992; Slomkowski et al., 2001). However, correlations among siblings' problem behaviors may be amplified in disadvantaged neighborhoods (Brody et al., 2003). In terms of developmental assets, a parenting style that combines high levels of control and monitoring with support and involvement (i.e., a no-nonsense style) and maintains a strong bond with extended family members provides significant sources of social capital, particularly for children of single African American mothers (Burton, 1995; McLoyd et al., 2000; Parke, 2004; Taylor, 2001).

The roles of prejudice, discrimination, racial identity, and spirituality in sibling dynamics and family life need to be examined in studies of African American siblings (e.g., Garcia Coll et al., 1996). Such research could increase understanding of siblings' roles in one another's racial socialization and experiences of discrimination. It could also, in turn, reveal links between child development and societal experiences. Furthermore, sibling dynamics need to be explored in Black immigrant families, and families that have siblings who vary in race and color (e.g., American Psychological Association, Task Force on Resilience and Strength in Black Children and Adolescents, 2008). Successful prevention and intervention programs for African American families increase understanding of the role of family-systemic mechanisms, including sibling modeling and mentoring, for positive adjustment in African American youth (e.g., Brody, Kogan, Chen, & Murry, 2008).

## Mexican American Families

Studies of siblings in Mexican American families have also focused on two-parent and single-parent families. Research suggests that adolescents' sibling relationships in two-parent families are characterized by both warmth and conflict (Updegraff, McHale, Whiteman, Thayer, & Delgado, 2005), which is consistent with studies of siblings in African American and European American families. In addition, positive sibling relationships in Mexican American families have been found to be linked with child well-being; this result is consistent with findings from other family contexts with the exception of families with antisocial children (e.g., Brody et al., 2003; Dunn & McGuire, 1992; East & Khoo, 2005; McHale et al., 2007; Updegraff et al., 2005).

Unlike the case with European American and African American families, understanding sibling experiences in Mexican American families requires an appreciation of the immigrant experience (Portes & Rumbaut, 1990), including the culture of origin, acculturation levels, and the nativity (i.e., first, second, or third generation) of the family members. For instance, upon arriving in the United States, immigrant children have to negotiate a balance between valuing their culture of origin and becoming immersed into the mainstream U.S. culture (e.g., Balls Organista, Marin, & Chun, 2009; Chun, 2006). Indeed, because children typically overcome linguistic and cultural barriers quickly, they may have to serve as cultural brokers for less acculturated siblings and parents. Furthermore, because of the family's lack of economic resources and social support, older siblings in immigrant families commonly take on caregiving and parenting roles (e.g., Fuligni, Yip, & Tseng, 2002; see also Walsh, Shulman, Bar-On, & Tsur, 2006).

The meaning of sibling experiences may vary depending on cultural values related to the importance of family (Marín & Marín, 1991; Updegraff et al., 2005). For example, preferential treatment of a sibling by a parent is often linked with adjustment problems for children in European American samples (McGuire, 2001). However, in a sample of Mexican American families, older siblings who embraced the cultural value of familism, which emphasizes support, interdependence, and loyalty among family members, were not more likely to have higher levels of depressive symptoms and risky behaviors when their parents regularly treated a younger sibling preferentially (McHale, Updegraff, Shanahan, Crouter, & Killoren, 2005). In the same sample, both older and younger siblings who reported high familism were more likely to report using solution-oriented and non-confrontational strategies to resolve sibling conflicts than were siblings reporting low familism (Killoren, Thayer, & Updegraff, 2008). Both strategies involve promoting harmony in relationships and may be in line with the collectivist values promoted in Mexican culture, whereas the controlling strategies typically found in studies of European American siblings may be more consistent with individualistic values found in U.S. culture (Killoren et al., 2008; see also Gabrielidis, Stephan, Ybarra, Dos Santos Pearson, & Villareal, 1997).

In Mexico, families typically have many children, along with a large extended family, and treat siblings in sex-typed ways (Cauce & Domenech-Rodriguez, 2002). One study found that when parents were more enculturated with Mexican culture than with Anglo culture, older sisters with younger brothers were granted significantly fewer privileges in the household than were older brothers with younger sisters (McHale et al., 2005). Furthermore, the same study found that children in Mexican American families with close ties to Mexican culture tended to spend many of their nonschool hours with siblings and cousins (Updegraff et al., 2005), and older sisters in these families tended to serve as caregivers for younger siblings (Cauce & Domenech-Rodriguez, 2002; Vega, 1990). Thus, families' cultural values, gender constellation, and sibship size are important contexts for sibling dynamics in Mexican-origin families, and sibling studies provide a window into links between child development and cultural values.

Teenage childbearing is common in Mexican American families (Martin et al., 2007). Studies by East and colleagues (which also included African American families) have shown that sisters' caregiving extends to teenage siblings' offspring in these families (East, 1998; East & Khoo, 2005; East et al., 2006). Results of these studies suggest that caring for young nieces and nephews results in both developmental costs (e.g., higher stress and lower grades) and benefits (e.g., higher life satisfaction and lower school dropout rate). Furthermore, taking care of young nieces and nephews in low-income, single-mother families was linked with high sibling warmth and increased levels of maturity among younger sisters. When older sisters were dominant or sibling conflict was high, however, younger siblings were at increased risk of early sexual behavior, pregnancy, and drug use.

Taken together, the findings in our review of families from different structures and ethnicities suggest that some correlates of sibling experiences, such as parental stress, economic strain, racism, and acculturation, are specific to certain ecological niches. Highlighting findings that appear to be consistent across contexts is tempting. For instance, studies have found that sibling positivity is associated with healthy development and resilience, especially for sister–sister pairs. Still, even this result may differ in unexplored family contexts, such as Asian American families and adoptive families. Furthermore, sibling positivity may need to be defined differently for boys and girls and in families of different cultural backgrounds. Consequently, we prefer to be cautious when discussing possible "universal" sibling processes. Instead, we encourage understanding processes *within* contexts defined by structure, ethnicity, and culture (e.g., Garcia Coll et al., 1996).

# Emerging Family Contexts

In this section, we discuss a selection of four U.S. family contexts, the study of which will further understanding of sibling experiences and ethnic and structural family diversity.

## Other Ethnic-Minority Families

Sibling experiences in other nonimmigrant ethnically diverse families (e.g., Native American families) have been largely neglected, but research on them could provide additional insight into the roles of discrimination, economic disadvantage, cultural values, and risk and resilience in children's development. In addition, no large studies of sibling or family experiences in the 28 Asian American subgroups in the United States have been conducted (Parke, 2004). Such studies are needed not only to understand sibling experiences and the acculturation process in other immigrant populations but also to learn about the role of family obligations in siblings' lives (Fuligni et al., 2002). Additional studies should examine sibling experiences in the context of ethnically diverse families living in extended, multigeneration, and multiethnic households (Burton, 1995; Taylor, 2001).

## Lesbian and Gay Families

From 1990 to 2000, there was a 314 percent increase in the number of households headed by same-sex partners, with gay and lesbian families living in 99.3 percent of U.S. counties at the turn of the century (Smith & Gates, 2001). Exploring sibling experiences in families headed by same-sex partners would further understanding of links among marginalization, family context, and sibling experiences (Patterson, 2000; Patterson & D'Augelli, 1998). And comparing these experiences in terms of whether or not the families live in states that allow same-sex marriage could help illuminate the joint influence of macrocontextual (e.g., laws and policies) and microcontextual influences (e.g., marriage) on sibling experiences. In addition, researchers could test hypotheses about the role of parental gender in links between parental differential treatment and children's development, connections which have been investigated only in heterosexual-headed households (e.g., McHale et al., 2005; Shanahan, McHale, Crouter, & Osgood, 2007). Studies of the experiences of sexual-minority individuals in their family of origin would shed light on the role of sibling relationships in identity and relationship development, especially given that a significant number of youth initially come out to their brothers and sisters (e.g., Allen & Demo, 1995; D'Augelli & Hershberger, 1993; Gottlieb, 2005; Savin-Williams, 1998).

## Adoptive Families

Behavioral genetic studies of siblings in adoptive families have examined genetic and environmental contributions to sibling relationship quality (e.g., Rende, Slomkowski, Stocker, Fulker, & Plomin, 1992; Stocker & Dunn, 1994) and to the differences between adopted and nonadopted siblings in adjustment and family experiences (e.g., McGue et al., 2007; Sharma, McGue, & Benson, 1998). Still, little is known about the nature of sibling processes in families with adopted children. In addition, research on sibling placement in adoptive or foster-care families would advance understanding of sibling contributions to risk and resilience during stressful transitions (Hegar, 2005; Linares, Li, Shrout, Brody, & Pettit, 2007). Studies of families with internationally adopted children could illuminate the role of siblings in the development of children's ethnic and racial identity and acculturation processes in multiethnic families (Lee, Grotevant, Hellerstedt, Gunnar, & the Minnesota International Adoption Project Team, 2006).

## Assisted Reproductive Technology

A more recent development in evolving family structures is the increasing use of assisted reproductive technology (ART). Golombok (2006) has reviewed research on parenting and child development in families that used ART, and most of this research has focused on singletons in order to avoid the complications associated with multiple births. Studies of families with twins and other multiples conceived through ART would further the literature on genetic contributions to sibling relationship quality (McGuire et al., 2010). Within-family studies of naturally conceived children suggest that there would be sibling differences in parenting experiences and children's outcomes in these families (e.g., Shanahan et al., 2008). In addition, family types have been evolving with the use of ART, including heterosexual women choosing to become single parents and lesbian or gay partners choosing to start a family together (Golombok, 2006).

# Conclusions

Sibling experiences provide a context for child development, a context that can differ at many levels within and across societies. Our review of studies of sibling experiences in ethnically and structurally diverse families points to the importance of context at multiple levels, from sex composition of the dyads to family structure to family policy to cultural beliefs. Sibling relationships are embedded in larger ecological niches. Diverse and evolving family contexts, even within societies, must be considered when describing the sibling experience and developing and testing theories of sibling dynamics. In addition, more sibling research is needed on families with complex structures and diverse ethnic and racial backgrounds to increase understanding of key developmental influences such as family stability, economic hardship, discrimination, and acculturation.

# References

Allen, K. R., & Demo, D. H. (1995). The families of lesbians and gay men: A new frontier in family research. *Journal of Marriage and the Family, 57,* 1–17.

American Psychological Association, Task Force on Resilience and Strength in Black Children and Adolescents. (2008). *Resilience in African American children and adolescents: A vision for optimal development.* Washington, DC: American Psychological Association.

Anderson, E. R. (1999). Sibling, half-sibling, and stepsibling relationships in remarried families. In E. M. Hetherington, S. H. Henderson, & D. Reiss (Eds.), *Adolescent siblings in stepfamilies: Family functioning and the adolescent adjustment.* Monographs for the Society for Research in Child Development, *64*(Serial No. 259, pp. 1–222).

Anderson, E. R., & Rice, A. M. (1992). Sibling relationships during remarriage. In E. M. Hetherington & W. G. Clingempeel (Eds.), *Coping with marital transitions: A family systems perspective.* Monographs for the Society for Research in Child Development, *57*(Serial No. 227, pp. 1–242).

Balls Organista, P., Marin, G., & Chun, K. M. (2009). *Psychology of ethnic groups in the U.S.* Thousand Oaks, CA: Sage.

Bernstein, A. C. (1997). Stepfamilies from siblings' perspectives. *Marriage & Family Review, 26,* 153–175.

Brody, G. H. (1998). Sibling relationship quality: Its causes and consequences. *Annual Review of Psychology, 49,* 1–24.

Brody, G. H. (2004). Siblings' direct and indirect contributions to child development. *Current Directions in Psychological Science, 13,* 124–212.

Brody, G. H., Ge, X., Kim, S. Y., Murry, V. M., Simons, R. L., Gibbons, F. X., et al. (2003). Neighborhood disadvantage moderates associations of parenting and older sibling problem attitudes and behavior with conduct disorders in African American children. *Journal of Consulting and Clinical Psychology, 71,* 211–222.

Brody, G. H., Kim, S., Murry, V. B., & Brown, A. C. (2003). Longitudinal direct and indirect pathways linking older sibling competence to the development of younger sibling competence. *Developmental Psychology, 39,* 618–628.

Brody, G. H., Kim, S., Murry, V. M., & Brown, A. C. (2005). Longitudinal links among parenting, self-presentations to peers, and the development of externalizing and internalizing symptoms in African American siblings. *Development and Psychopathology, 17,* 185–205.

Brody, G. H., Kogan, S. M., Chen, Y., & Murry, V. M. (2008). Long-term effects of the strong African American families program on youths' conduct problems. *Journal of Adolescent Health, 43,* 474–481.

Bronfenbrenner, U., & Morris, P. A. (1998). The ecology of developmental processes. In R. M. Lerner (Ed.), *Handbook of child psychology: Theoretical model of human development* (Vol. 1, 5th ed., pp. 993–1028). New York: Wiley.

Bullock, B. M., & Dishion, T. J. (2002). Sibling collusion and problem behavior in early adolescence: Toward a process model for family mutuality. *Journal of Abnormal Child Psychology, 30,* 143–153.

Burton, L. M. (1995). Intergenerational patterns of providing care in African-American families with teenage childbearers: Emerging patterns in an ethnographic study. In V. L. Bengtson, K. W. Schaie, & L. M. Burton (Eds.), *Intergenerational relations: Effects of social change* (pp. 79–125). New York: Springer.

Cauce, A. M., & Domenech-Rodriguez, M. (2002). Latino families: Myths and realities. In J. M. Contreras, K. A. Kerns, & A. M. Neal-Barnett (Eds.), *Latino children and families in the United States* (pp. 5–25). Westport, CT: Praeger.

Chun, K. M. (2006). Conceptual and measurement issues in family acculturation research. In M. H. Bornstein & L. R. Cote (Eds.), *Acculturation and parent–child relationships: Measurement and development* (pp. 63–78). Mahwah, NJ: Erlbaum.

Cicirelli, V. G. (1994). Sibling relationships in cross-cultural perspective. *Journal of Marriage and the Family, 56*, 7–20.

Cicirelli, V. G. (1995). *Sibling relationships across the life span*. New York: Plenum.

Conger, R. D., & Conger, K. J. (1996). Sibling relationships. In R. L. Simons (Ed.), *Understanding differences between divorced and intact families* (pp. 104–121). Thousand Oaks, CA: Sage.

D'Augelli, A. R., & Hershberger, S. L. (1993). Lesbian, gay and bisexual youth in community settings: Personal challenges and mental health problems. *American Journal of Community Psychology, 21*, 421–448.

Deater-Deckard, K., Dunn, J., & Lussier, G. (2002). Sibling relationships and social-emotional adjustment in different family contexts. *Social Development, 11*, 571–590.

Drapeau, S., Simard, M., & Beaudry, M. (2000). Siblings in family transitions. *Family Relations, 49*, 77–85.

Dunn, J. (1996). Siblings: The first society. In N. Vanzetti & S. Duck (Eds.), *A lifetime of relationships* (pp. 105–124). Belmont, CA: Thomson Brooks/Cole.

Dunn, J. (2007). Siblings and socialization. In J. Grusec & P. D. Hastings (Eds.), *Handbook of socialization: Theory and research* (pp. 309–327). New York: Guilford.

Dunn, J., Deater-Deckard, K., Pickering, K., Golding, J., & the ALSPAC Study Team. (1999). Siblings, parents, and partners: Family relationships within a longitudinal community study. *Journal of Child Psychology and Psychiatry, 40*, 1025–1037.

Dunn, J., & McGuire, S. (1992). Sibling and peer relationships in childhood. *Journal of Child Psychology and Psychiatry, 33*, 67–105.

Dunn, J., Slomkowski, C., & Beardsall, L. (1994). Sibling relationships from the preschool period through middle childhood and early adolescence. *Developmental Psychology, 30*, 315–324.

Dwyer, J. G. (2006). *The relationship rights of children*. New York: Cambridge University Press.

East, P. L. (1998). Impact of adolescent childbearing on families and younger siblings: Effects that increase younger siblings' risk for early pregnancy. *Applied Developmental Science, 2*, 62–74.

East, P. L., & Khoo, S. K. (2005). Longitudinal pathways linking family factors and sibling relationship qualities to adolescence substance use and sexual risk behaviors. *Journal of Family Psychology, 19*, 571–580.

East, P. L., Weisner, T. S., & Reyes, B. T. (2006). Youths' caretaking of their adolescent sisters' children: Its costs and benefits for youths' development. *Applied Developmental Science, 10*(2), 86–95.

Feinberg, M. E., & Hetherington, E. M. (2000). Sibling differentiation in adolescence: Implications for behavioral genetic theory. *Child Development, 71*, 1512–1524.

Fields, J. (2003a). *America's families and living arrangements: 2003* (Current Population Reports, P20-553). Washington, DC: U.S. Census Bureau.

Fields, J. (2003b). *Children's living arrangements and characteristics: March 2002* (Current Population Reports, P20-547). Washington, DC: U.S. Census Bureau.

Fuligni, A. J., Yip, T., & Tseng, V. (2002). The impact of family obligation on the daily activities and psychological well-being of Chinese American adolescents. *Child Development, 73*, 302–314.

Gabrielidis, C., Stephan, W. G., Ybarra, O., Dos Santos Pearson, V. M., & Villareal, L. (1997). Preferred styles of conflict resolution: Mexico and the United States. *Journal of Cross-Cultural Psychology, 28*, 661–677.

Garcia Coll, C., Crnic, K., Lamberty, G., Wasik, B. H., Jenkins, R., Garcia, H. V., et al. (1996). An integrative model for the study of developmental competencies in minority children. *Child Development, 67*, 1891–1914.

Gass, K., Jenkins, J., & Dunn, D. (2007). Are sibling relationships protective? A longitudinal study. *Journal of Child Psychology and Psychiatry, 48*, 167–175.

Golombok, S. (2006). New family forms. In A. Clarke-Stewart & J. Dunn (Eds.), *Families count: Effects on child and adolescent development* (pp. 273–298). New York: Cambridge University Press.

Gottlieb, A. R. (2005). *Side by side: On having a gay or lesbian sibling*. New York: Harrington Park Press.

Hegar, R. L. (2005). Sibling placement in foster care and adoption: An overview of international research. *Children and Youth Services Review, 27*, 717–739.

Hetherington, E. M., & Clingempeel, W. G. (1992). Coping with marital transitions: A family systems perspective. *Monographs for the Society for Research in Child Development, 57*(Serial No. 227).

Hetherington, E. M., Henderson, S. H., & Reiss, D. (1999). Adolescent siblings in stepfamilies: Family functioning and the adolescent adjustment. *Monographs for the Society for Research in Child Development, 64*(Serial No. 259).

Jenkins, J. M., Rasbash, J., & O'Connor, T. G. (2003). The role of the shared family context in differential parenting. *Developmental Psychology, 39*, 99–113.

Kaplan, L., Ade-Ridder, L., & Hennon, C. B. (1991). Issues of split custody: Siblings separated by divorce. *Journal of Divorce and Remarriage, 16*, 253–274.

Kempton, T., Armistead, L., Wierson, M., & Forehand, R. (1991). Presence of a sibling as a potential buffer following parental divorce: An examination of young adolescents. *Journal of Clinical Child Psychology, 20*, 434–438.

Killoren, S. E., Thayer, S. M., & Updegraff, K. A. (2008). Conflict resolution between Mexican origin adolescent siblings. *Journal of Marriage and Family, 70*, 1200–1212.

Kim, J., McHale, S. M., Crouter, A. C., & Osgood, D. W. (2007). Longitudinal linkages between sibling relationships and adjustment from middle childhood through adolescence. *Developmental Psychology, 43*, 960–973.

Kim, J., McHale, S. M., Osgood, D. W., & Crouter, A. C. (2006). Longitudinal course and family correlates of sibling relationships from childhood through adolescence. *Child Development, 77*, 1746–1761.

Kowal, A., & Kramer, L. (1997). Children's understanding of parental differential treatment. *Child Development, 68*, 113–126.

Larson, R. W., & Almeida, D. M. (1999). Emotional transmission in the daily lives of families: A new paradigm for studying family process. *Journal of Marriage and the Family, 61*, 5–20.

Lee, R. M., Grotevant, H. D., Hellerstedt, W. L., Gunnar, M. R., & the Minnesota International Adoption Project Team. (2006). Cultural socialization in families with internationally adopted children. *Journal of Family Psychology, 20,* 571–580.

Linares, L. O., Li, M., Shrout, P. E., Brody, G. H., & Pettit, G. S. (2007). Placement shift, sibling relationship quality, and child outcomes in foster care: A controlled study. *Journal of Family Psychology, 21,* 736–743.

Marín, G., & Marín, B. (1991). *Research with Hispanic populations.* Newbury Park, CA: Sage.

Martin, J. A., Hamilton, B. E., Sutton, P. D., Ventura, S. J., Menacker, F., Kirmeyer, S., et al. (2007). *Births: Final data for 2005 National vital statistics reports* (Vol. 56, No. 6). Hyattsville, MD: National Center for Health Statistics.

McGue, M., Keyes, M., Sharma, A., Elkins, I., Legrand, L., Johnson, W., et al. (2007). The environments of adopted and non-adopted youth: Evidence on range restriction from the sibling interaction and behavior study (SIBS). *Behavior Genetics, 37,* 449–462.

McGuire, S. (2001). Nonshared environment research: What is it and where is it going? *Marriage and Family Review, 33*(1), 31–57.

McGuire, S., Dunn, J., & Plomin, R. (1995). Maternal differential treatment of siblings and children's behavioral problems: A longitudinal study. *Development and Psychopathology, 7,* 515–528.

McGuire, S., McHale, S., & Updegraff, K. A. (1996). Children's perceptions of the sibling relationship during middle childhood: Connections within and between family relationships. *Personal Relationships, 3,* 229–239.

McGuire, S., Segal, N. L., Gill, P., Whitlow, B., & Clausen, J. M. (2010). Siblings and trust. In K. Rotenberg (Ed.), *Interpersonal trust during childhood and adolescence* (pp. 133–154). Cambridge, UK: Cambridge University Press.

McHale, S. M., & Crouter, A. C. (1996). The family contexts of children's sibling relationships. In G. H. Brody (Ed.), *Sibling relationships: Their causes and consequences* (pp. 173–195). Westport, CT: Ablex.

McHale, S. M., Crouter, A. C., & Whiteman, S. D. (2003). The family contexts of gender development in childhood and adolescence. *Social Development, 12,* 125–148.

McHale, S. M., & Pawletko, T. M. (1992). Differential treatment of siblings in two family contexts. *Child Development, 63,* 68–81.

McHale, S. M., Updegraff, K. A., Shanahan, L., Crouter, A. C., & Killoren, S. E. (2005). Gender, culture, and family dynamics: Differential treatment of siblings in Mexican American families. *Journal of Marriage and the Family, 67,* 1259–1274.

McHale, S. M., Whiteman, S. D., Kim, J., & Crouter, A. C. (2007). Characteristics and correlates of sibling relationships in two-parent African American families. *Journal of Family Psychology, 21,* 227–235.

McLoyd, V. C., Cauce, A. M., Takeuchi, D., & Wilson, L. (2000). Marital processes and parental socialization in families of color: A decade review of research. *Journal of Marriage and the Family, 62,* 1070–1093.

Noller, P. (2005). Sibling relationships in adolescence: Learning and growing together. *Personal Relationships, 12,* 1–22.

Nuckolls, C. W. (1993). *Siblings in South Asia: Brothers and sisters in cultural context.* New York: Guilford.

Parke, R. D. (2004). Development in the family. *Annual Review Psychology, 55,* 365–399.

Patterson, C. (2000). Family relationship of lesbians and gay men. *Journal of Marriage and the Family, 62,* 1052–1069.

Patterson, C. J., & D'Augelli, A. R. (Eds.). (1998). *Lesbian, gay and bisexual identities in families: Psychological perspectives.* New York: Oxford University Press.

Portes, A., & Rumbaut, G. R. (1990). *Immigrant America: A portrait.* Berkeley: University of California Press.

Reiss, D., Neiderhiser, J. M., Hetherington, E. M., & Plomin, R. (2000). *The relationship code.* Cambridge, MA: Harvard University Press.

Rende, R. D., Slomkowski, C. L., Stocker, C., Fulker, D. W., & Plomin, R. (1992). Genetic and environmental influences on maternal and sibling interaction in middle childhood: A sibling adoption study. *Developmental Psychology, 28,* 484–490.

Rowe, D., & Gulley, B. (1992). Sibling effects on substance abuse and delinquency. *Criminology, 30,* 217–233.

Savin-Williams, R. C. (1998). The disclosure to families of same-sex attractions by lesbian, gay, and bisexual youths. *Journal of Research on Adolescence, 8,* 49–68.

Shanahan, L., Kim, J., McHale, S. M., & Crouter, A. C. (2007). Sibling similarities and differences in time use: A pattern-analytic, within-family approach. *Social Development, 16,* 662–681.

Shanahan, L., McHale, S. M., Crouter, A. C., & Osgood, D. W. (2007). Warmth with mothers and fathers from middle childhood to late adolescence: Within- and between-families comparisons. *Developmental Psychology, 43,* 551–563.

Shanahan, L., McHale, S. M., Crouter, A. C., & Osgood, D. W. (2008). Parents' differential treatment and youth depressive symptoms and sibling relationships: Longitudinal linkages. *Journal of Marriage and the Family, 70,* 480–495.

Sharma, A. R., McGue, M. K., & Benson, P. L. (1998). The psychological adjustment of United States adopted adolescents and their nonadopted siblings. *Child Development, 69,* 791–802.

Slomkowski, C., Rende, R., Conger, K. J., Simons, R. L., & Conger, R. D. (2001). Sisters, brothers, and delinquency: Evaluating social influence during early and middle adolescence. *Child Development, 72,* 271–283.

Smith, D. M., & Gates, G. J. (2001). Gay and lesbian families in the United States: Same-sex unmarried partnered household: A Human Rights Campaign Report. Retrieved April 28, 2008, from www.urban.org/url.cfm?ID51000491

Snyder, J., Bank, L., & Burraston, B. (2005). The consequences of antisocial behavior in older male siblings for younger brothers and sisters. *Journal of Family Psychology, 19,* 643–653.

Stocker, C., & Dunn, J. (1994). Sibling relationships in childhood and adolescence. In J. C. DeFries, R. Plomin, & D. W. Fulker (Eds.), *Nature and nurture during middle childhood* (pp. 214–232). Malden, MA: Blackwell.

Sulloway, F. J. (1996). *Born to rebel: Birth order, family dynamics, and creative lives.* New York: Pantheon Books.

Taylor, R. (2001). *Minority families in the US: A multicultural perspective* (3rd ed.). Upper Saddle River, NJ: Prentice Hall.

Updegraff, K. A., McHale, S. M., Whiteman, S. D., Thayer, S. M., & Delgado, M. Y. (2005). Adolescent sibling relationships in Mexican American families: Exploring the role of familism. *Journal of Family Psychology, 19,* 512–522.

Vega, W. A. (1990). Hispanic families in the 1980s: A decade of research. *Journal of Marriage and the Family, 52,* 1015–1024.

Walsh, S., Shulman, S., Bar-On, Z., & Tsur, A. (2006). The role of parentification and family climate in adaptation among immigrant adolescents in Israel. *Journal of Research on Adolescence, 16,* 321–350.

Weisner, T. S. (1993). Overview: Sibling similarity and difference in different cultures. In C. W. Nuckolls (Ed.), *Siblings in South Asia: Brothers and sisters in cultural context* (pp. 1–17). New York: Guilford.

Whiteman, S. D., McHale, S. M., & Crouter, A. C. (2007). Competing processes of siblings influence: Observational learning and sibling deidentification. *Social Development, 16,* 642–661.

Zukow, P. G. (1989). *Sibling interaction across cultures: Theoretical and methodological issues.* New York: Springer-Verlag.

# Critical Thinking

1. Why is it important to consider ethnic and cultural issues in our attempt to understand how siblings matter in children's lives? What are some similarities and differences in sibling dynamics and impact across different ethnic groups in the United States?

2. How does the experience of racism and prejudice influence sibling dynamics in African-American families?

3. What are some new "emerging" kinds of families that need to be studied more to understand sibling experiences in different families?

# The Effects of Parental Undocumented Status on the Developmental Contexts of Young Children in Immigrant Families

Hirokazu Yoshikawa and Ariel Kalil

Approximately one in five American children has at least one foreign-born parent (Hernandez, 2004; Passel & Cohn, 2009). A substantial proportion of immigrants are undocumented (i.e., without federally recognized citizenship, legal permanent resident, or refugee status). There were 10.8 million undocumented immigrant adults in the United States as of 2009, more than a quarter of all foreign-born immigrants (Hoefer, Rytina, & Baker, 2010; Passel & Cohn, 2009). In 2008, 31% of children of immigrants in public K—12 schools in the United States, or 7% of all children in public school (roughly 4 million children), had at least one undocumented immigrant parent (Passel & Cohn, 2009). This represents an average of one or two children in each public school classroom in the country.

Current debates in immigration policy center on undocumented immigrants and their prospects for citizenship (Motomura, 2008; Preston, 2009). Nearly all of this debate concerns adults or adolescents and ignores young children with undocumented parents. This group is a large and growing subset of children in immigrant families (Tienda & Mitchell, 2006). This article describes the effects that parental undocumented status can have on developmental contexts experienced in early childhood. We exclude parent or child refugee status from our discussion because of this group's unique legal and contextual experiences (for a review of children in refugee families, see Guarnaccia & Lopez, 1998).

We focus on early childhood as a crucial but still overlooked period for the study of children in immigrant families, for several reasons. First, indicators of disadvantage have particularly strong effects when experienced in early childhood (e.g., poverty; Duncan, Ziol-Guest, & Kalil, 2010). Second, this is a period when foundational cognitive and social skills are developing; supports may make more of a difference here than later in development (Cunha & Heckman, 2007). Finally, 91% of children under 6 with at least one undocumented parent are themselves U.S. citizens (Passel & Cohn, 2009). This highlights the role of parental documentation status in affecting contexts of development that children may have access to, but cannot select themselves. We review developmental contexts including immediate postmigration contexts, social settings that parents and young children experience in their daily routines, and family processes.

Few data sets enable direct links between parent undocumented status and child development. The literature showing such direct links is in a very early stage of development because the majority of studies assessing children obtain no data on documentation. We therefore focus on comparing the developmental contexts of children of undocumented immigrants to those of children of documented immigrants and/or naturalized citizens. Developmental theory suggests that through children's experiences of those contexts (such as parental work, housing, access to public services and programs, care environments, and family processes), the effects of parental undocumented status can be transmitted to children's early cognitive, socioemotional, and health trajectories.

Given the paucity of existing data on connections between parents' legal status and children's outcomes, we also draw our evidence from three kinds of studies: those of groups that have high proportions of undocumented, those that have inquired about the citizenship status of parents, and ethnographic studies. In the Conclusion, we discuss future directions for research on this important but understudied topic in child development.

The little information we have about actual child development outcomes in these populations raises concerns. The only large-scale study to examine both parent documentation status and parents' reports of their children's development did so in a large sample of California residents (Ortega et al., 2009). It surveyed parents of young children about their documentation and citizenship status, as well as the general developmental status of their children, on a 10-item scale covering language, health, and socioemotional domains (unfortunately this study did not distinguish among different domains of development). The authors compared four groups: undocumented and documented Mexican immigrant parents, and Mexican and White

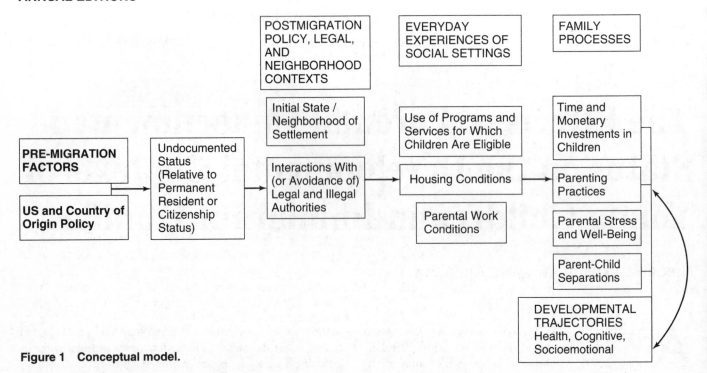

Figure 1    Conceptual model.

United States-born parents. After adjusting for confounding characteristics such as parental education, income, and language spoken at home, the study found that children of Mexican undocumented parents had higher developmental risk than children of United States-born White parents (Ortega et al., 2009). In other studies, food insecurity appears substantially higher among immigrant children with noncitizen parents than among those with citizen parents (Kalil & Chen, 2008). Mothers of 24% of low-income young children of nonnaturalized parents in a national sample reported that their children were in poor health, a figure that is significantly higher than low-income children of native (19%) and naturalized parents (20%; Kalil & Ziol-Guest, 2009). National studies show that, adjusting for a wide range of socioeconomic indicators, Mexican children (the group with the highest rates of undocumented status in the United States) score lower in reading and math skills at school entry than do children of other ethnic groups (Crosnoe, 2007; Fuller et al., 2009; Han, 2006), lower than children from immigrant groups with smaller proportions undocumented (such as Dominicans), and lower than children from racial/ethnic groups with comparably high rates of poverty, such as African Americans. These differences are reduced but not eliminated after controlling for indicators of socioeconomic status, language in the home, parenting, and goals for children. Thus, neither cultural nor economic explanations adequately explain disparities in early cognitive skills between groups that vary in parental undocumented status.

In contrast to the evidence on cognitive skills, early socioemotional indicators, such as problem behaviors or attention problems, do not differ among groups that vary in proportions of undocumented parents (Crosnoe, 2006). Nevertheless, early

childhood disadvantages in health and cognitive development are worrisome, given the long reach of these influences over the life span (Shonkoff, Boyce, & McEwen, 2009).

Our discussion centers on a conceptual model outlining mechanisms linking documentation status to children's developmental contexts (see Figure 1). The model encompasses, in addition to premigration factors in the country of origin and the United States, characteristics at three levels of children's developmental contexts: (a) immediate postmigration contexts; (b) experiences of proximal social settings such as access to and use of public programs and services (including preschool), housing quality, and work conditions; and (c) family processes. Each of these sets of contexts can transmit effects of parental undocumented status on children's health, cognition, and behavior. Factors in the model include direct consequences of undocumented status and mechanisms that can convey the influence of this status above and beyond the influence of other indicators of disadvantage, such as poverty and socioeconomic status.

## Premigration Characteristics

Premigration characteristics either advantage or disadvantage children of undocumented parents, compared to children of legal permanent residents or citizens. Selection processes (factors that shape parents' decisions and choices to migrate) can represent either negative or positive selection; they differ depending on comparison group, cohort, country of origin, and historical and policy context. For example, undocumented parents have lower levels of education and job skills than their documented counterparts in the United States, but somewhat higher levels of education and social capital than those in their sending regions who do not emigrate (Massey & Espinosa, 1997; Passel & Cohn, 2009). The "immigrant health paradox" is an example of positive selection: Immigrants with high rates of being undocumented, such as lower income Mexican immigrants, have better perinatal and postnatal outcomes than United States-born counterparts with roughly equal economic conditions (Scribner, 1996).

Immigration policies in the country of origin and the United States also influence the relative size, ethnic composition, and characteristics of both the undocumented flow into the country and the undocumented already residing in the United States. For example, policies establishing quotas of legal migration in the United States, economic policies in countries of origin, and emigration restrictions from countries of origin all shaped undocumented flows across the last century (Ngai, 2004). Because these premigration factors affect the composition and characteristics of the undocumented parent population, they can indirectly shape the development of children of the undocumented growing up in the United States.

# Immediate Postmigration Contexts

Transitions to undocumented status can occur through border crossing or overstaying a limited-term visa. Several contexts immediately following this transition might influence children. First, parents' fears of being deported can cause distress and anxiety, which could be transmitted to children through changes in parenting practices. Such effects can vary by geographic context of settlement. In 1996, provisions of the Illegal Immigration Reform and Responsibility Act made it possible for local law enforcement and other officials to rule individuals as inadmissible to the United States, thus initiating deportation without judicial oversight or review. Enforcement of deportation regulations thus varies by state, city, and even neighborhood.

Second, undocumented adults often owe debts to smugglers. The current price for an individual without documents to come to the United States from China, for example, is between $60,000 and $80,000 (Yoshikawa, 2011). A prolonged period of debt can reduce parents' ability to invest in children's learning, increase material hardship, compel them to work long hours, or increase psychological worry and distress. The adverse effects of these aspects of economic hardship on young children's development are well established (Gershoff, Aber, Raver, & Lennon, 2007).

Third, the neighborhood context can influence the development of children of the undocumented. A high concentration of coethnic residents can facilitate economic opportunities and information about programs for children (Zhou, 2001), but neighborhoods with high concentrations of low-income immigrants have fewer community-based resources (Small & McDermott, 2006) and can concentrate particularly disadvantaged residents and thereby disadvantage their children's achievement (Borjas, 2006). The literature is mixed on this issue, with most studies of children restricted to educational attainment (Chiswick & Miller, 2005); virtually no studies link young children's development in immigrant families to coethnic concentration.

# Everyday Experiences of Social Settings

Undocumented parents may experience differences in access to and enrollment of their children in public programs and services that make a difference in their everyday lives, and in the quality of their housing and work environments.

## Public Policy

Recent changes in federal welfare policy may have affected household economic security and the health and well-being of young children of undocumented parents. For this discussion, it is important to recall that the vast majority of children under 6 with at least one undocumented parent are in fact citizens and thus are eligible for many means-tested programs. As the main vehicle for welfare reform, the Personal Responsibility and Work Opportunity Reconciliation Act of 1996 (PRWORA) introduced restrictions on immigrants' eligibility for many health and social service programs, including cash welfare assistance (Temporary Aid to Needy Families, which replaced the Aid to Families with Dependent Children program), food stamps, and subsidized health insurance (Medicaid and the State Children's Health Insurance Program). Although undocumented immigrants were ineligible for these major public assistance programs both before and after PRWORA (Capps & Fortuny, 2006), steep caseload declines occurred in the wake of welfare reform among immigrant populations who remained eligible for assistance because of their children's United States citizenship (Fix & Passel, 1999; Haider, Schoeni, Bao, & Danielson, 2004; Van Hook & Balistreri, 2006).

Similarly, health insurance coverage and access to a regular source of health care have declined since 1996 among citizen children in low-income immigrant families, compared to low-income citizen children with United States-born mothers (Kalil & Ziol-Guest, 2009; Kaushal & Kaestner, 2005). Lurie (2008) found substantial declines since 1996 in health insurance coverage among citizen children of nonpermanent but not of permanent residents.

Together, these results suggest that parents with more precarious immigration statuses may be reluctant to use public programs in the wake of welfare reform, despite their children's eligibility. Ortega et al. (2007) found lower rates of health care use and regular medical care among undocumented immigrants than among the documented. In their large California sample, undocumented Mexicans had 1.6 fewer physician visits in the last year, and other undocumented Latinos had 2.1 fewer visits, than did their United States-born counterparts. Undocumented Mexicans were also less likely to have a usual source of care.

Undocumented parents may be reluctant to seek public assistance, even if their children are eligible, because of confusion about eligibility or fear that program use will hurt their children's future opportunities (Shields & Behrman, 2004).

Undocumented parents may not be aware of their United States-born children's eligibility for important benefits, in part because of low English proficiency but also because fewer members of their networks use these benefits than in networks of documented immigrants. One survey of low-income immigrants in New York City and Los Angeles in 1999 and 2000 showed that half the respondents answered the majority of questions about program eligibility incorrectly (Capps, Ku, & Fix, 2002). Immigrant noncitizens are less likely to be aware of community programs and health services than their native and naturalized citizen counterparts (Yu, Huang, Schwalberg, & Kogan, 2005). Children's development may be at risk if their parents fail to use needed programs and services. Such circumstances lead to missed opportunities for enhancing these children's development.

## Preschool Education

Groups with high proportions of undocumented immigrants appear to take up preschool education for their children at lower rates than groups with lower proportions (Crosnoe, 2006; Hernandez, Denton, & Macartney, 2008; Kalil & Crosnoe, 2009; Magnuson, Lahaie, & Waldfogel, 2006; Matthews & Ewan, 2006). For example, Mexican and Central American children ages 3–5 show particularly low rates of preschool enrollment (Matthews & Ewan, 2006). This pattern occurs even though parental preferences for preschool are not lower among these groups than among others (Garcia & Jensen, 2007). This is unfortunate given the benefits of preschool education for low-income children's cognitive development (Gormley, Gayer, Phillips, & Dawson, 2005).

## Housing and Work

Access to housing assistance is another policy-related challenge for families with undocumented parents. Because undocumented immigrants are categorically ineligible for federal housing subsidies or public housing, doubling up often occurs in their households. One study of undocumented farmworker households found that roughly 40% of farmworkers' homes had more than one adult per room and much lower rates of washers or dryers in the home than in the general United States rural population (Early et al., 2006). More crowded housing appears not only to lower children's academic achievement but also to raise their blood pressure and the likelihood of behavior problems at school (Evans, Lepore, Shejwal, & Palsane, 1998).

Finally, work conditions appear worse among undocumented than among documented workers, even after adjusting for human capital differences. A recent study found higher rates of wage violations (wages below legal minimum) among undocumented than among documented workers in Los Angeles, Chicago, and New York (Bernhardt et al., 2009). Also, substantially lower wage growth, very low autonomy or self-direction in job duties, and fewer benefits were reported among groups with high proportions than among low proportions undocumented in a sample of Latino low-income parents with young children (Yoshikawa, 2011). These differences were robust to controls for indicators of parental education. They may occur for multiple reasons, including reluctance to ask for wage increases, lower job skills, formal paperwork and identification requirements in better quality jobs, and language barriers. Research shows that these negative aspects of the low-wage labor market can hurt the cognitive and emotional development of low-income children (Johnson, Kalil, & Dunifon, 2010; Yoshikawa, Godfrey, & Rivera, 2008).

# Family and Child Processes

Some developmental contexts associated with undocumented status directly affect children's development, whereas others convey their influence through family processes. The influences of these mechanisms, we argue, occur above and beyond their status as mediating mechanisms for other contextual factors (such as poverty or neighborhood violence). Principles of multifinality and equifinality in developmental science (Cicchetti & Rogosch, 1996) suggest that different predictors can affect the same mechanisms, and that the different predictors (in this case, undocumented status and poverty) may have unique causal effects, even if they occur through similar mediators.

Some family processes are more implicated than others. A recent study found no evidence, for example, of differences among groups with high, moderate, and low proportions undocumented in parental goals for children's learning (Ng et al., 2009). Thus, it appears that undocumented parents care just as much about their children's learning. However, economic investments in children, which are linked to early language and cognitive skills, may be lower in families with undocumented parents. Such investments in the early years include books, toys, and other learning or print materials. Many facets of undocumented parents' experiences can limit their chances to make such these investments.

Other features of developmental contexts associated with undocumented status might increase parental stress. Fears of deportation, lower work quality, and crowded housing conditions can lead to psychological distress and parenting stress. Parental stress affects children's socioemotional development through parenting practices such as less warmth or more harshness, and through biological processes such as higher chronic levels of salivary cortisol (Ashman, Dawson, Panagiotides, Yamada, & Wilkins, 2002; Gershoff et al., 2007; Lupien, King, Meaney, & McEwen, 2000).

A particular concern for some groups of young children of undocumented parents is the fact that their parents send their infants and young children back to the country of origin for extended periods (Suárez-Orozco, Todorova, & Louie, 2002). Long-term separations during infancy appear to result from the high costs of child care, especially when family members in the United States who could take care of the infant are absent and debts to smugglers are large (as in the case of low-income Chinese immigrant parents; Yoshikawa, 2011). The long-term effects of parent—child separations in the first years of life are unknown; however, attachment theory would suggest that there may be adjustment problems after transition back to the United States in early childhood.

Undocumented parents also face the risk of involuntary (and sometimes permanent) separation from their children through loss of parental rights due to encounters with the criminal justice system in the United States. A recent study of 900 undocumented adults who experienced workplace arrests in three sites found that 500 children were affected, with over half of the children under the age of 5 and 66% of them United States citizens (Chaudry et al., 2010). Immediate effects on families included loss of child care; dramatic loss of income; difficulty obtaining basic needs for children such as food, diapers, formula, and clothing; and reluctance to go to agencies to obtain emergency assistance. Longer term changes occurred, such as social isolation, depressive symptoms and suicidal ideation among remaining caregivers, and anxiety, depression, and post-traumatic stress disorder in children.

## Conclusion

Early childhood is a crucial but still overlooked period for the study of children in immigrant families. Children of undocumented parents face unique challenges to their development, above and beyond socioeconomic risk. As we have described here, undocumented status is associated with adversity in several key contexts for child development. Whether and in what ways undocumented status is ultimately associated with children's developmental outcomes remains poorly understood. Unfortunately, significant data limitations have impeded progress, as it is rare for national data sets to collect information on immigrant parents' legal status. Nevertheless, developmental theory suggests that linkages are likely to exist, given associations of undocumented status with contextual characteristics that are known to affect children's development. Associations, however, may differ by developmental domain because of differences in associations between particular contexts and children's development. For example, early childhood education is associated with stronger impacts on early child cognitive skills than socioemotional (center-based care between birth and age 5 is associated with slight increases in antisocial behavior; NICHD Early Child Care Research Network, 2005). Any links between undocumented status and lower preschool enrollment rates may therefore have different implications for young children's cognitive versus socioemotional development.

We argue for more systematic collection of parents' legal status, as well as further theoretical work on the important contexts for development among children of undocumented parents. All such research must protect the identities of undocumented parents. Earlier research has done this sensitively, such as in ethnographies, in one-time data collection efforts that have not collected personal information, and in survey studies conducted by estimating numbers of the undocumented from the residual group identified through questions asking whether participants have citizenship and whether they have green cards or refugee status. We also again acknowledge that our conceptual model applies to early childhood development. A model that addresses the effects of parental undocumented status on adolescent development must include many other factors, including greater variation in youths' own legal status; knowledge and perceptions of their status, experiences of discrimination,

and different mechanisms of developmental effects, including, for example, youths' own work and family responsibilities. Progress in examining effects of parental documentation status on children of multiple developmental stages has the potential to inform not only basic knowledge in developmental science but also immigration and family policy.

## References

Ashman, S. B., Dawson, G., Panagiotides, H., Yamada, E., & Wilkins, C. W. (2002). Stress hormone levels of children of depressed mothers. *Development and Psychopathology, 14,* 333–349.

Bernhardt, A., Milkman, R., Theodore, N., Heckathorn, D., Auer, M., DeFilipppi, J., et al. (2009). *Broken laws, unprotected workers: Violations of employment and labor laws in America's cities.* New York: National Employment Law Project.

Borjas, G. J. (2006). Making it in America: Social mobility and immigrants. *The Future of Children, 16,* 55–71.

Capps, R., & Fortuny, K. (2006). *Immigration and child and family policy.* Washington, DC: Urban Institute.

Capps, R., Ku, L., & Fix, M. (2002). *How immigrants are faring: Preliminary evidence from Los Angeles and New York City.* Washington, DC: Urban Institute.

Chaudry, A., Capps, R., Pedroza, J., Castaneda, R. M., Santos, R., & Scott, M. M. (2010). *Facing our future: Children in the aftermath of immigration enforcement.* Washington, DC: Urban Institute.

Chiswick, B. R., & Miller, P. W. (2005). Do enclaves matter in immigrant adjustment? *City and Community, 4,* 5–36.

Cicchetti, D., & Rogosch, F. A. (1996). Multifinality and equifinality in developmental psychopathology. *Development and Psychopathology, 8,* 597–600.

Crosnoe, R. (2006). *Mexican roots, American schools: Helping Mexican immigrant children succeed.* Palo Alto, CA: Stanford University Press.

Crosnoe, R. (2007). Early child care and the school readiness of children from Mexican immigrant families. *International Migration Review, 41,* 152–181.

Cunha, F., & Heckman, J. (2007). The technology of skill formation. *American Economic Review, 97,* 31–47.

Duncan, G., Ziol-Guest, K., & Kalil, A. (2010). Early childhood poverty and adult attainment, behavior, and health. *Child Development, 81,* 292–311.

Early, J., Davis, S. W., Quandt, S. A., Rao, P., Snively, B. M., & Arcury, T. A. (2006). Housing characteristics of farmworker families in North Carolina. *Journal of Immigrant and Minority Health, 8,* 173–184.

Evans, G. W., Lepore, S. J., Shejwal, B. R., & Palsane, M. N. (1998). Chronic residential crowding and children's well being: An ecological perspective. *Child Development, 69,* 1514–1523.

Fix, M., & Passel, J. (1999). *Trends in noncitizens' and citizens' use of public benefits following welfare reform.* Washington, DC: Urban Institute.

Fuller, B., Bridges, M., Bein, E., Jang, H., Jung, S., Rabe-Hesketh, S., et al. (2009). The health and cognitive growth of Latino toddlers: At risk or immigrant paradox? *Maternal and Child Health Journal, 13,* 755–768.

Garcia, E., & Jensen, B. (2007). Helping young Hispanic learners. *Educational Leadership, March,* 34–39.

Gershoff, E. T., Aber, J. L., Raver, C. C., & Lennon, M. C. (2007). Income is not enough: Incorporating material hardship into models of income associations with parenting and child development. *Child Development, 78,* 70–95.

Gormley, W. T., Gayer, T., Phillips, D. A., & Dawson, B. (2005). The effects of universal pre-K on children's cognitive development. *Developmental Psychology, 41,* 872–884.

Guarnaccia, P. J., & Lopez, S. (1998). The mental health and adjustment of immigrant and refugee children. *Child and Adolescent Psychiatry Clinics of North America, 7,* 537–553.

Haider, S. J., Schoeni, R. F., Bao, Y., & Danielson, C. (2004). Immigrants, welfare reform, and the economy. *Journal of Policy Analysis and Management, 23,* 745–764.

Han, W. (2006). Academic achievements of children in immigrant families. *Educational Research and Reviews, 1,* 286–318.

Hernandez, D. (2004). Demographic change and life circumstances of immigrant families. *The Future of Children, 14,* 17–47.

Hernandez, D., Denton, S., & Macartney, S. E. (2008). Children in immigrant families: Looking to America's future. *Social Policy Reports of the Society for Research in Child Development, 22*(3), 1–22.

Hoefer, M., Rytina, C., & Baker, B. C. (2010). *Estimates of the unauthorized immigrant population residing in the United States.* Washington, DC: U.S. Department of Homeland Security.

Johnson, R. C., Kalil, A., & Dunifon, R. (2010). *Mothers' work and children's lives: Low-income families after welfare reform.* Kalamazoo, MI: W.E. Upjohn Institute for Employment Research.

Kalil, A., & Chen, J. (2008). Mothers' citizenship status and household food insecurity among low-income children of immigrants. *New Directions in Child and Adolescent Development, 121,* 43–62.

Kalil, A., & Crosnoe, R. (2009). Two generations of educational progress in Latin American immigrant families in the U.S.: A conceptual framework for a new policy context. In E. Grigorenko & R. Takanishi (Eds.), *Immigration, diversity, and education* (pp. 188–204). New York: Routledge.

Kalil, A., & Ziol-Guest, K. (2009). Welfare reform and health among the children of immigrants. In J. Ziliak (Ed.), *Welfare reform and its long-term consequences for America's poor* (pp. 308–336). Cambridge, UK: Cambridge University Press.

Kaushal, N., & Kaestner, R. (2005). Welfare reform and health insurance of immigrants. *Health Services Research, 40,*697–722.

Lupien, S. J., King, S., Meaney, M. J., & McEwen, B. S. (2000). Child's stress hormone levels correlate with mother's socioeconomic status and depressive state. *Biological Psychiatry, 48,* 976–980.

Lurie, I. (2008). Welfare reform and the decline in the health-insurance coverage of children of non-permanent residents. *Journal of Health Economics, 27,* 786–793.

Magnuson, K., Lahaie, C., & Waldfogel, J. (2006). Preschool and school readiness of children of immigrants. *Social Science Quarterly, 87,* 1241–1262.

Massey, D. S., & Espinosa, K. E. (1997). What's driving US-Mexico migration? A theoretical, empirical, and policy analysis. *American Journal of Sociology, 102,* 939–999.

Matthews, H., & Ewan, D. (2006). *Reaching all children? Understanding early care and education participation among immigrant families.* Washington, DC: Center for Law and Social Policy.

Motomura, H. (2008). Immigration outside the law. *Columbia Law Review, 108,* 2037–2097.

Ng, F. F., Godfrey, E. B., Hunter, C. J., Tamis-LeMonda, C. S., Yoshikawa, H., & Kahana-Kalman, R. (2009, April). Mothers' socialization goals for children in the first years of life: Developmental, ethnic and economic differences. In F. Ng & C. S. Tamis-LeMonda (Chairs), *Parental goals for children: the roles of cultural and social contexts.* Symposium presented at the biennial meeting of the Society for Research in Child Development, Denver, CO.

Ngai, M. (2004). *Impossible subjects: Illegal aliens and the making of modern America.* Princeton, NJ: Princeton University Press.

NICHD Early Child Care Research Network. (2005). Early child care and children's development in the primary grades: Follow-up results from the NICHD Study of Early Child Care. *American Educational Research Journal, 42,* 537–570.

Ortega, A. N., Fang, H., Perez, V. H., Rizzo, J. H., Carter-Pokras, O., Wallace, S. P., et al. (2007). Health care access, use of services, and experiences among undocumented Mexicans and other Latinos. *Archives of Internal Medicine, 167,* 2354–2360.

Ortega, A. N., Horwitz, S. M., Fang, H., Kuo, A. A., Wallace,S. P., & Inkelas, M. (2009). Documentation status and parental concerns about development in young US children of Mexican origin. *Academic Pediatrics, 9,* 278–282.

Passel, J., & Cohn, D. (2009). *A portrait of unauthorized immigrants in the United States.* Washington, DC: Pew Hispanic Center.

Preston, J. (2009, April 30). Democrats reframe debate on immigration. *New York Times,* p. A1.

Scribner, R. (1996). Paradox as paradigm: The health outcomes of Mexican Americans. *American Journal of Public Health, 86,* 303–305.

Shields, M. K., & Behrman, R. E. (2004). Children of immigrant families: Analysis and recommendations. *The Future of Children, 14*(2), 4–16.

Shonkoff, J. P., Boyce, W. T., & McEwen, T. S. (2009). Neuroscience, molecular biology, and the childhood roots of health disparities: Building a new framework for health promotion and disease prevention. *Journal of the American Medical Association, 301,* 2252–2259.

Small, M. L., & McDermott, M. (2006). The presence of organizational resources in poor urban neighborhoods: An analysis of average and contextual effects. *Social Forces, 84,* 1697–1724.

Suárez-Orozco, C., Todorova, I., & Louie, J. (2002). Making up for lost time: The experience of separations and reunifications among immigrant families. *Family Process, 41,* 625–643.

Tienda, M., & Mitchell, F. (Eds.). (2006). *Hispanics and the future of America.* Washington, DC: National Academy Press.

Van Hook, J., & Balistreri, K. (2006). Ineligible parents, eligible children: Food Stamps receipt, allotments, and food insecurity among children of immigrants. *Social Science Research, 35,* 228–251.

Yoshikawa, H. (2011). *Immigrants raising citizens: Undocumented parents and their young children.* New York: Russell Sage Foundation.

Yoshikawa, H., Godfrey, E. B., & Rivera, A. C. (2008). Access to institutional resources as a measure of social exclusion: Relations with family process and cognitive development in the context of immigration. *New Directions in Child and Adolescent Development, 121,* 73–96.

Yu, S. M., Huang, Z. J., Schwalberg, R. H., & Kogan, M. D. (2005). Parental awareness of health and community resources among immigrant families. *Maternal and Child Health Journal, 9,* 27–34.

Zhou, M. (2001). Chinese: Divergent destinies in immigrant New York. In N. Foner (Ed.), *New immigrants in New York* (2nd ed., pp. 141–172). New York: Columbia University Press.

# Critical Thinking

1. What are some ways that children's cultural background and experiences affect the development of children's social and cognitive skills?

2. Is a child's slow development simply due to the undocumented status of his or her parents or the disadvantages that come along with the status (e.g., type of job, health insurance, income)?

3. What kinds of policies would help these immigrant children succeed better in school and life?

This work was supported by grants from the National Science Foundation (NSF BCS-0721383) to Yoshikawa and a Foundation for Child Development Young Scholars grant to Kalil. We thank Ruby Takanishi for helpful comments on an earlier draft of this manuscript.

Correspondence concerning this article should be addressed to HIROKAZU YOSHIKAWA, Graduate School of Education, 704 Larsen, Harvard University, University, Cambridge, MA 02138; e-mail: hiro_yoshikawa@harvard.edu; akalil@uchicago.edu.

From *Child Development Perspectives*, vol. 5, no. 4, 2011, pp. 291–297. Copyright © 2011 by the Hirokazu Yoshikawa and Ariel Kalil. Published by the Society for Research in Child Development. Reprinted by permission of Wiley-Blackwell.

# Is Technology Ruining Our Kids?

**Not according to public health researcher Michele Ybarra, who outlined why, in general, there is little cause for alarm.**

Tori DeAngellis

Young people are using new technologies at ever-increasing rates, with 93 percent of young people now online, 73 percent on MySpace or Facebook, and 75 percent owning cell phones, up from 63 percent who owned cellphones in 2006, according to data from the Pew Internet American Life Project.

With this increased access comes greater worry for parents, teachers and counselors, whose anxiety is fueled by media reports of young people engaging in "sexting"—sending provocative photos of themselves to others via cell phone—and concerns that new technologies might create more avenues for bullying and harassment.

But are these fears realistic? No, said APA 2011 Annual Convention invited speaker Michele Ybarra, PhD, a public health and child mental health researcher who is president and research director of the nonprofit research organization Internet Solutions for Kids. Citing data from two ongoing studies, Ybarra said it's time to calm our nerves, save perhaps for a small group of young people who report being distressed by bullying and an even smaller number who "sext" and simultaneously report engaging in other forms of sexual activity.

"We need to better identify youth who are struggling and likely need individual help," said Ybarra. But at the same time, she said, we should refuse to give in to fear-mongering and hyperbolic statements about technology because the data simply don't support the idea that technology is changing or encouraging bullying, sexting or other types of harassment.

## Bullies Online

To examine how new technologies may be changing behaviors, including bullying and harassment, Ybarra tracked about 1,600 young people from 2006 to 2008 as part of the ongoing longitudinal Growing up with Media study funded by the Centers for Disease Control and Prevention. She asked young people ages 10 to 15 about levels of bullying—defined as ongoing, repetitive peer aggression or victimization that is marked by a power differential between bully and victim—and harassment,

a larger umbrella term that encompasses mean and rude comments, threatening and aggressive behaviors, spreading rumors and other annoying or hurtful behaviors.

Despite media reports suggesting an increase in the amount and intensity of online bullying, it's no more common or distressing than it was three years ago, Ybarra's data show. And many young people escape cyberbullying and harassment altogether: About 62 percent are not victims each year, compared with 24 percent who are harassed but not bullied, 13 percent who are both harassed and bullied, and 1 percent who are bullied only, she found.

Data on where and how bullying takes place also suggest inflated concerns about technology's impact, Ybarra said. About 40 percent of bullying still takes place in person, compared with 10 percent through phone calls, 14 percent by text messages, 17 percent online and 10 percent in some other way.

For many youngsters, bullying is also limited to a single place and communication type, her data also show: 21 percent who reported bullying said it happened only through one mode, while 11 percent said they were bullied via two modes, for example in person and online. When asked about distressing experiences, twice as many young people said they were very or extremely upset by the bullying that occurred at school compared to online. The one technological arena where bullying may be increasing is text messaging, but more tracking is needed to see if that is an actual trend, Ybarra said.

A small group of youngsters is cause for concern, however, she said: Twelve percent of those surveyed said they were bullied in several places and through several modes—in person, online and by phone, for example. In addition, about one in four study participants aged 12 to 15 who reported any bullying or harassment also reported high levels of distress, she found.

Given that other research she and others have conducted shows that young people harassed and bullied online are more likely to be bullied off line and to report more depression, suicidal ideation, alcohol use, social problems and poor caregiver relations, better monitoring to more quickly identify struggling youth is warranted, she said.

"These data suggest that some young people who are being harassed and bullied online are likely facing multiple challenges across multiple areas," she said.

## What about Sex?

The newer technologies also don't appear to be driving many more children and teens into accessing sexual content, Ybarra's data show. For the most part, they are still finding it the old-fashioned way: in TV shows, movies and music. Some 75 percent of young people said that at least some of the TV shows and movies they watched showed people kissing, fondling or having sex, while 69 percent said songs they listened to contained sexual content. By comparison, 19 percent of youth said that at least some of the games they played showed people kissing, fondling or having sex, and 25 percent said at least some of the websites they go to featured similar material.

"Yes, they're being exposed to sex online, and yes, they're being exposed to sex in video games," she said. "But if you want to affect the rates of young people's exposure to sexual material, I'd focus on television and music."

Ybarra's data also show that teens' rates of watching pornography rises by age but not across time. For instance, in 2010, young people were no more likely to visit X-rated websites than they were in 2006, although as they got older, they were more likely to seek it out.

"That's what you'd expect. These trends match the developmental trajectory of typical adolescent sexual development," she said.

Sexting, too, fails to match the hype, Ybarra said. According to Positive Youth Development, an ongoing study of 3,777 young people funded by the National Institute of Child Health and Development, only 3 percent of boys and 6 percent of girls ages 13 to 18 reported sexting—sending or showing someone sexual pictures of yourself where you are nude or nearly nude. Girls were twice as likely to sext as boys, and sexting increases as young people get older.

Because sexting is strongly associated with other types of sexual behavior including kissing, fondling and oral sex, sexting may be a marker of risky sexual behavior more generally, she added. But it's unclear whether the behavior of this small group should provoke serious worry, or whether in some cases it is simply a normal expression of developing sexuality, Ybarra said. In fact, stalking—both in person and via all technology types—is much more prevalent than sexting. And because stalking in any form is unwanted, unsolicited and potentially dangerous, it represents greater cause for concern, she said.

## The Bright Side

Despite doom-and-gloom prognoses about young people's entanglement with these technologies, they actually offer a wealth of ways to promote this age group's mental, social and physical well-being, Ybarra said. Examples include exercise programs like "Dance Dance Revolution" and websites for young people with chronic illnesses that can help them understand and manage their conditions.

Technology can likewise be a powerful social tool for young people, especially those who might feel isolated, her data show. Lesbian, gay, bisexual and transgender youth, for instance, are more likely than heterosexual youth to report using the Internet to make friends. They're also much more likely to say their online friends listen better and are more understanding, less judgmental and more likely to let them be themselves.

In sum, while new technologies might land some youngsters in more trouble than they would have gotten in otherwise, the Internet and cellphone are at least as likely to be a boon for this age group, Ybarra concluded.

"For young people who may feel more isolated and socially stigmatized—and in fact for young people in general—the Internet may be an incredibly positive influence that allows them to make friends and connect with others in healthy ways."

## Critical Thinking

1. Based on the evidence in this article, how concerned should parents and society be about the effects of technology on children?

2. Even if parents worry too much about technology affecting their children, should they still worry to some degree? Are there certain types of children who may be particularly vulnerable to negative effects of technology?

3. What are some positive effects of technology?

**TORI DEANGELIS** is a writer in Syracuse, N.Y.

# UNIT 5

# Cultural and Societal Influences

## Unit Selections

## Learning Outcomes

- Explain how globalization is shaping children's development in the 21st century in ways that child development in earlier eras was not affected.

- Describe ways in which children's understanding of globalization changes shape how children are influenced by such changes.

- Identify three concrete examples from American society that illustrate our emphasis on independence and individualism.

- Explain why it is not helpful to use independence and interdependence as a dichotomy or dualism. What is gained when we think of these values in more complex ways?

- Prepare a presentation for American parents to help them understand the possible advantages of promoting both independence and interdependence in their children.

- Design your own prevention program that would reduce the likelihood of post-traumatic stress for children who are abused or disturbed from other kinds of trauma.

- Critique the different kinds of treatment for PTSD offered in the reading.

- Explain to parents the ways in which their children learn eating habits in their early years and what methods can be adopted to teach them healthy eating practices effectively.

- Assess familiar techniques (e.g., those that your parents used) and programs that are designed to encourage healthy eating.

- Explain the ways in which adverse childhood experience can have long-term effects on an adult's mental and physical health.

- Justify why, in attempting to prevent medical illnesses like heart disease, efforts to reduce or counteract the effects of adverse childhood experiences are just as legitimate as efforts to lower cholesterol.

- Prepare a presentation for parents and teachers on ADHD and controversies surrounding its incidence and treatment

- Critique the different kinds of therapies for ADHD, from medical to behavioral.

- Relate to parents of children with autism the sources of gratification that can be found in the experience of developmental gains, seeing their child happy, spending time with their child, and other examples.

- Justify the need for more studies on the positives of caregiving for autistic children.

- Based on the research, advise pediatricians on how to increase chronically ill children's adherence to treatment.

- Design an educational program to help children and parents stick to their treatment programs.

- Describe the benefits of outdoor experience for the health and cognition of children as well as its long-term benefits in fostering a sense of responsibility for the environment.

- Advocate for the implementation of programs and practices that give children first-hand experience with nature.

- Explain how children may have a fundamental and developmentally important connection to nature.

- Reflect on the different psychological benefits for children that come from owning a pet in childhood.

# Student Website
www.mhhe.com/cls

# Internet References

**Association to Benefit Children (ABC)**
www.a-b-c.org
**Children's Defense Fund**
www.childrensdefense.org
**Children Now**
www.childrennow.org
**Council for Exceptional Children**
www.cec.sped.org
**Prevent Child Abuse America**
www.preventchildabuse.org

Social scientists and developmental psychologists have come to realize that children are influenced by a multitude of complex social forces. In this unit we present articles to illuminate how children and adolescents are influenced by broad factors such as economics, culture, politics, and the media. These influences also affect the family, which is a major context of child development, and many children are now faced with more family challenges than ever. In addition, analysis of exceptional or atypical children gives the reader a more comprehensive account of child development. Thus, articles are presented on special challenges of development, such as the effects of autism, child abuse, ADHD, globalization, chronic illness, and challenges associated with rising incidence of obesity and other circumstances.

Today's society is more complex than ever and children from at-risk families face growing challenges. New research has begun to focus on how the changing globalization of society may influence children's growth and development. For example, how is the advent of ubiquitous technology and communication access, privatization of health, education, and welfare institutions, and international political agreements affecting children today associated with risks or benefits for young children?

It is horrific to know that the reality is that each year, millions of children suffer child abuse at the hands of parents and others. The author of "More Support Needed for Trauma Interventions" describes how children may require a number of interventions and treatments to adjust. Although these articles are sometimes difficult to read, as future parents, teachers, and professionals, it is important for us to learn more about these difficult and challenging situations in order to find ways to improve and solve future problems for children and their families.

Our fast-paced, convenience-fueled lifestyles have forever changed America's palate and eating habits and in many ways have contributed to an epidemic of child obesity. In the past, experts have advocated for parents to help restrict their obese children's diets in order to see a drop in weight. Unfortunately, these efforts generally do not produce enduring and sustained weight loss in children. Instead, today experts are calling for parents, families, schools, and society to shift the focus from weight loss to making lifestyle changes for children that include integrating exercise into a daily routine and reconnecting children with nature and outdoor activity.

Some children must cope with special psychological, emotional, and cognitive challenges such as ADHD, autism, and chronic illness. Such children are often misunderstood and mistreated and pose special challenges. The author of "The Positives of Caregiving: Mothers' Experiences Caregiving for a Child with Autism" present positive, even joyful experiences of

Simon Jarratt/Corbis

resilient mothers who cope effectively with raising an autistic child and provide useful strategies for parents faced with similar situations. Similarly, in "Caring for Chronically Ill Kids," the author describes the challenges and parenting practices that may help families care for a child who suffers from a chronic illness. The author of "ADHD among Preschoolers" summarizes the debate and the research regarding the prevalence of ADHD among young children and helps parents understand both the pros and cons of medication and behavioral therapy and also discusses how schools can better support children with ADHD.

Finally, author Patrick Lee in "The Human Child's Nature Orientation" posits that young children are inherently grounded in a "nature orientation" that holds primacy for concepts and constructs related to animals, pets, plant life, parks, nature, and other outdoor settings and that this orientation shows developmental progression with age. He argues that this fundamental nature orientation is critical to the child's humanization process and also may have implications for 21st-century environmental issues and policies that affect children.

# Independence and Interdependence in Children's Developmental Experiences

CATHERINE RAEFF

A t least since the 1980s, it has been common to discuss cultural differences in behavior and development in terms of individualism and collectivism (Hofstede, 1980/2001). Individualism and collectivism refer to cultural ways of understanding and structuring independence and interdependence. Independence generally refers to aspects of human functioning that involve being a physically and mentally separate individual. Interdependence generally refers to aspects of human functioning that involve being connected to others. Insofar as major cultural differences in behavior and development involve independence and interdependence issues, it is important to consider child development in relation to the complexities of cultural understandings of independence and interdependence.

The goal of this article is to review theory and research that point to how independence and interdependence issues shape children's developmental experiences. First, a theoretical overview outlines a move from understanding cultures as either individualistic or collectivistic to discerning how aspects of both independence and interdependence are understood in culturally distinct ways. Then a review of cross-cultural research examines cultural conceptions of children's independence and interdependence and various ways of structuring each. This review is followed by a discussion of within-culture variability in conceptions of children's independence and interdependence.

## From Cultural Dichotomies to Cultural Complexities

Considerations of independence and interdependence in the social sciences were initially dominated by dichotomous perspectives that characterized cultures as either individualistic or collectivistic, with primary independence or interdependence orientations, respectively. Western cultures have been characterized in terms of independence, and European-American culture is usually considered to represent the epitome of an independence orientation. Independence cultures are assumed to value and promote such goals as self-expression, self-fulfillment, making individual choices, engaging in self-direction, and defining oneself separately from others. In contrast, the other

cultures of the world have been classified together as interdependence oriented. Interdependence cultures are assumed to value and promote such goals as, conformity, concern for others' needs, pursuing group interests, maintaining social cohesion, and defining oneself in relation to others. However, criticisms of dichotomous approaches emerged early (e.g., Turiel, 1983; Waterman, 1981), and arguments were subsequently made against labeling cultures as either individualistic or collectivistic, and against characterizing cultures in terms of either independence or interdependence.

One argument against such dichotomous characterizations proceeds from the basic premise that all people are physically and mentally separate and simultaneously socially connected. Accordingly, a meta-analysis of individualism and collectivism studies shows that *both* independence and interdependence are valued in diverse cultures (Oyserman, Coon, & Kemmelmeier, 2002). It is further argued that even though conceptions of independence and interdependence may conflict, independence and interdependence can also be understood as compatible and coexisting aspects of childrearing goals (Killen & Wainryb, 2000; Tamis-LeMonda et al., 2008). Kagitcibasi (2005) posited that self-direction and relatedness are universal and compatible human needs. Together, they comprise a cultural model of emotional interdependence whereby children are socialized to be self-directing, but not separate from others.

Another argument against dichotomous cultural representations of independence and interdependence is based on the position that cultures are heterogeneous, dynamic, and complex (e.g., Gjerde, 2004; Killen & Wainryb, 2000). Thus, even if a culture could be classified in terms of a preponderance of either independence or interdependence, it does not mean that the other is not important. To understand cultural complexities, it is necessary to discern cultural ways of understanding both independence and interdependence. Insofar as cultures are dynamic, they change historically. Classifying cultures in terms of either independence or interdependence reflects a static view of culture and does not account for changing conceptions of independence and interdependence.

A consensus is emerging that independence and interdependence are not always understood in opposition, and that cultures around the world value both. Thus, there is a move away from labeling cultures as either individualistic and independence oriented, or collectivistic and interdependence oriented. Instead, efforts are increasingly directed toward discerning culturally distinct modes of both independence and interdependence. Regarding child development, the question then becomes, How are both independence and interdependence understood and valued in relation to children's development in different cultures? Space limitations preclude a comprehensive review of relevant research. Accordingly, the empirical examples in the following discussion were chosen to emphasize cross-cultural comparisons and within-culture variability.

# Children's Independence and Interdependence across Cultures

The bulk of developmental research on independence and interdependence is descriptive, relying on parents' and teachers' responses to interviews and questionnaires to discern cultural conceptions of children's independence and interdependence. In addition, following from the position that development occurs as children participate with others in cultural practices (Rogoff, 2003), analyses have included observations of children as they engage in varied cultural practices. Cultural practices consist of "actions that are repeated, shared with others in a social group, and invested with normative expectations and with meanings or significances that go beyond the immediate goals of the action" (Miller & Goodnow, 1995, p. 7). Thus, analyses of children's participation in cultural practices can provide information about the structuring of children's independent and interdependent action. Moreover, insofar as cultural meanings or conceptions are enacted in cultural practices, such analyses can provide further insight into cultural ways of understanding and valuing children's independence and interdependence.

## Cultural Conceptions of Children's Independence and Interdependence

Research reveals varied cultural conceptions of independence and interdependence. For example, regarding interdependence, there are cultural differences in understanding relationships as voluntary and egalitarian, as duty based and hierarchical, and as empathy based (Miller, 2006). Regarding children's interdependence, one comparative study suggests that European-American parents want their children to engage with others by choice, whereas Latino parents expect their children to fulfill obligations to promote group welfare (Raeff, Greenfield, & Quiroz, 2000). These different conceptions of interdependence are in keeping with European-American traditions of voluntary and egalitarian relationships, and Latino traditions of valuing family duties and hierarchical relationships.

Cultural variability is especially likely for conceptions of independence and interdependence because these constructs encompass multifaceted components. In one comparative study of childrearing values (Wang & Tamis-LeMonda, 2003), European-American mothers favored interdependence in the forms of love and attachment to family and compassion and consideration, whereas Taiwanese mothers favored politeness, humility, getting along with others, and following social rules. Regarding multifaceted independence dimensions, the European-American mothers mentioned the importance of individuality more often than the Taiwanese mothers did, whereas the Taiwanese mothers mentioned the importance of achievement more often than did the European-American mothers. The Taiwanese mothers also viewed diligence and assertiveness as more important than did the European-American mothers, who, in turn, rated self-esteem more highly than the Taiwanese mothers did. These findings suggest that multifaceted components of independence and interdependence are understood and valued in culturally distinct ways.

More than coexisting orthogonally, cultural conceptions are parts of wider cultural value systems, whereby multifaceted independence and interdependence components are taken to be understood in relation to each other. For example, independence and interdependence may be understood as functionally dependent, whereby one "serves[s] the function of promoting the other" (Tamis-LeMonda et al., 2008, p.193). They may also be understood as mutually constitutive (Raeff, 2006a). Ethnographic interviews indicate that some middle-income American mothers value self-esteem in part because it enables children to "interact well with others and form healthy relationships" (Miller, Wang, Sandel, & Cho, 2002, p. 231). In turn, they believe that children's self-esteem should not become too high, lest children become "conceited, self-centered, egotistical, or self-promoting" (p. 232). In this European-American context, conceptions of independence and interdependence are mutually constitutive as self-esteem makes relationships possible and as relationships provide some parameters for self-esteem. In contrast, Miller et al. (2002) noted that the term *self-esteem* is not easily translated into Taiwanese, and that the Taiwanese mothers did not spontaneously mention self-esteem issues when interviewed. However, recall that in other research, mentioned above, other modes of independence are valued by Taiwanese mothers. Taken together, such research points to the importance of discerning cultural differences in how specific forms of independence and interdependence are understood and valued.

## Children's Independent and Interdependent Action
### Sleeping Arrangements

Research on children's sleeping arrangements has been a key source of data on the structuring of children's independent and interdependent action within cultural practices. Studies show that Western children are likely to sleep separately, which provides opportunities for fostering independent self-direction (Greenfield & Suzuki, 1998; Keller, 2007; Rogoff, 2003). In contrast, cosleeping is common around the world, as a means of fostering close and harmonious family relationships. At the same time, ethnographic research in a Mexican-Mayan community indicates that when children are about 5 years old, they can choose "when, how long, and with whom to sleep" (Gaskins, 1999, p. 40). Thus, there are cultural differences in how independent action is structured within the context of children's sleeping practices. Within separate-sleeping practices, self-direction involves relying on oneself to take care of one's own individual needs. Within cosleeping practices, self-direction involves making individual choices.

The structuring of children's sleeping practices is also informative in that it indicates how independent action and interdependent action are interrelated in culturally distinct ways. For example, research suggests that European-American parents favor separate sleeping for their children to improve their own sleep and also to preserve their dyadic relationship (Richman, Miller, & Solomon, 1988; Shweder, Jensen, & Goldstein, 1995). Thus, independence and interdependence are interrelated as children have opportunities to direct themselves in relation to others. Moreover, structuring children's sleeping practices to conform to parents' schedules is evident in the strategy of putting children to bed even when they are not tired. Thus, the independence of self-direction is inseparable from the interdependence of conforming to others' preferences. As suggested above, when children choose their cosleeping arrangements, the interdependence of group functioning depends partly on individual self-direction.

### Conflict Resolution

Much research has been conducted on the patterning of children's interpersonal interactions during waking hours in varied cultures, and some studies point to culturally distinct ways of structuring children's independent and interdependent action. For example, one study involved observations of conflict interactions between European-American and Guatemalan-Mayan 14-to 20-month-olds and their 3- to 5-year-old siblings when both wanted novel objects. European-American mothers typically treated the siblings equally and often encouraged turn taking so that both children had equal access to the objects (Mosier & Rogoff, 2003). In addition, the older siblings were adept at asserting their individual rights to the objects. In contrast, Guatemalan-Mayan mothers were more likely to ask the older sibling to give up his or her claim to the object and accommodate to the younger child, who is not yet considered capable of understanding the social consequences of personal action. In addition, the Guatemalan-Mayan older siblings found ways to cooperate with the younger children so that both could play with the objects.

These findings suggest that there are different modes of both independence and interdependence being practiced in the two cultural contexts. That is, in both cultures, "children seem to have been learning how to participate in their own community's approach to freedom of choice and social responsibility" (Mosier & Rogoff, p. 1055). Although each European-American child's individual claims to the coveted objects were satisfied by taking turns, each child also had to relinquish an object for some time. Thus, the assertion of individual rights was structured in relation to being considerate of the other. In addition, each child was directing him or herself in relation to the other.

The researchers explain that the Guatemalan-Mayan practice of privileging the younger child occurs within a cultural system of respect for individual freedom of choice. In turn, freedom of choice is believed to provide a basis for voluntary cooperation and to foster being responsible to the group. Thus, independent and interdependent action are mutually constitutive as group functioning is derived from self-direction and as self-direction benefits group functioning. Although the older siblings here gave up more than their European-American counterparts, this situation is one within the wider cultural context of respect for individual freedom and voluntary cooperation. It is assumed that by being accommodated to early in life, people go on to accommodate to others, thus promoting a network of mutual support for individual choices and goals. In addition, the older child's cooperation with the younger sibling enabled both children to "simultaneously meet their separate interests" (Mosier & Rogoff, p. 1056), thus coordinating the independence of pursuing individual goals and the interdependence of cooperation.

## Children's Independence and Interdependence within Cultures

As noted earlier, cultures are complex, dynamic, and heterogeneous, suggesting that cultural conceptions of children's independence and interdependence may be construed in varied ways within cultures. Developmental research points to varied sources of within-culture variability in conceptions of children's independence and interdependence, including societal processes, situational factors, and historical factors.

### Societal Processes

With regard to wider societal processes, it is argued that individuals in different power positions construct different perspectives and goals, which sometimes come into conflict (Gjerde, 2004; Turiel & Wainryb, 2000). Power differentials may be manifest in conceptions of independence and interdependence that vary by gender (e.g., Wainryb, 2006), ethnicity (e.g., Suizzo, 2007), and socioeconomic status. Ethnographic research in three urban American communities (Kusserow, 2004) shows how parents' conceptions of children's independence may vary in relation to their economic circumstances. Upper- and middle-income European-American parents favored a "soft individualism," characterized by "appreciating and developing one's psychological uniqueness and individuality" (Kusserow, p. 82). For them, the keys to happiness and success included developing children's "autonomy, uniqueness, individuality, and self-determination" (Kusserow, p. 84). In contrast, European-Americans in a tightly knit lower income community favored a "hard projective individualism" that was tied to fostering children's eventual economic upward mobility through self-determination, self-assertion, self-confidence, and perseverance. For European-American parents in the poorest community, which was also dangerous and violent, "hard protective individualism" prevailed, but in this case, independence was tied to the parents' "stories of struggle" (Kusserow, p. 57). Parents emphasized "not relying on anyone else" (Kusserow, p. 58), self-determination, and self-confidence as means for their children to overcome hardship.

## Situational Factors

Cultural conceptions are also construed in relation to concrete situational factors (Miller, 2006), which include the developmental characteristics of the people who populate a particular social setting. For example, parents' expectations for their children's independence and interdependence change as children develop (Raeff, 2006a; Tamis-LeMonda et al., 2008). In addition, in some contexts, parents may view independence and interdependence as conflicting and thus prioritize one over the other (Tamis-LeMonda et al., 2008). The self-esteem research mentioned earlier suggests that, in some situations, European-Americans prioritize fostering relationships over an individual child's self-esteem.

Different components of independence and interdependence may also be endorsed across contexts. Research in Japan shows that learning the distinction between inner and outer, or private and public, contexts is a key to understanding Japanese socialization values (e.g., Bachnik, 1992/1995; Doi, 1985/1988). Public or outer contexts include relationships with "meaningful 'outsiders' with whom one must enryo" (show restraint; Kondo, 1990, p. 150) in order to maintain social cohesion. However, people are more likely to express directly individual feelings in private or inner contexts, even if they contradict the feelings or opinions of others (Lebra, 1992/1995). Thus, independence in public contexts involves self-control, while independence in private contexts involves individual self-expression. This example also points to varied interrelations between independence and interdependence across contexts. In public contexts, social cohesion is dependent on self-control. In private contexts, close relationships foster self-expression.

## Historical Factors

An important aspect of cultural change involves historical changes in cultural conceptions. Assuming that aspects of both independence and interdependence are valued in culturally distinct ways, it is important to discern historical changes in conceptions of both independence and interdependence. For example, in the research described above regarding conflict resolution between young siblings, Mosier and Rogoff (2003) reported recent changes among mothers within the Guatemalan-Mayan community in relation to increased educational opportunities. Mothers with more education tended to follow the equal-treatment model, whereas mothers with less education tended to follow the privileged-treatment model. Insofar as both models entail culturally distinct modes of independence and interdependence, there have been changes in both independence and interdependence.

# Implications and Future Directions

Major cultural differences in development may be understood in terms of independence and interdependence issues. The research reviewed here indicates that cultural differences do not lie simply in how much independence or interdependence is valued but in how specific components of independence and interdependence are understood, valued, and structured. Within cultures, conceptions of children's independence and interdependence are dynamic as they vary across contexts and during development, as well as historically. In addition, conceptions of children's independence and interdependence are construed in relation to varied societal processes that permeate the exigencies of people's lives.

Consideration of the complexities of independence and interdependence can be applied in diverse developmental settings. For example, in the United States and around the world, school settings may be populated by immigrant children from cultures whose conceptions and practices sometimes come into conflict with those of the host culture (Greenfield, Keller, Fulgini, & Maynard, 2003). The situation may be further complicated by conflicting within-culture approaches to independence and interdependence. The research discussed here suggests that cultural conflicts such as these may be mitigated by considering that a particular child is developing different ways of understanding and structuring multifaceted components of independence and interdependence. Moreover, it might be possible to incorporate varied cultural approaches to independence and interdependence into school practices, as well as other settings populated by children of diverse cultural backgrounds.

Continued research is needed to discern how multiple facets of children's independence and interdependence are understood, valued, and structured in relation to situational factors and societal processes in different cultural contexts. In particular, there is a great need for research that focuses on discerning cultural ways of structuring children's independent and interdependent action within cultural practices. Such research would benefit not only from cross-cultural comparisons but also from within-culture comparisons of different cultural practices and children's engagement with different people. Varied observations of this nature would permit analyses of how others guide children's independent and interdependent action. Over time, developmental analyses could be directed toward discerning the development of children's independent and interdependent action (Raeff, 2006b). Research in these areas would permit identifying systematic cultural similarities and differences in conceptualizing and structuring children's independence and interdependence. Ultimately, addressing the ongoing dynamics of how independence and interdependence are understood and structured can further our knowledge of the complexities of culture and development.

# References

Bachnik, J. (1995). *Kejime:* Defining a shifting self in multiple organizational modes. In N. R. Rosenberger (Ed.), *Japanese sense of self* (pp. 152–172). Cambridge, UK: Cambridge University Press. (Original work published 1992)

Doi, T. (1988). *The anatomy of self: The individual versus society* (M. A. Harbison, Trans.). Tokyo: Kodansha International. (Original work published 1985)

Gaskins, S. (1999). Children's daily lives in a Mayan village: A case study of culturally constructed roles and activities. In A. Göncü (Ed.), *Children's engagement in the world: Sociocultural perspectives* (pp. 25–61). Cambridge, UK: Cambridge University Press.

Gjerde, P. F. (2004). Culture, power, and experience: Toward a person-centered cultural psychology. *Human Development, 47,* 138–157.

Greenfield, P. M., Keller, H., Fulgini, A., & Maynard, A. (2003). Cultural pathways through universal development. *Annual Review of Psychology, 54,* 461–490.

Greenfield, P. M., & Suzuki, L. K. (1998). Culture and human development: Implications for parenting, education, pediatrics, and mental health. In I. E. Sigel & K. A. Renninger (Eds.), *Handbook of child psychology* (Vol. 4, pp. 1059–1109). New York: Wiley.

Hofstede, G. (2001). *Culture's consequences: Comparing values, behaviors, institutions, and organizations across nations.* Thousand Oaks, CA: Sage. (Original work published 1980).

Kagitcibasi, C. (2005). Autonomy and relatedness in cultural context: Implications for self and family. *Journal of Cross Cultural Psychology, 36*(4), 403–422.

Keller, H. (2007). *Cultures of infancy.* Mahwah, NJ: Erlbaum.

Killen, M., & Wainryb, C. (2000). Independence and interdependence in diverse cultural contexts. In S. Harkness, C. Raeff, & C. M. Super (Eds.), *Variability in the social construction of the child. New Directions for Child and Adolescent Development, 87* (pp. 5–21). San Francisco: Jossey-Bass.

Kondo, D. K. (1990). *Crafting selves: Power, gender, and discourses of identity in a Japanese workplace.* Chicago: University of Chicago Press.

Kusserow, A. (2004). *American individualisms: Child rearing and social class in three neighborhoods.* New York: Palgrame Macmillan.

Lebra, T. S. (1995). Self in Japanese culture. In N. R. Rosenberger (Ed.), *Japanese sense of self* (pp. 105–120). Cambridge, UK: Cambridge University Press. (Original work published 1992)

Miller, J. G. (2006). Insights into moral development from cultural psychology. In M. Killen & J. G. Smetana (Eds.), *Handbook of moral development* (pp. 375–398). Mahwah, NJ: Erlbaum.

Miller, P. J., & Goodnow, J. J. (1995). Cultural practices: Toward an integration of culture and development. In J. J. Goodnow, P. J. Miller, & F. Kessel (Eds.), *Cultural practices as contexts for development. New Directions for Child and Adolescent Development, 67* (pp. 5–16). San Francisco: Jossey-Bass.

Miller, P. J., Wang, S., Sandel, T., & Cho, G. E. (2002). Self-esteem as folk theory: A comparison of European American and Taiwanese mothers' beliefs. *Parenting Science and Practice, 2,* 209–239.

Mosier, C. E., & Rogoff, B. (2003). Privileged treatment of toddlers: Cultural aspects of individual choice and responsibility. *Developmental Psychology, 39,* 1047–1060.

Oyserman, D., Coon, H. M., & Kemmelmeier, M. (2002). Rethinking individualism and collectivism: Evaluation of theoretical assumptions and meta-analyses. *Psychological Bulletin, 128,* 3–72.

Raeff, C. (2006a). *Always separate, always connected: Independence and interdependence in cultural contexts of development.* Mahwah, NJ: Erlbaum.

Raeff, C. (2006b). Multiple and inseparable: Conceptualizing the development of independence and interdependence. *Human Development, 49,* 96–121.

Raeff, C., Greenfield, P. M., & Quiroz, B. (2000). Conceptualizing interpersonal relationships in the cultural contexts of individualism and collectivism. In S. Harkness, C. Raeff, & C. M. Super (Eds.), *Variability in the social construction of the child. New Directions for Child and Adolescent Development, 87* (pp. 59–74). San Francisco: Jossey-Bass.

Richman, A. L., Miller, P. M., & Solomon, M. J. (1988). The socialization of infants in suburban Boston. In R. A. LeVine, P. M. Miller, & M. M. West (Eds.), *Parental behavior in diverse societies. New Directions for Child and Adolescent Development, 40* (pp. 65–74). San Francisco: Jossey-Bass.

Rogoff, B. (2003). *The cultural nature of human development.* Oxford, UK: Oxford University Press.

Shweder, R. A., Jensen, L. A., & Goldstein, W. M. (1995). Who sleeps by whom revisited: A method for extracting the moral goods implicit in practice. In J. J. Goodnow, P. J. Miller, & F. Kessel (Eds.), *Cultural practices as contexts for development. New Directions for Child and Adolescent Development, 67* (pp. 21–39). San Francisco: Jossey-Bass.

Suizzo, M. (2007). Parents' goals and values for children: Dimensions of independence and interdependence across four U.S. ethnic groups. *Journal of Cross-Cultural Psychology, 38,* 506–530.

Tamis-LeMonda, C. S., Way, N., Hughes, D., Yoshikawa, H., Kalman, R. K., & Niwa, E. Y. (2008). Parents' goals for children: The dynamic coexistence of individualism and collectivism in cultures and individuals. *Social Development, 17,* 183–209.

Turiel, E. (1983). *The development of social knowledge: Morality and convention.* Cambridge, UK: Cambridge University Press.

Turiel, E., & Wainryb, C. (2000). Social life in cultures: Judgments, conflict, and subversion. *Child Development, 71,* 250–256.

Wainryb, C. (2006). Moral development in culture: Diversity, tolerance, and justice. In M. K. Killen & J. G. Smetana (Eds.), *Handbook of moral development* (pp. 211–240). Mahwah, NJ: Erlbaum.

Wang, S., & Tamis-LeMonda, C. S. (2003). Do child-rearing values in Taiwan and the United States reflect cultural values of collectivism and individualism? *Journal of Cross-Cultural Psychology, 34,* 629–642.

Waterman, A. (1981). Individualism and interdependence. *American Psychologist, 36,* 762–773.

## Critical Thinking

1. What does it mean to say that a culture values independence rather than interdependence (and vice versa)?

2. How do parents' views on children's sleeping arrangements and conflict resolution reflect a culture's values regarding independence and interdependence?

3. What does within-culture variability refer to? Why is it important to recognize how a single culture can vary within itself on any trait or value instead of just focusing on how different cultures are different on those traits or values?

From *Child Development Perspectives*, vol. 4, no. 1, 2010, pp. 31–36. Copyright © 2010 by Catherine Raeff. Published by the Society for Research in Child Development. Reprinted by permission of Wiley-Blackwell.

# More Support Needed for Trauma Interventions

Treatment for child trauma works, but too often, children don't have access to it.

BETH AZAR

In the wake of the Penn State *sexual abuse* scandal, legislators are looking for ways to protect children from abuse. Less than two weeks after Penn State officials were charged with perjury and failing to report suspected child abuse, Sen. Robert Casey Jr. (D-Pa.) introduced legislation that would pressure states to have and enforce laws requiring all adults to report suspected child abuse and neglect.

Decades of research spell out the long-term consequences that abuse can have for children. The ongoing CDC "Study of Adverse Childhood Experiences," for example, shows that children who are abused and neglected have an increased risk of severe mental and physical health problems, including *posttraumatic stress disorder*, *depression*, *suicide*, *substance abuse*, chronic obstructive pulmonary disease, ischemic heart disease and liver disease.

But just as important as identifying cases of abuse is supporting treatments that help victims recover. Psychologists have developed evidence-based interventions that can reduce the harmful effects of child abuse. The key is ensuring that all individuals who experience abuse have access to these evidence-based treatments, so they don't become victims for life, says psychologist Anthony Mannarino, PhD, vice chair of the department of psychiatry, Allegheny General Hospital, Pittsburgh, and professor of psychiatry at Drexel University College of Medicine.

"With treatment, these kids can have the resilience to overcome their experience," says Mannarino, who through APA submitted written testimony to a Dec. 13 hearing on child abuse held by the Senate Health, Education, Labor and Pensions Subcommittee on Children and Families. "Being a victim doesn't have to become who they are or how they define themselves. But if they don't get help and their families don't participate, they can have long-standing difficulties."

## Scope of the Problem

The Penn State case serves to remind the public that child abuse is all too common in the United States. Although estimates vary greatly depending on the source, the Fourth National Incidence

Study of Child Abuse and Neglect, released in 2010, found that in 2005–06, one child in 25 in the United States, or 2.9 million children, experienced some kind of abuse or neglect. Most of those children—77 percent—were neglected. Of the 29 percent of those children who were abused, 57 percent were physically abused, 36 percent were emotionally abused and 22 percent were sexually abused.

Estimates of the percentage of abused children who will suffer long-term consequences vary widely. One review of research on child maltreatment—including physical and sexual abuse as well as neglect—published in the 2004 *Posttraumatic Stress Disorder In Children and Adolescents: Handbook*, found that PTSD rates ranged from 20 percent to 63 percent. In her studies, psychologist Sheree Toth, PhD, director of the Mt. Hope Family Center in Rochester, N.Y., and associate professor at the University of Rochester, finds that as many as 90 percent of maltreated infants have insecure or disorganized attachment. "The bright side is that there are evidence-based treatments that can dramatically improve the prognosis for these kids," says Toth. "We've shown that with intervention we can greatly decrease rates of insecure and disorganized attachment."

## Interventions That Work

A study published in 2006 in *Development and Psychopathology* by Toth and her colleagues showed that before intervention, 90 percent of a group of 137 maltreated infants had disorganized attachment and only one infant had secure attachment. Of the 50 infants who subsequently received one of two evidence-based therapies—infant-parent psychotherapy or a psychoeducational parenting intervention—58 percent had secure attachment a year later. In comparison, only one child among the 54 who received the standard treatment available in the community had secure attachment a year later.

Other researchers have shown positive results using evidence-based treatments to decrease the incidence of PTSD, depression, aggression and other behavioral problems seen in abused children. Mannarino, for example, has spent more than 25 years developing and testing an intervention called Trauma-Focused Cognitive Behavioral Therapy (TF-CBT) to treat children age 3 and older who have post-traumatic stress symptoms from abuse. In 12 to 16 sessions, children and their non-offending parents or caregivers learn about the specific effects trauma can have on emotions and behavior, and develop skills to manage their emotional distress, including relaxation techniques and how to use words to express their feelings.

In addition, the therapists help the children construct a narrative about their experience. "We talk about the idea of making the unspeakable speakable," says Mannarino. "By showing them that it's OK to talk about it, it makes the experience less overwhelming."

Many child abuse experts agree that, to date, TF-CBT has a strong base of empirical support as an intervention to treat trauma in children, with 10 randomized controlled trials, all showing its effectiveness. The studies show that as many as 85 percent of children treated with TF-CBT get markedly better on measures of shame, PTSD and depression, says Mannarino. Parents improve as well, showing less depression and emotional distress, better parenting skills and having a better outlook for the future.

Another highly regarded intervention is Alternatives for Families: A Cognitive Behavioral Therapy (AF-CBT), whose senior developer is David Kolko, PhD, professor of psychiatry, psychology and pediatrics at the University of Pittsburgh School of Medicine. AFCBT is designed to address individual and family involvement in conflict, coercion and aggression, including hostility and anger, mild physical force and child physical abuse. Its focus on physical abuse includes joint and individual work involving the alleged perpetrator—in most cases abusing parents or caregivers—and the child at various times throughout treatment. Working with the adult offender makes treatment complicated clinically, says Kolko, and may require additional time, but his team sees good results from this integrated approach.

Kolko also directs a program that provides services to the adolescent sexual offender, called Services for Adolescent and Family Enrichment. His program—which is funded by the local court system—has kept data on more than 250 cases and finds a two-year recidivism rate of only 1.5 percent, he says.

Unfortunately, access to these evidence-based treatments for child abuse is "pitiful," says Toth. Because researchers have developed them in university settings, they're mostly available near big medical centers. In addition, only 45 percent of graduate programs and 51 percent of internships that train psychology students to treat abused or otherwise traumatized children use TFCBT, according to two studies published in December in *Psychological Trauma*: Theory, Research, Practice, and Policy and Training and Education in Professional Psychology.

That's why Mannarino is putting much of his efforts these days into training and dissemination of TF-CBT around the country.

"Despite our ability to treat these kids, the real truth is that most kids who are abused are never properly treated," says Mannarino. "They grow up bearing the scars of unfortunate victimizations and wind up having serious adult problems, including depression, psychiatric hospitalizations and a general overuse of health services because they didn't get the help they needed."

# Critical Thinking

1. What are the barriers to the implementation of evidence-based practices?

2. How might psychologists increase public awareness of evidence-based practices?

3. What are the different types of treatment for PTSD and which do you think seems most effective?

4. How has the Penn State sexual abuse scandal changed how we view sexual abuse?

**BETH AZAR** is a writer in Portland, Ore.

# ADHD among Preschoolers

Identifying and treating attention-deficit hyperactivity disorder in very young children requires a different approach.

BRENDAN L. SMITH

Preschoolers can be inattentive or hyperactive even on the best of days, so it can be difficult to accurately diagnose attention-deficit hyperactivity disorder. But a growing body of research has shown that early treatment can help struggling children and frazzled parents.

The diagnosis of young children with ADHD is "very contentious" since there is a blurry line between common developmental changes and symptoms of the mental disorder, says ADHD researcher Stephen Hinshaw, PhD, chair of the psychology department at the University of California at Berkeley. "The symptoms for ADHD are very ubiquitous and very age-relevant," he says. "It's hard to know if you're seeing the signs of a disorder or just the signs of a young kid."

Hinshaw and some other researchers believe ADHD can be reliably diagnosed in children as young as 3 after thorough evaluations. In one study of school-age children, mothers reported that symptoms of ADHD appeared at or before age 4 in two-thirds of the children (*Journal of Developmental & Behavioral Pediatrics,* Vol. 23, No. 1).

Researchers disagree about whether ADHD is overdiagnosed, which may lead to unnecessary medication of healthy children. There is a tendency to overdiagnose young children with ADHD because of a lack of understanding about normative development in toddlerhood and the early preschool years, says Susan Campbell, PhD, a psychology professor at the University of Pittsburgh who has researched ADHD for more than three decades. "The only reason to diagnose a young child is to access appropriate services to help the child and family," she says. "Sometimes the earlier the better."

Overall, more children of all ages are being diagnosed with ADHD since there is greater awareness of the disorder and improvements in treatment, says Russell Barkley, PhD, a psychologist and professor at the Medical University of South Carolina who studies ADHD. Some inaccurate media reports have fueled a public misperception that ADHD is overdiagnosed, Barkley says. But only 20 percent of children with ADHD received any treatment in the 1960s and '70s, compared with roughly 70 percent to 80 percent today, he says.

"The rise in diagnosis is not bad news. It's good news," Barkley says. "Frankly, we were doing an awful job 20 or 30 years ago."

## Medication Issues

Often the first line of treatment for ADHD in school-age children is medication with stimulants, which have been found to be generally safe and effective. But drugs have less positive results for preschoolers. "I'm very opposed to the use of medication with young children because we don't really know the implications for brain development," Campbell says.

Approximately 4 million children—or 8 percent of all minors in the United States—have been diagnosed with ADHD, and more than half of them take prescription drugs. Methylphenidate hydrochloride (Ritalin) is the most commonly prescribed medication, but its use in children under 6 years old hasn't been approved by the Food and Drug Administration, which cites a lack of research for this age group. As a result, doctors are prescribing methylphenidate off label for preschoolers with ADHD.

The most comprehensive study on medication of preschoolers with ADHD showed mixed results for 3- to 5-year-old children. Funded by the National Institute of Mental Health, the multisite Preschool ADHD Treatment Study enrolled 303 preschoolers and their parents in a 10-week behavioral therapy course. Children with severe symptoms who didn't respond to therapy were given low doses of methylphenidate or a placebo. The medicated children showed a marked reduction in symptoms compared with the placebo group, according to the study results published in 2006.

> "It's crazy to me that we use the same criteria for a 3-year-old as we do for a 35-year-old."
>
> —George Dupaul, Lehigh University

More troublesome, though, was the fact that almost a third of parents reported that their medicated children experienced moderate to severe side effects, including weight loss, insomnia, loss of appetite, emotional outbursts and anxiety. Eleven percent of the preschoolers dropped out of the study because of their reactions to methylphenidate. During the study, the medicated children also grew about half an inch less in height and weighed about three pounds less than expected based on average growth rates (*Journal of the American Academy of Child & Adolescent Psychiatry,* Vol. 45, No. 11).

"The bottom line to me is for this age group, I don't believe stimulant medication is a first-line treatment," says George DuPaul, PhD, a professor of school psychology at Lehigh University who studies ADHD.

## Embracing Other Methods

Parental training and school-based interventions can be effective in treating preschoolers with ADHD, DuPaul says. His book, "Young Children With ADHD: Early Identification and Intervention" (APA, 2011), co-written with Lehigh University colleague Lee Kern, PhD, describes one of their studies of nondrug interventions with 135 preschoolers with ADHD.

Parents were given 20 training sessions on behavior problems, basic math and language skills, and child safety since children with ADHD often suffer accidental injuries because of their hyperactivity and impulsivity. One group of children also received individual assessments in the home and at preschool or day care. Both groups of children showed marked improvements in ADHD symptoms, although there was no significant advantage for the children with individual assessments (*School Psychology Review,* Vol. 36, No. 2). One limitation of the study was the lack of a control group because of ethical considerations about providing no treatment.

While older children can sometimes be taught to manage their ADHD symptoms, the training of preschool children has been more difficult, in part because cognitive-behavioral therapy doesn't work, Barkley says. Preschoolers with ADHD are delayed in communication skills, and language hasn't been internalized yet, so they can't use mental instructions or self-monitoring to change their behavior.

"It failed so we abandoned that after multiple studies found it had little or no influence," Barkley says.

But some behavioral management techniques are effective, including a token reward system and praise to provide extra motivation for preschoolers with ADHD, Barkley says. Teachers can seat children with ADHD near the teacher's desk and provide detailed explanations of class rules and disciplinary procedures, such as time-out or loss of tokens. Frequent class breaks and shorter work assignments also can help maintain children's attention and reduce outbursts.

Symptoms of ADHD can be exacerbated in children by impulsive parents who also have ADHD, Campbell says. Parents who are quick to anger and who frequently use physical punishment also can be detrimental. "There is going to be an interaction between the genetic risk and the support or lack of parental support the child has," she says.

## Looking Ahead

As the diagnosis of preschoolers with ADHD has increased, so have questions about the lack of age-specific symptoms in the Diagnostic and Statistical Manual of Mental Disorders, Fourth Edition. "It's crazy to me that we use the same criteria for a 3-year-old as we do for a 35-year-old," DuPaul says.

Scheduled for publication in 2013, the fifth DSM edition should require a greater number of symptoms for diagnosing young children with ADHD and more age-specific symptoms instead of generic descriptions such as fidgeting or running around and climbing, DuPaul says. "How do we apply that to a 17-year-old kid in a high school classroom?" he says. "They don't run about and climb on things."

Despite the risks, early identification and treatment of ADHD can provide substantial benefits for children and their families, Campbell says. "It can help so that when the child gets to the first grade, he isn't the only child no one else wants to play with and no teachers want in their class," she says.

## Critical Thinking

1. How can you tell if a child has ADHD or is he or she is just being a normal preschooler?

2. Do you think ADHD is overdiagnosed? If so, why, and if not, why not?

3. Are there ways to treat ADHD other than medicine? What might be better versus poorer choices?

# The Positives of Caregiving: Mothers' Experiences Caregiving for a Child with Autism

MICHAEL K. CORMAN

The documentation and representation of the experiences of caregivers of children with autism and other developmental disabilities has been one dimensional at best, with a pervasive focus on the stresses, burdens, and parental coping associated with caregiving (Grant, Ramcharan, McGrath, Nolan, & Keady, 1998). Much of this focus is warranted. For example, sources of stress (stressors) for caregivers of these children are numerous and might include the autistic traits themselves (DeMyer, 1979; Tomanik, Harris, & Hawkins, 2004), social stigmas from the general public and health practitioners (Gray, 1998, 2002a, 2002b), and the social support system that is intended to alleviate stress (Corman, 2007a; DeMyer, 1979; Gray, 1998).

This multitude of stressors can have an immense effect on individuals in the family, including parents and siblings (DeMyer, 1979; Kaminsky & Dewey, 2001; Schopler & Mesibov, 1994), extended family members (Gray, 1998), and, depending on how caregivers cope, the possible life gains that the individual with autism can make (Schopler & Mesibov, 1994). For example, parents often experience a combination of emotional problems (such as depression, isolation, and feelings of being a failure as a parent), physical problems (fatigue, ulcers, headaches, fluctuation in weight, dermatitis, and other physical health conditions), career problems (limited or no employment—specifically for mothers and career changes), and negative effects on the marriage (marital discord often ending in divorce; Gray, 1998, 2002a). Parents also report feelings of guilt, isolation, doubts of their ability to care for their child, anger toward the symptoms of autism, increased physical and psychological tensions, frustrations, lack of life satisfaction, and feelings of exhaustion and old age (DeMyer, 1979; Gray, 2002b). Last, because of the unique and often complex symptomatology associated with autism, such as a lack of verbal communication, variant cognitive functioning, and severe behaviors, comparative studies have reported that the burden of caregiving for children with autism is greater than that of parenting a child with other disabilities (Weiss, 2002), such

as mental retardation, Down's syndrome, cystic fibrosis, and chronic and fatal physical illness.

Caregiving for a child with autism is stressful! But what about the positive side of caregiving? The narrow focus on the stressful and negative aspects of the caregiving experience offers only partial insights into the experiences of caregiving for children with chronic conditions. There is a need for research to examine the other side of the spectrum, the positive and often joyous side of parenting children with disabilities. The purpose of this article is to provide insight into that positive side by exploring the experiences of mothers of children with autism through in-depth interviews. Although these mothers portrayed an experience that was often stressful, they also discussed many joys of caregiving. This article attempts to strike a balance with the majority of research that focuses on the negatives of caregiving; it will show that caregiving for children with autism is not solely stressful. These findings have theoretical and practical implications. First, this article provides a brief overview of the literature on the positives of caregiving for individuals with chronic conditions.

## Literature Review

Most caregiving research focuses solely on the negative aspects of the experience (Chappell, Gee, McDonald, & Stones, 2003), which may be indebted to the pathological models of stress that guide such inquiries. For instance, Pearlin, Lieberman, Menaghan, and Mullan's (1981) framework of the stress process focuses on the stressors (antecedents to stress) associated with caregiving and pays specific attention to the many related relationships, and the developing and changing nature of these relationships over time, that eventually lead to stress (see also Pearlin, Mullan, Semple, & Skaff, 1990). Lazarus and Folkman (1984) offered a framework that focuses on the more individual and psychological components of what they called the *stress-coping process*. They suggested that it is how stressors are appraised, in addition to individual resources, that determines whether or not an event is stressful (Lazarus & Folkman, 1984). Although these conceptualizations are useful for exploring the stressful aspects of caregiving and how individuals cope, they are limited in that they fail to address any positives of caregiving in a systematic way; positives have been left by the wayside (Kelso, French, & Fernandez, 2005). As Grant et al. (1998) suggested, such a singular view fails to account for other important dimensions.

Research on caregiving has only recently considered gratification and the role of positives in the caregiving experience. For example, in Susan Folkman's (1997) seminal study of caregiving for men with HIV/AIDS, she discussed how positive states of mind can co-occur with negative states. She reported that "despite high levels of distress, people also experience positive psychological states during caregiving and bereavement" (p. 1207). Folkman described four psychological states associated with coping: (a) positive reappraisal, (b) goal-directed problem-focused coping, (c) spiritual beliefs and practices, and (d) the infusion of ordinary events with positive meaning. All four states have an underlying characteristic, that is, the appraisal of positive meanings occurring within a stressful event, which she referred to as *meaning-based coping*.

Grant et al. (1998) explored the positives of caregiving by interviewing 120 caregivers of individuals with intellectual disabilities. They described rewards and caregiver gratification as emerging from three sources: (a) the relationship between caregiver and care receiver, (b) intrapersonal characteristics of the caregiver, and (c) the desire for positive outcomes or the avoidance of negative affect. They also found that many of the gratifications expressed by caregivers were related to, or a product of, successful coping strategies, supporting Folkman's (1997) findings.

More recently, Chaya Schwartz (2003) defined caregiver gratification as "fulfilling parental duties, a better idea of 'what's important in life', learning about inner strengths, aware of personal limitations, learning to do new things, satisfaction from doing what's right, personal growth, [and] becoming more self-confident" (p. 580). In her study of 167 primary caregivers of individuals with mental, developmental, or physical disabilities, she found that caregivers who were younger, unemployed, and had poor health were more likely to experience caregiver gratification. In addition, she found the only characteristics of the child that factored into experiencing gratification were the age of the child (younger children) and the type of disability (having a physical rather than a mental disability). Last, subjective (perceived stress) rather than objective burden (the level of care required) was associated with less caregiver gratification (Schwartz, 2003). Schwartz speculated that the gratification parents experienced might be a product of how they perceived or created meaning in their caregiving role.

In the field of autism, research has only provided marginal insights into the more rewarding aspects of caregiving. For instance, in a study about narratives published on the Internet by parents, Amos Fleischmann (2004) found that in addition to the demanding aspects of caregiving, a majority of websites focused on the positive essence of individuals with autism and the caregiving experience, with an emphasis on parents' positive relationship with their child and joyous experiences derived from caregiving. Fleischmann's study is supported by other research on the contributions people with disabilities make to their families: families might benefit in terms of strengthened family ties, compassion and fulfillment, and happiness (Pruchno, 2003).

Despite the shortcomings of Pearlin et al. (1981, 1990) and Lazarus and Folkman's (1984) models, they allow for a scope that looks beyond adjustment and toward positives (Kelso et al., 2005). This is apparent in Folkman's (1997) work on caregiving for individuals with HIV/AIDS (see also Folkman & Moskowitz, 2000a, 2000b). Using these insights, the positives of caregiving are defined in this article as experiences or events that caregivers appraise as positive and sometimes joyous. It is important to note that if this definition seems ambiguous, it is because the positives of caregiving remain relatively uncharted, lacking conceptual clarification (Grant et al., 1998). Based on mothers' reflections, this article explores the positives of caregiving for a child with autism. In doing so, a more complete understanding of these parents' lived experiences emerges, with important contributions to the broader constellation of caregivers of children with chronic conditions.

# Method
## Participants

Results reported in the next section were drawn from a larger study that explored mothers' experiences of caregiving for a child with autism, before and after their child was placed outside of the home (either in foster care, a group home setting, or a treatment-care facility, hereafter referred to as *placed* or *placement*). Interviews occurred between November 2005 and February 2006. Nine mothers participated in total; 6 lived in British Columbia, and 3 lived in Alberta, Canada. The average age of mothers was 46, with a range between 35 and 62 years old. For 7 out of the 9 mothers, family income ranged between $30,000 and more than $100,000. One mother responded "middle class," and another chose not to answer. As of the first interview, the children with autism were between the ages of 8 and 18, with the average being 14 years old. The age of these children at the time of placement was 6–15, with an average of 11 years old. Mothers were purposively chosen because they are usually the primary caregivers (Gray, 2003) and are therefore more likely to be involved in the day-to-day ups and downs of caregiving. Furthermore, a unique sample of mothers was chosen; their experiences were so stressful that their child was ultimately placed outside of the home (see Corman, 2007a). Although this study did not aim to be generalizable, it was assumed that if this sample experienced positives, caregivers in less stressful circumstances (e.g., caregivers of a child with less severe autistic characteristics and other disabilities) would also experience them. Therefore, these findings are potentially transferable to other constellations of caregivers.

A diagnosis of autism was reported by 7 out of the 9 mothers during the initial contact, with the remaining 2 mothers reporting a diagnosis of pervasive developmental disorder (PDD) and PDD not otherwise specific (PDD-NOS). Mothers also reported co-occurring conditions, including Landau-Kleffner syndrome, obsessive compulsive disorder, mental handicap, epilepsy (for three children), and Down's syndrome. Two of the mothers had a female child, and 7 had a male child. Although I refer to a generalized *autism,* it is important to note that there is no all-or-nothing form of autism but rather a continuum of severity, known as autism spectrum disorders (Wing, 1988). Based on mothers' descriptions, these children would most likely fall within the moderate to severe end of the spectrum.

## Research Design

In-depth, semistructured interviews were conducted based on transcendental phenomenology (Moustakas, 1994), a qualitative research strategy and philosophy that allows researchers to identify the essence of experience as it relates to certain phenomena as described and understood by participants of a study (Creswell, 2002). Mothers were interviewed at their homes and asked to retrospectively talk about their caregiving experiences. Questions were geared toward exploring the positives and joys of caregiving, the demands of caregiving, and how mothers coped, focusing on the times before and after out-of-home placement. The portion of the interviews reported in the analysis below are based on the questions that explored the positives during the early years prior to placement (approximately 0–8 years of age, depending when the placement process was activated) and after their child left home. Interviews lasted on average 2.24 hours with a range of 1.5–3 hours. The interviews and the numbers of mothers interviewed continued until sufficiency and saturation of information were reached.

Interviews were transcribed in their entirety and analyzed based on a modified approach offered by Moustakas (1994), specifically intended for the analysis of qualitative data. Eight steps were followed: (1) identifying patterns in the data based on the lived experiences of participants, (2) reducing the data by identifying unique aspects of experience, (3) organizing the data into core themes that represent the experience of participants, (4) validating step 3 by reviewing the complete transcript of participants, (5) constructing an individual textural description of the experience presented by each participant, (6) based on step 5, constructing a clear account of the dynamics of the experience, (7) combining steps 5 and 6 to create a textural-structural description of each participant that incorporated the experiences of participants, and (8) combining individual textual descriptions of each participant into one that represents the experience presented by the group as a whole.

To assist in the process just described, insights offered by Moerer-Urdahl and Creswell (2004) were followed. Initially, significant statements within each participant's transcripts were identified, with a primary focus on understanding how individuals viewed different aspects of their experiences as they related to the positives and joys of caregiving. The goal here was to ground or contextualize the positives of caregiving to gain a better understanding of the distinct character of positives as described by mothers. The data were then broken down into themes based on the experiences of mothers. Once themes were developed, a detailed description of the experience of each mother as it related to the themes that emerged was provided. Conclusions were then drawn in accordance with the lived experiences expressed by participants. The product of this process was the grouping of statements into the themes discussed in the next section.

# Results
## Pockets of Child Development

All parents expressed the positives during the early years of their child's development as "pockets" because they were "kind of few and far between." Positives discussed by mothers included their child developing, seeing their child happy, times devoid of negative autistic traits or maladaptive behaviors (as perceived by the mother) that are often associated with autism, spending time with their child, unique and/or positive personality traits of their child, and knowing or discovering what was wrong with their child. I discuss each in the following paragraphs.

**Developmental gains.** With a diagnosis on the autism spectrum, parents are often left in ambiguity because of the nature of the disability; they do not know how much their child will develop in the years to come. As a result, mothers described feelings of joy when their child started to make developmental gains. For example, one mother discussed how she was "very pleased" when her child progressed in developmental areas, such as "when he started to speak." Another mother commented on her child's success in learning new tasks; "Oh yeah, his success still makes me feel good, no matter what. Like I remember when he learned how to wave good-bye. That made me cry that day [laugh]." Another mentioned the "little milestones that parents take for granted, I think are tremendous."

Another mother discussed how watching her child was "hugely satisfying . . . it makes it all worth it when you start to see a little bit of language or a behavior, or a skill emerge." For some mothers, this gave them hope for their child's future. One mother explained, "I think . . . a little bit of joy with a child that's seriously handicapped goes a long way. It gives you a lot of hope."

**Child being happy.** All mothers experienced positives derived from seeing their child happy. Although this might seem like a common experience of all parents, it is important to contextualize this side of caregiving in that many mothers viewed their child as being chronically unhappy. One mother put it best, "just to see him happy, because all through his life he's lived either withdrawn or anxious, or afraid of doing things." When mothers saw their child happy, they were especially happy. For example, joy arose for one mother when she watched her child enjoy his favorite activity. She explained:

> You see this bright-eyed little boy at the top of the slide, that was his favorite activity was going down the slides. So when you see him at the top of the slide with this big grin on his face, those kinds of times were really exciting for me. . . . I just knew that he enjoyed that.

Seeing her child happy made her feel "really good . . . That is sort of what we hope our kids are going to feel." Another mother described, "when he's happy and having a really good time, then I'm happy. It's like I'm just a normal parent."

**Times devoid of negative autistic traits or maladaptive behaviors.** Mothers also talked about times devoid of negative behaviors (negative autistic traits), which they thought of as "normal" times. For instance, one mother described how when her child "didn't throw his food . . . [or] didn't have any feces smearing in the bathroom," these were more positive times. Others experienced positives when their child "hadn't pinched another child or hit another child." One mother went on to explain, "So any time he was cooperating . . . times that he was being and not bothering anybody. . . . If I heard that he sat for five minutes in his desk, or he sat in circle time without poking the next person." During these times, some mothers expressed being "really happy."

**Spending time with your child.** Despite many of the difficulties, all mothers described the positives of spending time with their child. For instance, one mother discussed how she and her child would go swimming together and go down to the beach to spend time together. Her child "loved it" and always "liked hanging off me." She described how there were so many "nice times" that they spent together. Another mother described how she felt "just connected" to her child because of the times they spent together, specifically "the caregiving part . . . being hands on, physically connected." She talked about how she "really enjoyed" the connection she had with her child: "We're connected on a different level." This mother concluded:

> I guess having a child with autism, you connect with them on a completely different level than I think you would with other children because you don't have language. He's also mostly nonverbal, so physical connections are really important; it's the way you communicate that's beyond words I guess, so I think that's part of it.

For this mother, what might be viewed as a demanding aspect of caregiving was in fact very joyous for her.

**Unique and/or positive personality traits of their child.** Individuals with autism often have a variety of challenges, including maladaptive behaviors, difficulty in communicating with others, difficulty listening and following directions, and other co-occurring medical conditions. However, individuals who have autism are heterogeneous; the severities of impairments vary from person to person (Gray, 2003; Seltzer, Shattuck, Abbeduto, & Greenberg, 2004). Nonetheless, the positive side of this uniqueness often goes unrecognized. All mothers in this study recognized the uniqueness of their child. In doing so, they expressed many positives derived from the unique personality traits of their child.

For example, mothers discussed how their child was "real sweet" and showed affection. Another mother talked about her child being a "very warm individual. . . . We were blessed that way, I guess; very cuddly, quite attached to your close family members." Other personality traits included being "very funny, like she's got a good sense [of humor] . . . she's quite a little

monkey," and being "a very good-natured kid . . . he still has a happy disposition." Despite the negative traits mothers dealt with throughout their caregiving experience, which sometimes worsen or change as their child ages into adulthood (Gray, 2002a), mothers described the many unique personality traits of their child as a positive side of caregiving.

**Knowing or discovering what was wrong with their child.** Common perceptions of receiving a diagnosis on the autism spectrum suggest that the experience is devastating, and often it is (Mansell & Morris, 2004). In fact, for many of the mothers in this study, the autism diagnosis represented the loss of the child that was or could have been. One mother explained how "the day that I found out [I was floored] because there's nothing like that in my family, and we've always been high achievers . . . and I don't know where that [diagnosis] came from."

Although some mothers described receiving the diagnosis of autism as very burdensome—"it was sad, it's pretty devastating, to have a child who's not typical"—for others, the receipt of the diagnosis was not a stressful experience but a positive one. With a diagnosis, mothers were relieved to finally know what was wrong with their child after having entered into multiple systems of care in search for answers and supports. For example, after receiving a diagnosis, one mother described how "all of a sudden you know . . . because up until this point everybody's been asking me 'Why is he doing this? What's he doing?' And I'd be going 'I don't know; I don't know.' I really had no answers for anybody." With a diagnosis, answers started "coming out." With these answers, mothers described a positive experience derived from knowing and understanding.

Furthermore, the receipt of a diagnosis allowed the mother to gain access to specialized services and supports for her child, such as intervention therapy, and herself, such as respite, and set out a pathway of care for her child.[1] The ability to take action was positive, and often a relief, because now the mother was able to help her child. One mother expanded upon this point:

> I'm very much a doer, and so when you have a diagnosis, then you can look at putting the pieces together to move forward and do something; especially I hear so much about early development and early intervention. It was right around the time that the money was being made available for early intervention, and I didn't want to waste a minute, especially knowing that that money would dissolve when he was 6.

## The Impacts of Positives

Parents did not just describe the positive side of caregiving, they also discussed how the positives interacted with negative and stressful experiences (i.e., their stress-coping process). For example, the positives associated with their child developing gave mothers hope. One mother, like many parents of children with autism, worried about her child's future (Ivey, 2004). When her child started to make developmental milestones, she began to have a more positive outlook for her child's future.

This hope impacted the concerns and worries she had for her child's future. She went on to explain how the positives "are the things that keep you going . . . a little bit of joyful experience gives you . . . the ability to go on."

On a more general note, one mother described how the positives of caregiving had an impact on her stress-coping process.

Well they (the positives) kept me going . . . it wasn't all negative. It kind of gave me hope to continue on, like every day is a new day kind of thing. . . . It gave me a reason to get up in the morning so I wouldn't be waking up going "oh no, I have to deal with another day" sort of thing . . . any time you have any kind of joy or positive feelings then that . . . just gives you a really good feeling that you can continue over the next period of time.

Another mother explained:

[The positives] just keep you going. Without the moments of comic relief, without the joys, without those moments of connection where he catches your eye directly for 1 minute and you actually have his gaze directly, without those things, you'd go stir crazy. Those are the things that feed you. I get a huge amount of strength from the tiniest little things.

Despite the demands of caregiving, mothers experienced a multitude of positives during their caregiving years, many of which brought joy to their lives.

## Positive Reflections on Their Overall Caregiving Experience

All mothers spoke about personal transformation as a result of their caregiving years. This transformation included learning from their experience and growing as a person. It is important to note that these positive reflections are not linked to any specific event but were a product of their caregiving experience as a whole. Furthermore, it is important to contextualize this positive side of caregiving: All mothers eventually placed their child with autism due to a number of factors, including their child's maladaptive behaviors increasing drastically, "getting more intense" and more difficult to deal with over time, a failure in the support system that was intended to alleviate stress, and a general inability to cope with the demands of caregiving, leading to mothers experiencing severe distress and feeling that they "couldn't go on" (Corman, 2007a). However, despite this experience of severe distress, all mothers ultimately reflected positively on their caregiving experience as a whole.

For example, one mother explained the learning involved in caregiving where she not only "learned a lot about autism, but I learned a lot about people, and I would have missed that . . . it was a really wonderful thing." Another explained how "the biggest positive is just the learning that came out of that for us as a family, but for me in particular as a person. But I think it's shaped all of us, it certainly has shaped [my husband and daughter] as well as me."

Others described caregiving as making them stronger as a person. One mother mentioned how she "became a fighter, just kind of like an advocate for the family but also for [my child with autism] . . . So, yeah, definitely it makes you stronger. And it makes you tougher in a way." Her experience also made her realize what is "important . . . So, you realize what's really important and don't sweat the small stuff." Another mother described her child with autism as being one of her greatest teachers in life:

I mean, I don't even know who I would be if I hadn't had May . . . it's kind of a weird thing, but in my life, she's been kind of one of my key teachers. She's kind of forced me to kind of examine parts of myself that I don't know if I ever would have got to if I didn't have her. And, she forced [my husband] and I to kind of deal with issues that might have taken us years . . . It's been a struggle, and sometimes I've hated her for it, [but] nobody has taught me so much.

Mothers also discussed how the caregiving experience made them more empathetic:

My husband and I were asked one time about the biggest thing that we got from Sam. I think it was the gift of patience 'cause I have patience unlimited, you know . . . 'cause once somebody's dumping milk out in your front yard [laugh], it's amazing how much patience you have.

# Discussion and Conclusion

Despite the demanding aspects of caregiving for children with autism, and it is often very demanding, caregivers experience many positives and joys from their role as caregivers. However, the majority of research focuses on the negative and more stressful aspects of the caregiving experience. Breaking away from this preponderance of research in the field of autism, this article highlights some of the positives of caregiving that mothers experienced during the early years of their child's development and overall reflections on their caregiving experience after their child left home. When asked to discuss the positives of caregiving, all mothers expressed a multitude of positives directly related to their caregiving role (Chappell et al., 2003; Folkman, 1997; Grant et al., 1998; Schwartz, 2003). Others derived positives from finding the "positive essence" in their child (Fleischmann, 2004) and achievements of their child (Grant et al., 1998). More unique positives included discovering what was wrong with their child in the face of not knowing.

## Implications for Practice

Many practical implications arise from this study. Although caregiving for children with autism is demanding, this article suggests that the positives and joys that emerge from this role are not only important but also have a specific function. Whereas current research describes the positives of caregiving as a *product* of successful coping—the adaptational function of positives (see Folkman, 1997; Grant et al., 1998)—parents in this study discussed how positives had an impact *on* their stress-coping process, rather than being simply a product of it. In other words, positives also occur outside of the stress-coping process, and interact with it, affecting how mothers experience stressors and negative outcomes, potentially impacting their ability to cope at different times. This finding expands on the function of positives within the caregiving experience; they go beyond adaptational function to being a core aspect of caregivers' experiences.

Furthermore, the importance and function of the positives and joys of caregiving is most apparent when they are not present. In the larger study that contributed to this article, all mothers described severe distress and solely negative outcomes during the time leading up to and immediately following the placement of their child, a time devoid of any positives or joys of caregiving. One mother described it best: "When the stresses got to be too much, the joy of everything started to disappear." Does a lack of positives impact caregiver well-being and a caregiver's ability to cope? Cummins (2001) explained that most caregivers are able to describe positives derived from their caregiving role; when they are unable to do so, the demands of their role are likely to be intolerable. Grant et al. (1998) further explained that without the positives of caregiving, it may not be possible for caregivers to feel as if they are able to continue encountering the stressful circumstances corollary to their role. As such, it might be concluded that the positives of caregiving are an integral part of parents' ability to cope, to the point that when they are not present, parents may not be able to continue caregiving. Policy and practice implications directly follow from these findings in that a lack of positives might be an indicator of the current state of a caregiver's well-being or lack of well-being. It might be an indicator for professional services and supports that additional supports are needed to proactively assist those in crisis or on the brink of crisis. Furthermore, policies need to be developed that are proactively geared toward preventing a crisis or assisting those on the brink of a crisis rather than solely intervening once the crisis emerges. Of equal importance, this examination of positives provides future families of children with autism and other disabilities a better understanding of the experience of caregiving as a whole—an experience that is very demanding at times but also has many positives.

How families cope with the demands associated with caring for a child with autism not only influences the well-being of the family but also possible life gains that an individual with autism can make (Schopler & Mesibov, 1994). Current research on caregiving for children with autism attempts to promote the use of successful coping strategies and resources to improve the quality of life of the caregiver and care receiver (Dunn, Burbine, Bowers, & Tantleff-Dunn, 2001; Gray, 1994, 1998). One practical implication that might inform research, policy, and practice on successful coping is the need to promote and draw attention to the positives of caregiving both within service agencies and for those caregiving for children with autism and other disabilities. If services and supports are able to enhance the positive aspects of caregiving by drawing attention to them, parents might be able to cope more successfully with the difficulties of caregiving. In addition, it might

be beneficial for services and supports to facilitate the joys of caregiving by drawing attention to the strengths of the caregiver and the positive contribution their child with a disability makes to their family (Pierpont, 2004). The strengths-based perspective and active interviewing are two resources that service providers might draw upon to help facilitate and draw attention to the positives of caregiving.

The strengths-based perspective is one orientation that might assist those whose work intersects with individuals with disabilities and their families in drawing attention to and facilitating the identification of the positive and joyous aspects of caregiving. This perspective shifts away from pathological conceptions of persons with disabilities and the experiences of caregiving to more qualitative and holistic understandings, aligned with the positives of caregiving discussed earlier. By focusing on strengths (see Cohen, 1999; Early, 2001), this perspective has the potential to assist service providers in gaining a more complete understanding of the caregiving experience and perceiving their experiences in a more positive light, which has the potential to increase caregivers' quality of life and the quality of care they provide (Berg-Weger, Rubio, & Tebb, 2001).

In addition to the strengths-based perspective, and complementary to it, insights offered by the reflexive and linguistic turns in sociology could be of use to service providers and researchers alike as a resource or tool to draw upon to explore the positives of caregiving and draw attention to them. One approach aligned with this shift is "the active interview," which is a methodological and analytical approach to interviewing that conceptualizes the interview as an active meaning-making process between interviewee and interviewer, who both participate in the coproduction of knowledge. The interviewer (i.e., service provider), in the context of exploring the positives of caregiving, might invite or "incite" the interviewee (i.e., caregiver) to talk about and reflect on the positives of caregiving. Traditionally, this approach might be viewed as leading the respondent, resulting in a social desirability bias (Esterberg, 2002; see also Cummins, 2001). However, the active interview suggests that interviewers are inevitably embedded and implicated in the meaning-making processes of respondents. Holstein and Gubrium (2002) explained:

> This is not to say that active interviewers merely coax their respondents into preferred answers to their questions. Rather, they converse with respondents in such a way that alternate considerations are brought into play . . . encouraging respondents to develop topics in ways relevant to their own everyday lives . . . to provide an environment conducive to the production of the range and complexity of meanings that address relevant issues. (pp. 120–121).

Furthermore, in the context of the positives of caregiving, the active interview is not solely concerned about the positives; it suggests that there is usefulness in inviting individuals to think about the positives and honor participants in the meaning-making process. As such, I suggest that this approach can provide a more fruitful examination of the caregiving experience as a whole by assisting researchers and service providers in exploring and gaining a better understanding and appreciation of the positives of caregiving. This process might also facilitate families and caregivers in talking about and reflecting upon their experiences in a more positive and joyous light (Berg-Weger et al., 2001).

## Directions for Future Research

The findings from this study suggest that future research should focus on the factors that lead to positives of caregiving, which might identify and assist in the development of services, supports, and specific interventions that will potentially facilitate improved outcomes for individual caregivers, care receivers, and the family as a whole. As such, there is a need to explore links among positives, social supports, coping, and appraisal processes of caregivers of children with autism and other chronic conditions. Furthermore, future research should investigate these links to determine how the facilitation of positives might affect caregivers' lived experiences. Also, as mentioned earlier, it is important to examine positives and joys not only in relation to stressors but also as a significant factor throughout the entire stress-coping process.

Last, this study focused on the retrospective experience of mothers whose children were under 18 years old. However, for the first time in history, large numbers of people with autism are reaching old age (National Advisory Council on Aging, 2004; Seltzer et al., 2004). As a result, parents now "face a lifetime of caregiving responsibilities" (Kim, Greenberg, Seltzer, & Krauss, 2003, p. 313). However, very little is known about this constellation of caregivers and care receivers. There is need to explore the experiences of individuals with autism, their caregivers, and families as they age over the life course.

## Note

1. In British Columbia and Alberta, for instance, institutional services and supports are attached to a diagnosis of autism (see Corman, 2007b).

## References

Berg-Weger, M., Rubio, D., & Tebb, S. (2001). Strengths-based practice with family caregivers of the chronically ill: Qualitative insights. *Families in Society: The Journal of Contemporary Human Services, 82*(3), 263–272.

Chappell, N., Gee, E., McDonald, L., & Stones, M. (2003). *Aging in contemporary Canada*. Toronto, Canada: Pearson Educational Publishers/Prentice Hall.

Cohen, B. (1999). Intervention and supervision in strengths-based social work practice. *Families in Society: The Journal of Contemporary Human Services, 80*(5), 460–466.

Corman, M. K. (2007a). *Primary caregivers of children with autism spectrum disorders—An exploration of the stressors, joys, and parental coping before and after out-of-home placement.* (Masters Thesis, University of Victoria, Canada, 2007). Available from the Electronic Theses and Dissertations website: http://hdl.handle.net/1828/1227

Corman, M. K. (2007b, August). *Panning for gold—An institutional ethnography of health relations in the process of diagnosing*

*autism in British Columbia*. Paper presented at the meeting of The Society for the Study of Social Problems, New York.

Creswell, J. (2002). *Research design: Qualitative, quantitative, and mixed methods approaches* (2nd ed.). Thousand Oaks, CA: Sage Publications.

Cummins, R. (2001). The subjective well-being of people caring for a family member with a severe disability at home: A review. *Journal of Intellectual & Development Disability, 26*(1), 83–100.

DeMyer, M. (1979). *Parents and children in autism*. Washington, DC: V. H. Winston & Sons.

Dunn, M., Burbine, T., Bowers, C., & Tantleff-Dunn, S. (2001). Moderators of stress in parents of children with autism. *Community Mental Health Journal, 37*(1), 39–52.

Early, T. (2001). Measures for practice with families from a strengths perspective. *Families in Society: The Journal of Contemporary Human Services, 82*(2), 225–232.

Esterberg, K. G. (2002). *Qualitative methods in social research*. Boston: McGraw-Hill.

Fleischmann, A. (2004). Narratives published on the Internet by parents of children with autism: What do they reveal and why is it important? *Focus on Autism and Other Developmental Disabilities, 19*(1), 35–43.

Folkman, S. (1997). Positive psychological states and coping with severe stress. *Social Science & Medicine, 45*(8), 1207–1221.

Folkman, S., & Moskowitz, J. T. (2000a). Positive affect and the other side of coping. *American Psychologist, 55*(6), 647–654.

Folkman, S., & Moskowitz, J. T. (2000b). Stress, positive emotion, and coping. *Current Directions in Psychological Science, 9*(4), 115–118.

Grant, G., Ramcharan, P., McGrath, M., Nolan, M., & Keady, J. (1998). Rewards and gratifications among family caregivers: Towards a refined model of caring and coping. *Journal of Intellectual Disability Research, 42*(1), 58–71.

Gray, D. (1994). Coping with autism: Stresses and strategies. *Sociology of Health & Illness, 16*(3), 275–300.

Gray, D. (1998). *Autism and the family: Problems, prospects, and coping with the disorder.* Springfield, IL: Charles C. Thomas Publisher.

Gray, D. (2002a). Ten years on: A longitudinal study of families of children with autism. *Journal of Intellectual & Development Disability, 27*(3), 215–222.

Gray, D. (2002b). 'Everybody just freezes. Everybody is just embarrassed': Felt and enacted stigma among parents of children with high functioning autism. *Sociology of Health & Illness, 24*(6), 734–749.

Gray, D. (2003). Gender and coping: The parents of children with high functioning autism. *Social Sciences & Medicine, 56*, 631–642.

Holstein, J. A., & Gubrium, J. F. (2002). Active interviewing. In D. Weinberg (Ed.), *Qualitative research methods* (pp. 112–126). Oxford, UK: Blackwell.

Ivey, J. (2004). What do parents expect? A study of likelihood and importance issues for children with autism spectrum disorders. *Focus on Autism and Other Developmental Disabilities, 19*(1), 27–33.

Kaminsky, L., & Dewey, D. (2001). Sibling relationships of children with autism. *Journal of Autism and Developmental Disorders, 31*(4), 399–410.

Kelso, T., French, D., & Fernandez, M. (2005). Stress and coping in primary caregivers of children with a disability: A qualitative study using the Lazarus and Folkman process model of coping. *Journal of Research in Special Educational Needs, 5*(1), 3–10.

Kim, W., Greenberg, S., Seltzer, M., & Krauss, W. (2003). The role of coping in maintaining the psychological well-being of mothers of adults with intellectual disability and mental illness. *Journal of Intellectual Disability Research, 47*(4–5), 313–327.

Lazarus, R., & Folkman, S. (1984). *Stress, appraisal, and coping.* New York: Springer Publishing.

Mansell, W., & Morris, K. (2004). A survey of parents' reactions to the diagnosis of an autistic spectrum disorder by a local service: Access to information and use of services. *Autism, 8*(4), 387–407.

Moustakas, C. (1994). *Phenomenological research methods.* Thousand Oaks, California: Sage Publications.

Moerer-Urdahl, T., & Creswell, J. (2004). Using transcendental phenomenology to explore the "ripple effect" in a leadership mentoring program. *International Journal of Qualitative Methods, 3*(2), 1–28.

National Advisory Council on Aging. (2004). *Seniors on the margins: Aging with a developmental disability.* Canada: Minister of Public Works and Government Services Canada.

Pearlin, L., Lieberman, M., Menaghan, E., & Mullan, J. (1981). The stress process. *Journal of Health and Social Behavior, 22*(4), 337–356.

Pearlin, L., Mullan, J., Semple, S., & Skaff, M. (1990). Caregiving and the stress process: An overview of concepts and their measures. *The Gerontologist, 30*(5), 583–594.

Pierpont, J. (2004). Emphasizing caregiver strengths to avoid out-of-home placement of children with severe emotional and behavioral disturbances. *Journal of Human Behavior in the Social Environment, 9*(1/2), 5–17.

Pruchno, R. (2003). Enmeshed lives: Adult children with developmental disabilities and their aging mothers. *Psychology and Aging, 18*(4), 851–857.

Schopler, E., & Mesibov, G. (1994). *Behavioral issues in autism.* New York: Plenum Press.

Schwartz, C. (2003). Parents of children with chronic disabilities: The gratification of caregiving. *Families in Society: The Journal of Contemporary Human Services, 84*(4), 576–584.

Seltzer, M., Shattuck, P., Abbeduto, L., & Greenberg, J. (2004). The trajectory of development in adolescents and adults with autism. *Mental Retardation and Developmental Disabilities Research Reviews, 10*(4), 234–247.

Tomanik, S., Harris, G., & Hawkins, J. (2004). The relationship between behaviours exhibited by children with autism and maternal stress. *Journal of Intellectual & Developmental Disability, 29*(1), 16–26.

Weiss, M. (2002). Hardiness and social support as predictors of stress in mothers of typical children, children with autism, and children with mental retardation. *Autism, 6*(1), 115–130.

Wing, L. (1988). The continuum of autistic characteristics. In E. Schopler & G. Mesibov (Eds.), *Diagnosis and assessment in autism* (pp. 91–110). New York: Plenum Press.

# Critical Thinking

1. For what practical reasons is it important to study the positive and not just negative aspects of the experience of caregiving for an autistic child?

2. How exactly might identifying and being aware of the positives of caregiving for an autistic child affect the experience of the caregiver and the success in coping with the highly documented stresses of caregiving?

**MICHAEL K. CORMAN,** MA, is a doctoral student in the Department of Sociology at the University of Calgary and a part-time faculty member in the Department of Sociology & Anthropology at Mount Royal College in Calgary, Alberta. His research and teaching interests include the sociology of health and illness, aging, institutional ethnography, caregiving and autism spectrum disorders, health care work, and critical research strategies. Correspondence regarding this article can be sent to the author at mkcorman@ucalgary.ca or University of Calgary, Department of Sociology, Social Sciences 913, 2500 University Drive NW, Calgary, AB, T2N IN4 Canada.

**Author's note**—I would like to thank Dr. Neena L. Chappell for her continued support throughout the larger study that contributed to this article and the preparation of this manuscript.

# Caring for Chronically Ill Kids

Many parents are struggling to manage their children's care. Here's why.

ELIZABETH LEIS-NEWMAN

It's the news no parent wants to hear: Your child has been diagnosed with a chronic, potentially life-threatening illness.

Luckily, treatments for diseases like asthma, diabetes and cystic fibrosis have made these diseases manageable. But the latest research on parents' involvement in children's chronic illnesses indicates that parents may be struggling to find a balance between letting their children take responsibility and letting go too soon, which puts their children at risk for medical complications that can lead to hospitalization.

When this under-supervision occurs, it can be for a number of reasons, psychologists say: a lack of understanding about a disease, the potential for the primary caretaker to become depressed and ill-equipped and, in later years, a parent who is simply worn out by teenage rebellion. Parents, it seems, may be giving over the child's care to the child too early, says Suzanne Bennett Johnson, PhD, a Florida State University School of Medicine professor and APA's 2012 president.

"We do have some parents who stymie the child by exerting too much control, but there's a clinician's fallacy about the over-involved parent," she says.

What parents and health-care providers need, she and others say, are more realistic expectations of children's abilities to manage such illnesses.

## Lack of Understanding

Psychologists and physicians can begin to address this problem by making sure the parent and child understand the severity of the illness and the potentially fatal impact of not treating it thoroughly, says Johnson.

That can be difficult when the child's symptoms are not consistently present, says Kristin A. Riekert, PhD, who co-directs the Johns Hopkins Adherence Research Center. In a 2003 study in *Pediatrics* (Vol. 111, No. 3), Riekert and other researchers at Johns Hopkins University looked at asthmatic children in Baltimore elementary schools to see which parents were giving the physician-prescribed asthma medication. They found that poor communication between a physician and the primary caregiver led to the child's underuse of asthma medicines. In addition, they found that caregiver beliefs about asthma management were the most significant factor in whether the child's medication protocol was followed. In addition, a lack of time during a meeting with a physician was often cited as the main reason for poor communication—indicating physicians need to spend more time explaining the disease and the treatment.

Health-care providers also need to remember that with diseases like asthma, the parent wants to see a difference when a child uses a medication, Riekert says. A child may skip using his inhaler for a few days and appear fine, for example, and the parent may believe that he or she doesn't really need it. "It's not uncommon to see a reaction of 'no symptoms, no asthma,' among inner-city families," Riekert says.

This dynamic also can be true of epilepsy. Avani Modi, PhD, assistant professor of pediatrics at Cincinnati Children's Hospital Medical Center, is conducting a five-year study funded by the National Institutes of Health that examines adherence to anti-epileptic medications for children with new-onset epilepsy. She says some parents may fail to give the child his or her medications on a day-to-day basis, but then administer the medication each day right before seeing the child's physician—the phenomenon known as white-coat compliance.

"This can be dangerous with epilepsy as the physician measures the drug levels every time the child goes in [for a clinic visit]," says Modi. "If the parent has just started giving the medication, it may not be indicative of what is going on most of the time and clinical decisions may be made on this false level."

So far, her data indicate that roughly 40 percent of children newly diagnosed with epilepsy adhere almost religiously to the medication protocol, with 13 percent completely dropping off and the other 47 percent taking medications only some of the time. The only medical/sociodemographic factor that correlates with adherence is higher socioeconomic status—nothing else, including the epilepsy type or medication, matters.

## Adolescent Turmoil

No matter which chronic illness a child has, adherence falls off around adolescence, researchers say. Teenagers yearn for privacy, and resent their parents asking them to keep their bedroom or bathroom doors open in case of a medical emergency. "There is growing evidence that the patient, family and health-care team need to anticipate, in a collaborative manner, how care will be handled during adolescence," says Anne E. Kazak, PhD, a professor of pediatrics in the University of Pennsylvania School of Medicine. "At the end of adolescence, after all, most teens will be more autonomous in general as they enter early adulthood."

Plus, after what can be as long as a decade of dealing with a child's chronic illness, parents may be tempted to turn over the medical management once the child hits 13.

"That may not be developmentally appropriate," Modi says. While adolescents are old enough to understand a disease, she says, often they do not see the consequences of ignoring the treatments.

"With a disease like CF, an hour a day of medication and therapy takes them away from their social activities, from their friends, from their clubs. It's not malicious, but they forget to keep up and the consequences can be serious," she says.

Parents may think they need to lay off nagging their teens to take along their insulin to a friend's house or packing their inhaler before a day out. Riekert remembers a teenage CF patient who went on at length about how much he hated his parents nagging him. When she asked what would help him manage his CF, he grumbled, and said, "for them to bug me."

"It can be accepted as a necessary evil," Riekert says.

A parent simply being in the same room as their child during CF treatment raises compliance, says Alexandra Quittner, PhD, a psychology professor at the University of Miami.

"Parents and medical teams don't understand that the parent doesn't have to set up the treatment," she says. "We need to remind the parent how important their presence is. It's like a child sitting at the kitchen table doing his homework—he is more likely to do it if the parent is there."

What else improves adherence among teens? More time with mom and dad, according to a 2006 study by Modi and Quittner published in the *Journal of Pediatric Psychology* (Vol. 31, No. 8). In the study, they asked adolescents about barriers to adherence and what would motivate them to be more compliant.

"We have been very surprised—often when a child is asked what he or she would like to receive as a reward, it's a special outing with his or her mother or father," Quittner says. "It's important to spend that time together."

Modi encourages parents to think of their child managing his illness as a process akin to learning how to drive.

"There needs to be a learner's permit," she says. "At some point, you let go, but there needs to a bridge to the child managing his or her medication. We work with parents on that so by the time the child is 17 or 18, they can relinquish control."

## Depression and Anxiety

One of the more common challenges parents face when managing the care of their chronically ill children is that they simply may not have the ability to cope. "Generally, the research shows that when moms are depressed, adherence will go down," Johnson says.

New insight on that problem is coming from the first large-scale international study to evaluate levels of depression and anxiety among children with cystic fibrosis and their parents.

The study evaluated nearly 1,000 mothers and 182 fathers.

"What we are seeing is that 30 percent of [mothers] meet the clinical criteria for depression . . . double the rate of a regular sample," says Quittner, principal investigator for the study, known as the TIDES International Depression/Anxiety Epidemiological Study.

The study also found that more than 55 percent of the children's primary caregivers were anxious. These parents feel isolated and stressed by such challenges as obtaining insurance when a child has a pre-existing condition and the financial strain of co-payments for doctors' visits and medications.

In particular, says Quittner, "mothers often don't get enough support from their spouse and they end up handling the load."

The preliminary results of her study indicate that health-care providers need to spend more time evaluating depression and anxiety. "We are going to recommend annual screenings of both children with CF and their parental caregivers for anxiety and depression, and recommend paths for intervention," Quittner says.

Guiding these parents toward treatment will likely improve their child's health.

The other good news for struggling parents is that the difficult years of a child's illness can make the family stronger, Johnson says. A 2006 study in the *Journal of Pediatric Psychology* (Vol. 31, No. 4) by researchers Lamia P. Barakat, PhD, Melissa A. Alderfer, PhD, and Kazak, indicated that adolescent cancer survivors and their mothers reported at least one positive outcome stemming from the illness, with 86 percent of mothers saying that cancer "had a positive impact on how they think about their lives."

"There's a tendency to assume that a chronic illness will be a negative experience for the family," Johnson says.

"While it is stressful, families are quite resilient, and psychologists should emphasize that."

It's also important for health-care providers to be sympathetic to parents. Even when efforts fall short, parents are dedicating a major chunk of their lives to managing their child's illness, says Kazak. "Most families are doing the best they can," she says.

# Critical Thinking

1. Do most children will chronic illness take their medicines? In what ways do parents contribute for better or worse to helping their children's to their treatment programs?

2. How does a child's age and developmental stage influence their adherence to a treatment program for a chronic illness?

# The Human Child's Nature Orientation

Patrick C. Lee

The purpose of this article is to explore the hypothesis that the human child has a basic and developmentally significant orientation toward nature. To frame the discussion, two points should be made clear at the outset. First, the child's nature orientation is not proposed as a competitive alternative to what might be called a "human orientation." Quite the contrary, it is understood, on both evolutionary and developmental grounds, to be fundamental to the child's *humanization* process. Second, the term *nature* is used here in an inclusive and intuitively recognizable sense, referring to animals, pets, plant life, parks, streams, woodlots, irrigation ditches, mud, sand, overgrown and abandoned city lots, and so on.

Unfortunately for the position taken here, the models and/or theories that have most deeply characterized child studies over the years share a strongly anthropocentric worldview. These include, among others, traditional behaviorism and learning theory, social learning theory, various psychoanalytic approaches, formal structuralist (e.g., Chomsky) and/or constructivist approaches (e.g., Piaget, Kohlberg), Vygotsky's social constructivism, Bronfenbrenner's misleadingly labeled "ecological" model, and—in its chosen emphasis—attachment theory. What these accounts share in common is a view of child development as overwhelmingly determined by the forces of human society, culture, and history. Explicit attention to the child's experience of nature is much more the exception than the rule.

But this imbalance is correctible. In fact, one of the conventional approaches, constructivism, has recently been modified by Peter Kahn to explore the child's nature orientation (Kahn, 1997, 1999, 2002, 2006). There are also a small number of studies grounded in attachment theory that examine the attachment value of children's pets (e.g., Rost & Hartmann, 1994; Triebenbacher, 1998). Analogously, Bronfenbrenner's "ecological" approach could easily be extended to nonhuman settings such as those listed above: parkland, nature trails, neighborhood woodlots, and the like.

This article is not the first to point out the field's self-limiting anthropocentric bias. Others who have explicitly expressed a need for a complementary ecological and/or evolutionary orientation include Kaplan and Kaplan (1989, pp. 198, 203), Melson (2000, p. 376; 2001, pp. 4–5, 7–21, 188 ff.), Heerwagen and Orians (2002, pp. 29, 33, 57), Bjorklund (1997), Simpson and Belsky (2008, p. 150), Kahn (1997, p. 54; 1999, p. 87), Mithen (1996, pp. 61–71), and Serpell (1999).

Why the recent stirring of interest in the child and nature? The field's concern is probably a subset of the larger society's concern about environmental issues. Since 1960, the human population of Earth has more than doubled, and in approximately the same time frame, our footprint on the planet—that is, our use of water, arable land, and fossil fuel—has more than *tripled* (Harrison & Pearce, 2000, pp. 12–14; Hunter, 2000, pp. 12–13, 37). An important part of reducing our footprint is raising and educating children who themselves will have the awareness, knowledge, and will to reduce it further. For the field, this is arguably one of the most critical issues of the 21st century.

This article pursues three interwoven objectives: (a) to make a case for the developmental significance of the child's nature orientation; (b) to show that this orientation does not threaten, but rather complements, enriches, extends, and interacts with the standard anthropocentric view of the child; and (c) to briefly review empirical findings that a have good fit with the nature-orientation hypothesis. I start by laying out an evolutionary framework for the adaptive significance of the human child's nature orientation, then proceed to the developmental case.

## Evolutionary Background of the Child's Nature Orientation

There are two major hypotheses that posit humanity's interaction with animals as a central driving force in human evolution: sociobiologist E. O. Wilson's "biophilia" (1984) and paleoanthropologist Pat Shipman's "animal connection" (2010). Wilson argues that the tendency to orient toward other life forms—observing their behavior, figuring out when and how to approach or avoid them, and so on—would have made such a contribution to our species' fitness during evolution that it would have spread throughout the human gene pool. In fact, the plausibility of Wilson's hypothesis has encouraged several child developmentalists to adopt a modified version of biophilia—one that incorporates both innate and learned features—as a heuristic starting point to their research on the child-nature relationship (cf. Kahn, 1999, p. 34; Melson, 2000, p. 375; Kellert, 2002, p. 129).

As far as it goes, Wilson's position is compatible with Shipman's, but Shipman takes the matter a lot further. She argues that humanity's connection to animals is the "underlying link"

(2010, p. 519) among the three well-known adaptive strategies that, taken together, distinguish humanity from all other species: complex use and production of tools, symbolic behavior (language, art, ritual, etc.), and domestication of plants and animals. In her view, the "animal connection" is so fundamental to the human type that it at least qualifies as a fourth diagnostic indicator of our species and may even be our foundational adaptive strategy. In this scenario, the other three strategies (tools, symbols, and domestication) would serve as particular expressions of, and vehicles for, the animal connection.

Put briefly and concretely, Shipman's position is that throughout our evolution, the human line has been preoccupied with animals. We obsessively observe them; use tools to scavenge them, hunt them, and process their carcasses; symbolically merge with them in myth and ritual; compile and communicate information about them; draw, carve, and sculpt representations of them; and domesticate them into "living tools." We also reciprocally exchange adaptations with them—we select them for human-friendly features (e.g., domesticability), even as they select us for animal-friendly features, such as the ability to tolerate animal-transmitted diseases (e.g., mumps, measles, the common cold). Finally, we bring them as companions into our families and homes.

In other words, over evolutionary time, the *humanization* of our species has involved sustained, close, and progressive interaction with animals and their habitats. Our children have been right at the center of all this, spontaneously, routinely, and unavoidably participating in the animal connection. By Shipman's account, this connection would be as typical and defining of human childhood as is acquiring language and drawing pictures (symbolic behavior), playing rule-bound games (ritual), digging holes with sticks and pulling wagons (tool use), and keeping pets (domestication).

Wilson's and Shipman's hypotheses about humanity's *evolutionary* background generate several questions regarding the human child's *developmental* foreground. For example, is there good evidence for the child's having a special orientation toward animals and other features of nature (e.g., pets, mud play, etc.)? If so, does this orientation undergo qualitative change with age? Does the child's nature orientation potentiate or interact with other aspects of the developmental process, such as linguistic, cognitive, moral, or affective development? Does the child's human support system facilitate or obstruct the child's nature orientation? Do children with disabilities benefit from interaction with animals? And so on.

## Is There Evidence of a Special Child–Nature Relationship?

Despite its understandably anthropocentric bias, the large literature on early language and affect offers an occasional study indicating that the young child is precociously oriented toward nature. Nelson (1973, pp. 32–33), for example, found that seven animal names (e.g., *cow, duck, horse,* etc.) are commonly included in toddlers' first 50 words and that toddlers use the terms *dog* and *cat* more than any other words except *mommy* and *daddy.* Related to this point, Serpell (1999, pp. 87–88)

rightly notes the high frequency of animal characters in children's stories and animal decorations and toys in children's environments. There is also evidence that living animals—that is, family pets—can, like stuffed teddy bears, serve as Winnicott's (1953) "transitional objects" (cf. Triebenbacher, 1998), or even as attachment figures in their own right when human caregivers are absent or ineffective (cf. Rost & Hartmann, 1994).

Somewhat related to pets' attachment value are the benefits that companion animals bring to children with disabilities. For example, an observational study by Mader, Hart, and Bergin (1989) showed how trained companion dogs enhance the social acceptability of wheelchair-bound children in shopping malls. These children received more than twice as many friendly greetings from strangers than did a matched sample without companion dogs. Perhaps the most systematic research in this area stems from A. H. Katcher's work with 9- to 15-year-old boys diagnosed with severe conduct and oppositional defiant disorders in a residential treatment facility (Beck & Katcher, 1996, pp. 143–147; Katcher, 2002; Katcher & Wilkins, 2000). These boys spent 5 hr a week at the facility's "Companion Zoo," where they cared for a variety of indoor and outdoor animals, such as rabbits, tropical fish, frogs, chickens, sheep, and so on. Carefully conducted observations showed a marked decrease in antisocial behaviors alongside improvements on all measures of symptomatology and social aptitude, as contrasted to a matched sample of boys who had Outward Bound experience. Interestingly, these results were achieved not because the animals "cared" for the boys but because of the boys' taking care of the animals.

It is also relevant to ask what research such as the foregoing tells us about the child's human support system. If caregivers participate in the child's acquisition and use of animal names, tell animal stories to the child, decorate the child's environments with animal representations, and incorporate pets as members of the family, then the child's human surround would seem to actively *support* his or her propensity to affiliate with nature. If biophilia and the animal connection have contributed in an important way to human fitness, then it would be adaptive for caregivers and child therapists to convey biophilic (nature-approaching) and—when safety is at risk—biophobic (nature-avoiding) messages to the child. It would be maladaptive for them to shut out nature. Viewed this way, the child's human support system does not see the child's nature orientation as competing with the ongoing process of human socialization. Rather, caregivers spontaneously interpret the orientation as compatible with, perhaps even contributing to, the humanization process—just as Shipman (2010) would predict.

## Does the Child-Nature Relationship Change With Age?

I briefly consider four promising approaches to the developmental question of whether the child–nature relationship changes with age: (a) Stephen Kellert's child survey research, (b) Peter Kahn's child interview studies, (c) the relatively large body of research on the child's animate-inanimate distinction, and (d) observational studies of children's behavior in natural settings.

## Kellert's Survey Research

Kellert and Kahn both pursue a double agenda: to identify developmental levels in children's ideas about nature and to discover whether children's understanding of nature–human interaction includes a clear moral–ethical dimension.

Kellert (1996, pp. 37–51; 2002, pp. 129–138) began his investigation by positing several "values," some antagonistic to human–nature relations, and some friendly. Using survey methodology, he studied the prevalence of these values in the thinking of 3- to 17-year-olds and identified four age-related periods (later reduced to three). Without going into the particulars of each period, it is fair to say that Kellert's research yielded several straightforward age-related trends. In general, he found that, with age, three negative values *decreased* and three positive attitudes *increased*. The survey responses of the youngest children were characterized by fear and avoidance of unfamiliar animals (not family pets), attitudes of control and dominion, and a utilitarian, self-serving perspective on nature. During the middle-childhood and preadolescent period, this pattern of negative attitudes was progressively replaced by more positive values, which in turn achieved strong expression by adolescence. The older participants reported an ecological appreciation of the complex relations between organisms and their habitats; a naturalistic orientation toward conservation, wild animals, and wild nature; and moral concern for nature's well-being, backed up by a strong sense of stewardship.

## Kahn's Interview Studies

In contrast to Kellert's use of survey methodology, Kahn (1997, 1999, 2002, 2006) has employed the semistructured interview technique associated with Piaget and Kohlberg. He has conducted four studies with youngsters from first grade to college level to classify the reasoning, most particularly the moral—ethical reasoning, that underlies their relation to nature. His probing interviews yielded three age-related moral orientations: anthropocentric, biocentric, and "compositional." The anthropocentric type assigns value to nature because of the benefits it provides to humanity. In contrast, biocentric reasoning sees nature as having inherent value, that is, moral standing in its own right. Compositional reasoning coordinates the other two types into a more comprehensive and integrated framework (Kahn, 2002, pp. 98–100).

One study of elementary school children showed anthropocentric reasoning occurring at each grade level, whereas the biocentric type jumped from use by only 7% of first graders to 56% of fifth graders. In another study that added eighth graders, Kahn found that both types of reasoning increased with age (1997, pp. 44–45). A third study, which included older high school and college students, showed even further increases in biocentric thinking. Moreover, there were step-by-step increments of higher order compositional reasoning from only 3% of fifth graders to 71% of college-age participants (Kahn, 2002, pp. 97–101).

In addition, by fifth grade, some of Kahn's participants began to show awareness that environmental pollution harmed not only animals and plants but abiotic nature as well (e.g.,

water and air). This finding suggests that the child's orientation toward nature goes beyond a simple focus on animals to incorporate other dimensions of natural ecology, including the impact of human activity on ecosystems (Kahn, 2006, pp. 463–464).

## The Child's Animate–Inanimate Distinction

Although research on the development of the animate–inanimate distinction is not usually understood as addressed to the child's nature orientation, it can be fruitfully reframed as such. Doing so shows, first, the precocious development of this subset of the child's nature orientation; second, the functional relation between the distinction and Shipman's animal connection; and, third, the potentially rich contribution the animal connection makes to cognitive, perceptual, and behavioral development (cf. recent reviews by Gelman & Opfer, 2002; Rakison & Poulin-Dubois, 2001).

By 2–3 months of age, infants clearly distinguish a living person from a doll, a musical mobile, or a toy monkey (Gelman & Opfer, 2002, p. 153). By 9 months, babies differentiate birds from airplanes and animals from vehicles, and they attribute behaviors like drinking and sleeping to novel animals but not to novel vehicles (Mandler & McDonough, 1993, 1996). They are also more attracted to real animals than to their fake counterparts (Ricard & Allard, 1993).

Three- to 4-year-old children typically interpret self-generated or goal-directed movement as diagnostic of life and recognize life as a precondition to these kinds of movement. They identify even unfamiliar animals (photos of a praying mantis, an echidna, etc.) as animate and judge them capable of self-generated movement (Gelman & Opfer, 2002, p. 161; Massey & Gelman, 1988). Four-year-olds understand that artifacts do not die but that animals and plants have to die and that they "stay dead after they die" (Gelman & Opfer, 2002, p. 160). By age 4½ years, children define plants as animate because, like animals, plants grow, change shape, and heal themselves when scratched; they also recognize that the opposite applies to inanimate objects (e.g., tables don't grow and, when scratched, don't heal on their own).

By age 4½ years, then, children seem to have consolidated a robust and elaborate animate–inanimate distinction, which serves as the foundation for a naïve theory of biology and for a number of other broadly applicable conceptual distinctions—for example, between different kinds of causality (such as physical contact vs. action at a distance) and between different categories of change and movement (such as internally generated vs. externally imposed, linear vs. nonlinear, goal-directed vs. random). On these grounds, the animate–inanimate distinction seems to be more fundamental and broadly adaptive than most other categorical distinctions, such as those based on shape, color, size, and so on.

Moreover, for the animal connection to have been as adaptive as Shipman (2010) claims, it must have incorporated an all-but-foolproof version of the animate–inanimate distinction. Viewed this way, the distinction would seem to be both a developmental instantiation of, and an evolutionary precondition to, the animal connection.

In summary, the animate—inanimate distinction in early child development may play a role roughly analogous to the animal connection in human evolution. Both processes are viewed as "fundamental . . . foundational . . . central . . . deeply rooted" in their respective disciplines (Gelman & Opfer, 2002, pp. 151, 163, 166; Shipman, 2010, pp. 522, 525). The adaptive advantage conferred by the animal connection over evolutionary time would seem to innately predispose the human child to an early and fundamental sensitivity to life and its properties: growth and reproduction; contingent, goal-directed, and self-generated movement; and so on. Moreover, the connection's adaptive payoff would likely have encouraged the child's caregivers to nurture this predisposition. Interestingly, the best evidence for or against the caregiver-nurturance hypothesis would probably be generated by developmental (not evolutionary) investigations. The earlier point made about contemporary caregiver support of the child's nature orientation would seem to speak to the nurturance hypothesis.

## The Need for Systematic Observational Studies

Although Kahn's and Kellert's developmental accounts may differ on some details, they generally agree on the overall direction of children's understanding of nature. Even so, the current state of developmental research calls for at least one caveat. Both Kahn and Kellert relied exclusively on children's *verbal reports* for their findings. But so far, there have been no comparably systematic investigations of age-related changes in children's *behavior* vis-à-vis animals or natural settings.

Of course, there have been more than a few observational reports on children's play and behavior in countryside, parks, zoos, playgrounds, vacant urban lots, and so forth (e.g., Nabhan & Trimble, 1994; Pyle, 2002; Sobel, 1993; Wood, 1993). Wood's observational study (1993), for example, shows that toddlers and preschoolers enthusiastically play with mud, sand, and water in natural settings—an attitude not revealed in the negative verbal reports of Kellert's youngest participants (2002). But such accounts, however rich and insightful, are typically not cast in a full and systematic developmental framework. The problem with this mix is that it leaves us ignorant of the correspondence between what children say about nature and what they actually do in natural settings.

## Closing Considerations

The goal of this article has been to explore the hypothesis that the human child has a basic and developmentally significant orientation toward nature. In the process, I have drawn upon research and informed commentary from two disciplines, trying to integrate them into a coherent account of the child's relationship with nature. At present, however, this line of inquiry is still relatively underdeveloped, leaving several major questions unresolved.

First, is the child's nature orientation innate, learned, or both? Unsurprisingly, the evolutionary approach tends to emphasize the genetic tracking of strongly adaptive human behaviors, such as those described by Wilson (1984) and Shipman (2010). The human infant's precocious ability to make fairly sophisticated animate–inanimate distinctions in the 1st year of life also suggests a genetic component. On the other hand, the evident support of the child's caregiving system argues for a strong nurturing role in the acquisition of a nature orientation. Moreover, a small but growing body of evidence and commentary indicates that *non*facilitative experiential inputs—for example, the incremental urbanization and computerization-virtualization of childhood experience—may permute the child's nature connection into a disconnection (Kareiva, 2008; Louv, 2008; Pergams & Zaradic, 2008; Pyle, 2002; Rideout, Foehr, & Roberts, 2010). At this point, the available evidence suggests that the child's nature orientation is a function of interaction among hereditary, experiential, and developmental factors.

Second, where do we go from here? Again, in an area as underdeveloped as this, it would be premature to advance a confident list of testable, falsifiable hypotheses. At present, we need the kind of research that identifies *patterns of correspondence* among relevant variables: for example, as already noted, between children's verbal reports (e.g., the Kahn and Kellert studies) and their actual behavior in natural settings (e.g., Wood, 1993), between parental attitudes toward nature and the child's access to nature (e.g., visits to national parks, unsupervised play in natural settings), between school-based programs that promote the acquisition of "ecological intelligence" (Goleman, 2009) and the development of Kahn's biocentric and compositional levels of reasoning about nature, between pet ownership and Kahn's levels of reasoning, and so on. Once an adequate baseline of correspondence patterns is in place, this area can begin to formulate testable cause-and-effect hypotheses: for example, that pet ownership would partially mitigate the nature-blunting effects of the child's computer time; that the closer the child–pet relationship, the greater the mitigation effect; and so on.

Finally, are there other topics that might fall under the general rubric of the child's nature orientation? Due to space limitations, several related lines of inquiry have gone unmentioned. These include, for example, the developmental precursors and consequences of animal abuse in childhood (cf. Ascione, 2005; Ascione & Arkow, 1999; Melson, 2001, pp. 159–187); how children's oral and written nature stories might shape their attitudes toward nature (cf. Serpell, 1999), and adults' retrospective reports of their childhood experience of nature (cf. Chawla, 1986, 1990; Cobb, 1977).

In conclusion, the child-and-nature focus proposed here shows promise on both scientific and policy grounds. First, it calls attention to features of childhood that are overlooked by the field's dominant emphasis on the child's sociocultural context. Second, it has already generated a modest body of empirical findings. Finally, it would better position the field to address 21st-century environmental issues and policy as they affect the child.

# References

Ascione, F. R. (2005). *Children and animals: Exploring the roots of kindness and cruelty.* West Lafayette, IN: Purdue University Press.

Ascione, F. R., & Arkow, P. (Eds.). (1999). *Child abuse, domestic violence, and animal abuse: Linking the circles of compassion for prevention and intervention.* West Lafayette, IN: Purdue University Press.

Beck, A., & Katcher, A. (1996). *Between pets and people: The importance of animal companionship.* West Lafayette, IN: Purdue University Press.

Bjorklund, D. F. (1997). The role of immaturity in human development. *Psychological Bulletin, 122,* 153–169.

Chawla, L. (1986). The ecology of environmental memory. *Children's Environments Quarterly, 3,* 34–42.

Chawla, L. (1990). Ecstatic places. *Children's Environments Quarterly, 7*(4), 18–23.

Cobb, E. (1977). *The ecology of imagination in childhood.* New York: Columbia University Press.

Gelman, S. A., & Opfer, J. E. (2002). Development of the animate-inanimate distinction. In U. Goswami (Ed.), *Blackwell handbook of child cognitive development* (pp. 151–166). Malden, MA: Blackwell.

Goleman, D. (2009). *Ecological intelligence.* New York: Broadway Books.

Harrison, P., & Pearce, F. (2000). *AAAS atlas of population and environment.* Berkeley: University of California Press.

Heerwagen, J. H., & Orians, G. H. (2002). The ecological world of children. In P. H Kahn Jr. & S. R. Kellert (Eds.), *Children and nature: Psychological, sociocultural, and evolutionary investigations* (pp. 29–63). Cambridge, MA: MIT Press.

Hunter, L. M. (2000). *The environmental implications of population dynamics.* Santa Monica, CA: Rand.

Kahn, P. H., Jr. (1997). Developmental psychology and the biophilia hypothesis: Children's affiliation with nature. *Developmental Review, 17,* 1–61.

Kahn, P. H., Jr. (1999). *The human relationship with nature: Development and culture.* Cambridge, MA: MIT Press.

Kahn, P. H., Jr. (2002). Children's affiliations with nature: Structure, development, and the problem of environmental generational amnesia. In P. H. Kahn Jr. & S. R. Kellert (Eds.), *Children and nature: Psychological, sociocultural, and evolutionary investigations* (pp. 93–116). Cambridge, MA: MIT Press.

Kahn, P. H., Jr. (2006). Nature and moral development. In M. Killen & J. G. Smetana (Eds.), *Handbook of moral development* (pp. 461–480). Mahwah, NJ: Erlbaum.

Kaplan, R., & Kaplan, S. (1989). *The experience of nature: A psychological perspective.* Cambridge, UK: Cambridge University Press.

Kareiva, P. (2008). Ominous trends in nature recreation. *Proceedings of the National Academy of Sciences, 105,* 2757–2758.

Katcher, A. (2002). Animals in therapeutic education: Guides into the liminal state. In P. H Kahn Jr. & S. R. Kellert (Eds.), *Children and nature: Psychological, sociocultural, and evolutionary investigations* (pp. 179–198). Cambridge, MA: MIT Press.

Katcher, A. H., & Wilkins, G. G. (2000). The centaur's lessons: Therapeutic education through care of animals and nature study. In A. H. Fine (Ed.), *Handbook on animal assisted therapy: Theoretical foundations and guidelines for practice* (pp. 153–177). San Diego, CA: Academic Press.

Kellert, S. R. (1996). *The value of life: Biological diversity and human society.* Washington, DC: Island Press.

Kellert, S. R. (2002). Experiencing nature: Affective, cognitive, and evaluative development in children. In P. H. Kahn Jr. & S. R. Kellert (Eds.), *Children and nature: Psychological, sociocultural, and evolutionary investigations* (pp. 117–151). Cambridge, MA: MIT Press.

Louv, R. (2008). *Last child in the woods: Saving our children from nature-deficit disorder.* Chapel Hill, NC: Algonquin Books of Chapel Hill.

Mader, B., Hart, L., & Bergin, B. (1989). Social acknowledgements for children with disabilities: Effects of service dogs. *Child Development, 60,* 1529–1534.

Mandler, J. M., & McDonough, L. (1993). Concept formation in infancy. *Cognitive Development, 8,* 291–318.

Mandler, J. M., & McDonough, L. (1996). Drinking and driving don't mix: Inductive generalization in infancy. *Cognition, 59,* 307–335.

Massey, C., & Gelman, R. (1988). Preschoolers decide whether pictured unfamiliar objects can move themselves. *Developmental Psychology, 24,* 307–317.

Melson, G. F. (2000). Companion animals and the development of children: Implications of the biophilia hypothesis. In A. H. Fine (Ed.), *Handbook on animal assisted therapy: Theoretical foundations and guidelines for practice* (pp. 375–383). San Diego, CA: Academic Press.

Melson, G. F. (2001). *Why the wild things are: Animals in the lives of children.* Cambridge, MA: Harvard University Press.

Mithen, S. (1996). *The prehistory of the mind: A search for the origins of art, religions and science.* London: Thames and Hudson.

Nabhan, G. P., & Trimble, S. (1994). *The geography of childhood: Why children need wild places.* Boston: Beacon Press.

Nelson, K. (1973). Structure and strategy in learning to talk. *Monographs of the Society for Research in Child Development, 38* (Serial No. 149).

Pergams, O. R. W., & Zaradic, P.A. (2008). Evidence for a fundamental and pervasive shift away from nature-based recreation. *Proceedings of the National Academy of Sciences, 105,* 2295–2300.

Pyle, R. M. (2002). Eden in a vacant lot: Special places, species, and kids in the neighborhood of life. In P. H. Kahn Jr. & S. R. Kellert (Eds.), *Children and nature: Psychological, sociocultural, and evolutionary investigations* (pp. 305–327). Cambridge, MA: MIT Press.

Rakison, D. H., & Poulin-Dubois, D. (2001). Developmental origin of the animate-inanimate distinction. *Psychological Bulletin, 127,* 209–228.

Ricard, M., & Allard, L. (1993). The reaction of 9- to 10-month-old infants to an unfamiliar animal. *Journal of Genetic Psychology, 154,* 5–16.

Rideout, V. J., Foehr, U. G., & Roberts, D. F. (2010). *Generation M²: Media in the lives of 8- to 18-year-olds.* Menlo Park, CA: Henry J. Kaiser Family Foundation.

Rost, D. H., & Hartmann, A. (1994). Children and their pets. *Anthrozoös, 7,* 242–254.

Serpell, J. (1999). Guest editor's introduction: Animals in children's lives. *Society and Animals, 7,* 87–94.

Shipman, P. (2010). The animal connection and human evolution. *Current Anthropology, 51,* 519–538.

Simpson, J. A., & Belsky, J. (2008). Attachment theory within a modern evolutionary framework. In J. Cassidy & P. R. Shaver (Eds.), *Handbook of attachment: Theory, research, and clinical applications* (pp. 131–157). New York: Guilford.

Sobel, D. (1993). *Children's special places. Exploring the role of forts, dens, and bush houses in middle childhood.* Tucson, AZ: Zephyr Press.

Triebenbacher, S. L. (1998). Pets as transitional objects: Their role in children's emotional development. *Psychological Reports, 82,* 191–200.

Wilson, E. O. (1984). *Biophilia: The human bond with other species.* Cambridge, MA: Harvard University Press.

Winnicott, D. W. (1953). Transitional objects and transitional phenomena. *International Journal of Psychoanalysis, 34,* 89–97.

Wood, D. (1993). Ground to stand on: Some notes on kids' dirt play. *Children's Environments, 10*(1), 3–18.

# Critical Thinking

1. What evidence does the article provide for a child having a developmentally significant orientation toward nature?

2. How does the child's nature orientation hypothesis enhance or complement anthropocentric models of child development?

3. Identify some of the age-related trends in a child's nature orientation. What might these trends suggest about cognitive, moral, and emotional development?

4. How can we use biophilia and animal connection to educate children about environmental conservation? What can children teach us?

Correspondence concerning this article should be addressed to **Patrick C. Lee**, 128 Walmer Road, Toronto, ON, M5R 2X9, Canada; e-mail: patricklee2312@gmail.com.

© 2012 The Author
Child Development Perspectives © 2012 The Society for Research in Child Development DOI: 10.1111/j.1750-8606.2012.00232.x

From *Child Development Perspectives*, vol. 6, no. 2, 2012, pp. 193–198. Copyright © 2012 by the Patrick C. Lee. Published by the Society for Research in Child Development. Reprinted by permission of Wiley-Blackwell.

# Test-Your-Knowledge Form

We encourage you to photocopy and use this page as a tool to assess how the articles in *Annual Editions* expand on the information in your textbook. By reflecting on the articles you will gain enhanced text information. You can also access this useful form on a product's book support website at www.mhhe.com/cls

NAME:                                                                          DATE:

TITLE AND NUMBER OF ARTICLE:

BRIEFLY STATE THE MAIN IDEA OF THIS ARTICLE:

LIST THREE IMPORTANT FACTS THAT THE AUTHOR USES TO SUPPORT THE MAIN IDEA:

WHAT INFORMATION OR IDEAS DISCUSSED IN THIS ARTICLE ARE ALSO DISCUSSED IN YOUR TEXTBOOK OR OTHER READINGS THAT YOU HAVE DONE? LIST THE TEXTBOOK CHAPTERS AND PAGE NUMBERS:

LIST ANY EXAMPLES OF BIAS OR FAULTY REASONING THAT YOU FOUND IN THE ARTICLE:

LIST ANY NEW TERMS/CONCEPTS THAT WERE DISCUSSED IN THE ARTICLE, AND WRITE A SHORT DEFINITION: